'Urgent, incisive and hugely readable. The authors—two of our most brilliant advocates for women's rights—make visible the often-hidden ways in which patriarchy remains so resilient.'

Monica Ali, bestselling novelist

'This is a scholarly and thoughtful book—inspiring and challenging. There's an idea on every page and outrage in every chapter. Ambitious in its scope, looking at women's struggle for equality in seven countries, it still manages to tell individual stories of heroism. A frightening story of spreading patriarchy—and the heroines that stand against it.'

Philippa Gregory, author of *Normal Women*

'Two brilliant feminist writers survey the world and the inequality that is still meted out to women everywhere. This heartbreaking book describes ongoing patriarchal power in all its cruel manifestations, cataloguing the ways in which gains made by women are being subverted and rolled back through the rise of populist nationalisms. A powerful condemnation but also a call to arms!'

Baroness Helena Kennedy LT KC

'My two favourite women to think with have been thinking with each other about why patriarchy does not die, and more importantly, how it adapts and shapeshifts in different contexts. This book helps us imagine how to dismantle the systems that deny women freedom.'

Liz Kelly, former head of the Women's National Commission, UK

'A vital, passionate and superbly written global dispatch from two of the most respected stateswomen of feminist activism.'

Samira Ahmed, journalist and broadcaster

'Wherever one stands in the debate over the meaning of patriarchy, this is a valuable investigation of the place in which women find themselves across the globe, and of their resistance to oppression.'

Kenan Malik, *Observer* columnist and author of *Not So Black and White*

'In this powerful series of dispatches from the front lines of women's oppression, Campbell and Gupta document patriarchy's remarkable resilience. While they tell shocking stories of violence against women, they also celebrate the awesome wit, courage and creativity of feminist resistance. What an essential, intelligent and ultimately uplifting book!'

Anne Karpf, sociologist, journalist and author of *How Women Can Save the Planet*

'What becomes clear when reading this brilliantly researched but disturbing book, is that the patriarchy is still very much with us, in different forms, wherever you are. And progress for women seems to crucially depend on the flexibility that is permitted within a given social system, principally developed by men.'

Vicky Pryce, author of *Women vs Capitalism*

'A must-read. Campbell and Gupta reveal the myriad political, cultural and economic soils in which patriarchy can survive or reemerge—even after it appeared to be rolled back. But they graphically show that locally rooted, feminist-informed resistance also persists—from El Salvador to Saudi Arabia to South Africa. Every chapter here opened my eyes.'

Cynthia Enloe, author of *Twelve Feminist Lessons of War*

'At times enraging but ultimately inspiring, this landmark book of our contested and troubled times vividly tells how patriarchy—or, more accurately, patriarchies—have adapted and endured, enmeshed within capitalism. This is a crucial report from the front lines—and an invigorating call to arms.'

Carne Ross, author and former senior British diplomat

'Drawing on extensive research and countless conversations with women around the world, the authors offer a powerful, wide-ranging analysis of patriarchy—showing how it may vary in degree across countries and cultures yet retains a persistent and recognisable form. They remind us of the enduring link between patriarchy and war, violence and dehumanising politics. The path forward lies through feminist collective action.'

Halla Gunnarsdóttir, Leader of VR Union, Iceland

'Beautifully written and deeply researched. Campbell and Gupta expose the patriarchal foundations of capitalism, religion and the state that oppress and, all too often, destroy women. They also offer hope: from small enclaves of local resistance to Rojava's feminist-forward society, they grace us with the examples, tools and fortitude we need right now to fight for a liberated future.'

Debbie Bookchin, journalist, author and co-founder of the Emergency Committee for Rojava

'Campbell and Gupta unravel the intricate threads of global misogyny with clarity and grace. They show how patriarchy doesn't collapse—it recalibrates, feeding off neoliberalism, nationalism and silence. A transformative journey into the heart of feminist thought.'

Maryam Aldossari, academic and writer

PLANET PATRIARCHY

BEATRIX CAMPBELL
RAHILA GUPTA

Planet Patriarchy

Global Tales of Feminism and Oppression

HURST & COMPANY, LONDON

First published in the United Kingdom in 2025 by
C. Hurst & Co. (Publishers) Ltd.,
New Wing, Somerset House, Strand, London, WC2R 1LA
© Beatrix Campbell and Rahila Gupta, 2025
All rights reserved.

Distributed in the United States, Canada and Latin
America by Oxford University Press, 198 Madison Avenue,
New York, NY 10016, United States of America.

The right of Beatrix Campbell and Rahila Gupta to be identified as the authors of this publication is asserted by them in accordance with the Copyright, Designs and Patents Act, 1988.

The extract from *The Doctor and the Saint* is reproduced here with the kind permission of Arundhati Roy.

A Cataloguing-in-Publication data record for this book
is available from the British Library.

ISBN: 9781805262879

This book is printed using paper from registered sustainable
and managed sources.

www.hurstpublishers.com

Printed and bound in Great Britain by Bell & Bain Ltd, Glasgow

Revolutions can, and often have, begun with reading.

Arundhati Roy, *The Doctor and the Saint*

*In memory of Kamila Zahno, whose generous
contribution made this book possible.*

Our abiding regret is that she did not live to see the end result.

CONTENTS

Preface	xiii
Introduction	1
1. El Salvador: The Currency of Violence	39
2. Raqqa to Riyadh: The Copy and the Template	85
3. Russia: We Will Get Up off Our Knees	131
4. China: I Ask for the Swiftest Horse	179
5. South Africa: White Capitalist Men Got What They Wanted	219
6. Iceland: Paradise?	261
7. Rojava: 'The Street Was Open to the Women'	295
Conclusion	339
Acknowledgements	355
Notes	363
Index	443

PREFACE

Rahila Gupta and Beatrix Campbell

We, the authors, share almost a century of political activism between us, as well as shared experiences and life histories, as a black and a white woman inspired by Women's Liberation, raised in countries with enmeshed colonial histories—India and the UK—in activist families with revolutionary aspirations. At the launch of her book *The End of Equality*, Beatrix Campbell posed a number of inspiring questions around the synergy of neopatriarchy and neoliberalism, a new articulation of men's dominance—from violence to budgets, from incomes to the politics of time and space. Rahila Gupta's lifetime immersion in black feminist activism through her membership of Southall Black Sisters gave her an insight into what it is like to stand at the crossroads of race, class and sex, a no man's land, as it were. Rahila was present at Beatrix's book launch and felt those questions could do with further scrutiny. This led to our collaboration on this book.

When we embarked on this project, originally titled 'Why Doesn't Patriarchy Die?', we knew it would provoke hostility and a certain bemusement—surely the answer was obvious. As Rahila's partner said, of course democracy is the best political regime for women and the one most damaging to patriarchy. But we have democracy in Sweden and India, and the two societies couldn't be more different in the way they impact women's lives.

As soon as we tweeted about the project, seeking crowdfunding via Byline, a platform for journalists, some wag, no, misogynist, responded that this was like asking, 'Why Doesn't Godzilla Die?'; another tweeter helpfully explained that this meant that 'Awesome things are forever, ha!', which led the original twit to clarify that 'just like Godzilla, patriarchy theory is fiction'. In case our little female brains hadn't quite got it, he then went on to dazzle us with science—'Why Is the Force of Gravity 32 Feet per Second Square?' He was upbraided by another witty friend, showing a faux sympathy with feminists, 'Mathematics is oppressive. It's the language of the Patriarchy.' The next tweet told us that our question had already been answered by Steven Goldberg's book *The Inevitability of Patriarchy*, which was based on the premise that men are biologically superior to women, a book that was published in 1973. Sadly, the '70s term 'male chauvinist pig' was now out of fashion. But by the standards of a twitterstorm, this was a breeze.

What deserved more serious attention but still didn't put us off our quest was an irate email from an academic who said 'it is obvious why patriarchy does not die: it suits men to maintain it and women often internalise their own oppression for a host of reasons. Please don't write to me again.' If the collusion of women was a factor perpetuating the continuity of patriarchy, then surely that itself merited further study. A Kurdish woman, growing up in the Rojava women's revolution, said in exasperation: 'If you remove women from the patriarchal set-up, it would collapse.' Of course! Was the answer so obvious that no one had tackled this question? Were we barking up the wrong tree? We were driven by wanting to arrive at a place, an analysis that activists could use to inform their practices and attempt to weaken patriarchal institutions wherever they were.

PREFACE

We suspect that a more sophisticated version of these attitudes is prevalent on the editorial boards of some publishers. Initial excitement at our project would be replaced with interminable tinkering with the proposal before it was dropped altogether. We think that a Nancy Fraser view of feminism continues to dominate in some circles, including elements of the left, a view that is essentially a modernised version of the trope that feminism is the Trojan horse that betrayed the class struggle.

On the other hand, among our supporters and donors, there appeared to be real excitement at the prospect of engaging with the big questions—sometimes we get so caught up in our specific little corners that we forget to map the contours of the room itself.

We were not able to visit all the countries in our book, although that had been the original plan. The COVID-19 pandemic thwarted our travel plans. The political conditions in China, Russia and Saudi Arabia were perilous to journalists, particularly freelancers unfamiliar with the terrain, and dangerous for interviewees; and Russia has become even more so after its full-scale invasion of Ukraine. We were advised by our interviewees in all these countries that we would gain nothing from visiting as people would be too scared to speak to us, face to face.

Given the lack of space, the feminist groups that we have looked at in each of the countries are, of necessity, the more prominent and long-established ones. But there is lots of feminist activity at grassroots levels that may be doing the work of raising the feminist consciousness of its members or working on very local issues whose importance must not be discounted simply because they do not make an appearance in our discussions.

At the very least, whether we answered the question we set ourselves or not, we hope that we have presented a picture of the current state of patriarchal relations in each of the countries we selected.

INTRODUCTION

Rahila Gupta and Beatrix Campbell

We started writing this book while the world held its breath, and our observations and analysis could only partly be confirmed before travel opened up again. Our breath had been stolen from us by the COVID pandemic; the inability to breathe became a meme of resistance against oppression, from George Floyd's cries of 'I can't breathe' as a police officer kneeled on his neck in the US city of Minneapolis in May 2020, to the schoolgirls of Iran who were gassed for refusing to wear the hijab in 2023.[i] In the face of entrenched power, voices were raised for 'Woman, Life, Freedom' by the Kurdish and Iranian women's revolution and in support of #BlackLivesMatter, which reached the ears of the world but have since faded away. We witnessed the extinguishing of breath in Gaza and the livestreaming of the genocide into our living rooms,[ii]

---

[i] The death of twenty-two-year-old Iranian-Kurdish woman Mahsa Jina Amini in 2022 after being arrested for improper dress by the morality police sparked an unprecedented wave of protests against the hijab that has been seen as a women's revolution by many activists.

[ii] The 7 Oct. 2023 lethal raid by Hamas into Israel and the retaliatory genocidal bombing of Gaza.

which has revealed the weakness of global governance and the debilitation of democracy by a triumphant neoliberalism, unburdened by the ideals of human rights and egalitarianism.

Authoritarian and right-wing populism flourishes in the twenty-first century: it is as though we have lived through an era of democracy on sufferance. Democratic institutions like the media and the judiciary have been hollowed out; checks and balances eroded; NGOs and the welfare state undermined. Trump's return to the White House in early 2025, hurling executive orders in every direction, reveals the apparent ease with which basic human rights may be reversed and provides succour to the dictators of the world. This is a perverse 're-wilding' that renews the spaces where patriarchy thrives and women's rights suffer, posing new challenges for feminist resistance to what we see as a historic crisis.

Meanwhile, muted breath is the order of the day in domestic spaces around the world, as was most horrifically demonstrated by the case of Gisèle Pelicot in France. Dominique Pelicot, her husband, would regularly drug her to unconsciousness to enforce her compliance before offering her in online chatrooms 'catering to swingers' to be raped by random men, which he filmed, shared on his networks and stored on his computer. The case revealed the supreme self-confidence of men assured of impunity, not just by the elaborate schemes of a man who delivered a comatose body to them, his property, with his explicit blessings to do what they wanted with her, but by patriarchal society itself. An egregious example of the rape culture faced by women that Gisèle Pelicot tried to singlehandedly overturn; to make 'shame swap sides' from victim to rapist by renouncing her anonymity.[1]

This book has been a long time in the making, during a period when the concept of patriarchy has acquired currency in the popular and political lexicon. Feminists debate whether the concept is capacious or dynamic enough to hold a historical trajectory and make sense of the transnational and national realities

INTRODUCTION

aired here. We agree with Angela Saini in *The Patriarchs* that it is more accurate to talk in terms of patriarchies.[2] This book will investigate what makes a patriarchy so resilient—how it shapes and is shaped in turn by diverse political and economic systems: capitalism, socialism, democracy, dictatorship and theocracy. We wanted to find the fissures and contradictions in 'regressive modernisation',[3] to identify how feminist resistance unsettles the new order and understand how patriarchy undermines feminist solidarity through race, class, religious and national divisions. We examine what the patriarchy has done to women in Saudi Arabia and the ISIS caliphate at one end of the spectrum and, at the other, how patriarchy plays out in Rojava, North East Syria, where a women's revolution is in progress; El Salvador, China, Russia, South Africa and Iceland are the other countries under our microscope. The 'slow poison of patriarchy' spreads,[4] and its nemesis is feminism. However, unsupported and alone, can it be an adequate antidote?

Patriarchy is different from all other systems of oppression—it is institutional and individual, it operates in public and in the most private and intimate of spaces: the home and the body. A description of slavery as at once 'the most public institution *and* the ground of the institution's most terrifying intimacies' applies to patriarchy too.[5] Patriarchy disparages, disempowers *and* depends on women. Men's dependence is disguised in their dominance and destruction. Edith Elizondo, who works with the families of disappeared women in El Salvador, argues that 'men learn to dominate on the bodies of women. So that's why women are useful, because their bodies are a training ground for men to learn their trade.'[6]

Our motivation in writing this book was to understand our times and their implications for feminist politics and activism. We take as our starting point that patriarchy, in its many different versions, exists in every society in the world and has done so for thousands of years—islands of matrilineal[iii] and matrilocal[iv] societies notwithstanding. Some scholars, usually male,[7] have argued that patriarchy's universality and resilience is explained by biology, as if male authority is a natural outcome of biological attributes, a view that has crystallised into 'common sense'. But Raewyn Connell, an Australian theorist of masculinity, explains that masculine and feminine cultures only arise in a system of gendered relations, historical processes that refer to 'bodies and what bodies do'. Gender, Connell insists, is a culture that 'exists precisely to the extent that biology does not determine the social'.[8] Saini reminds us that, '[b]y thinking about gendered inequality as rooted in something unalterable within us, we fail to see it for what it is: something more fragile that has to be constantly remade and reasserted'.[9] It is politics, not biology, that produces patriarchy.

Our question is: How does patriarchy articulate with different political and economic systems? Some feminist academics reject the concept of patriarchy, in part because they believe it constructs women as passive and does not differentiate between the levels of oppression faced by women at a specific time and place.[10] We argue that patriarchy, like feminism, is always contingent: it makes and is made within 'conducive contexts', spaces and conditions that enable gender inequality.[11] The working definition of patriarchy we are using is not controversial—it is a system that facilitates the oppression, exploitation and control of women by men. It has been theorised variously as the 'gender order',[12] 'the sex/gender system'[13] and 'phallocentrism or phallogocentrism'.[v]

[iii] Where kinship is traced through the female line and inheritance is often passed down from mother to daughter.

[iv] Where men live with the wife's family after marriage.

[v] Term originally coined by Jacques Derrida to mean the privileging of the masculine.

INTRODUCTION

Connell breaks it down into its constituent parts: an overarching national and global order that includes gender regimes—like those found in corporations and institutions—that shape and are shaped by gender relations between institutions and between individual women and men.[14] As these elements are not always in alignment and change over time, this approach carries optimism, for it feels less forbidding a task to bring about change in one of these constituent parts than confronting a monumental patriarchy. British sociologist Sylvia Walby also breaks it down, examining patriarchy as it operates in the mode of production, in paid work, in the state, male violence, sexuality and cultural institutions, but she warns that 'the elimination of one does not lead to the demise of the system as a whole';[15] patriarchy instead settles into a new shape and configuration.

In assessing the robustness of patriarchy in the countries we have studied, we have kept some of the following questions in mind: the degree of separation between the public and private spheres and the visibility or invisibility of women in the public sphere; the presence and implementation of equality laws and the re-shaping of labour markets; violence and sexual exploitation; gender equality culture, that is, rights over our own bodies, property and children; the construction of particular masculinities; the sharing of domestic work between men and women and the relation between paid and unpaid work; and the role of religion. We will investigate why education, employment, access to resources and political power, internationally recognised markers of equality, have not proved sufficient to help women escape patriarchal structures.

We have chosen countries that illuminate different patriarchies: demographic masculinisation of the population and state capitalism in China; the interdependence of church and state in post-communist Russia; the highest levels of femicide and the most restrictive abortion laws in El Salvador; how an egalitarian constitution has failed to save post-apartheid South Africa from being one of the most unequal and violent societies in the world; the conundrum of Iceland, where feminism created the space to breathe and flourish despite the neoliberal character of its political economy; the construction of religious nationalism by Saudi Arabia and its offspring ISIS, where patriarchy is manifest in its starkest form; and a women's revolution in Rojava, North East Syria, where remnants of patriarchy still resist change.

To examine the articulation of patriarchy with different political regimes, we chose Russia and China for their post-communist status, with the first being a pseudo-democracy and the second an autocratic state. El Salvador was initially chosen for this book as a democracy in which the state was in hock to gangs, but in the process of writing it has turned into yet another so-called democracy that has delivered authoritarian rule by one man, Nayib Bukele, whose popularity grew when he threw 1 per cent of the population into prison without due process to rid the country of gangs. Saudi Arabia's regime, which falls somewhere between a monarchy and theocracy, is the most reliant on patriarchy. We chose Iceland because it is a functioning democracy and is consistently at the top of the global index on gender equality; and Rojava because it is a revolutionary society explicitly committed to 'real' democracy and the ending of patriarchy. Apart from Rojava, all the other political regimes are underpinned by neoliberal economics, which reveals that neoliberalism has no inherent need for democracy, whatever the West may cynically or naively claim. In fact, true democracy is antagonistic to neoliberalism and vice versa.

Although the United States is not one of our countries, its shadowy influence has shaped developments in all the countries we discuss. The country's search for profit, resources and national security trumps any consideration of women's rights, democratic values and social justice. A US presence permeates the disasters of global politics. In El Salvador, the United States funded a right-wing government's attempts to crush an insurgency that

INTRODUCTION

arose out of poverty and the absence of human and civil rights. While the insurgency was not explicitly feminist, women were present on the frontline and supply lines in large numbers, many of whom were politicised by the struggle but also destroyed by it. In Rojava, once the Kurdish forces had played their part in the US coalition to defeat ISIS, there was no support—financial, moral or political—for the women's revolution taking place there. In the Middle East and North Africa, Timothy Mitchell, an American academic, observes that '[a]s a rule, the most secular regimes ... have been those most independent of the United States. The more closely a government is allied with Washington, the more Islamic its politics.' Iran is the only exception.[16] Those regimes that struck out on their own were undermined, unsupported or targets of CIA coup attempts—Egypt under Nasser, republican Iraq, the Palestine national movement, post-independence Algeria, the Republic of South Yemen, Ba'athist Syria with Nasser in Egypt but successful in Iraq, where the downfall of the government ushered in Saddam Hussein. Yet these were the regimes whose political agendas included land reform, women's rights, free education and healthcare.

Point of departure

In the 1990s the world was re-configured: the Berlin wall was knocked down; China embraced capitalism; the Soviet Union collapsed; and a new phase of neo-liberal capitalism[iv] was inaugurated by Ronald Reagan and Margaret Thatcher in the late 1970s which became hegemonic by the 1990s. In 1979-80 Deng

---

[vi] The term neoliberalism was coined in the 1930s, but neoliberal ideas entered the mainstream in the 1970s when Keynesian economics became discredited in the US and the UK and became the dominant economic form in the 1990s.

Xiaoping launched the 'Four Modernisations' programme, market-oriented reforms that opened up China's economy to foreign capitalist investment which aligned with the global trend of neoliberal economic policies. The Soviet leader Mikhail Gorbachev's democratisation was met by an attempted coup in 1991. It was defeated but the Soviet Union was fatally wounded. The rot had begun in 1979 when the Soviet Union invaded Afghanistan to support its Communist government against the US-backed mujahideen, setting in motion a chain of events that reverberates still today: a global Islamist movement, the collapse of communism and the rise of neoliberalism as the only ideological answer to the world's problems.

The new world order ushered in a new sexual settlement—a new era of male domination, buttressed in many parts of the world by religion. While we have provided some historical context, spanning the twentieth century where necessary, we have, in the main, confined ourselves to the period beginning in the 1990s, which represented a significant break with the past for much of the world. In both Russia and El Salvador, the turn to neoliberalism was accompanied by a flowering of the women's movement—an energetic, sometimes raucous, autonomous women's movement emerged. A major shift in the status quo took place: the signing of the Peace Accords in 1992 in El Salvador; the end of the Soviet Union in 1991; and the dismantling of apartheid between 1990 and 1994 in South Africa. Gorbachev's policies of glasnost ('openness') and perestroika ('restructuring'), implemented in the 1980s, allowed a liberal feminism to take root in the USSR, one that set itself against the uniformity of Soviet-era gender stereotypes and in favour of individual choice. Similarly, in El Salvador, women guerrillas who came out of the bloody armed struggle against the state, feeling betrayed by their exclusion from the Peace Accords, discarded the burden of male comradeship and began to organise

INTRODUCTION

autonomously. The Peace Accords were finally signed by the government in order to satisfy the World Bank, which was offering El Salvador a structural adjustment loan that demanded the end of the civil war.

The second turning point was in 2011, the Arab Spring uprisings that the former president of Tunisia, Moncef Marzouki, speaking in 2024, described as Arab volcanoes that will continue erupting.[17] Though the Arab Spring is widely considered a failure, no mainstream narrative has pointed out that the genuinely democratic women's revolution in Rojava, which now occupies nearly one-third of Syria—a grassroots, anti-patriarchal, multi-ethnic, secular and ecologically sustainable democracy—was made possible by the Arab Spring. The reverberations were even felt in Saudi Arabia. A drive to get more women into work began in 2011, when it was also announced that women would be given the right to stand and vote in municipal elections.

In Russia, the 2010s marked the transition of feminism from a liberal to a more radical movement. During this decade, feminism became a word that women proudly adopted, a badge worn on the lapel and not hidden under layers of cloth. Maria Alyokhina of Pussy Riot attributes a certain magic to 2011, the year of the Snow Revolution.[18] Large-scale protests against what many Russians saw as fraudulent elections began in 2011 and continued until 2013. At the time, those involved thought it was the start of a bigger revolution, but it was not to be.[19]

For Iceland, the turning point was 1975, when 90 per cent of women went on an all-day strike that led to their Equal Rights Law the following year and the election of the world's first female president in 1980, the repercussions of which resonated right into the twenty-first century, not just in Iceland but throughout the world.

Saudi Arabia has faced several points of turmoil in its short history: 1979 was a moment of reckoning for the monarchy, when the Iranian Revolution brought Ayatollah Khomeini to power. Saudi Arabia responded by ceding greater power to the religious authorities in social and religious matters, which removed the limited freedoms Saudi women enjoyed. The Soviet invasion of Afghanistan also took place in 1979. Saudi and US support for Osama bin Laden's mujahideen mired the Soviets in a foreign adventure that hastened the end of communism, creating an ideological vacuum that was filled by religious fundamentalism. The US deemed this to be a threat more easily controlled than communism. All of this was a setback for women.

The origins of patriarchy

We do not know and may never know the origins of patriarchy. All we know is that it seems to saturate recorded history. However, notions of eternal, natural patriarchy are being unravelled: archaeologists are re-interpreting the first humans' representations of themselves in the Ice Age between 20,000 and 40,000 years ago that dispatch to the dustbin of history the modern myth of the stereotypical hunter, the hairy hulk, a fearless family man, slaying beasts bigger than himself. The Venus of Hohle Fels in Germany made 40,000 years ago from a mammoth tusk and the glistening Moravian 'Black Venus' fashioned from clay and crushed bones 27,000 years ago, are small yet massively voluptuous figurines found beside scattered relics of bone and fibre—suggestive clues of the invisible sexual politics of the Ice Age.[20] It seems these women were their own subjects: they made their own art, sculpted and carved, hunted and fished, grew and harvested plants, wove baskets and fabrics and nets that they used to wear, fish and snare. The discovery of these prehistoric technologies is shedding 'new light not only on the labour of a heretofore unrecognized segment of Upper Paleolithic people, women, but also on the high value of their labour'.[21]

INTRODUCTION

We do not have the space to engage with the extensive literature on the origins of patriarchy, much of it driven by a sense of intrigue about a time when men did not rule, of which the latest is Saini's *The Patriarchs*.[22] However, the anthropological and archaeological literature suggests there was no single event, no 'big bang', but an uneven and gradual assertion of male power across societies and historical periods. The growing research into early matrilineal societies reveals that power was much more diffuse: women had greater sexual freedom and property rights and lived in societies that could definitely not be described as patriarchal, even if brothers and uncles had some authority.[23] Matrilineal societies existed in pockets in Asia, Africa and the Americas until the nineteenth and early twentieth centuries, when many of these societies were forced, through a process of attrition, under colonisation to align with European patriarchal gender norms. The state of Kerala in India abolished matriliny altogether only as late as 1976.[24] We are not arguing that patriarchy did not exist in these societies before colonisation but that other templates of organising society had been available. Even today, there are pockets of matrilineal societies, albeit so few as to feel like anomalies. The Mosuo community in China, for example, has become famous for its 'walking marriage', where men may visit a woman on a nightly basis but return to their own homes, where they are responsible for raising their nephews and nieces but not their own children. The community preserved their traditions while their remote area was inaccessible to tourism, but today they are on the cusp of change, heading towards a more traditional patriarchal model. Umoja, the women-only village in Kenya, led by a matriarch, was set up as recently as 1990 for women wanting to escape male violence.[25] Umoja has been a source of inspiration to the women in Rojava (see Chapter 7), who have also set up a women-only village, Jinwar. Anthropologist Gerda Lerner argues that there is historical evidence to show that there were egalitarian societies but believes there is no hard evidence to conclude that matriarchies existed once upon a time.[26]

White feminist scholars date the beginning of feminist resistance to the famous 1848 Seneca Falls Convention of middle-class women in the United States. As Saini points out, however, the indigenous women who had lived there in egalitarian societies for over 200 years had veto rights over any future wars: 'So, the middle-class American women who met to fight for equality in Seneca Falls in 1848 were asking for a small slice of what native American women in the same area had had, as a matter of course, for centuries before them.'[27]

Patriarchy and capitalism: A toxic co-dependency?

Patriarchy existed before capitalism, which most commentators date to the sixteenth century but which utterly transformed the economy of England and the colonies with the onset of the industrial revolution in the late eighteenth century. Feminist historians and economists have triggered 'titanic' debates about what can—and cannot—be inferred from official records and histories of the economy, work, waged and unwaged, gender and generation. Feminist scholars have analysed the defeat of women in modernity: how patriarchy shaped the context, the nest, from which the economic esprit and engine of our era, capitalism, emerged and achieved world domination. They have shown the transition from a family economy—to which women, children and men contributed—to the creation of the male breadwinner[28] in the 'symbiotic structural relationship between inherited patriarchal relations and nascent industrial capitalism'.[29] To this must be added the irreducibly important excavation of slave ownership, which funded investment in capitalist enterprise.[30]

Heidi Hartmann, American economist, notes that '[c]apital accumulation encounters pre-existing social forms and both

INTRODUCTION

destroys them and adapts to them. The adaptation of capital can be seen as a reflection of the *strength* of these pre-existing forms to persevere in new environments.'[31] Sociologist Gary Blank relies on this analysis to argue that 'this opens the door to an historical account of how capitalism instantiates and transforms patriarchy, rather than why capitalism logically requires patriarchy'.[32]

Historian Barbara Taylor's pioneering book *Eve and the New Jerusalem: Socialism and Feminism in the Nineteenth Century* reminds us that the socialist and feminist movements that were a rebuke to patriarchal capitalism are marked by breaks, retreats and ruptures, defeats and forgettings.[33] By the second half of the nineteenth century, the British labour movement—one of the largest mass movements in the country—had been captured: it became a men's movement. What the compulsory domestication of women gave to men was both domination and dependence on women for their maintenance and the ecology of their everyday life and, with that, control over women's bodies, space and time. This was expressed in the patriarchal concept of the male breadwinner whose wages would sustain the whole family, which defined the labour movement's wage-bargaining priorities for a century—despite the evidence that at any one time half the men were not fathers with dependent children, that in any case the wage did not adequately sustain their families and that despite institutional and cultural barricades, women were always working: paid and unpaid. The family wage was 'illusory', said pioneering suffragist, social reformer and feminist politician, Eleanor Rathbone; it was 'a crucial foundation of male power'.[34] Rathbone and women's movements campaigned for the 'family allowance'—a child benefit paid directly to the mother—as an unequivocal assertion of *social* responsibility for the care of children. Trade unions continued to bargain for men's 'family wage' in the 1970s, despite women's movements' successes in securing equal pay and opportunities legislation.

Hartmann reports that the end of the family wage has led some commentators to predict the demise of patriarchy, arguing that 'as women are increasingly able to earn money they will increasingly refuse to submit to subordination in the family, and that since the family is oppressive particularly to women and children, it will collapse as soon as people can support themselves outside it'.[35] Hartmann disagrees with this view, as do we, because patriarchy has proved to be more resilient, partly by disguising itself as as 'natural' as the air we breathe.

We started our research with the notion that patriarchy was a pillar of capitalism but discovered that there are tensions between the two systems that sometimes reinforce patriarchy and sometimes weaken it, tensions that have been exploited and intensified by various political movements. The connection between the two has been theorised extensively, but we do not have the space to do justice to those debates. Under pressure from feminist demands, capitalist solutions can sometimes be found to ameliorate the worst effects of patriarchy. The appallingly low rate of conviction in rape cases globally has driven women, particularly in countries like the US and the UK, to pursue civil prosecutions with higher rates of success and in which financial damages are paid to victims. Price Waterhouse Coopers (PwC), one of the big four multinational accounting firms, a beacon of capitalism, estimates that if the gender pay gap across the Organisation for Economic Co-operation and Development was reduced to that of Sweden's, it would result in a gain of $5.8 trillion to GDP in OECD countries.[36] PwC ascribes this gap mostly to what feminists have described as the motherhood penalty—the loss of earnings resulting from childbirth and childcare—and argues for 'policy solutions that aim to redistribute unpaid childcare more equally between women and men' and increase the low take-up in paternity leave.

Population control, which has been central to capitalist economics, has directly impacted women's reproductive rights. At a

INTRODUCTION

time of falling populations in the West, the cost of pensions and care for the elderly cannot be met with lower numbers of younger people in work. Combined with the neoliberal impulse to shrink the welfare state, rising nationalism and anti-migrant populism, the pressure on women to produce more children, particularly from right-wing populist sources, is increasing. A 2021 report finds that 30 per cent of countries, Russia, El Salvador and China among them, now have pronatalist policies, which include restrictions in access to abortion, as compared to 10 per cent in the 1970s.[37] However, with women's higher levels of education and participation in the labour market and greater awareness of rights, as in Russia and China, pronatalist policies struggle to be effective.

Capitalism is chameleon-like: it adapts to political pressures and changing values. It has no principles other than turning a profit. Hence its longevity and success. It is commonly argued that capitalism does not see the colour of money (i.e. race), although it will capitalise on racism to divide and rule the workforce and extract maximum profit. The same applies to the sex/gender of money. Social theorist Michèle Barrett stresses that the oppression of women is enacted by other factors and not necessarily 'the logic of capitalism'.[38] This is demonstrated by new policies on gender equality and inclusion—enhancements to parental-leave policies, bereavement and baby-loss leave, and a new menopause policy—announced by Deloitte, one of the other big four accounting companies. The firm has also introduced cover for assisted fertility treatment and gender dysphoria as part of its private medical insurance.[39] A report in *Forbes* tells us that shareholder activism has been used to drive gender equality. A Microsoft shareholder resolution in 2020 went beyond the issue of gender pay equity to call for disclosures to tackle sexual harassment in the wake of the #MeToo movement.[40] It is political action by feminists that has drawn attention to workplace inequalities, the gender pay gap, sexual harassment at work and domestic violence at home, to which capitalism responds with corporate social responsibility policies that burnish a company's public image and enhance their profits.

Neoliberalism

The current, more aggressive phase of capitalism is underpinned by neoliberalism, a predominantly economic philosophy that was first implemented in Chile in the 1970s, based on the shrinking of the state, the privatisation of government services and a reliance on the individual rather than the collective, which has been devastating for women. There is no such thing as society, Thatcher famously declared—that is the key political idea underpinning neoliberalism, which flourishes in dictatorships and democracies alike. Yet women's rights groups, some of which identify as feminist, have emerged in these inhospitable conditions, particularly in Russia and El Salvador. How are we to understand this convergence of neoliberalism and feminism?

We profoundly disagree with Nancy Fraser, who believed that second-wave feminism in the UK in the 1970s 'served to legitimate a structural transformation of capitalist society',[41] an argument that embodies classic left suspicions that feminism has weakened the class struggle. While there may have been a convergence of the two in terms of historical period, it is not a causal relationship but a case of capitalism assimilating the opposition in order to neutralise it. As Rahila Gupta has argued elsewhere, '[i]f part of the project of neoliberalism is to shrink the size of the state, it serves its purpose to co-opt the feminist critique that the state is both paternalistic and patriarchal'.[42] Neoliberalism provides an illusion of freedom—traditional forms of exploitation, such as prostitution and pornography, are presented as freedom and empowerment. Neoliberalism is rhetorically gender neutral—

INTRODUCTION

the marketplace welcomes the qualified professional, and anyone, it is said, can be an astrophysicist or an entrepreneur. Achieving gender equality becomes an individualising project: lean in, try harder, look better, thinner, younger. Sheryl Sandberg, successful executive at Facebook until she stepped down in 2022, became the poster girl of this new 'feminism' with her book, *Lean In*, in which she argued that the onus was on women to step up and take on leadership roles.[43] While work outside the home is no longer frowned upon, the successful woman juggles the demands of both home and a career and draws upon her femininity as a source of power in the workplace. The system does nothing to ease this double burden by providing good-quality, reasonably priced childcare. When this obliges women to choose between the two options, the narrative presents it as one of choice and freedom, valorises the stay-at-home mum and produces research on the diminished life choices of children who grow up without the full attention of their mothers.

Neoliberalism appears to laud virtues central to democracy and feminism—freedom, equality, empowerment and participation—but hollows them out in support of a pro-market agenda. The pragmatism of capital, in its latest neoliberal guise, appears everywhere on view, as we will demonstrate in the individual chapters. The neoliberal assumption that countries that emerge from a period of conflict and embrace democracy will gradually move towards peace has been belied by both El Salvador and South Africa—and Africa and Latin America generally—where violence and crime have been major destabilising features. Violence has a particular significance for women given its masculine and misogynistic presentation. Just as there is nothing inherently peaceful about democracy, there is nothing to suggest that democracy is inherently inimical to patriarchy. If violence is an expression of unequal power relations, and democracy is more and more a thin cover for neoliberalism rather than a force for equality, then this undermines any expectations we might have for women doing better under democracy.

The labour of love

The domestic occupies an unstable place in conceptions of the political: it is simultaneously regulated by the church and state and yet deemed a uniquely private domain, where the 'writ of the state runs out at the gate of the family home', wherein men and children are naturally nurtured and disciplined by women.[44] The family, in all its modern variations, has been both comfort blanket and hair shirt for women. As the primary site on which patriarchy is reproduced and reinforced, states around the world have made attempts to buttress it. Even as the family implodes through poverty, violence and immigration in El Salvador or divorce and single parenthood in Russia, it is kept afloat as an idea, reinforced by conservative laws and politicians' speeches.

Both Abdullah Öcalan, imprisoned leader of the Kurdish struggle for self-determination (see Chapter 7), and Engels claim that families enslave women. Engels described the marital relationship in economic terms, viewing the man as the 'bourgeois' and the woman as the 'proletariat'.[45] His 1884 work *The Origin of the Family, Private Property and the State* made the case for the abolition of the family as the economic unit of society and the primary location of women's oppression. It was Engels who pointed out that the word family originally referred to the number of slaves held by one man. His description of the 'modern' family could easily apply to families in the twenty-first century: 'The modern individual family is based on the open or disguised domestic enslavement of the woman; and modern society is a mass composed solely of individual families as its molecules.'[46] While the degree of domestic enslavement may vary across cultures and countries, this assertion remains broadly true and indicates how far feminism has to traverse.

INTRODUCTION

The recognition that the family is the micro unit through which a patriarchal system asserts itself led to a number of experiments to 'abolish the family', as in the early days of the Soviet Union and in the many attempts at communal living in societies as diverse as Israel and hippy communes in the West. Is there a way to radicalise the family without abolishing it, as the various failed attempts seem to suggest an irreplaceable need for human intimacy? The nuclear family (as well as the joint family system in countries like India) has been subtly changing, with rates of marriage dropping worldwide, women getting married later and choosing in greater numbers to have either no or fewer children, more women in the workforce and in education and more enlightened LGB and T policies.

The work of care, or 'social reproduction', is a decisive preoccupation of feminist politics that is announced in the radical notion of 'the personal is political', one of the founding theories of the Women's Liberation Movement in the 1960s,[47] in 'domestic labour' debates in the 1970s and more recently feminist expansion of the theory of social reproduction: 'If workers' labor produces all the wealth in society, then who produces the worker? Put another way: what kinds of processes enable the worker to arrive at the doors of her place of work every day so that she can produce the wealth of society?' Social reproduction theory is concerned with that question—it embraces the reproduction of life itself and the complex network of social processes that produce human beings' conditions of existence.[48]

The work of care, unlike other economic activities, cannot be reduced to a product; it has been deemed a cost rather than a benefit and ranked low in political priority. The very nature of care as a personal relationship between care giver and care recipient does not automatically hold in the market. 'Care is a personal service, not just the production of a product that is separable from the person delivering it,' argues economist Susan Himmelweit;[49] it requires presence: it cannot be impersonally dispatched or digitalised. By what criteria can we measure the time, qualities and feelings that comprise receivers' needs, or the affection, regard and responsibility animating the giver?[50]

In a world dominated by neoliberal ideology, in which the unpaid and paid work of care has been both demanded and disparaged, depleted, devalued and privatised, the COVID-19 pandemic that spread across the world in 2020 exposed 'what is of value in an economy'. Economist Mariana Mazzucato says that '[t]he areas that we thought of as "high value"—finance or real estate, for example—are not the components of society that we regard as "foundational"'. The pandemic forced governments to re-define 'essential' work: 'Our most valuable, irreplaceable citizens are those who work in health and social care, education, public transport, supermarkets and delivery services.'[51] These jobs are performed primarily by women, people of colour and migrants. Feminists have drawn attention to the failure of GDP to take account of unpaid care and domestic work. The effect of this gendered myopia is to erase the invisible work upon which individuals' and societies' survival depends—what it is, who does it, where it happens. This is illuminated dramatically in India, where the poorest women workers expend inordinate amounts of time travelling to and from employment and then perform unpaid domestic labour and the work of care. These activities that don't appear in GDP statistics in effect subsidise the marketised economy and state provision.[52] Women from the Caribbean to Africa and the Pacific Rim have to leave their own families to become part of what Sonya Michel and Ito Peng describe as 'transnational care migration' to the Global North.[53]

The politics of care, therefore, is not only central to everyday life; it is a global issue. It is, argues social policy scholar Fiona Williams, 'central to strategies of social justice' in the context of an international crisis of care,[54] at the heart of which are the

INTRODUCTION

women who constitute around half of the world's migrant workers. Across the world, the patriarchal division of domestic labour is being buffeted by women's labour force participation and by the dependence on migrant domestic workers—a dependence that reproduces gender, class and racial hierarchies. The populist politics of the Global North—the beneficiary of migrant care providers—sponsors the anti-migrant political hatred starkly visible in Trump's anti-migrant policies. The harms of present generations are, argues Williams, connected, therefore, to the unrecognised colonial sufferings of past generations. The political ethic of care that is vital to everyday life is knotted in historic global inequalities, says Williams, that 'are now playing out in the most intimate of spaces'.[55]

Undoubtedly, migration is a feminist issue.

Masculinity under patriarchy

What kinds of masculinities are promoted by patriarchy? There was no single model of masculinity that emerged from our research. While there were commonalities in construction of the ideal masculine type—muscular, sporty, adventurous, decisive, attractive to women, the 'hard man' like Putin of Russia or Bukele of El Salvador—there were differences even between them, with Bukele sporting a 'metrosexual' look rather than a bare-bodied approach. While a heavily tattooed body announced a certain kind of gangster masculinity in El Salvador, it was no longer a sign of hegemonic masculinity under Bukele's strategy of arresting and imprisoning all tattooed bodies in a deliberate conflation with gang membership. Those masculinities dubbed by women as toxic or deviant are often welcome in patriarchal societies, like Russia, where feminism is ridiculed and has little currency. Anna Adrianiva, Russian feminist, while acknowledging the prevalence of the military man as masculine ideal, a Putin prototype, argues that the oligarchs' enormous wealth and influence have popularised a softer masculine ideal among younger men working in high tech or the international corporate sector.[56] Elon Musk challenged the head of Facebook, Mark Zuckerberg, to a cage fight; his claim that it would be fought for charity did not disguise the bare-knuckle masculinity that lay behind it.[57]

We have also seen the rise of toxic, criminal masculinity, the sigma male, as embodied by the likes of Andrew Tate, whose proud acceptance of the label 'misogynist' and whose claim to women's bodies as if they were his birth right are the kind of blatant patriarchal attitudes that belong to a previous era.[58] While the internet may have been the medium that amplified his voice, that it has been widely and enthusiastically received especially by young men,[59] perhaps as a backlash to the perceived crisis of masculinity provoked by the #MeToo movement and feminism in general, is frightening. This presumptuous ownership of women's bodies finds echoes in the incel (involuntary celibates) subculture among men who are seen as 'losers', pathetic models of masculinity in their failure to attract women, but who are also, in fact, a variant of male supremacism.[60] Hegemonic masculinity is built on the negative ideology of what it means to be a man, usually imposed upon boys during the socialisation process; it is characterised by physical strength, sexual conquest (of women) and financial success.[61] However, Connell has argued that it would hardly be hegemonic if only negative traits were attached to it,[62] as hegemony also requires consent from subordinate groups. It must include attributes like being a father, sustaining a sexual relationship and bringing home a wage.

A BBC Radio 4 programme on patriarchy sought to emphasise that men do not benefit from the system by listing the following issues: men die earlier than women, are more likely to commit suicide, are incarcerated in greater numbers, are more likely to be the victim of a violent crime and are more likely to be unemployed.⁶³ True, but what the analysis omitted was the context: many of these issues arise because of male power, their presence in public spaces, their violence towards women and ideals of masculinity that prevent them from expressing emotion and seeking help. What the programme also did not make clear is that masculinities are shaped by race and class,⁶⁴ nationalism and ideology.

The way in which public space is available to men is strikingly seen in the development of youth gangs in places like Russia and El Salvador: 'Countless generations of boys around the world grow up playing and fighting in the streets, in a space of freedom from adult control, where they can assert their masculinity, develop friendships, and protect their turf.'⁶⁵ This freedom has never been available to women, and those who venture into public spaces fear sexual harassment and assault.

The sexual prowess of leaders and the number of attractive women in their entourage and fan base also ensure their winnability in democratic elections or continued popularity in dictatorships. Political scientist Valerie Sperling, writing about Putin and Russia, explains how masculinity plays a useful role in legitimising political authority:

> Instances where political actors bring to bear masculinity, femininity, sexualization, and homophobia as political legitimation tools occur in a wide range of political contexts: in semi-authoritarian regimes like contemporary Russia's, in more authoritarian regimes like China's, and in democratically inclined regimes like those in Western Europe and the United States. It is patriarchy, not political regime type, that produces the use of gender norms as instruments of political authority-building.⁶⁶

The readiness to engage in war is the ultimate signifier of manliness and masculinity. Putin's invasion of Ukraine, initially with the support of the Wagner group and Yevgeny Prigozhin, who set a new low in toxic masculinity, enhanced the hard man approach. As Sperling observes: 'Gender norms can be used in politics to undermine the authority of undemocratic regimes, for instance, by labelling political leaders as unmanly.'[67]

The Kurdish movement for self-determination recognises the toll that masculinity takes on men and not just women. A Kurdish activist said:

> Öcalan always asked the women, did you kill the man in your head? And this is a really good question. If you don't succeed to kill masculinity in your mind, you cannot succeed to be yourself. This is the theory of *xwebûn*, to be yourself. If you can't be yourself, you cannot be in a collective, you cannot be in relation with other people, in a symbiotic way.[68]

Unlike many radical feminists in the West who believe in organising autonomously and leaving men to work on their masculinity, Kurdish women do both—they set up independent structures while working on educating men and 'killing their masculinity'. Another Kurdish woman said:

> We can't leave the men to change themselves because they have a connection with patriarchy, using this power over women in private life. But the main question is how we are going to push them to deal with their masculinity. For this we have two things; we have to have a very strong autonomous organisation to be strong against this manipulative masculinity. ... And on the other hand, we have to educate them.[69]

In El Salvador, too, women talked about their work in reshaping masculinities and saw it as a necessary part of feminist activism.

Political and economic factors play a role in the construction of masculinity. Deniz Kandiyoti believes that the increased level of violence against women in the Middle East is not a sign of the strength of the old patriarchal order but of weakness, a sign of masculinity's profound crisis.[70] According to Peggy Watson, the creation of market economies in Eastern Europe following the fall of the Berlin wall 'fundamentally entails the construction of a "man's world" and the simultaneous propagation of masculinity in the public sphere, with domestication and the marketing of women. The degradation of feminine identity is an inevitable corollary of this process.'[71]

Violence against women

Violence against women remains the unyielding nub at the heart of the relationship between men and women. The figures are damning. There is a culture of disbelief that minimises women's experiences, with a refusal to name, recognise and record acts of violence, a narrative capture that allows shame to be attached to the beaten woman rather than the man doing the beating and a lack of consensus on the limits and circumstances—this is the irreducible evidence of the health of patriarchy. Political attention to men's violence as a political problem has been intermittent and ad hoc and always contingent on the presence of women's movements that confronted domestic abuse. Public awareness grew 'when feminism was strong and ebbed when feminism was weak'.[72] With the renewal of feminist activism in the 1960s and the Women's Liberation Movement in the UK, sexual violence was restored to the political and academic agenda not as a problem of hapless men's incontinent loss of control or passion but as strategic and purposive. A major achievement of feminism in our time, according to feminist scholars and activists Elizabeth Frazer and Kimberly Hutchings, has been to transform the meaning of political violence by reframing 'what is and is not violence' and, therefore, 'what is and is not political'. Feminism instead names 'sexual and domestic violence against women as an exercise of power, embedded in and reproducing patriarchal privilege and the subordination of women'.[73]

The first refuges for women escaping violence at home were established in the UK and the US in the early 1970s. In 1978, the Women's Liberation Movement passed what became known as its seventh demand: 'Freedom for all women from intimidation by the threat or use of violence or sexual coercion regardless of marital status; and an end to the laws, assumptions and institutions which perpetuate male dominance and aggression to women.'[74] Laws tackling domestic violence were subsequently passed in the US and the UK in the 1970s and 1980s. By 2006, international activism against men's violence culminated in the UN Secretary General's report *Ending Violence against Women: From Words to Deeds*: 'Patriarchal disparities of power, discriminatory cultural norms and economic inequalities serve to deny women's human rights and perpetuate violence. Violence against women is one of the key means through which male control over women's agency and sexuality is maintained.'[75]

Globally, a third of women have endured physical and/or sexual violence by their intimate partners, reports the World Health Organization.[76] The issue is rife with paradox. Naming acts of violence against women is harder because so much of the violence has been normalised. It is harder than naming racism because racist acts are usually located outside the day-to-day reality in the home, perpetrated by the 'other', whereas so much sexual violence stems from our 'own'. There is a theoretical issue with measuring violence. There are hierarchies of violence or, more precisely, a hierarchy of meanings attached to violence. Violence in the domestic sphere, for example, is seen as acceptable or normalised as compared to violence in the public arena. The focus on public violence invalidates the terror that many women and children live with on a daily basis within the 'refuge' of the private sphere. Following the lead of a number of scholars, a report produced by Scottish Women's Aid, *Everyday Terrorism: How Fear Works in Domestic Abuse*, drew parallels between domestic violence and terrorism, partly motivated by the need to dissolve the boundaries 'between forms of violence that are usually framed as public, political and spectacular, and forms of

INTRODUCTION

violence that are usually framed as private, apolitical and mundane'.[77] Where the issue sits in governmental priorities, globally, is revealed by ministries for public security having a higher status than those concerned with violence against women. In fact, in many countries there is no special portfolio for women. Physical violence with visible consequences attracts a more effective police response than coercive control and mental or emotional abuse. Additionally, no research has been done to differentiate the severity of violence experienced. The number of incidents alone cannot help us understand whether the violence in Iceland is of a different category from the violence in El Salvador.

Every single country examined in this book has legislated against violence against women. We live in an era where violence against women is almost universally recognised as a crime, but everywhere the legislation is wanting and could be improved, and everywhere there is a failure of implementation, even where the laws pass muster. In Russia, the punishment for domestic violence has been downgraded. In El Salvador, the law is surprisingly comprehensive, including 'symbolic' and 'patrimonial' forms of violence (see Chapter 1) in its definition of domestic violence, which are not to be found in UK law, and yet until recently El Salvador had the highest number of femicides in the world. Iceland, which consistently ranks as the country with the greatest levels of gender equality in the world, still celebrates Husband's Day, when the menfolk are spoiled by their wives and girlfriends with traditional delicacies such as ram's testicles and sheep's head jelly.[78] And the rate of violence against women—one in four women report sexual or physical violence[79]—is similar to that of the UK. Joan Smith, journalist and campaigner, has revealed a strong link between men engaged in acts of public terror and their personal history of domestic violence either as perpetrators, victims or witnesses.[80]

The economic costs of domestic violence, in work, health and education, are vast: in healthcare alone, the cost is estimated at

27

billions of dollars.⁸¹ Making an economic case to the government on the scourge of domestic violence, as opposed to a solely human rights case, of the number of working days lost, the consequential economic costs to the criminal justice system or the health service, is also an effective way of getting governments to respond. By pointing to how patriarchy damages the interests of capital, the hope is that in the interests of profitability, that particular 'limb' of patriarchy will be weakened by the state acting in the interests of capital. Conversely, demonstrating the savings achieved by appropriate intervention by the women's sector strengthens the argument for increased funding, as Southall Black Sisters has sought to do.⁸²

Sexual violence, which overlaps with domestic violence, is also a way of controlling and disciplining women, an expression of power, contempt and hatred of women, in its many forms: sexual harassment, assault, rape, pornography and prostitution. Of all the forms of sexual violence, pornography and prostitution are the most contested, not least between feminists. Critics argue that pornography harms producers and consumers; that it deforms masculinity; that it normalises violence and rape; that it distorts and hijacks authentic sexuality, especially in adolescents; and that it reinforces sexist and misogynist attitudes towards women. It is everywhere; our culture is saturated with it more than ever. Not surprisingly, the porn industry attempts to counter these arguments but, more dishearteningly, so do so-called sex-positive activists: by pointing to the absence of definitive research on the causal links between the consumption of porn and rape; by using that classic neoliberal trope of 'choice' to defend women's right to participate in its production; by calling it censorship; and by traducing it as anti-sex. Gail Dines, feminist academic and activist, insists, however, 'I am pro sex and that's why I'm anti porn ... because the most anti sex imagery I've ever seen is in pornography. Porn, really, is to sex [what] McDonald's is to food.'⁸³

INTRODUCTION

Like pornography, prostitution too is a fault line that remains unresolved. What makes prostitution hard to challenge is the patriarchal trope that it is inevitable, necessary and universal. Even those academics who see prostitution as a form of work rather than violence against women accept that 'sex work is critical to an analysis of the lived intersectionality of capitalism and patriarchy in individual and collective lives'.[84] This is one of the major schisms in feminist activism across the world—whether prostitution is a form of work, no better or worse than any other 'waged-labour' under capitalism and in need of good trade union representation to improve working conditions, or a form of violence against women.

We explore how prostitution was treated in the early years of the Soviet Union partly because it chimes with the modern abolitionist movement, even though the Bolsheviks did not theorise or understand violence against women beyond ascribing it to capitalism. They introduced policies to criminalise punters and found ways of rehabilitating women rather than criminalising them. They sought to abolish prostitution and thought it would gradually wither away in a communist state. These attempts are not widely known today. What survives today is Russian revolutionary Alexandra Kollontai's equation of prostitution with marriage, as both institutions provide unfettered access to women's bodies in return for financial gain, a view expressed by a number of celebrated feminists like Simone de Beauvoir and Mary Wollstonecraft. This argument is marshalled by radical feminists to disparage both institutions and used by left circles to defend prostitution as a rational option because it is no different from marriage, a widely accepted bourgeois institution. The rise in same-sex marriage, the introduction of rape in marriage laws in all but approximately thirty-two countries and the drop in marriage rates in favour of cohabitation are all factors that serve to weaken the analogy.[85] Just as prostitution is used to condemn all that is wrong with marriage, it is used by Marxists to condemn all that is wrong with waged labour following on from Marx's statement that 'prostitution is only a *specific* expression of the general prostitution of the *labourer*'.[86]

The idea that both marriage and prostitution provide a framework of consent makes it quite difficult to get convictions for rape, especially in prostitution. Rape conviction rates are low across the world; the reporting rates, legal definitions of rape and conviction rates are so variable that it is difficult to assess its real prevalence. The following comparison makes the point well: in India, with the world's biggest population at 1.4 billion, more than 31,000 rapes were reported in 2022,[87] while in England and Wales, with a population of merely 60 million, nearly 68,000 rapes were recorded in 2023/4.[88] Post-conflict societies do appear to have a higher rate of violence towards women and girls, as we note in El Salvador and South Africa. However, qualitative research of women's stories of rape shows that there is a widespread culture of disbelief that ends up re-traumatising women who take the initial bold step of reporting the rape. This culture of disbelief is slowly being dislodged as we have seen with the success of the #MeToo movement in bringing down powerful men and heinous cases like that of Gisèle Pelicot, the predictable backlash notwithstanding.

A shocking UN account published in March 2016 on South Sudan says that soldiers were allowed to rape in lieu of wages.[89] If rape is a central tool of patriarchy, then using rape to prop up a failing regime, unable to pay its soldiers, demonstrates how patriarchy undergirds authoritarian rule. Rape is now recognised as 'an extremely effective wartime weapon. It is strategically used to shame, demoralize and humiliate the enemy. By systematically raping women and girls, armed groups assert power and domination over not only the women, but their men as well.'[90] The gendered political economy (plundering of natural resources,

INTRODUCTION

looting, pillage, smuggling of various kinds) of 'new wars' contributes to the logic of persistence. Armed groups benefit from sustained violence. The military priority is the making and maintaining of violent masculinities to engender terror, plunder and rape.[91] Violations of human rights are used to subordinate the population. While these features may have been present in 'old wars', what is new is the flagrant abandoning of the rules of engagement: the indiscriminate bombing of schools and hospitals. In old wars, men within the military forces of the state were regularly depicted as heroic, courageous and 'just' warriors selflessly protecting their country and 'their' women and children. Gender hierarchy was thus key to nationalist goals and symbolism. Designated the 'rape capital of the world',[92] the Democratic Republic of the Congo is the archetype of contemporary warfare—an ensemble of national and international, religious and economic interests—at the heart of which is the treasure of cobalt and other precious metals vital to twenty-first-century electronics. Since 1996, the conflict has led to an estimated 6 million deaths and rampant rape.

Any survey of violence against women reveals the battle over the female body, lying bleeding and torn in the street and home, both metaphorically and physically: instrumentalised by the state as a mechanism of population control; straitjacketed by religious forces in a bid to police sexual morality; raped by soldiers as a means of desecrating the 'honour' of the enemy; and beaten by men in the name of love.

Feminist resistance

Given that violence has been so central to the shaping of modern masculinity, and violence against women is extensive in all societies, it is not surprising that pacifism and non-violence are central elements of feminist thought. This has led, in some cases, to the refusal to contemplate violence as a defensive tool to be used by the powerless to escape their oppression: in the defence of their revolution against Islamo-fascist groups like ISIS, the women of Rojava took up arms, and some women have killed their abusive partners as the ultimate escape from a life of abuse. There is no doubt that women toting guns gain respect from their male comrades and enemies as the women of Rojava have attested, but using the master's tools to dismantle the master's house—to paraphrase Audre Lorde—is a vexed question for feminists who want to campaign according to feminist values.

A peasant woman in El Salvador, Domitila Ayala Mejía, who joined the Farabundo Martí National Liberation Front (FMLN) guerrilla movement aged twenty, related how acquiring a gun transformed her position at home. She had been prevented from going to school by her father because he was afraid she would use her literacy skills to write love letters to men. When she started sneaking out in the middle of the night for military training, the father was convinced that she was cavorting with men. The parents doubled her domestic chores as punishment and threatened to kick her out. One day when she was out, the father searched her bedroom and found a gun under her pillow. Since that day, her father showed her the kind of respect that he only reserved for men.[93] It could be argued that this kind of respect, based on masculine values of weaponry and violence, does not represent a true transformation of patriarchal values. Kurdish women also report newfound respect from men since joining the defence forces and valiantly fighting against ISIS. They cannot afford the privilege of non-violence given the challenges their revolution faces. They see self-defence not exclusively in terms of gun toting but as a whole philosophy of life and politics, of preserving a feminist culture against the predations of men in daily life, not just in war.

In non-revolutionary conditions, feminists campaign for the right to live free from violence using the framework of human

INTRODUCTION

rights, one of the tools available in the fight for social justice. Historically, this framework prioritised abuses by the state, but feminists expanded this to criminalise violence perpetrated by private individuals and non-state actors. The opening up of the private sphere to the glare of the law, of demonstrating that the violence faced in the home was a legitimate arena for intervention by the state, is seen as one of the successes of feminist activism. There have been a number of landmark cases in which international courts have ruled against states on the basis of their failure to protect women against violence by individuals.[94] Marieme Helie-Lucas, founder of Women Living Under Muslim Laws, fought a long battle with human rights organisations like Amnesty International to get them to condemn the violence of non-state actors such as religious fundamentalists, often directed against women and religious and sexual minorities, in countries like Algeria, rather than seeing them merely as victims of the state. She argues that 'by ignoring the crimes committed against women by Muslim fundamentalist non-state actors, they have also created a hierarchy of rights in which women's rights come last, after religious rights, cultural rights and minority rights'.[95] At the same time as certain groups are privileged above others, some academics, notably Samuel Moyn in *The Last Utopia*, have argued that human rights are a distraction or displacement from more important issues of structural injustice.[96] While acknowledging that there are similarities between the 'heroic victim' of human rights discourses and the 'self-responsibilizing individual of neo-liberalism', the academic Kate Nash argues that there are divergences in which individuals are valorised and how human rights discourses foreground those individuals with a specific 'relation to structures of injustices', which entails constructing 'individuals as necessarily belonging to groups. In this respect, human rights although fundamentally rights of individuals, validate collectivist solutions to problems that are simultaneously those of individuals *and* groups.'[97]

PLANET PATRIARCHY

The human rights framework is not available to activists in Saudi Arabia, Russia, China or El Salvador. Saudis have left the country because even the mildest criticism of the regime brings brutal punishment in its wake. It is from the diaspora that they hope to bring about change. The ability of states to reach out into the diaspora and kill dissidents begs the question of how effective political action can be from outside the country even though social media holds the potential of uniting a scattered population. The limitations on actions from outside the country are acknowledged by Ella Rossman, a young feminist who is part of the Russian diaspora of activists hoping to bring about change within Russia. Activists are leaving Russia in droves. Those who remain and spoke to us for this book have asked to be anonymised when only a few months ago, during research for the book, they were not worried about being quoted in their own name.

When the space for feminist activism is squeezed, feminists adopt various tactics to survive. In Russia, women will use feminist language when talking to Western audiences but couch the same message in human rights language for home audiences. There have been concerted efforts to diminish and dismiss feminist challenges to the status quo by framing them as culture wars, as simply being about one worldview as opposed to another, to delink them from the material basis that makes women's lives substantively different, a development to which feminists themselves have contributed by getting heated up about identity politics. Other kinds of framing, like in Russia and El Salvador, turn feminism into a dirty word. It is no surprise that patriarchal forces will do everything possible to discredit a term and a movement whose stated goal is the overthrow of patriarchy. Women's centres have responded by providing more gender-neutral spaces or feel pressured into allowing male perpetrators into women-only spaces for counselling. Resistance by women especially under authoritarian regimes may be successful

INTRODUCTION

if they are not overtly feminist. Some scholars have attributed the downfall of the junta in Argentina in 1983 to the significant role played by the Mothers of the Plaza De Mayo or Mothers of the Disappeared, who

> responded to the dictatorship's inhumanity with a 'counter-performance' highlighting their own traditional gender authority as mothers. Rather than contesting the masculinity of the junta (e.g., by accusing the generals of weakness), the Mothers used their gender performance (relying on a traditional femininity based in motherhood) to accrue value for their political position as opponents of the regime.[98]

The regime found it difficult to be heavy handed with them in a culture that respects 'motherhood', so it was a case of co-opting patriarchal values in the fightback. In El Salvador, the fightback against the lack of abortion rights is framed in medical terms with regard to the wellbeing of mother or foetus. Progressive women in Saudi Arabia may quote the Qur'an, as do other Muslim women in Islamic societies, in order to cut the ground from under their opponents. However, we have seen from the way religion has been used as a cosh against women's rights in Russia, El Salvador and Saudi Arabia that secularism is very important for women. Both Russia and El Salvador have nominally secular constitutions, but the church is so powerful that it can and does prevent the passing of women-friendly laws.

Another strategy of feminist resistance in authoritarian states is to make common cause with men, partly because both are repressed by the state. The view that both will be liberated by democracy and that state patriarchy takes pre-eminence over the struggle against patriarchal men drives many Saudi women to fight alongside men—much like the Marikana women in South Africa who stood in solidarity with their men, who were massacred when they engaged in an unofficial strike against the Lonmin platinum mine where they worked. Global south feminists in the UK may set up autonomous women's groups but do work in alliance with men in campaigns against policing of black communities and state racism—a reflection of the multiple discriminations they face—even though these men may not support their struggles against patriarchy. Women who fought alongside male comrades in major battles against the state, as in El Salvador's twelve-year civil war or the long struggle against apartheid in South Africa, find it really hard to acknowledge the betrayal and even sexual violence they faced from male comrades. While many feminist groups organise autonomously and guard their independence zealously, different contexts and times demand different strategies.

The outlook is bleak

The obstacles facing feminism continue to be huge, the bright flame of Rojava notwithstanding. Depressingly authoritarian leaders who deploy machismo and traditional patriarchal norms in pseudo-democratic regimes like Russia or El Salvador regularly notch up 80 per cent or more in popularity ratings. We are on the cusp of a world that may be rewritten and reshaped beyond all recognition by the new incumbent of the White House. Dissidents cannot survive in countries like Saudi Arabia, El Salvador, Russia or China. Intolerance of dissent is not an environment conducive to the challenges feminism poses to the status quo.

Feminists are mostly fighting a defensive battle. Even the institutionalisation of abortion rights in the French constitution in 2024 is not necessarily a sign of progress but an anxious attempt to forestall a development like the overturning of the historic Roe v. Wade judgment in the US.[99] Many of the new freedoms are illusory, and the framings have changed. The concept of choice, the freedom to sell your body in sexual transactions, is seen by some as a new freedom. Feminist demands are

INTRODUCTION

framed as culture wars, which has the impact of diminishing the importance of their demands. Women's rights have become one of the dividing lines in the ideological struggle between liberal democracies and authoritarian states: the very fact of it being seen as a marker of modernity in the West makes it a sign of the West's decadence in countries like Russia, Saudi Arabia and El Salvador. Second-wave feminism's founding slogan 'the personal is political', which made women aware that their individual experience of oppression had a systemic cause and proved an important spur to political action, has been subverted by the avatars of neoliberalism like Sandberg,[100] who promote individual solutions in order to undermine collective action. Mazzucato argues that 'capitalism is incompatible with feminism'.[101] While feminist demands seeking parity with men on pay and representation in public spaces are causing change, albeit at a glacial pace, where capitalism cannot be made to bend, otherwise it will break, is the feminism that seeks equality, across class, with other women. Capitalism can accommodate mobility within classes and a certain amount of mobility between classes, but it cannot exist without the class structure.

A global political trend appears to be an unprecedented nostalgia for some glorious, racially pure, past—a nationalist ideology that can mobilise people behind dictators—to a time when women knew their place, which was firmly at home. Putin looks back to the days of imperialist Russia bolstered by the Russian Orthodox Church, Trump's desire to Make America Great Again looks to replicate America at the beginning of the twentieth century[102] and Modi promotes a Hindu nationalist agenda by harking back to a golden period of Hindu rule before Muslims invaded in the eleventh century.[103]

We hope we have managed to shed some light on the questions we posed at the beginning of this chapter. What this book shows is the inherent instability of patriarchy, that 'there's no single moment when patriarchal values decisively "won"'.[104] In fact, as we researched each of the countries, we found that if you went far back enough in history there were stories of amazing women's resistance, even if, in the current moment, like in Russia, China, Saudi Arabia or El Salvador, the prospects for feminism look particularly bleak. Women are waiting, watching and acting: waiting, watching and preparing for the tipping point. As Gary Younge reminds us, in relation to the ebb and flow of the #BlackLivesMatter movement and the combustibility of political anger, 'no energy is ever lost', and 'there is oil on the ground' waiting for that spark.[105] Much of this book, intended equally for activists as much as the general reader, is a search for that oil on the ground and the spark.

1

EL SALVADOR

THE CURRENCY OF VIOLENCE

Rahila Gupta

El Salvador is a country where the president, Nayib Bukele, has brought peace to the streets by sending prostituted women to imprisoned gang leaders to get them to stop their men killing people at random. In no other country, it seems, is the ruling regime's reliance on patriarchy so obvious and brutal. That women are included on a list of material incentives for prisoners, such as mobile phones and PlayStations, makes the objectification of women complete.[1] When these deals failed because the government did not keep its side of the bargain, the gangs went on a killing spree. Gangs, also run along staunchly patriarchal lines, have been a feature of Salvadoran society since the end of a twelve-year civil war from 1980 to 1992 between the Marxist–Leninist umbrella group the FMLN (Farabundo Martí National Liberation Front) and a US-backed government that used a scorched earth policy and death squads to visit terror upon the population. It ended in a stalemate. The Peace Accords of 1992 saw the FMLN being set up as a political party but did not deal with the structural poverty and inequality that drove the FMLN to take up arms in the first place and that gave rise to the gangs following the civil war.

In the areas controlled by the FMLN and the refugee camps in neighbouring countries to which activists had fled, there was an opportunity to put ideas of democracy and equality into practice. Some women found their collective voice and began to engage in a feminist struggle with the predominantly male leadership to highlight patriarchy as a separate but equally significant system of exploitation as capitalism. However, my conversations with feminists who were active in the FMLN have given rise to a very mixed picture, with some women claiming to have found feminism in the 1990s after the war. This coincided with the rise of free-market, neoliberal forces that relied on the control of women's bodies and reproductive rights as a vote winner in a deeply religious society. These neoliberal forces set themselves up as guardians of the family's sanctity, a useful tool in deflecting attention from poverty. An interesting dynamic emerged—using patriarchal ideology to deflect from the shortcomings of capitalism. Whether the flowering of feminist consciousness happened in the '80s or '90s, there is no question that the civil war unleashed a political momentum for rights, equality and justice. Many of the women's organisations active today, which were set up in the 1990s, had roots in the FMLN women's sections. This chapter aims to track the spectacular loss of this political momentum and the vicious ways in which patriarchy has closed in on the spaces for feminist activism.

Every society tells itself a story about itself, an imagined and relative set of shared values that contains both aspiration and reality and is dynamic but also restrictive in that it becomes impossible to imagine another way of doing things. The Salvadoran social imaginary is 'characterized by violence, inequality, machismo, and religious conservatism',[2] all coordinates of patriarchy that map out the subordination of women. It has been argued that 'violence has become intrinsic to how Salvadorans imagine and perform democracy as well as to how El Salvador's democracy works',[3] which explains both the popularity of the *mano dura* (iron fist) policies against the gangs and also the fact that gangs are merely the visible eruption of a body politic whose veins are fuelled by violence. The impact is felt on both the imagination and the body.

A politics of fear

After ninety-two people were killed over one weekend in March 2022, Bukele announced a 'state of exception', dubbed a 'state of deception' by activists,[4] which has been renewed each month up until the time of writing in early 2025, in which a number of constitutional rights were suspended. Official figures reveal that 81,000 people—over 1 per cent of a population numbering around 6.5 million—have been rounded up and thrown into prison without due process or regard for civil liberties.[5] El Salvador has moved from one premier league position to another—top in global homicide rates to the most number of people in prison, relative to population. Of those imprisoned, it is estimated that nearly 60 per cent are innocent. So far, 7,000 people have been released after two years in prison without charges and without evidence for their arrest in the first place.[6]

As Joan Didion observed on her visit in 1982, El Salvador is a place of magic realism, 'in which no ground is solid, no depth of field reliable, no perception so definite that it might not dissolve into its reverse'.[7] Nothing has changed; in some ways, it has got worse as the Bukele government in its attempt to rewrite the narrative simply does not release statistics of the dead and disappeared, nor does it acknowledge the existence of violence against women. Clanci Rosa, editor of *Revista la Brújula*, a digital feminist publication, explains the lengths she has to go to in order to get information or statistics, mostly without success.[8] There are behind-the-scenes battles between feminists and government officials over the use of language in manuals and the inclusion of words like equality, patriarchy and feminism.[9]

It is therefore difficult to know what to make of the reported drop in homicides by almost half, a reduction that validates Bukele's hard-line approach and has made him extremely popular in El Salvador. The government has not released any statistics since November 2022. Nor can the accompanying drop in femicides be taken at face value, with the decline being disputed by feminists whose experience on the ground does not support this claim. ORMUSA (Organización de Mujeres Salvadoreñas), a leading feminist organisation, does a body count based on media reports, which, by definition, will be an underestimate as not all murders are reported in the press. They also point out that the rates began to drop before Bukele came to power in 2019.[10] ORMUSA's figures for 2022 stand at sixty-eight femicides, almost a quarter of the number recorded in 2017. Sylvia Juárez, lawyer at ORMUSA, and others point out that there are no figures for disappearances, many of whom may have been killed. In 2021, four times more girls (mostly under the age of seventeen) than boys were reported missing.[11] Since 2019, at least four mass graves have been discovered,[12] one with possibly forty women in it, with no figures broken down by sex available for the others.[13] While femicide may represent the extreme end of the violence, activists argue that it takes place within a continuum of violence against women that more than doubled between 2021 and 2023. Carmen Urquilla of ORMUSA said: 'Just because women aren't bleeding on the street, doesn't mean that they are safe.'[14]

EL SALVADOR

Femicide in El Salvador has some disturbingly specific features, including (1) the savagery of the attacks, which often involve removal of victims' wombs, breasts, and heads, (2) the rape and/or other forms of extreme sexual abuse, (3) the deliberate destruction of identifying features through burning or other means, (4) the ritualization of the crime and/or crime scene, and (5) the political significance and messaging of the murders.[15]

Combined with a total ban on abortion, even when the woman's life is at risk, El Salvador is one of the worst places in the world for women, particularly poor women. Without any sense of irony, El Salvador celebrates 25 March, towards the end of International Women's Month, as the Day of the Unborn Child and uses it to call for respect for life.[16] The obligatory single motherhood that is imposed on women not allowed the escape route of abortion is the kind of limited space in which feminist organisations hope to make a difference—to achieve some relief for the women by getting men to own up to their paternity and so provide for the child.

Religion, both Catholicism and Evangelism,[17] is deeply embedded in El Salvador, which accounts for the criminalisation of abortion—a feature of many Latin American societies. In order to shore up their authority, governments need to keep the church on side. It did not take long for Bukele, whose decisions are based on daily data sent to his mobile phone that measure his popularity,[18] to become ostentatiously religious, including a U-turn on abortion. In 2013, as mayor of Nuevo Cuscatlán for the left-wing FMLN party, Bukele criticised 'defenders of life' who opposed a life-saving abortion for a Salvadoran woman named Beatriz and accused them of 'fanaticism' in a tweet.[19] But once he became president, Bukele backtracked on commitments to LGBT rights as well. In a Facebook post, he wrote, 'I've decided, so that there is NO DOUBT, TO

NOT PROPOSE ANY TYPE OF REFORM to ANY ARTICLE that has to do with the RIGHT TO LIFE (from the moment of conception), marriage (maintaining only its original design, A MAN AND A WOMAN), or euthanasia.'[20] He even invoked God to justify his assault on democracy. In order to pressure a reluctant Legislative Assembly to approve funds for his ill-defined security plan, he mobilised a large crowd of people outside the building to support him and instructed the army and the police to occupy the assembly building. To the assembled crowds, he declared: 'None who have gone against God have triumphed.' Democracy comes a poor second to divine right, especially one enforced by violent means.

In terms of the central question of our book, why doesn't patriarchy die, we find a pincer-like movement between the gangs, the church and the brutal state, not always coordinated, which refreshes the institution of patriarchy and squeezes the breath out of any feminist movement. A law was passed in April 2022, apparently intended to criminalise the passing of messages between gangs but worded so broadly that anyone caught sharing information about the gangs could be punished with up to fifteen years in prison. Rosa, editor of *Revista la Brújula*, says they initially avoided covering the issue of disappearances as much of it was gang-related and they were unclear if they could even mention the word 'gangs'. As it is mostly women who go in search of their loved ones, Rosa realised they could no longer avoid the issue. Even if they are quoting a woman who blames the 'gangs' for the disappearance of her family member, Rosa will run it past a lawyer, a cost they can hardly afford. As she says: 'Given the state of our prisons, it is not something I would wish to risk. There are enough martyred women.'[21] Sports shirts do not carry the numbers 13 or 18 because it could be seen as a reference to the two main gangs, MS-13 and Barrio-18.

EL SALVADOR

Many of our interviewees, while talking, would put their mobile phones at arm's length for fear of being recorded. Israeli software, Pegasus, has been widely used in unlawful surveillance of journalists and activists.[22] Unless praising him, nobody mentions Bukele in public for fear of being overheard. Nicknames, such as Don Cerote—'Don of turds'—which rhymes nicely with Don Quixote, abound. When whiling away the time in a public square in the Centro Histórico of San Salvador, we got chatting to a local woman who pointed to a couple of soldiers standing nearby and whispered that they might be listening in.[23] And she was a self-confessed admirer of Bukele or, at least, claimed to be. We were advised not to hold our interviews in our hotel dining area for the same reason.

Edith Elizondo, who runs Ixchel, a feminist organisation based in Casa de Safo, a delightful women's centre with murals and brightly coloured walls, generously offered us a safe meeting space in their courtyard. A fellow guest at the hotel we were staying at, a Salvadoran returnee from the US, told us that her daughter did not come with her because she has extensive body tattoos. People with tattoos are being rounded up on suspicion of being gang members. Creating a climate of fear, as any woman who is trapped in a situation of domestic violence knows, is as effective at controlling behaviour as taking punitive action. Feminists say they have not seen such a patriarchal government since the 1970s. Such governance sets the tone for ordinary men to behave with impunity, and women are celebrated only for their role as mothers. When gangs literally got away with the murder of women, it allowed other men to believe they would face no consequences for their murderous actions.[24] This is the territory through which we will take a ride to understand how women's choices are constrained everywhere they turn and how the reinforcement of the patriarchal norms of society contributes to the popularity of a populist ruler.

PLANET PATRIARCHY

Oil on the ground

It is impossible to understand the current situation in El Salvador without looking at the civil war from 1980 to 1992, as the long tail of repercussions is still rippling through the country. The roots of the violence stretch back to the Spanish invasion and colonisation of the country in the sixteenth century, when the indigenous people were massacred and their lands taken from them. The inequality of land distribution, which continues to this day, lies behind many of El Salvador's problems. In the nineteenth century, fourteen of the most important families controlled all the country's wealth and agricultural production and held most of the political power. The descendants of the original fourteen families of the coffee oligarchy, as they came to be known,[25] have metamorphosed into eight business conglomerates that dominate economic life in El Salvador today. Patriarchy has played a significant role in maintaining structural inequalities, elite power and concentration of political and economic capital. Arranged marriages, conducted by the patrefamilias of these families, in which women had no choice, were a key tool in cementing power. This trend has continued in the boards of the privatised companies since the 1990s, where the links are both matrimonial and entrepreneurial. Ainhoa Montoya, lecturer in Latin American studies at the University of London, observes that '[i]t was precisely through intermarriage and entrepreneurial alliances that the Salvadoran elites reproduced their power over time thereby following dynastic patterns similar to those of other Latin American elites'.[26]

The more immediate conditions that created the possibility of revolutionary consciousness that erupted in the civil war date from the mid-1960s onwards, when teachers, workers and peasants began organising in the trade union movement, which women began to join to make class-based but not necessarily

EL SALVADOR

feminist demands. An inspiring anecdote from 1979,[27] on the eve of the civil war, when state repression was particularly intense, describes the militancy of 190 striking women workers who occupied an American glove factory. The US ambassador got involved and talked to the company's lawyer about the strike. The women presented a list of thirty-one demands, including soap in bathrooms, which reveals the terrible conditions in which they worked and which for menstruating women would have made life very difficult. But the ambassador dismissed that demand as 'frivolous'. More audaciously, they also demanded a 100 per cent wage increase and the firing of workers who did not join the strike. This was described as 'clearly unacceptable'. To gain leverage over the company, the women took five US citizens hostage, including the company president and several executives.

Organising peasant militias became critical to the work of preparing for the insurgency, especially in light of the increased violence they were facing from the government in the 1970s. It has been estimated that state repression of the rise in worker activism led to 800 deaths per month in that decade,[28] heavily outnumbering the deaths caused by gang violence in the post-war period. Military training had to be undertaken at night-time to avoid detection. I met an FMLN fighter, an illiterate peasant woman, who used to grow corn for a living. She thinks she may be sixty-nine years old; her poverty is visible in a mouth caving in on itself without teeth to give it shape. They would meet at 1 am to have political conversations and get military training, which included handling guns and defusing bombs. At first, women cooked the food and 'serviced men's needs', but when the fighting got serious, the women took up arms too. Her eyes well up as she remembers the massacre of seven pregnant women by the army, a memory she says she will take to her grave. They were not allowed to bury their bodies, so they were left to be eaten by wild animals.[29] For women, involvement with the FMLN was an additional commitment to their domestic responsibilities. Both men and women had taken to sleeping in the hills at night to avoid capture by the National Guard and death squads.

In Gary Younge's words, there was oil on the ground.[30] The spark came when Archbishop Óscar Romero was shot dead in 1980. There is considerable debate about whether he was a proponent of liberation theology; what is not disputed is that he sided with the poor and denounced the repression of the government and the death squads once he was appointed archbishop. Joaquín Villalobos, a former commander of the FMLN, wrote: 'Before they killed Monseñor, we were tens of guerrilla fighters; after it, we were thousands.'[31] A few months later, five peasant revolutionary groups came together under the umbrella of the FMLN. There were important differences of emphasis in the revolutionary praxis of each of the groups, including the degree to which they were influenced by feminist demands. It was a recognition of the failure of electoral and reform-based politics that drove the groups towards revolutionary struggle. The FMLN identified as Maoist. The Founders of one of the groups in the FMLN, the Popular Liberation Forces (Fuerzas Populares de Liberación, FPL), defected from the Communist Party because they found it too reformist, although they recognised that reform-based movements that raised their members' political consciousness could act as a bridge to revolution. But the ideological influences were diverse, and the church played a surprisingly important role.

Liberation theology

Liberation theology reflected the fervour of the 1960s postcolonial movements that were throwing off their chains everywhere. The Vatican too appeared to come under the influence of these movements. The Second Vatican Council, which took place in the '60s, was called by the pope to make theology relevant to a changing world. The debate centred on whether salvation was to be found in this or the next world and whether the church had a role to play in the struggle for social justice and freedom from oppression and poverty. This was to have a particular impact on the Latin American bishops who met to discuss the ideas of the council in Colombia in 1968, which led to the development of liberation theology.[32]

In the 1970s, small groups of people got together in parishes to study the Bible, but the focus was on action rather than prayer and introspection. Some ended up joining unions, others were recruited by the FMLN into the revolutionary struggle. There is no doubt that liberation theology was an important catalyst in raising the revolutionary consciousness of peasants, in particular by drawing attention to the human causes of poverty that could be challenged rather than a divine explanation that taught forbearance of suffering as a virtue in itself: 'In the 1970s and 1980s, mourning rituals rooted in liberation theology politicized and connected individual deaths to a collective struggle that sought to create heaven on earth.' The linking of the sacred and secular, in this way, reinforced the power of each.[33]

The FPL was a member group of the FMLN, recruited from the ranks of these politicised peasants, who, in turn, pressured the FPL to be more open to religion. The FPL declared that radical Christianity was compatible with Marxist thought. If evidence of its success were needed, then it came in the brutal killing of members of CEBs (Comunidades Eclesiales de Base), the Christian Base Communities as they were known, by the government's death squads. 'Be a Patriot, Kill a Priest', became a common death squad slogan.[34] Priests had poles stuck up their anuses.[35] It became illegal to read the Bible and sing religious songs. Archbishop Romero condemned the heavy-handed repression of peasants and working classes and lobbied the US government to stop its military aid to El Salvador. At Romero's funeral, there were 100,000 mourners. The government opened fire and killed over thirty people. While liberation theology condemned violence, it recognised that the injustice inflicted upon the poor was a form of violence that required a robust response.[36] Romero was reputed to have said about the rich, months before being murdered, 'it is time to hand over the rings so that their fingers are not cut off'.[37]

While liberation theology did not address issues of gender inequality, some scholars have argued that it was the first time that women were exposed to leftist politics and ideas of class equality, from which the progression to women's rights was a natural one.[38] Women were also able to bend religious views, such as the glorification of women as mothers, to their advantage. CO-MADRES, founded by a group of mothers to campaign for information about their 'disappeared' sons, occupied Catholic churches and reached out to other women in the same situation in relative freedom from the authorities. Another group, the Christian Committee for the Displaced of El Salvador, which was mainly made up of women and elders, was also seen as unthreatening until it started speaking up for the refugees and demanding an end to the war. The group operated in refugee camps—after the civil war, 2 million people had been internally displaced, and there were 1 million refugees—populated mostly by women who set up structures of participatory democracy and taught themselves skills traditionally associated with men, like carpentry, mechanics and leadership.[39]

It has been a long time since the sting was pulled from the tail of liberation theology. Only pockets of resistance remain. We attended Romero's birthday celebrations on 15 August 2023 at the Metropolitan Cathedral of San Salvador to see what remained of his ideas in a country that worships Bukele. As the only saint of El Salvador, portraits and statues of Romero are ubiquitous. The conservative church has co-opted Romero as their figure-

EL SALVADOR

head, to borrow his stardust while ignoring his teachings, much like the capitalist co-option of militants like Che Guevara.

The cathedral, which has a cavernous, echoing basement (the crypt) and an upper ground floor with an ornate altar, is the perfect metaphor for the split between the radical and conservative wings of the church. The Crypt community of Catholics is radical and small in number and like all radical movements lives literally and metaphorically underground. We were embraced by the Crypt community, a dozen of whom came together after Sunday mass to talk about their hero, the resistance to his ideas from the church and to lament the return of the poverty, injustice and inequality in El Salvador that had sparked the civil war. Romero is reputed to have said that the law is like 'a poisonous snake which only bites the barefoot'. One of the priests, who was officiating at the mass, welcomed us and wanted to know why we were interested in Romero. As we had been warned by some of our interviewees not to talk about the book, I said it was because my father was a communist. The priest had very little English, but he lifted his hands to heaven in a gesture of supplication and said, delightedly, 'Congratulations'. With one word, he had eliminated the chasm between the secular and religious left. The Crypt community continues some of the radical traditions of the early Christian Base Communities in providing legal, psychological and humanitarian assistance to relatives of those who disappeared in the civil war and the families of those arbitrarily detained under Bukele's regime. The congregation collects food baskets for families on limited resources. However, it does not take a position on abortion rights. Romero himself had been opposed to abortion.[40]

Women in the FMLN: a contested history

The road to the civil war was littered with bodies, killings that were mostly carried out by the government against anybody who dared question government policy, let alone resist it. During the war itself, more than 75,000 people were killed. Contrary to the carefully constructed image of the FMLN as terrorists that fuelled US support for the government, it was government forces and death squads that committed 85 per cent of the acts of violence. The FMLN was responsible for 5 per cent of cases. The rape and torture of women was a central strategy of government forces, knocking out the heart of the communities of resistance.[41] More than 25 per cent of the population is estimated to have fled El Salvador during the civil war, with most moving to the United States, of which a large number settled in California.

The tactics used by the Salvadoran army and death squads shortly after they returned from training in the US are described in bloodcurdling detail by Noam Chomsky:

> [A] peasant woman ... returned home one day to find her three children, her mother and her sister sitting around a table, each with its own decapitated head placed carefully on the table in front of the body, the hands arranged on top 'as if each body was stroking its own head'.
>
> The assassins, from the Salvadoran National Guard, had found it hard to keep the head of an 18-month-old baby in place, so they nailed the hands onto it. A large plastic bowl filled with blood was tastefully displayed in the centre of the table. According to Rev. Santiago, macabre scenes of this kind aren't uncommon.
>
> People are not just killed by death squads in El Salvador—they are decapitated and then their heads are placed on pikes and used to dot the landscape. Men are not just disembowelled by the Salvadoran Treasury Police; their severed genitalia are stuffed into their mouths.
>
> Salvadoran women are not just raped by the National Guard; their wombs are cut from their bodies and used to cover their faces. It is not enough to kill children; they are dragged over barbed wire until the flesh falls from their bones, while parents are forced to watch.[42]

EL SALVADOR

In 1981, the FMLN launched an unsuccessful offensive to bring down the government. After the failed resistance, women in their thousands joined the movement as combatants or radio operators, medics and couriers and came to be known collectively as Las Compas. By 1983, the FMLN held a quarter of the country, which increased to a third by the end of the decade. Although these areas were constantly targeted by government forces, the FMLN held sway, which allowed the women's arm of the FPL, AMES (Asociación de Mujeres de El Salvador), set up in 1977, to move around and organise with a fair amount of ease. The extent to which patriarchy was dismantled within the resistance movement is contested. According to María Candelaria Navas, an AMES activist and grande dame of Salvadoran feminism, AMES had declared themselves to be revolutionary feminists because class struggle was seen to be insufficient for the liberation of women. Nevertheless, Navas also believed that the women's movement in the 1980s was not really feminist and became so only in the post-war period. She argued that issues like wage increases and childcare should be categorised as feminine demands, while a demand for abortion rights should be seen as a gender-specific demand that challenges sexism.[43] This is debatable, but in the process of joining the political struggle, women had to overcome patriarchal barriers in the family only to be confronted by the same attitudes within the movement itself, all of which gave rise to a feminist consciousness.

Even the more positive accounts of women's achievements recognise that they came about because of ideological struggle and were mainly driven by pragmatism. Abortion was freely available, for example, because the movement could not afford to lose women to pregnancy. A parallel society was in operation in the liberated territories, which represented a direct challenge to the national government's capitalist interests. Instead of waiting for the revolution to be victorious, peasants set up democratically run councils imbued with their values and revolutionary goals.[44] This was partly necessitated by the drain the civil war placed on the resources needed for services in the liberated territories— schools, health clinics, craft workshops and food collectives. AMES was active in these councils, ensuring that women took on leadership roles.[45] In their ideological work, they connected women's practical demands around childcare, domestic responsibilities and intimate relationships to their overarching analysis of how capitalism intersected with patriarchy. Deysi Cheyne, however, who worked in communications and diplomacy with the FMLN, says she found feminism after the civil war.[46] The most generous description she could apply to any feminist consciousness within the FMLN was to call it an intuitive feminism.[47] Some FMLN members say that only FMLN members were living in those territories, so the idea of democratically run councils did not ring true for them. Possibly the most feasible explanation was given by Raúl Martinez, legal advisor to the FMLN president of the Legislative Assembly until 2015. Each zone controlled by the FMLN was surrounded by disputed areas and zones of expansion in which people were not safe, as both the army and FMLN were attempting to wrest control of the area. Those areas were usually evacuated by the civilian population because of the danger to life. Martinez believes that the partial perspectives were a result of individual experience of the zone in which people lived.[48]

Between 27 to 34 per cent of the FMLN cadre was made up of women. The ideological starting point of the FMLN in relation to women was typical of left-oriented militant struggles around the world: capitalism was the root cause of all inequality, including gender inequality. Initially, FMLN women guerrillas also attributed gender inequality to capitalism rather than patriarchy. They pointed out how capitalism used the bodies of women to sell products. They believed that sexism, produced by capitalism, constructed relationships between men and women as primarily sexual. In time, AMES developed a more sophisticated praxis and theoretical position. As a result of their organising work with the women, they moved away from the FPL position and argued that the revolution had to overthrow both patriarchy and capitalism by highlighting the patriarchal foundations of capitalism.[49] Unusually for left and Marxist–Leninist groups of the time, the FPL believed that various sectors must organise for their own interests and did not believe that the women's struggle for their rights would deflect attention from the main struggle.

The two largest groups in the FMLN, the FPL and the ERP (Ejército Revolucionario del Pueblo), had the greatest number of women, with most of them in combatant roles. Support roles such as cooking and healthcare were often carried out by older men. The FMLN had a hierarchical military structure. The high command was made up of the all-male leaders of each of the five constituent groups. Each of the five FMLN groups set up their own women's organisations with varying degrees of autonomy. The ERP had the largest number of women in its command structure—four in total.

A positive reading of the achievements of women in the FMLN argues that militants came to recognise, under pressure from the women activists, that women's liberation was not something to be considered after capitalism had been overthrown: '[The] women resisted male-centric definitions of the revolutionary subject, which marginalized the labor, bodies, and needs of women.'[50] For instance, women fought to collectivise food production among both men and women and to gain access to sanitary napkins. There is a story about the huge tensions generated by the question of who would cook tortillas, seen to be emasculating women's work. In one particular camp where women got up at 3 am to make tortillas for the whole camp, men demanded that they wake up at 1 am to wash before food preparation as they had been dirtied in the act of sleeping with men. As the camp was run by a woman, she ordered the men to get up at 3 am instead to prepare tortillas. Some women demanded that the men should also wake at 1 am to wash as they had been sleeping with women. In the end, the measure was dropped when men refused to eat tortillas made by men.[51]

Contraception pills were made available, and medics were trained to carry out abortions. Cheyne, who was with the FMLN during the civil war, says there was no policy as such, but ad hoc arrangements existed to allow women to have abortions on a case-by-case basis if they so wished.[52] A leading feminist and ex-guerrilla, Morena Herrera, looking back, believes it was a missed opportunity for women to have embedded the right to choice argument in the consciousness of their comrades. However, this new openness to abortion dissipated in the post-war years, leading to some of the most restrictive abortion laws in the world and the most horrific 'miscarriages' of justice, literally speaking, when women who have miscarried their babies are handed long sentences for murder. Those women who wanted to keep their child would be sent off to refugee camps in Nicaragua or Costa Rica. These were camps where the FMLN carried out training and recruitment, an important adjunct to the struggle in El Salvador, at a safe distance from the marauding death squads. AMES women had a strong presence there: the aim was to train women for leadership positions on their return to El Salvador and to make links with the wider Central and Latin American women's network, including in North America.

Outside the territories controlled by the FMLN, the government writ on abortion ran large. The 1973 Penal Code, which remained in effect until 1997, criminalised abortion with three exceptions: to save the mother's life, in cases of rape and in cases of foetal deformities.[53] Today, there are no exceptions. Sentences can stretch up to fifty years. The stark choice facing women is to proceed with the pregnancy, no matter what the consequences, or face life imprisonment unless you can afford to fly out of the country to procure an abortion abroad.

Sexual violence and rape were reported to be infrequent within the ranks of the FMLN and were more likely to be perpetrated by the commanders than the rank and file. Rape was apparently punishable by death. All reported civilian rapes were carried out by state forces. Not a single one of the 450 cases that were reported to the United Nations Truth Commission was attributed to the FMLN.[54] For many of the militants, it was important to be seen to hold high moral standards in order to find favour with the mainly peasant base of their support. The women combatants also felt the need to be exemplary and became, in universally recognisable ways, the receptacles of group honour, except this time it was revolutionary honour, and arguably the women exercised more choice in taking on this role than they would when they were the vehicles of male honour for their family or community.

However, many of the feminists and ex-guerrillas I met provided anecdotal evidence of rape within the FMLN. Herrera describes an incident of rape and how it was dealt with in an FMLN camp. A cook was raped by three men in a camp Herrera was visiting. Although the men were recognised as rapists, the woman was also condemned for being a provocateur and ultimately given the same punishments as the men. In the first punishment, they were shot at with rubber bullets to frighten them into believing they would be killed before being made to travel to other camps to acknowledge their mistakes; the other punishment was to dig a deep trench. Herrera questioned why the woman was treated as equally culpable. She was told that her opinion did not count because she was a visitor. She was second in command at the front, but she knew instinctively that she would have been disregarded even if she had been stationed at that camp. Feminism was a dirty word, a petty bourgeois phenomenon, a word she would not have wanted to own during the war even though she questioned the status quo.[55]

In a 1982 radio interview, FPL commander Ana María stated that 'the role of women in our revolutionary process is of great historical transcendence ... a great percentage of Salvadoran women have liberated themselves from the ties of the current system'.[56] Looking back on that time, women revolutionaries talk about how political education discouraged machismo, which was soon replaced by compañerismo—'comradery'—in which men participated in childcare and domestic work. Other scholars dismiss this portrait of women's roles in the movement, arguing instead that women were encouraged to use their femininity as a tool to build bridges with the local community, who were an important part of the guerrillas' support network. As women are traditionally seen as teachers, they were used to spread the revolutionary doctrine. They were also used as couriers as they were less likely to be suspected.[57] The FPL valorised peasant women, singing their praises for their commitment to the revolutionary struggle, attending meetings and preparing for revolution, despite the long hours of domestic work, field work and childcare for sick children. An article in their periodical, *Campo Rebelde*, praised mothers for their 'clean heart, pure feelings, and noble ideals'.[58] This tendency to essentialise the goodness of women finds echoes in Abdullah Öcalan's statements on women (see Chapter 7).

María was ultimately murdered in 1983 with an ice-pick, a killing orchestrated by the FPL leader Comandante Marcial, who then committed suicide.[59] María's death precipitated the winding down of AMES in 1984; the torchbearer of feminism was extinguished early in the civil war, which may explain why some women found feminism after the war.

Militarily, there was a stalemate until 1989, when the FMLN mounted another offensive and even occupied parts of the capital,

EL SALVADOR

San Salvador, retreating only when the army started bombing their positions in residential neighbourhoods, which put local populations at risk. Although this offensive failed, it became clear to the government and the US that the FMLN could not be defeated militarily. Peace talks followed soon after. Additionally, the ARENA (Alianza Republicana Nacional) government had signed its first structural adjustment loan with the World Bank in 1991, which required the privatisation of government-run services, the cutting of subsidies and taxes and reduction of the budget deficit. This neoliberal programme could not be instituted while the country was fighting a civil war. This was a major reason why the government came to the table to sign the Peace Accords. The agricultural elite had been damaged by the civil war and were gradually migrating to the industrial and finance sector, which could only be profitable in a more stable environment. The progressive opposition moved its focus from the struggle against military dictatorships to neoliberalism.[60] The FMLN accepted 'the market as the operating principle of the economy' as long as it delivered social justice and the end of poverty, a major concession.[61] The Peace Accords did not benefit women and did not address the question of women's rights. Higher-ranking FMLN officials benefitted from access to loans, land and employment. As women were generally in the rank and file, unless they were connected to a high-ranking FMLN official, they did not do so well.[62]

Dousing fire with petrol

The young undocumented migrants who had fled the civil war arrived in the US lacking skills and employment opportunities and facing discrimination. They joined criminal networks that morphed into two rival gangs, Mara Salvatrucha (MS-13) and Barrio-18, involved in prostitution and drugs. Gangs have been a deeply embedded feature of Salvadoran society since the late 1980s, when the United States began deporting young Salvadoran gang members with criminal records just as the country was emerging from a traumatic civil war. Though 4,000 gang members were deported, in 2017 it was estimated that only 1 per cent of gangs had originated in the US. Interestingly, as the US leadership of the gangs was replaced by local Salvadorans, the gangs became more sexist.[63]

There are continuities between the days of the civil war and the thirty years that followed, when gang rule, to a greater or lesser extent, held sway. People had got used to living in a country that was divided into small parcels of land whose frontiers could not be crossed without grave danger. During the war, the country was divided into army- and FMLN-controlled areas. Under the gangs, neighbourhoods were controlled by either the MS-13 or Barrio-18.[64] What changed was the direction from which the violence came: first the state, then the gangs; today, it is the state again. Under Bukele, the cost of gang-free streets is the high price of indiscriminate violence from the state. When gangs took over the running of poor neighbourhoods, the violence emerged from within. Its face was known. It did not reduce the sense of terror, but, like women living in situations of domestic violence, people navigated their way around it.[65]

Both hard-line and conciliatory measures against the gangs failed: the *mano dura* policy introduced by the ARENA party in 2003 was Central America's first anti-gang initiative. Under the first FMLN government, voted into power in 2009, a government-brokered truce between the rival gangs in 2012 brought some relief to the population for a short period of time, but that too failed for various reasons, including the US withdrawal of funding from those municipalities where gang members were involved in the truce, yet another example of the irrationality of US policies given that gang involvement had brought peace to that neighbourhood.[66] Estimates of the number of gang members in El Salvador have fluctuated wildly from 30,000 to 70,000, with Bukele putting the number at 95,000. The kind of suffocating control gangs exerted over their areas is reminiscent of the way in which ISIS kept control of its caliphate. It was a vice-like grip on everything that came under their sway—territories, resources, populations, gang members and even their girlfriends.

Having visited El Salvador, it is easy to visualise gang members guarding entrances to poor communities identified by 1-story shacks with brightly coloured walls and corrugated iron roofs. Faint outlines of graffiti with MS-13 or Barrio-18 sprayed on the outer perimeter walls are still visible. You would stray into these areas at your peril, especially if you belonged to a rival gang. Soyapango, a satellite city of San Salvador, the capital, where the national bus terminal is located and where we had to go to catch buses to other parts of the country, used to be in the grip of gangs. A social worker described what life was like when it was run by gangs and her work involved supporting single mothers and their sons, where the men were either dead or in prison, with the goal of preventing young children joining the gangs. She had to duck behind walls to avoid the exchange of gunfire as she went about her business. The main source of gang income was extortion, which ranged from demands made of poor women selling pupusas, a type of thick pancake made from cornmeal or rice flour, their national dish, to charging bus companies thousands of dollars for plying their streets. The director of public transportation gave the example of bus route 29, which paid $12,000 monthly for 100 buses.[67]

The fracturing of families and communities caused by emigration and the 75,000 reported to have been killed in the civil war left young men without family and a sense of belonging. The gangs served as a type of surrogate family, providing 'a sense of self-worth, and a sense of belonging to a group that cares about their welfare and survival'.[68] Gang membership was primarily a search for cultural identity and the 'respect' accorded to gang members out of fear. Scholars have asserted that identity is a more dangerous motivation for violence than 'turf'. Much of the killing was done as a show of loyalty and affirmation of identity rather than an encroachment on territory.[69] Extortion impoverished the victims but did not raise enough money to trickle down to all gang members. While the gangs did not provide services that the state would normally provide, they would determine who could access state services, like buses or schools. If, for any reason, the state wanted to enter gang-controlled territory, it would have to be well armed. The elite did not directly suffer the gang's extortionate behaviour, but they incurred extra costs in recruiting and paying for armed guards to accompany them and stand outside their department stores and luxury hotels.[70]

The gangs' hyper-machismo has been described as a form of 'protest masculinity',[71] a response to social exclusion and perceived lack of respect for a poor, uneducated, unemployed demographic of young men. This narrative sees much of the violence against women as collateral of internecine gang conflicts and the need to maintain status among peers through 'control of women'. The early lives of women who joined the gangs were often inscribed by violence and neglect. Without the options of employment and education, gang life becomes a 'less bad' option, a possibility of escape from home and reconfiguration of some of the traditional behaviours expected of women.[72] In ways similar to the FMLN's reliance on women, women in gangs had a dual role to play. They were expected to withstand and dish out violence like any man would, but they were also expected to take on the 'female' roles of caring and cooking. They would be expected to act as mules carrying drugs and arms, spying on rival gangs and smuggling goods into prison as they were less likely to draw attention to themselves, much the same rationale that lay behind

EL SALVADOR

FMLN women acting as couriers: 'Once females have entered into relationships with a gang member—or have been targeted for such a relationship—they are considered to be that gang member's *jaina* or *morra*, his property and, at times, the property of the gang itself.'[73] They were expected to be totally faithful to their men on pain of death but not to expect fidelity from their men. Homegirls (as they were known) were treated like toys and shared freely among the members.[74] Rebuffing the advances of a gang member could mean death. The initiation ceremony for women entering gangs was often sex with gang members. Where they were offered a choice between sex and beatings, they often opted for the latter as it would assert their right to be treated like one of the 'homies' even though they were entering a turbo-charged patriarchy. This was the paradox that circumscribed their actions: they were agents as well as victims. The exercise of violence gave them power and status within the group and was not just a means of self-defence.[75]

Although some women in gangs could gain full membership and even rise to leadership positions, power was ultimately concentrated in the hands of the men. It has been estimated that of the 500,000 Salvadorans dependent on the income generated by gang members, many are women—girlfriends, wives, mothers and cousins. It is women who congregate outside prisons waiting for news of their loved ones, giving up their domestic chores and their jobs for days on end, further impoverishing families where the main breadwinner was in prison.[76] While male prisoners can rely on their female relatives for support, women prisoners are often abandoned entirely, having broken with the patriarchal stereotype of women as submissive and caring. Women with children, while appreciating the time that prison gives them for parenting, are also keenly aware that the children can remain with them only until the age of five.

A woman who was interviewed on Radio Victoria explained why she cannot report domestic violence or any other crime to the police. If she does, the gang turns up to say that the police are not allowed into their territory and she and her family will have to leave the area if they persist in their complaints: 'The truth is that getting home every night in this country is a daily achievement, it's a miracle. It's something you give thanks to your life, God, and anyone you want.' Her solution was to 'burn them all'.[77] That is exactly what Bukele has done. Having tried the route of sweeteners such as women and phones in a secret pact with gang members and failed, Bukele declared a 'state of exception' in a reprise of the *mano dura* policies that had not worked before.

The statistics on the latest crackdown are horrific. In 2024, over 3,000 children were in prison, 1,000 of whom had been convicted and given sentences of up to twelve years.[78] Before the 'state of exception', the highest estimate of gang membership was 70,000. As many gang members have left the country and there is still some gang activity in rural areas, the fact that 81,000 people are in prison suggests that many of those behind bars are innocent. People are rounded up on arbitrary grounds such as their appearance—judged by their tattoos—or perceived nervousness. The very signifier of their masculinity and gang membership—tattoos—has been their undoing. Since 2016, the law has criminalised people with only the flimsiest of connections to gangs, including those who receive 'direct or indirect benefit' by having relations 'of any nature' with gangs,[79] which mostly impacts women dependants. Silvia Juárez estimates that up to 60 per cent of those who have been imprisoned have no connection with gangs. Many are put away on the basis of neighbours reporting someone to the authorities as a form of revenge for local infighting. A woman fruit seller was thrown into prison because the number of a gang member, who might have called her randomly, was found on her mobile phone. Juárez highlights the class and ethnic dimension of Bukele's hard-line policies, which have landed most heavily on poor, indigenous people.[80]

EL SALVADOR

The streets have become heavily militarised, and fear of gangs on the streets has now been replaced by fear of soldiers.[81]

Many people have died in prison—nearly 300 at the latest count[82]—with some of these deaths being attributable to the conditions in prison: overcrowding, lack of hygiene, poor food, poor medical services and internecine gang violence. Bukele has rationed food, space and sunlight as his weapons against the gangs in prison. He has also launched measures to prevent prisons from becoming recruiting grounds for new gang members, which had been the unintended consequence of the *mano dura* policies of the past. He has experimented with living arrangements inside prison, which had become notorious as alternative headquarters for gang leaders directing activities on the outside—ending the segregation of gangs so that they are constantly at loggerheads with each other and unable to use prison as their new HQ. In a tweet in April 2023, he claimed that prisons are no longer the command centres for the gangs: 'There are no more parties, drugs, graffiti, prostitutes.'[83]

In February 2023, the investigative news website El Faro reported that the gangs had ceased to exist in any meaningful way—a conclusion reached by high-level gang members who have absconded from the country. Critics of the policy are not sure that the gangs have been decimated as claimed. The peace brought about by state violence appears to be fragile and tremulous given that so many innocents have been rounded up without due process. In 2016, the Central Reserve Bank estimated that gang violence had cost El Salvador around $4 billion.[84] In his crackdown on gangs, Bukele doubled the level of investment in his security infrastructure, mainly a massive recruitment drive of military personnel to put his Territorial Control Plan into action, to $250 million *dollars* in 2022.[85] In purely financial terms, this strategy could be seen as cost-effective. This is being funded by a budget deficit that some experts believe will be unsustainable over the longer term. Feminists argue that the savings made from massive cuts to health and education services and the funding of women's organisations have been 'siphoned off to security and building prisons and buying arms and putting soldiers on the streets'.[86] Unless Bukele plans to keep gang members locked up indefinitely, which looks highly likely by the length of sentences being dished out, any prospect of humane solutions to the problem of youth unemployment were dashed by an announcement in September 2023 in which $30 million will be siphoned off from the funding of a vocational training organisation, INSAFORP (Instituto Salvadoreño de Formación Profesional), to his Territorial Security Plan.[87] Financial institutions believe that the reduction in crime could lead to greater foreign investment in El Salvador. This game of ping pong between government and gangs over who directs the violence and deaths, this investment in death to build an environment that is good for business, is a form of necro-capitalism that is seen at its clearest in El Salvador.[88]

The state of emergency grants the government powers to intercept the correspondence of ordinary citizens without the need for a court order; freedom of assembly has been banned, and detainees no longer have the right to free legal representation. Bukele's response on X to those international human rights groups anxious about this turn of events was to remark that '[i]f they love the gang members so much, come get them, we'll give them to them two for one'.[89] An amendment to the criminal law in July 2023 introduced mass trials of 900 people belonging to the same criminal networks.[90] Political dissidents face the same fate—imprisonment on flimsy evidence without due process.

A broad church

The only escape routes for men and women in gangs are death, church or migration. Women might be able to leave if they are pregnant and want to give their child a new life. One in-depth study of women in gangs suggests that members are able to 'calm down', that is, become inactive by requesting withdrawal from the most dangerous activities while still retaining gang membership.[91] The number of women who wanted to 'calm down' was large, but if they were in prison, they would receive no support from the gang and might even face the prospect of score settling from the gang once released.[92] The investigative platform Insight Crime tells the story of Flaca, a woman gang member who did not flinch as she was whipped for thirteen seconds as part of her initiation into MS-13. She chose this over the other initiation ceremony reserved for women, the *trencito* (little train) of men queuing up to rape them. She was brutal in the torture and killing of gang enemies, particularly rapists. She stuck a broomstick up the anus of one of them and made him suck his own penis to teach him a lesson before killing him. She stuck it out for a number of years. Finally, after three years in prison, she joined the church in 2018, where she was shunned. She finally found a church for ex-gang members where she was the only woman. She stopped drinking, smoking and having sex. She went from seeking abortions to becoming an anti-abortionist. At one level, there was no difference in the control exerted over her body and mind by the church and the gangs.[93]

Gang members predominantly follow Evangelical religions whose teachings do not challenge their patriarchal attitudes. Elvis, a gang member turned pastor in an Evangelical church, 'uses the story of Adam and Eve to justify his belief that women are corrupters of men'.[94] Religion and gang membership are closely interlinked; God and Satan live side by side. The two institutions, if they can be called that, are part of the same neighbourhood. The church cannot ignore the economic and social pressures that act upon their congregations and are shaped by the congregations. Given the criminalisation of abortion and widespread rape and sexual violence, single mothers form a sizeable part of the demographic. The churches respond to that by providing rescue centres. Although the church's teachings go against typical barrio values, and those who violate the code of behaviour are disciplined on issues like domestic violence, alcohol or drug consumption, they are never expelled. Poor neighbourhoods face an absence of running water and sewerage systems, poor-quality education, decrepit buildings, a high dropout rate of youngsters who take on work to support their families and poor health services—all of these things affect gang members equally, who, apart from the tattoos and weapons that make them intimidating, do not actually have a physique to match. Migration, high unemployment and economic need have devastated families. There are many women-headed households, and in some families, both parents have migrated to the US, leaving children with their grandparents. Top of the list of good jobs is work in a grocery store.[95]

At the other end of the spectrum, Nubia Lazo, wearing vagina earrings and appearing to delight in using explicitly sexual metaphors in a religious setting, runs a Sunday mass for the 'LGBTQI' community, who also fail to fit in anywhere else. She is so welcoming that she has had the seventeen-page mass translated into English for my benefit. Lazo's sermon is fiercely feminist, condemning phallocentric culture, which is faintly amusing given that the congregation is made up of gay men, apart from one lesbian couple. She said the feminist focus was deliberate because she was talking to a group of men. I suspect it may also have something to do with our presence. We got chatting to some members of the congregation. I asked a gay man why there were hardly any lesbians present.[96] According to him, most lesbians were atheist, and unless they were 'butch', most felt safer to pass as 'hetero'. He also acknowledged that as a man he fared better under patriarchy, notwithstanding his homosexuality. One of

EL SALVADOR

their affirmations of faith read: 'I believe in a non-binary God whose pronouns are plural ... I believe in Jesus Christ, their child, who wore a fabulous robe and had two dads.' That was quite a stretch from the traditional teachings of Christianity. Wouldn't it be simpler to create another set of beliefs from scratch? To which they responded unanimously that it was important to reform the institution from within.

Made in the USA

Evangelism was a gift from the United States. The Central American Mission (CAM) played a central role in putting down Protestant roots in El Salvador. They were later joined by the Baptists and remain a significant presence today.[97] The backlash against liberation theology from inside and outside the church and the realignment of the Catholic Church with political and social elites opened the door to competition from a number of religious denominations from the US such as the Evangelicals, Mormons and Jehovah's Witnesses, including those churches that preached the 'gospel of prosperity', the idea that wealth will come to those who follow God.[98] Today, Catholicism is practised by 50 per cent of the population and Protestant Evangelism by 36 per cent,[99] of which 70 per cent are poor and uneducated.

The entanglements between the US and El Salvador are many and varied. The relationship has been more damaging than beneficial to El Salvador. The most unexpected fact about the gangs of El Salvador is that they were made in the United States. The death squads during the civil war were funded and trained by America. The Salvadoran military regime received $4.5 billion in US economic and military aid. In the 1980s, US policy towards Central America was essentially the global Cold War writ small. Ronald Reagan, in particular, was keen to contain the spread of communism and attempted to do so with a mixture of strong-arm tactics through military aid and free markets, enveloped in ideas of Christian fundamentalism and right-wing nationalism. There was no concern for human rights, which Jimmy Carter, the previous president, had injected into US foreign policy even though he too had been concerned with maintaining US dominance. It is no coincidence that the Peace Accords were signed shortly after the fall of the Soviet Union.

The irrationality of US policy towards its Central American and Latin American neighbours can be summed up thus: the US imposes policies that create the conditions of hunger, poverty and violence that drive 'illegal' immigration to the US. The precarity induced by US immigration policy pushes people into criminal networks, which then provides the US with the perfect cover story to deport them, thus exporting criminality back to countries with weak institutions. To try to curtail immigration, the US provides funding for job creation, an apparently rational solution undercut by self-interest: the schemes are based in areas like extractive industries, which are damaging to El Salvador's environment, or free trade zones, which operate a highly exploitative regime for workers, mainly women, and essentially benefit the US corporate sector. The classic route to the US is fraught with danger. Almost a quarter of migrants-to-be return to El Salvador. Another 30 per cent remain in transit countries such as Guatemala or Mexico. Juárez believes that if paying child support was made mandatory and implemented, it would weaken the interest in migration.[100]

Despite low-skilled and low-paid immigrant jobs, remittances from the over 3 million Salvadorans working in the United States totalled $7 billion in 2021, representing 24 per cent of El Salvador's GDP.[101] There is not enough data differentiating the pattern of remittances by sex, but global World Bank figures dating from 2016 reveal that the amounts women migrants remit represent a bigger proportion of their income than that of men because they generally earn less, even when similarly qualified, as they are over-represented in the poorly paid domestic and care sectors.[102] Women's remittances are also more reliable and long term than those of men, even though the individual sums remitted are smaller. In this way, women play a beneficial role for both economies—allowing the richer economy to provide essential services in the care and health sector for a fraction of the costs it would incur if relying on local workers. So the patriarchal system deals a double whammy to women. A greater vulnerability to male violence and poverty, often converging in single motherhood, drives women to migrate. Having been denied education at home and only being able to acquire skills in childcare and domestic work, women attract no wages in El Salvador and are poorly recompensed in the destination countries.

The FMLN government, which was in power from 2009 to 2019, expanded social services for the poor and for women but did not break with the neoliberal model, partly due to pressure from the Obama administration because the model benefitted US corporations. The entire country, and particularly San Salvador, is bursting with malls filled with US fast-food chains. US policy in Central America is to make infrastructure funding conditional on the recipient countries implementing neoliberal policies regardless of the government's political colours.[103] 'The road leading from neoliberalism to state capture must be understood better if we are to prevent other societies—in the US and elsewhere—from traveling it.'[104] This is what has happened in places like El Salvador, and human rights organisations are now wringing their hands about the suspension of democratic rights. The US is El Salvador's largest trading partner and largest 'humanitarian' donor. It has been suggested that Bukele's interest in promoting the Bitcoin currency, a failed and deeply unpopular policy, is a bid for independence from America and other world institutions like the International Monetary Fund, which may be reluctant to provide aid given the suspension of human and civil rights in Bukele's crackdown on gangs.[105] All this may change under Trump's second term as president given his administration's embrace of cryptocurrency and Trump's public love-in with dictators like Bukele.

Feminism in peacetime

When the war ended, many women left the FMLN to organise autonomously. Herrera set up Las Dignas and subsequently La Colectiva Feminista, two prominent feminist organisations still active today. Some scholars argue that the post-revolutionary feminist movement inherited the FMLN's sectarian tendencies and divided according to which group they sprang from.[106] Some have concluded that despite the sexism of male-dominated leftist movements,[107] like the FMLN, and the subordination of feminist politics to party politics, the women played a significant, if not a leadership, role on the frontline, in the supply lines and in influencing the theoretical understandings of the oppressive role of patriarchy among the FMLN cadre. What the civil war taught the women was resilience, a quality that holds them in good stead in their ongoing political struggles.

Las Dignas, one of the leading feminist groups in El Salvador today, began life as an offshoot of National Resistance—Resistencia Nacional, or RN—one of the five parties affiliated with the FMLN. The relationship between the two deteriorated when the women began to challenge the leadership, so after the civil war Las Dignas went its own way. According to Herrera, accusations of sexual promiscuity and lesbianism were used to smear them.[108] ORMUSA is the only major feminist organisation not to have roots in the FMLN. Over 100 women's organisations had been established in El Salvador by 1991, a year before the Peace Accords were signed, working at a national or regional level. The women used the experience they gained in struggles with their male comrades during the civil war to challenge government bodies and ministries to incorporate gender issues into their policies. In the post-war period, women's groups 'have brought to the table for discussion issues such as abortion, reproductive rights, deadbeat dads, domestic violence (including marital rape), unequal working conditions for women, and many others'.[109] These issues were not discussed in public before, and the fact that they entered the national consciousness is attributed to the work of women. The funding the sector received from large international donors like the European Union and the US Agency for International Development also helped the sector to grow and 'professionalise' into an NGO sector. This was a double-edged sword in that they lost some control over their own agendas in accepting this funding and it sowed division in the competition for resources, a recognisable phenomenon worldwide.

In the post-civil war era, feminists faced multiple setbacks, not least the total criminalisation of abortion in 1998, until women-friendly laws were introduced under the leftist FMLN presidencies from 2009 to 2019, including the 2011 law on gender violence (LEIV). President Salvador Sánchez-Cerén, in office from 2014 to 2019, prioritised programmes to empower women for the first time in El Salvador's history,[110] but there was no liberalisation of abortion. LEIV, which is still on the statute book, categorises violence against women as psychological, sexual, physical, symbolic, economic and patrimonial. The symbolic and patrimonial categories have not entered the lexicon of many other states' legal systems, like the UK, where, paradoxically, the level of violence and brutality against women is less extreme.

Juárez, of ORMUSA, elaborates on the way in which 'symbolic' violence is understood in practice. Any anti-woman expression, be it in advertising, digital or non-digital spaces, in the law, in art or the use of language, can be prosecuted. She gave the example of a police officer who might say, 'I don't want to work with women because they are gossips.' The usual punishment is fines, but it could also have a negative impact on his job prospects. Only 4 per cent of claims end up in court, most of which are targeted at poor or rural men. I asked her about the huge gap between such radical steps to deal with misogyny and the fact that El Salvador has the most restrictive abortion laws in the world and the highest rates of femicide. Her response was poetic: 'It is like putting a new roof on an old structure.' She believes that men feel threatened by the progress women have made towards equality and rush to 'reset the patriarchal button'.[111] Machismo, described as 'the cult of virility ... arrogance and sexual aggression in male-to-female relationships',[112] permeates all Salvadoran institutions and is reinforced by the religious conservatism upheld by the Catholic and Evangelical Churches in El Salvador.

Juárez also helps to clarify the meaning of patrimonial violence and how it can be distinguished from economic violence, which forms part of the definition of domestic violence in UK law. Patrimonial refers to the already existing property of the woman such as money, photos, family goods, properties and bank savings, which the man may seize without her consent. Economic abuse relates to the support that would be beneficial to her survival but that is not offered or is withdrawn by the man. The subtle difference between the two was clarified by the following example. If a woman owned a car that her husband sold without her permission, that would amount to patrimonial violence. However, if her husband refused to support her application for a bank loan to purchase a car, something that is not yet in existence but adversely affects her ability to meet her needs, that would fall under the category of economic violence. The law enshrines an enlightened approach to violence against women, but half of the institutions in El Salvador do not pay heed to LEIV. Apparently, 'some judges have deemed the law as unconstitutional and deliberately refuse to implement it because they claim that it "unequally protects women with respect to men"'.[113]

Despite a half-baked attempt to use a more enlightened approach to gangs and a focus on the rights of women and other minorities, FMLN leaders turned out to be corrupt and returned to the *mano dura* policies of the conservative ARENA government. In the 2019 elections, FMLN's support sank to around 14 per cent of the vote. Bukele's decisive victory, winning 53 per cent of the vote, represented a break from the old binary of FMLN versus ARENA. He had been expelled from the FMLN for his biting public criticism of their performance and set up his own New Ideas party. As mayor of Nuevo Cuscatlán and San Salvador from 2012 to 2018 on an FMLN ticket, Bukele appeared to be socially progressive, setting up scholarship programmes for young men as a way of diverting them from gang membership and promoting pro-choice and same-sex marriage proposals that proved too challenging for a deeply Christian country and were duly discarded in order to win votes and power. In a speech to university students when he was mayor in 2013, he asked if people would like a populist president. When faced with a stony silence, he said, 'Nobody? No one? Well, I do. The dictionary defines "populism" as a political doctrine that aims to defend the interests and aspirations of the people. It's a paradigm. We have been told that populism is bad. I'd rather have populism than individualism.' As a true populist, he is swayed not by ideology but opinion polls.[114] According to feminists, Bukele's macho authoritarian style of governing 'reinforces the macho mindset of Salvadoran men and also those women who admire strong, powerful men'.[115] Although drugs are banned in El Salvador, it is widely believed that Bukele is a heavy user of cocaine. Among progressives, the fervent hope is that they are 'one overdose away from a change of regime!'

The absence of gangs on the streets has not made the streets that much safer for women. According to Juárez, 'this idea of sexual violence being tied up with the gangs is not correct. There is evidence which shows that sexual violence in El Salvador hasn't changed since the gangs have been put away.'[116] While she conceded there was greater freedom of movement on the streets, it had come at a huge cost. The belief that gangs were responsible for all violence against women has been used by the government to cut funding to women's projects because the streets are now gang-free.[117] In fact, the government has been extremely successful in creating a narrative that denies the existence of violence against women, denies enforced disappearances, does not release figures of femicides and has stopped funding the Observatorios de Violencia that monitor violence and the local health officials who kept track of teenage pregnancies.[118] Alerta Raquel, a project set up by Elizondo of Ixchel in the name of a young woman, Raquel, who is missing to this day, to support women looking for their missing relatives, keep its own database and reports that 245 women and girls disappeared between the start of 2020 and August 2023.

Women's organisations are also being harassed. ORMUSA is harassed on X and social media; its website comes under digital attack and goes down twice daily. Worst of all, a government representative is based in the office who reports back to the government on any irregularities. As ORMUSA's books are in order and its finances are transparent, they have nothing to fear, but this is a form of harassment. There is also a bill that has not yet been passed that will make it difficult for organisations to accept international donations as they will be expected to share 40 per cent of the funding with the government.[119] The government has a department that monitors dissident statements on social media. Anyone who declares herself a feminist can expect a tirade of abuse, which has a chilling effect on all criticism of government policy. Venues that agree to host feminist conferences are leaned on by the government to withdraw the offer.[120] Feminists believe that there is what they call a 'patriarchal pact' between the church, which includes Christians of all denominations, and Bukele's government, so he will not relent on abortion and LGBT rights; the church does not criticise him, and sex education has recently been dropped from school curricula.[121]

Over the bodies of women

Sexual violence is rife. Even though underreporting is likely to be extensive, a US-funded report found 5,211 cases of sexual violence against women in 2022, of which 3,135 cases involved girls under eighteen, and 1,184 cases involved girls under twelve.[122] Teenage pregnancies caused by men who are often twenty years older have become so normalised that they are not seen as a crime and go unreported.[123] Given the lack of options, it is not surprising that there is a high suicide rate among pregnant women, especially pregnant teenagers. The left-leaning digital outlet El Faro has described El Salvador as a haven for child rapists.[124]

Given the high rate of child pregnancies, Norma Leticia Lobos, an official in the Secretariat of Women in a local municipality who says she was 'born with a feminist chip embedded in her', vows to continue her work on sex education in schools regardless of the new directive banning sex education from schools and of the danger to her life and the possible loss of her job, which is a fate suffered by other dissidents. She points out the irony of the president's new law, 'Nacer con cariño' (Born with love), on supporting new mothers and babies when teenage pregnancies are exacerbated by a ban on sex education and a ban on abortion. She says: 'I can't celebrate a twelve-year-old giving birth when I know her rapist is out there.'[125] She relies on a measure of protection that people in El Salvador get from their personal networks. Her work on domestic and sexual violence brings her into contact with police officers and government officials. She describes how a police officer turned up at her door with a search warrant on the suspicion that she hosted meetings of gang members. When he recognised her, he did not carry out the search. There is some measure of local autonomy in municipalities, but the room for feminist action is limited and constantly under assault.

The 'Nacer con cariño' law is part of a trio of laws with romantic names in which women are subjects of rights solely based on their roles as mothers. The other two are the 'Believe Together' law ('Ley Crecer Juntos para la Protección Integral de la Primera Infancia, Niñez y Adolescencia', on the protection of childhood and adolescence), and the awkwardly translated 'Love Turned into Food' law ('Ley Amor Convertido en Alimento', on breastfeeding), which asserts the 'absolute priority of children's rights' and requires the mother to breastfeed exclusively for six months. The very fact that a law has been passed on this issue is enough to strike terror in the hearts of mothers who cannot breastfeed for whatever reason. There is a frightening internal coherence between these laws and those governing abortion, where the child's right to life is prioritised over the mother who becomes dehumanised; simply a carrier of more valuable lives. If the state can commandeer women's breasts, Juárez argues the state should also take control of men's penises.[126] But there are also contradictions. The 'Believe Together' law stipulates the right to sex education, yet Bukele has instructed that sex education be removed from the school curriculum under pressure from religious forces. The law replaces 'LEPINA' ('Ley de Protección Integral de la Niñez y Adolescencia'), which activists argue provided better protection for young girls, where sex with a minor was seen as rape and hospitals were obliged to report the rapist and initiate a search for him. Some feminists believe that it is in the interests

EL SALVADOR

of patriarchy to keep women out of the public sphere, starting with keeping girls out of school once they are pregnant.[127]

El Salvador outlawed abortion in 1998, making it one of eight countries in the world with a total ban. Abortion laws are so strict that miscarriages and even stillborn foetuses can be construed as abortions, and women can be jailed for murder with sentences of thirty to fifty years. In this context, feminists cannot frame the debate on abortion in terms of women's choice or bodily autonomy. The cases on which they campaign are egregious ones like the famous Beatriz case in which fifteen medical specialists unsuccessfully recommended that her pregnancy should be ended because her health was fragile and her anencephalic (without a brain) foetus would die shortly after birth.[128] In June 2021, a poor woman, Lesly Ramirez, who had received no sex education and therefore did not understand the changes in her body, became pregnant and gave birth to a baby in a toilet at the age of nineteen. She was convicted of aggravated homicide because the authorities said she had stabbed her child and sentenced her to fifty years in prison. She had been trying to cut the umbilical cord in the dark as they had no electricity.[129] Herrera, president of the Citizen Group for the Decriminalization of Abortion, established in 2009, tells me proudly that they have freed seventy-two women to date using a variety of penal and legal strategies including 'pardons' and commuted sentences.[130] At the time of writing, there were only two women left in prison. This is a class issue as much as a sex issue. It is mostly poor, often uneducated women who end up in prison as the rich can either leave the country to get an abortion or pay privately for healthcare. There are eight government hospitals with a prosecutor based in each whose role is to denounce all obstetric emergencies as criminal abortions. There are none in private hospitals.[131]

Nubia Lazo, a lay Anglican priest who spoke out on TV in favour of limited abortion rights, had to escape to Costa Rica in

2011 within four days of the broadcast because a member of Opus Dei wrote an article condemning her stance, leading to threats against her and her son.[132] Despite the draconian laws, girls use herbs to induce abortions in schools. If they start haemorrhaging and are taken to hospital, the doctors will report them, and they will go to prison.[133] Doctors remove the girls' uteruses so that they can be used as evidence in court.[134] The men who rape these girls escape scot-free. As Juárez powerfully argues, children who die of malnutrition because men do not provide child support to the women and girls they have impregnated is a form of 'masculine abortion' that is tolerated by society. There are 26,000 demands for child support each year.[135] While procreation is seen to have economic value under capitalism in providing cheap labour, El Salvador's underdeveloped economy has little use for human capital as workers—it exports one-third of its surplus population through migration to economies that can make use of their labour. This may be an example of where the demands of patriarchy diverge from the demands of capitalism. Equally, it could be said that the prop provided to the economy by the huge remittances sent back by these surplus workers is an example of patriarchy and capitalism working in concert.

The reversal in the already-limited abortion rights began in the mid-1990s when El Salvador was in a transitional moment and the right realised it was a good way of putting clear water between themselves and the FMLN. In 1994, in the first elections since the Peace Accords, the conservative ARENA party won around 45 per cent of the vote and was forced to sit alongside the FMLN, which won around 21 per cent of the vote, the enemy they had fought bitterly for over twelve years. In the same year, the UN World Conference on Population and Development, which called for abortion rights for women, was denounced by the pope as a First World strategy to control 'Third World' populations. The local Catholic church took up the call with highly charged rhetoric comparing abortion to 'Nazi death camps', and ARENA politicians seized upon the issue as an effective strategy to vilify the FMLN's enlightened pro-women policies and implicitly their entire 'communist' agenda. By drawing attention to their own 'sanctity of the family' agenda, ARENA deflected the left's demands for policies to deal with poverty. The 1995 World Women's Conference in Beijing also served to strengthen the Christian right in El Salvador. In the official organ of the Catholic Church, Orientación, 'feminismo is invariably portrayed as being the exact antithesis of machismo—that is, a dichotomous reflection whose intention is to replace patriarchal authoritarianism with a symmetrical matriarchal equivalent'.[136]

By the time of the second post-civil war election in 1997, the anti-abortion campaign had found its voice in the group Foundation Yes to Life (Fundación Sí a la Vida), which mobilised powerful lobbies in support of a total ban. The FMLN could not command enough votes to liberalise the abortion laws in the Legislative Assembly, so a total ban on abortion was passed into law, despite being only one seat behind ARENA and despite women making up 18 per cent of those present. In the 1999 presidential election, not content with the total ban, the right went further and demanded that the constitution be amended to redefine life as beginning with conception. Realising that the abortion issue was a vote winner, the FMLN withdrew its party-wide opposition and allowed individuals to vote with their conscience. That too passed.

There was only one more way left to milk the issue after these legislative changes, and that was to argue that the law was not being implemented and that 'killer mothers' were getting away with it.[137] As Herrera put it, 'people's attachment to religion is instrumentalised to impose an agenda and norms of conduct that do not respond to public health and rights recognition criteria, but rather to the visions and mandates of church hierarchies'.[138]

Under feminist pressure, the FMLN government agreed to make improvements to its sexual and reproductive health policies but insisted that the words 'right to' sexual health be removed.[139] So squeezed is the space for feminist action that many of the feminists look back with regret to 2017, when there was a moment when things could have gone their way on liberalising the abortion laws in the Legislative Assembly. A bill tabled by Lorena Peña, an ex-guerrilla fighter, member of the FMLN and founder of Las Mélidas, a prominent feminist organisation, might have received the requisite number of votes, but Peña failed to show up for the debate, either because she was ill or because she was facing pressure from the FMLN to step back. Nobody knows, but the disappointment of feminists is captured by the semi-humorous trope doing the rounds to this day, 'Lorena Peña isn't coming down.' Of course, as activists themselves will acknowledge, there is no way of knowing whether they had enough votes. But the episode illustrates the difficulties faced by women in bringing about change in a hostile environment.

There is a logical consistency between the high rates of femicide and the total ban on abortion—a complete disregard for the lives and bodies of women. A 2017 survey of violence against women found that 67 per cent of Salvadoran women had experienced violence at some point in their lives. Nearly three out of every four acts of sexual violence take place in the victims' homes, and 70 per cent of victims are under the age of twenty.[140] Salvadoran law defines femicide as the killing of a woman with 'motives of hatred or contempt for her condition as a woman'. Some scholars have 'proposed the term feminicide, rather than femicide, to underline the role of state negligence in these crimes and the intersection of power dynamics and cultural and socio-economic factors'.[141] Feminicide is also the term applied to state killing of women. Femicide is punishable by twenty to twenty-five years' imprisonment, a lower sentence than in cases of abortion, while aggravated femicide is punishable by thirty-five to fifty years in prison. However, the reality on the ground is the familiar lack of implementation, a worldwide phenomenon. In El Salvador, that has been aggravated by the presence of gang violence, which was hardly policed and allowed men to kill women and attribute it to gangs. The impunity granted to perpetrators by this inaction symbolises the lack of value attached to women by the patriarchal system.

Conclusion

This is a very complicated moment for the feminist movement in El Salvador. There was widespread consensus on this question among the women to whom we spoke. For all of the FMLN government's failures, and the familiar disappointment that feminists express in their left comrades, the 'doors of dialogue' were open to feminists until 2019. The gains were limited, but several women-friendly laws were passed to prevent and prosecute violence against women. However, with poor implementation, femicide figures remained high. Draconian abortion laws have lost none of their teeth, thanks partly to the stranglehold of religion and political parties' focus on vote-winning policies. Since then, Bukele has shut feminists out of government. Cheyne feels that feminists are disorientated—having got used to being consulted, they have not been able to devise a political strategy to deal with a hugely popular leader whose politics are hard to pin down.[142] If there are any positives to be gleaned, it is that feminists have made use of the limited spaces available for manoeuvre to the best of their ability, like finding bubbles of oxygen in polluted waters. Herrera asserts that it is important to celebrate the small victories because the road to freedom is a long one. While the movement may be weak, it is united apart from the competition for funds and some intergenerational tensions. The fight against abortion, disappearances and for a life free of violence is part of a common agenda. The transgender issue has not divided the feminist movement in El Salvador. Transgender and non-binary people are also seen as victims of patriarchy. There is no abolitionist movement in terms of the sex industry, another divisive issue in Western feminism.

The violence unleashed by Bukele's policies qualifies the political system in El Salvador as a form of necro-capitalism. While the term necro-capitalism might be applied to a number of different countries, El Salvador appears to be the perfect fit. Cameroonian critical theorist Achille Mbembe coined the term to describe 'the role of extreme violence in the functioning of larger biopolitical orders':

> [N]ot merely a state's 'right' to kill and to organise people to be killed (as opposed to live), but to expose them to extreme violence and death and reduce entire segments of populations to the barest and most precarious existence. All in order to preserve the established economic and political hierarchies of the capitalist system.[143]

While Mbembe focuses on the racial dynamic behind necro-capitalism and the criminalising of poor indigenous people, of which El Salvador is certainly an example, there is also a gender dynamic, not taken into account in Mbembe's theory, in which the state builds its power on the bodies and lives of women, where certain masculinities are criminalised, but the difference between the state and gangs is arguably paper-thin. Feminists and other human rights activists will need to be prepared to play the long game now that Bukele, like other populist dictators who have come to power by democratic means, has set aside the constitution that allows only one five-year term, having been re-elected in 2024.

2

RAQQA TO RIYADH

THE COPY AND THE TEMPLATE

Rahila Gupta

In the middle of Deera Square in Riyadh, the capital of Saudi Arabia, is a storm drain. Not normally a remarkable feature of public spaces, by any means, except that very little rain falls in Saudi Arabia. Perhaps there is a clue in its colloquial name, the Chop Chop Square. This is where public executions used to take place, usually beheading by sword on a Friday. Since King Salman and his son Mohammed bin Salman—widely known as MBS—came to power in 2015, and contrary to the liberal modernising image that MBS likes to project, the number of executions annually has gone up by a staggering 82 per cent, averaging about 130 killings per year. On 12 March 2022, eighty-one people were killed in a single day.[1] That storm drain comes in handy, although most executions, especially the political ones, now take place behind closed doors. Nobody knows when the last execution was carried out in Deera Square. Filming of the executions is forbidden; political prisoners—always referred to as terrorists—are executed in prisons, and public executions are not announced in advance. Sharia law dictates that the execution of murderers must be carried out in public, and the victim's family is allowed to watch,[2] but the recent gentrification of the square makes it hard to imagine it as a place of butchery.

This veil of secrecy, possibly as a nod to its Western allies, is the only thing that separates Saudi executions from those that were carried out in another part of the Middle East, the short-lived ISIS caliphate (2014–19) stretching across Iraq and Syria.[3] Nearly 1,600 executions were carried out in 2017 alone,[4] many of which were filmed and released on the internet, and beheaded bodies were left on display as part of their gory self-aggrandisement. As a terrorist group, it was even less accountable to global governance rules or restricted by trade relationships than Saudi Arabia. However, it has been argued that public executions acted as a tool of state-building, allowing ISIS to exert authority through fear and 'enabling it to evolve from an insurgency into what it perceives as a state'.[5] To some extent that applies to Saudi Arabia too.

Until ISIS came on the scene, Saudi Arabia, Afghanistan under the Taliban and Iran were considered the apotheosis of religious rigidity, the first two belonging to the Sunni branch of Islam and the other Shi'a. But ISIS saw the Saudis as *kaffirs*, insufficiently strict adherents of Salafism, the ultra-conservative branch of Sunni Islam professed by ISIS and on which the governance of Saudi Arabia is based. According to Carmen bin Ladin (CBL), of dual Iranian and Swiss heritage, raised in Switzerland and married to one of the Bin Laden brothers from 1974 to 1988, '[t]he Saudis are the Taliban, in luxury'.[6] While Saudi Arabia does not massacre towns and villages at point-blank range like ISIS, both believe in the 'importance of living by the Koran and ruling by the sword'.[7]

RAQQA TO RIYADH

Debate has raged over whether Saudi Arabia funded ISIS and what the precise connections between the two might have been. When Abu Bakr al-Baghdadi, one-time leader of ISIS, damned Saudi Arabia as 'the serpent's head'—the primary antagonist against the advancement of pure Islam[8]—he summed up the relationship perfectly but not in the way he intended. ISIS represents—we still cannot talk about it in the past tense—the natural outcome of the billions of petrodollars that Saudi Arabia has poured into madrassas (Islamic schools), mosques, the training of clerics and printing of free Qur'ans across the world from Africa to Asia to the Far East and even the migrant communities of America and Europe from the 1970s onwards.[9] The rise of political Islam, increased tensions and reduced freedoms for women have been noted in every country where Muslim communities have glittered with Saudi gold. In fact, the money was donated on condition that recipients enforced strict Islamic codes, minimised education for women, banned alcohol and enforced fasting during Ramadan.[10] CBL believes that most of Saudi society agrees with the ideas of Osama bin Laden and claims that the Bin Laden family still maintain an intricate network of relations with the Saudi royal family. Whatever the ideological differences between the various strands of hard-line Islam, they arise from the serpent's head. The difficulty for Saudi Arabia was to convincingly disavow responsibility for their offspring when it was Saudi religious teachings that were responsible for the way they turned out. From the Saudi point of view, as long as America had its back, there was no pressure to be convincing.

No book on global patriarchy can be complete without an exploration of the position of women in, unarguably, the most egregious example of the oppression of women—ISIS. Although much weakened in Syria, it is still active in parts of Africa and Afghanistan, as demonstrated by the audacious attack on a Moscow concert hall in March 2024.[11] By examining the most extreme version of patriarchy promoted by a religious philosophy rooted in the seventh century and blended with jihadism, a modern interpretation of the Islamic concept of struggle, it is possible to see clearly the dangers for women when hard-line Islam is unadorned by the makeovers taking place as Saudi Arabia loosens the straitjacket of Wahhabism, a strain of Salafism. ISIS threw patriarchy into sharp relief, taking ideas present in all religions and cultures—men demanding unfettered access to women's bodies, their reproductive and domestic services—to an extreme. Their central belief, shared in common with Wahhabism—'The Prophet [Muhammad] Warned Us Of Corruption And *Fitnah* (rebellion) That Will Be Spread On The Earth Because Of Women'[12]—runs through the organisation's governance structures. The age-old justification for patriarchy, as a suppression of the evil that is women, still resonates.

Rise and fall of ISIS

Many commentators have ascribed the growth of ISIS to the political vacuum in Iraq following the US-led invasion of 2003 and the fall of Saddam Hussein, fuelled by the sense of injustice felt by the Sunnis in Shia-dominated Iraq, who were looking for vengeance and found an outlet in Al-Qaeda in Iraq (AQI), the precursor of ISIS led by Abu Musab al-Zarqawi, which attempted to counter the ascendance of Shias. Almost all the founder-members of AQI, later renamed ISIS, were thrown together by the Americans in Camp Bucca in Iraq. According to a senior ISIS official: 'If there was no American prison in Iraq, there would be no ISIS now. Bucca was a factory. It made us all. It built our ideology.'[13] Seventeen of the twenty-five most important ISIS leaders spent time in US prisons.

When Zarqawi was killed by the Americans in 2006, it threw AQI into disarray, nearly destroying them as a significant actor until the 'Arab Spring' spread to neighbouring Syria and gave them another shot in the arm.[14] Assad released jihadis from Syrian prisons in 2012 as part of a two-pronged strategy to divide the opposition, turning it from a peaceful, democratic opposition to an armed one led by jihadis, which then gave him the excuse to retaliate with brute force. Saudi Arabia too released religious prisoners and encouraged them to join the fighters in Syria.

In March 2013, Raqqa became the first major Syrian city to fall to jihadi groups, and ISIS subsequently took advantage of the jihadis' infighting to take over the city in January 2014. Despite their deep unpopularity among the local population, ISIS established themselves through their use of the carrot and stick. ISIS bought the loyalty of populations in newly conquered lands. They 'distributed free or heavily subsidized bread, cracked down on crime, and cleaned up the streets'.[15] In Mosul, citizens reported that roads were kept in fairly good repair despite the regular bombings and that the supply of electricity was much improved. ISIS also attempted to provide health services, with Raqqa reportedly having the best health service in Syria.[16] However, the system was not all it appeared to be: it provided free healthcare to ISIS fighters but charged local civilians exorbitant rates. An anonymous eyewitness account of life in Raqqa described the breakdown in services, the exorbitant taxes levied by ISIS, the price of basic goods becoming unaffordable and the unavailability of gas and petrol.[17]

Unlike Saudi Arabia, ISIS was a challenge to US interests in the region and had to be decimated. The US coalition, which included major European powers, supported the most reliable boots on the ground, the Kurdish-led Syrian Defence Forces (SDF), with air-cover, military training and arms. The SDF were engaged in an existential battle with ISIS to protect their fledgling revolution, based on an anti-patriarchal, secular ideology that acted as a red rag to ISIS. The SDF's determination and discipline led to a village-by-village pushing back of the borders of the 'caliphate' until the dramatic fall of its capital, Raqqa, in 2017. The once-mighty ISIS caliphate was eventually reduced to a postage stamp-sized area and ultimately smoked out of its final redoubt, Baghouz, in 2019.

Economic underpinnings

Contrary to the popular belief that ISIS's wealth was derived from oil revenue and the selling of looted antiquities, it has emerged from the paperwork seized after their rout in Mosul, Iraq, that their tax revenue from agriculture was greater than oil revenue by a factor of six. The strategy of the US coalition of bombing oilfields was therefore misguided. Rukmini Callimachi, journalist at the *New York Times*, found an abandoned suitcase bulging with paper in a bombed-out building in Iraq:

> The documents describe how it made money at every step in the supply chain: Before a single seed of grain, for example, was sown, the group collected rent for the fields it had confiscated. Then, when the crops were ready to be threshed, it collected a harvest tax …
>
> The trucks that transported the grain paid highway tolls. The grain was stored in silos, which the militants controlled, and they made money when the grain was sold to mills, which they also controlled. The mills ground the grain into flour, which the group sold to traders.
>
> Then the bags of flour were loaded onto trucks, which traversed the caliphate, paying more tolls. It was sold to supermarkets and shops, which were also taxed. So were the consumers who bought the finished product.
>
> In a single 24-hour period in 2015, one of the spreadsheets in the briefcase shows, the Islamic State collected $1.9 million from the sale of barley and wheat.[18]

All kinds of other taxes were levied from citizens for rubbish collection services, provision of electricity, water, phone lines and so on. In Northern Iraq, Patrick Cockburn writes 'that people would not eat at any restaurant that wasn't up to date with its tax payments to ISIS lest the place be bombed while they were dining'.[19]

By contrast, Saudi Arabia used its oil wealth to buy off its population with a no-tax economy. It is important to note the extent to which the US and other Western countries, who like to boast of their women-friendly societies, are implicated in sustaining deeply entrenched patriarchal societies like Saudi Arabia. Timothy Mitchell, a professor at Columbia University, examines the unacknowledged role that political Islam has played in the development of global capitalism, which he dubs 'McJihad', meaning that 'capitalism appear[s] to operate, in certain critical instances, only by adopting the social force and moral authority of conservative Islamic movements'.[20] When oil was discovered, and Ibn Saud, founding monarch of Saudi Arabia, turned to the Americans for help with extraction, he did a deal with the religious establishment, who were opposed to a foreign, colonising presence. In return for their cooperation, they were given a substantial portion of oil revenues to fund their proselytising activities. Aramco, the national oil company, invested in Saudi Arabia's infrastructure, local Saudi enterprises and paid royalties amounting to millions and later billions to the royal family. The religious authorities were given free rein over the moral and social order, using sharia to justify its *fatawa*—religious opinions, in plural—to suppress dissent and entrench a deeply patriarchal society.

Having silenced internal opposition to their embrace of US imperialism, the Saudis faced opposition from the nationalist governments of Egypt and Iraq. With the help of Aramco, the Saudi government devised and funded an Islamist political movement to undermine President Nasser of Egypt. William Eddy, the CIA agent on Aramco's staff, called for 'a moral alliance between Christians and Muslims against the common threat of communism'.[21] The CIA attempted coups in both countries, whose governments had made progress on women's rights, land reforms and universal education, and succeeded in toppling the government in Iraq.

This detour into the political economy of oil demonstrates how US imperialism and economic interests override women's freedoms. Profits from oil were only possible if Saudi Arabia cooperated with the US in maintaining an artificial scarcity of oil, switching the supply on and off as dictated by market conditions. And Saudi Arabia itself relied on an ultra-conservative branch of Islamism to head off opposition from a number of directions. Keeping two such polarised allies content was a difficult juggling act. Over the years, some of the most serious threats to the power of the Saudi monarchy have come from the same religious forces they had promoted who have grown tired of the corruption and luxurious lifestyles of the Saudi royal family. Saudi Arabia dealt with political unrest by exporting young imprisoned religious activists to overseas wars. In the 1980s, it sent 12,000 prisoners to Afghanistan to fight against Soviet communism alongside Osama bin Laden.[22]

Drawing devotees to the cause

The strategies followed by ISIS and Saudi Arabia were obviously different because they were at different stages of development and their needs were different, but they shared the same crusading impulse. Once ISIS had acquired a vast swathe of land stretching across Iraq and Syria, the challenge was to populate it and make it grow, to attract both men and women who had fully signed up to the ISIS ideology, as the loyalty of local populations, predicated on fear, could not be relied upon. Saudi Arabia's oil-rich economy, on the other hand, used cash rather than ideology to attract much-needed labour to the country. As mentioned earlier, they chose to spread their ideology around the world in the service of creating an Ummah, a supra-national global community of Muslims dedicated to Wahhabism, which is ultimately responsible for the rise of groups like ISIS. They recruited predominantly from the Muslim populations of poorer countries on the Asian subcontinent, the Philippines, Indonesia and Africa for domestic and unskilled work and among Europeans and Americans for the more skilled jobs. According to the Saudi census of 2022, the percentage of foreign migrant labour in Saudi Arabia stood at nearly 42 per cent of the population despite the Saudisation policy, initiated to encourage the employment of Saudi nationals in the private sector, that has been followed enthusiastically by MBS since 2017.[23]

ISIS used sophisticated propaganda methods to attract recruits to the cause, with different strategies aimed at women and men, often young girls and boys. ISIS understood the power of ideology as a call to action. Their journal, *Dabiq*, celebrated the fact that al-Baghdadi launched attacks in Canada, America and Australia 'with nothing more than words and a shared belief in the act of worship that is jihād'.[24] Although I have only seen the digital version, *Dabiq* appears to be as glossy as an in-flight magazine, with full-page, graphic photographs of bloody scenes, portraits of fighters and Western leaders—all male of course. The only pictures of women were those of corpses, but their faces were pixelated much like the public images of women in Saudi Arabia. In one particularly tragic Saudi case in 2018, a man could not identify his wife who had died in an accident because she had never lifted her veil, even in their most intimate moments.[25]

ISIS ideology blamed the oppression of Muslims on a Western Christian conspiracy. To provide downtrodden Muslims with a new sense of purpose and self-esteem, they harked back to the period between the seventh and eleventh centuries, when the 'caliphate was the most powerful and advanced polity in the whole of western Eurasia'.[26] ISIS is an exclusive and excluding club in which Saudi Arabia, the Muslim Brotherhood and al-Qaeda are considered apostates. This strategy is paradoxically both divisive and cohesive, building brand loyalty among its followers through the heroic self-sacrifice that commitment to a higher ideal and membership of the group requires. Their ideology acquired heft from their material success: '[T]he closer ISIS came to realizing its territorial ambitions, the less religion played a part in driving people to join the organization.'[27] In the first, most comprehensive statistics, 41,490 people from eighty countries joined ISIS in Iraq and Syria, up to 13 per cent of whom were women and 12 per cent children. An estimated 850 jihadists travelled from the UK.[28] Women were not the only temptation for new recruits; land and free housing were also part of the allure. Of that figure, 145 women left the UK to become 'jihadi brides', as they are popularly known.[29] These young women, sometimes only teenagers, who had been brought up in comparatively liberal Muslim families living in the West, were giving it all up to migrate to this fundamentalist 'state'. Why? The question 'why?' lingers unanswered despite or because of our extensive knowledge of life under ISIS. An almost farcically savage form of patriarchy was constructed around the living entombment of women, covered head to foot, where even the seductive lure of eyes had to be veiled when women dared to venture into public spaces. Life under ISIS involved dress codes, especially for women, that were brutally enforced; beheadings of dissenters and criminals with heads on poles; the killing of gay men; the banning of cigarettes, alcohol and music—a narrow, prescriptive, ideologically pure Islam. Women were beaten for breaching the dress code or if they were caught walking on the street alone.

Some researchers believe that 'jihadi brides' is a reductive term because it implies that the women are naïve and vulnerable to manipulation. In fact, that has been the primary argument made by lawyers on behalf of Shamima Begum—that she had been 'groomed' by ISIS, a child at fifteen—arguing for her right to return and face justice in the UK.[30] While that right should certainly be granted, it appears that she was not as innocent as she has claimed. According to my Kurdish sources, there are videos of her as an adult forcing a three-year-old child to watch while her mother is raped and beheaded, as well as videos showing her whipping a woman on her lower back, buttocks and feet for transgressing the strict dress code. But researchers argue that the 'jihadi brides' were making considered choices, seeking empowerment in ways that fitted neither traditional nor Western gender norms. They reported that their interviewees were making statements like, 'This is in line with my religion, my political beliefs, the fact I want to live how I want.'[31]

Saudi women, on the other hand, chafed against similar restrictions, fought back and sought to leave the country in search of asylum in more welcoming countries as soon as travel restrictions were lifted in 2019. Based on an analysis of the social media accounts of twelve women who self-identified as ISIS supporters and migrated to Syria,[32] half of whom originated in the UK, the researchers ascertained their commitment to Islam, the extent of their enthusiasm for or disillusion with ISIS, the facts of their life, whom they married or whether they had children.[33] As complaints had to be disguised, it became even more difficult to draw conclusive observations. Many of their social media posts, when they were not exchanging recipes or handing out tips on how to dress or what to bring for the journey to Syria, simply regurgitated official ISIS positions. There was not much evidence of nuanced thinking—the world was divided into two camps: that of *iman* (belief) or *kufr* (unbelief). The researchers found that '[l]ike their male counterparts, the women within our sample who migrate to ISIS territory talk at length about the oppression of Muslims throughout the world'.³⁴ They often shared gruesome pictures of dead Muslims, killed by Western forces, to build a sense of shared victimisation at the hands of the West. One woman rewinds a beheading video and asks for 'more beheadings please'.³⁵ The researchers conclude that 'the women hope to contribute to the creation of an ideologically pure state. They also hope to contribute to ISIS's state-building as mothers, nurses or teachers.'³⁶

Women were not there as fighters. However, in the last days of the caliphate, women were encouraged to become jihadis,³⁷ an accommodation with pragmatic needs that is also apparent in Saudi Arabia as religious edicts are discarded in the move to a post-oil economy. In October 2017, an article entitled 'The Duty of Women in Waging Jihad against the Enemy' was published in the weekly ISIS newspaper *Al-Naba*. Women were called on to prepare themselves as 'mujahidat', female holy warriors, to 'support the mujahideen in this battle'. After the fall of the caliphate, there have been reports of ISIS women carrying out or planning terrorist actions in Western Europe. In her book *Your Fatwa Does Not Apply Here*, Karima Bennoune describes how fundamentalist doctrine operates by denying 'the possibility of interpretation and reinterpretation even while its adherents engage in both'.³⁸

From their social media posts, it is clear that women can access other roles in ISIS only once they have accepted the role of 'bride'. One woman writes:

> I have stressed this before on twitter but I really need sisters to stop dreaming about coming to *Shaam* [Syria] and not getting married. *Wallahi* [I swear to God] life here is very difficult for the *Muhajirat* [sisters] and we depend heavily on the brothers for a lot of support. It is not like the west where you can casually walk out and go to Asda/Walmart and drive back home ... even till now we

have to stay safe outside and must always be accompanied by a *Mahram* [chaperone].³⁹

It was rare to hear even mildly critical posts of the *mahram* system by newly arrived women in Syria. However, it was possible to read between the lines and pick up complaints about the absence of proper medical facilities, irregular electricity supplies and Western-style luxuries. Women were allowed to work in *hisba* (Islamic morality enforcement) teams and as teachers, doctors and nurses to service other women in their strictly segregated society. In ISIS lands, the *mahram* system is sacrosanct within a strict interpretation of sharia, just as it was in Saudi Arabia. But the *mahram* rule could be suspended: an article in *Dabiq* urged women to migrate to the caliphate on their own if necessary, saying it was justified by scholars, such was their need for procreation.⁴⁰ Though the women saw this migration as commitment to a higher goal, they also talked of the pain of having to leave their families, and some of them yearned to see their mothers again. One woman consoled herself with the thought that '[t]he family you get in exchange for leaving the ones behind are like the pearl in comparison to the Shell you threw away into the foam of the sea which is the Ummah [Muslim community]'.⁴¹

Even though the bulk of their daily routine was domestic work—cooking and cleaning and looking after children—it was elevated by the knowledge that they were fulfilling their religious duty. The very real prospect of widowhood, being married to an ISIS fighter, was seen as an honour. They acquired special status through the 'martyrdom' of their husbands, though this was sometimes the point at which a European migrant would decide to return home. However, women were often married off before the stipulated mourning period of four months was over. There were reports that widows were being married off again in as little as a week.⁴² An article in *Dabiq* provided lengthy advice on how a widow must deport herself. She was not allowed to adorn herself by wearing jewellery, make-up or perfume: 'If they have errands the[y] must run them during the day, and return by sunset. If they're lonely, they can meet up with other women during the day but they must not gossip or backbite only use the sessions for religious education or maintaining family ties.'[43] The only time women would be justified in leaving their husbands is when the men have become apostates either by expressing doubt in their religion or supporting democracy.[44] Umm Sumayyah, possibly the only female contributor to *Dabiq*, urged women to come to the caliphate because it is their duty, saying of those who have arrived that '[t]hey are as fragile as glass bottles but their souls are those of men with ambitions almost hugging the heavens. Yes, these are the ... sisters who performed *hijrah* to the lands of the Islamic State.'[45] She recounts stories of women who abandoned riches. In one story, she even glorifies the loss of a baby during a pregnant woman's journey to the caliphate, saying it 'is better for him [to die in the caliphate] than to die through the curriculum of the tawāghīt's [apostate's] schools'.[46] In Saudi Arabia, the situation is the polar opposite. When the *mahram* system was partially liberalised in 2019, so that women could apply for their own passports and travel without male permission, it led to an exodus of women fleeing Saudi Arabia for either domestic or political reasons.[47] 'It's a sad thing that we, as Saudi women, the first step we take to protect ourselves is to run away from our country and lose our citizenship,' said Saudi activist and journalist Khulud al-Harithi. 'We are from a country where there are no wars or crises that could force a woman to seek asylum.'[48]

Part of ISIS's success can be attributed to the fact that they were media savvy and knew how to use modern methods of communication to get their message across. Anna Erelle (not her real name), a French journalist who set up a fake Facebook account in the name of Mélodie in order to research the world of ISIS, describes the effectiveness of ISIS communication strategies:

Jihadism 2.0's new communication strategy has hit the mark. The Islamic State has inundated YouTube with ultraviolent videos that stick in the minds of thousands of Westerners lobotomized by the group's swiftness of action and execution of threats. ... These days, would-be jihadists aren't drawn by easy money, guns, or drug dealing. Instead they dream about being respected and gaining recognition. They want to be 'heroes'. Becoming the neighborhood bigshot and hanging out over PlayStation is one thing; playing war and creating a state is quite another.[49]

The role ISIS carved out for their women is perfectly captured in Erelle's memoir. After she posted a video on Facebook on the exploits of Abu Bilel—who turned out to be a high-ranking ISIS official, an emir, close to al-Baghdadi—he unexpectedly contacted her. Within forty-eight hours, he professed his love for her and asked her to join him in Syria, marry him and join the jihad. Their whole 'relationship' lasted only a month:

I love you more than I've loved anyone. You should be here with me. I can't stand to think of you in that corrupt country ... You should see how happy the women are here. They used to be like you—lost. One of my friends' wives has arranged a program for your arrival. After your shooting lessons, she'll take you to a very beautiful store, the only one in the country that sells fine cloth. I'll pay for everything. You'll establish your own little world here with your new friends ... Brick by brick, we'll build a better world, a place where *kafirs* won't be allowed, and we'll carve a name for ourselves in history. I have found a huge apartment for you! If you bring friends, I'll find an even bigger one. You take care of orphans and the wounded during the day, while [I'm] fighting. We spend our evenings together ... *insha'Allah*.[50]

This is the ISIS message, personalised. Although there is a reference to shooting lessons, the rest of the passage makes it clear that her role would be one of domesticity. He urges Mélodie to remember to buy some lingerie and to do everything to please her future husband. Given the emphasis on women as mothers and the ISIS critique that women in the West are treated as sexual objects, this is one of their many contradictions. Erelle believes that ISIS men have a preference for European Muslims or converts because they are not 'close-minded' like Syrian women, who are not 'imaginative' in what they will do with their husbands.[51] These designated patriarchal roles for women are common to almost any society in the world. What is exceptional is the degree of unfreedom.

The Ezidi enslavement

However, women as wives still commanded a modicum of respect as potential mothers, and the men had to show a certain amount of restraint. Sex was a vital recruitment tool for male fighters both in this life and the hereafter (the hadith, the sayings of the prophet, promise seventy-two virgins in paradise to jihadists who die in battle). One of ISIS's single most notorious actions was the widely publicised abduction of thousands of Ezidi women from Mount Sinjar, Iraq, in 2014, when ISIS mounted a siege of the area. Rape in war is usually an expression of the power of the victors and a calculated humiliation of the conquered through the dishonouring of their women. But Matthew Barber, who researches Ezidi culture, believes the real purpose of the ISIS offensive was to capture Ezidi women to meet the sexual needs of their fighters. The Ezidis, who spoke Kurdish, were not considered to be Muslims: they were 'deviant', 'devil worshippers', and their women were therefore fair game. There are echoes of this too in Saudi society, where domestic workers mainly from Asia and Africa are seen as fair game for sexual and labour exploitation: 'Any woman who was not a Muslim was considered a prostitute,' observed Princess Sultana, a granddaughter of the founding monarch of Saudi Arabia.[52]

Over 6,000 Ezidis, mostly women and children, were abducted and enslaved. The ISIS fighters had come to Sinjar prepared:

> The captives were taken to the nearest town, where ISIS separated the young unmarried girls from their mothers, forced them into buses that had been prepared in advance, with curtains over the windows, and drove them to their destined point of sale, where they were stripped naked and examined for breast size and good looks. The prettiest virgins, who fetched the highest prices, were auctioned off at the slave market in Raqqa, where buyers haggled to drive the prices down.[53]

The way slaves were distributed was divinely ordained. According to a UN official: 'There is a hierarchy: sheikhs get first choice, then emirs, then fighters. They often take three or four girls each and keep them for a month or so, until they grow tired of a girl, when she goes back to market.'[54] One of the most horrific stories to emerge was that of a nine-year-old girl who was brutally raped by a middle-aged fighter who tore her vagina; she was then made to have FGM (female genital mutilation) surgery, after which he tried to rape her again.[55] Women who tried to resist were killed or put out in the sun for long periods of time or thrown into prison. Yet over 2,000 women managed to escape with the help of a network of Ezidi men or by bribing smugglers. Over 300,000 Ezidis are still languishing in Northern Iraq, including many of the traumatised women who escaped ISIS.[56] Alongside this story of victimisation are also stories of Ezidi women who were trained by the YPG (Yekîneyên Parastina Gel)/YPJ (Yekîneyên Parastina Jin) defence forces of the Rojava revolution (see Chapter 7) to join the battle against Raqqa.

The ISIS Research and Fatwa Department issued a pamphlet for its fighters with twenty-seven FAQs on how to deal with Ezidi women. I have chosen three of them as examples of the lengths they were prepared to go to place a framework of religiously sanctioned rules on their interactions with Ezidi women, a process that explicitly sanitises and legitimises the enslavement but is bloodcurdling to read:

> Question 5: Is it permissible to have intercourse with a female captive immediately after taking possession [of her]?
>
> If she is a virgin, he [her master] can have intercourse with her immediately after taking possession of her. However, if she isn't, her uterus must be purified [first].

This last sentence suggests that ISIS fighters were not allowed to rape a pregnant woman. To ensure she was not pregnant, they were enjoined to wait until she had her first period, that is, when her uterus would be purified. For this reason, at a slave market, a girl would often be asked the date of her last period by a prospective buyer.

> Question 13: Is it permissible to have intercourse with a female slave who has not reached puberty?
>
> It is permissible to have intercourse with the female slave who hasn't reached puberty if she is fit for intercourse; however, if she is not fit for intercourse, then it is enough to enjoy her without intercourse.

Vast freedoms are conferred on an ISIS fighter to 'enjoy her without intercourse'.

> Question 19: Is it permissible to beat a female slave?
>
> It is permissible to beat the female slave as a [form of] *darb ta'deeb* [disciplinary beating], [but] it is forbidden to [use] *darb al-takseer* [literally, breaking beating], [*darb*] *al-tashaffi* [beating for the purpose of achieving gratification], or [*darb*] *al-ta'dheeb* [torture beating]. Further, it is forbidden to hit the face.[57]

Another article from *Dabiq* provides a theological justification for the enslavement of Ezidi women, making clear that the slavery of women for sexual purposes was essential for men to have a religiously sanctioned sexual outlet:

[A] number of contemporary scholars have mentioned that the desertion of slavery had led to an increase in *fāhishah* [adultery, fornication, etc.], because the shar'ī alternative to marriage is not available, so a man who cannot afford marriage to a free woman finds himself surrounded by temptation towards sin. In addition, many Muslim families who have hired maids to work at their homes, face the *fitnah* [act of rebellion] of prohibited *khalwah* [seclusion] and resultant *zinā* [adultery] occurring between the man and the maid, whereas if she were his concubine, this relationship would be legal.[58]

The practice of 'temporary marriages' that might last a day or even a few hours was in evidence among ISIS commanders, according to a report in *The Independent*. The practice is also used extensively in Saudi Arabia, though it is hard to distinguish it from casual sex, except that it is authorised by a fatwa. The Ezidi women were not even accorded the 'privilege' of a fatwa because they were devil-worshippers. This is a divinely ordained rape culture. This 24/7 availability of a woman's body is worse than prostitution, yet any suggestion that the two are comparable enrages Umm Sumayyah. In 'Slave-Girls or Prostitutes?', she asks: 'Are slave-girls whom we took by Allah's command better, or prostitutes—an evil you do not denounce ... What is wrong with you? How do you make such a judgment?'[59] *Kufr* women were legitimate targets for slavery, and marrying them was considered an act of apostasy.

The construction of male sexuality under ISIS is typically patriarchal: male sexuality is rampant and uncontrollable, and religiously sanctioned ways of regulating it in a way that does not destabilise society must be found. Pornography, casual sex and dating were not sanctioned. ISIS fighters caught using pornography faced the lash, although there are reports that it has been found in huge quantities on ISIS computers. (Bin Laden was also a heavy consumer).[60] Polygyny, concurrent marriage to multiple women, is sanctioned for very 'noble' reasons such as financially supporting widows, divorcees and infertile women who have no market value while at the same time providing the man with alternatives to fulfil his needs while a woman is menstruating or giving birth.[61]

The complementary role that 'believing women' must play, as a counterpart to men's rampant sexuality, is to ensure that they will 'lower their gaze and guard their private parts ... and to wrap their veils over their chests and not expose their adornment'.[62] This is the position adopted by ISIS literature and the manifesto produced by the Al-Khansaa Brigade, the all-female morality police.[63]

Notion of apostasy

Apostasy is a tool of political control, and the fear of being declared an apostate kept dissent to a minimum. It allowed ISIS to keep their conquered populations quiescent while they fought their battles with the Syrian and Iraqi states, the Kurds and the other Islamist factions. The road to apostasy is a minefield of dos and don'ts. From the ridiculously sublime: Muslims cannot criticise the enslavement of *Kufr* women, that is, Ezidis;[64] they must not describe Islam as a religion of peace; they cannot call for the unity of Shias and Sunnis; they cannot promote interfaith alliances with Jews and Christians; they cannot believe that democracy is compatible with Islam;[65] to the sublimely ridiculous: in her memoir, Erelle describes how Abu Bilel sees her via a video link blowing on her tea to cool it down and gets very angry 'because under sharia, it is written that you should not change the nature of things'.[66] In 2015, ISIS banned the keeping of pigeons above the roofs of houses on pain of fines, imprisonment and flogging. The reason for this is that pigeons 'are harming one's Muslim and Muslim women neighbours, revealing the genitals [of the pigeons]'.[67] While such absurd examples have not been reported in Saudi Arabia, there is no freedom of religion—

apostasy, which includes criticism of Islam, conversion to another religion or advocating secular principles, is punishable by death.[68] When ISIS took charge of Mosul, it suspended one of the daily duties of the Directorate of Agriculture, the measuring of rain: 'Rain, they said, was a gift from Allah—and who were they to measure his gift?'[69] The same article goes on to list the range of crimes for which people could be thrown into prison—'eyebrow plucking, inappropriate haircuts, raising pigeons, playing dominoes, playing cards, playing music and smoking the hookah'.[70] In maths lessons in schools, ISIS replaced the plus sign (+) with the letter (z) because the cross is associated with Christianity.[71] These strictures were embedded in their educational system.

Education

Deepening commitment to the cause is essential to longevity and sustainability. ISIS knew that. They provided training for new recruits and introduced fundamental changes to the schooling of the next generation of children: 'New recruits join training that ranges from two weeks, one month, 45 days, six months up to one year. Inside the camps, students receive a mix of military, political and sharia orientation, usually given by around five instructors.'[72] Those recruits who could not stomach the more brutal aspects of ISIS practice would be sent back to 'strengthen' their faith.

There are conflicting reports on whether girls were allowed to go to school. According to Save the Children, only boys were allowed to go to school.[73] By the age of fourteen, they were considered old enough to become fighters. Initially, men and boys were encouraged to join the fighting forces, until the need for fighters grew severe enough to justify conscription. Some families tried to keep their children home because they were unhappy with them being taught how to make bombs and being exposed to ISIS films that showed beheadings. However, a Syrian citizen journalist suggests that girls did go to school, but ISIS discouraged the mixing of genders, even among very young children attending grade one, and were strict about separating female students from their teachers:

> The education situation is most dire in ISIS-controlled territories. Schools there follow an Islamic, Sharia-based curriculum that has eliminated and banned subjects that the group claims 'inspire depravity' including art, music, social studies, history, and philosophy. In its place, ISIS has instituted a mandatory study of Islamic law and jurisprudence; changed methods of Arabic-language instruction to rely on religious and medieval texts; removed all photographs and drawings from the classroom; and revised textbooks in such a way that course materials and learning models rely upon Islamic sources such as the Quran.[74]

ISIS banned the study of novels but retained the teaching of English, keeping a beady eye on the need for a future generation of people skilled at global communications. Mention of democracy, nationalism, moneylending and voting was forbidden. They shut down university courses in law, philosophy, archaeology and hotels and tourism. They invested heavily in the teaching of medicine: medical students paid no fees, and their board and lodging and all other needs, like textbooks and transport, were taken care of.[75] A journalist writing in 2016 claimed that books reflecting Wahhabi ideology in ISIS schools are the same as those found in Saudi Arabia.[76] All public schools in the kingdom are free, gender-segregated and follow the Arabic curriculum while putting a heavy emphasis on Islamic studies.[77] Textbooks preaching intolerance of Jews and Christians are common in both. When King Faisal proposed mass schooling for girls in the 1960s, he had to placate religious opposition by ensuring that girls were educated by religious scholars, assuring them that 'education was not meant to challenge traditional gender expectations but to confirm women in their role as good mothers who could educate their children in piety and respect for Islamic tradition'.[78]

Nadia, a Saudi dissident, was taught as a schoolgirl in the '90s that feminism, like socialism, was evil. Students were given a list of proscribed books, a list that she immediately searched on the internet and started reading. Nadia describes the irony of the Saudi educational system, which produces Islamist radicals and then imprisons them when they challenge the monarchy, remarking that 'the West gets told that the Saudi Government is protecting the West from this animal by keeping them in a cage and controlling them'. The radical religious agenda is pumped out by the media and the clerics, who are chosen by the government itself: 'During the *Jummah* [Friday] prayers the eulogy the imam reads and the main topics get chosen by the government. So it doesn't matter if you go to this mosque or the other mosque. Everybody will listen to the same eulogy.'[79]

The end of the 'caliphate'

In the end, neither brutality nor ideological rigour guaranteed ISIS rule. Its intensely narrow understanding of Islam had made too many enemies: it had isolated itself from the other Islamist groups, the populations under their control had grown increasingly disenchanted and the firepower of the US coalition along with the dedication of the Kurdish-led forces to annihilate them was too much to resist. The liberation of Mosul in July 2017 and Raqqa in October 2017 sounded their death knell, at least in terms of their territorial ambitions in the Middle East. However, as mentioned earlier, this should not be seen as the end of ISIS.

ISIS ideology continues to flourish in an unexpected part of Syria: the prisons in Rojava (North East Syria), which held 12,000 ISIS fighters, and the refugee camps housing 39,000 ISIS families, mostly women and children, as of February 2025, down from around 100,000.⁸⁰ A hardcore minority of ISIS women, mostly foreign, has taken on the role of the morality police. According to *The Times*, at least three women and one man were killed in 2019.⁸¹ The women have been killed by the *hisba* women for refusing to wear the veil, denouncing ISIS or for having an affair. The children are reportedly growing more ferocious than their fathers, attacking the *asayiş* (Rojava police) with a barrage of rocks even while they were accompanying a vaccination team. During the Turkish invasion of Rojava, many of the ISIS fighters escaped when some of the camp guards were distracted by the battle for survival against the Turks. Meanwhile, many countries have refused to repatriate their citizens. Surprisingly, the ISIS patriarchal project is being kept alive by its victims, the women of ISIS.

Wahhabism in Saudi Arabia has created a society eerily similar to the ISIS caliphate in its literalist interpretation of Islam. The failure of ISIS would suit MBS, who is keen to weaken ties with Wahhabism to authenticate his modernist credentials. According to the Begin–Sadat Center for Strategic Studies:

> If ISIS should prevail, that would mean the *salafist* doctrinarians will have finally taken over the jihadist movement. A victory of the *salafist* trend as embodied by ISIS would be an important development for Saudi Arabia, because ISIS presents a much graver ideological threat to the kingdom, which has based its very legitimacy on *Wahhabi* (or *salafist*) doctrine.⁸²

Saudi Arabia emphasises the active role it has played in the international coalition to defeat ISIS. In 2014, President Obama lauded the kingdom for agreeing to 'to host our efforts to train and equip Syria opposition forces' to fight ISIS.⁸³ A briefing produced by the Saudi embassy in Washington in 2019 boasts that '[a]s of March 2017, Saudi Arabia has flown 341 sorties against ISIS in Syria, the second largest number after the United

States'.[84] The same briefing claims that 'Saudi Arabia is hunting down the men, cutting off the money and destroying the mindset that ISIS and other terror organizations create and rely on.' In truth, as commentators have pointed out, 'when it came to Islamist terrorism, the Saudis were the arsonists and the firefighters in one'.[85] Saudi Arabia sees itself as the main target of ISIS attacks: 'Saudi Arabia has faced more than 60 terrorist attacks by Daesh and Al-Qaeda, more than 25 of them since 2015. More than 200 citizens and policemen have been killed in terrorist attacks.'[86] ISIS used the master's tools to try and dismantle the master's house. But Saudi attempts to put clear water between themselves and ISIS does not weaken the central argument of this chapter, which explores the ideological affiliations between the two and demonstrates how governance based on the precepts of fundamentalist religions represents the death knell for feminist aspirations.

Saudi Arabia set up the Global Centre for Countering Extremist Ideology (ETIDAL) in 2017 to counter the jihadi mindset. The security agency described feminism, homosexuality and atheism as extremism but apologised soon after to quell the furore in the West.[87] Many women activists have been monitored and harassed by ETIDAL. Saud al-Qahtani, MBS's right-hand man and founder of ETIDAL, was present in the torture sessions of Loujain al-Hathloul, who was detained for protesting against the driving ban. Any 'liberalisation' on the part of Saudi Arabia, much of which is a chimera, as I will argue below, reveals a reluctant response to the pressures of being part of a global community of nations, which is not a consideration for ISIS, who pride themselves on being the true upholders of the Salafi torch. Saudi Arabia cannot afford the ideological purity of ISIS, who consequently deride Saudis as *kafirs* who are trying 'to establish the filth of democracy'.[88] It seems as if the international community too has been persuaded by the superficial changes, enough to elect Saudi Arabia as chair of the UN Commission on the Status of Women in 2024.

Pendulum of freedoms

Until the recent 'liberalisations', Saudi Arabia was universally seen as a regressive place where religion and governance were so welded together that women had no hope of exercising even minimal freedoms. This gave rise to debates among scholars as to whether Saudi Arabia was a theocracy, with some concluding that theo-monarchy would be a more accurate description, while others believe it to be a straightforward monarchy.[89] It has also been described as an Islamic state governed by a monarchy.[90] As Article 8 of Saudi Arabia's Basic Law of Governance (equivalent to their constitution) states that '[t]he system of government in the Kingdom of Saudi Arabia is established on the foundation of justice, "Shoura" [consultation] and equality in compliance with the Sharia (the revealed law of Islam)', the view that Saudi Arabia is a theocracy has its justifications.[91] However, the apparent ease with which MBS is pulling away from the power of clerics today establishes the sovereignty of the royal family and suggests that the description of Saudi Arabia as a monarchy is more accurate.

Writing in the early 2000s, anthropologist Madawi al-Rasheed described the Saudi monarchy as 'politically secular' and 'socially religious'.[92] Some of the ambiguity can be traced to the origin story of Saudi Arabia, and some of it lies in Wahhabi theology, in which the total fusion of politics and religion is a central feature. Muhammad Al Atawneh, an academic based in Israel who has written extensively on Islamic law, explains that 'Wahhabi political theory is based on the premise that the purpose of government in Islam is to preserve the *shari'a* and to enforce its dictates [sic].'[93] The rulers were required to consult with the *ulama*, also known as the Al-Shura Council, set up in 1971, religious scholars steeped in sharia, who issued *fatawa*, usually non-binding advice on social, religious and governance matters, from time to time. Only by royal decree could it become binding. For example, the *fatwa* that prohibited women from driving was issued in 1990 and justified by quotations from the Qur'an that it was for the protection of women who might encounter dangerous situations while driving alone but was made into law by the Saudi Ministry of the Interior.[94]

Since the 1940s, the Saudi monarchy has sought to rein in the power of the religious authorities. Saudi Arabia has executed a complicated dance in controlling, diminishing or enhancing religious forces at various times in its history—the markers of this opening and closing of doors are signified by the freedoms provided or denied to women. It has been argued that these freedoms are as much a sign of acceding to Western pressure as a check on the power of Islamists within Saudi Arabia.[95] As is well known, where business interests are concerned, Western pressure is merely lip-service. Under the Taliban's first reign in Afghanistan in the 1990s, a US diplomat remarked that 'the Taliban will probably develop like the Saudis did. There will be Aramco, pipelines, an emir, no parliament and lots of Sharia law. We can live with that.'[96] The king can set the agenda of the Shura Council and has the power to hire and fire scholars, who are ultimately accountable to him. Paradoxically, the Shura Council has both had its influence extended and diminished. Being absorbed into the government has allowed it to influence the work of several ministries, but the very act of co-optation has also reduced its independence. On at least four key occasions, the Shura Council has provided the kind of legitimacy the monarchs needed to quell any unrest in the kingdom: in 1979, with the occupation of the Mecca Mosque and the Islamic revolution in Iran; in 1990, when the stationing of American troops in Saudi Arabia in response to a possible attack from Kuwait was opposed by the Islamic reform movement; in the wake of jihadi attacks on Saudi territory in 2003; and in 2011 so as to prevent an Arab Spring-type uprising.[97]

There were *fatawa* prohibiting the public mixing of sexes, compelling restaurants to provide separate spaces for families dining out, prohibiting women from working in hotels and prohibiting men from providing services to women. Imported films, except for educational documentaries, were not allowed, because they contradicted the principles of sharia, even for private viewing. Hairdressing establishments for women were shut down. Music and singing parties at weddings were prohibited. Other than the bride, weddings were single-sex affairs. Women could visit clothing stores and tailors only when accompanied by a *mahram*.[98] CBL reports that wealthy women shopped by asking their drivers and servants to return home with a large selection of clothes or shoes, which the women tried on at home before returning anything they didn't like.[99]

The current iteration of the kingdom founded in 1932 by King Abdulaziz was the third attempt, a jihadi project that bears comparison with the setting up of the ISIS caliphate. The king recruited the Ikhwan or 'Brethren' from Bedouin tribes and indoctrinated them with the Wahhabi ideology: 'Armed with fanatic fervour and the firm desire to die as martyrs in the war against infidels, the Ikhwan could not be stopped.'[100] He was successful in melding the disparate regions, tribes and clans into one kingdom, using religious nationalism as the glue. All the Saudi kings to date, including the current king, Salman, were fathered by the original Saudi king, Abdulaziz Saud, who had fifty-four children by twenty-two wives. This was an unspoken rule of succession now broken by MBS, the crown prince, a grandson, faced with the reality that there are no more eligible surviving sons. Abdulaziz also had concubines, women he could marry for an hour or one night.[101]

RAQQA TO RIYADH

The first attempt at establishing a kingdom came about as the result of a pact between the ultra-conservative cleric Abd al-Wahhab, who wanted to restore Islam to the glory of the seventh century, and Ibn Saud in 1744. It was agreed that Abd al-Wahhab and his descendants would exercise control over religious and social affairs, while Ibn Saud would be the military and political lead. As neither of them could do it alone, they swore their allegiance to one another and promised to share power in the future kingdom.[102] The pact lasted, even though the kingdom of Saud came and went. Today, MBS is attempting to rewrite the origin story by reducing the role of Abd al-Wahhab in the formation of the kingdom. MBS has started celebrating a 'Founding Day' that started seventeen years earlier, in 1727, when Ibn Saud was just an emir of a small town.[103]

The Saudi monarchs have responded to various international threats to their legitimacy by doubling down on their Islamist credentials. The Saudis countered the rise of Arab nationalism in the region under Nasser in Egypt in the 1950s and '60s by fostering the Muslim Brotherhood, which faced persecution by Nasser and ultimately escaped Egypt. In time, the Muslim Brotherhood grew to challenge the Saudi monarchs and is currently considered a terrorist organisation. Another turning point for Saudi Arabia, as indeed for the entire Muslim world, was 1979, when the overthrow of the shah of Iran brought Ayatollah Khomeini and the clerics to power. The lesson it contained was a dangerous one for the Royal House of Saud: it was possible for the monarchy to be unseated by religious forces. More specifically, Khomeini claimed that Islam is fundamentally opposed to monarchy.[104] Instead of clamping down on the power of the clerics as might have been expected, the Saudi monarchs sought to placate them by giving in to their demands for a society run on a more sharia-compliant basis.

There are a number of personal and political accounts of the freedoms enjoyed by Saudi women before the 1979 Iranian

Revolution, which may come as a surprise to the casual observer. CBL recounts the life of wealthy Saudi women during her ten years in Saudi Arabia in the 1970s. Alongside gleaming new roads and buildings came freedoms for women like walking unveiled in the malls.[105] As a member of the influential Bin Laden family, building contractors to the royal family with a contract for the renovation of Mecca and Medina, which raised their status above that of others in the merchant class, they were immune from many of the common harassments of the religious police. She could invite people to barbecues and drink beer at events where the sexes mixed freely, as the *mutawa* (religious police) did not raid the houses of royalty or the influential.[106] A visiting European journalist, Karen Elliott House, confirmed that the 1970s was a relatively liberal decade. She did not have to wear an *abaya* (which began to be enforced on girls aged twelve onwards in the 1990s) and had attended dinner parties where Saudi men and women mixed and sipped alcohol, although driving was still out of the question for women.[107]

However, the mood soured after 1979, when Mecca was occupied by religious extremists, a huge shock to the Saudi royal family, and the heavily Saudi-supported mujahideen began fighting the Soviet Union in Afghanistan. Women started wearing thick black stockings under their *abayas*, veiling again, wearing gloves; the *mutawa* began breaking into homes and smashing hi-fis, confiscating alcohol, beating and imprisoning the consumers; and children's dolls could not be sold because they showed human images.[108] Women were prevented from doing sport in case they damaged their reproductive organs.[109]

When the events of 9/11 left their scars on the Western psyche and it was discovered that fifteen of the nineteen al-Qaeda jihadis were Saudi nationals, the kingdom responded with a trickle of gender equality.[110] It had the same response after the Arab Spring in 2011. Saudi women had long fought for the right to vote and to stand in local elections. This right was announced in 2011 and finally granted in the 2015 elections, when twenty women were elected. Saudi academic Madawi al-Rasheed sees this as a divide-and-rule policy: 'Authoritarian states need women as allies against men who challenge the state and criticize its general exclusion of the population from the decision-making process.'[111] In 2013, in another mark of liberalisation, King Abdullah appointed thirty women to the Shura Council,[112] overriding the grand mufti who led the council who was not happy with the idea of the mixing of sexes, another example of the tensions between religion and royalty.

The first concrete achievement made by these highly educated women with backgrounds in science and medicine was the approval of a law that would allow women to apply for loans in their own right, regardless of their marital status. They promoted the Saudisation of labour policies to provide employment opportunities for Saudi women. They argued against the driving ban, pointing out that women in the desert and rural areas drove anyway because it was essential and there was nothing in the Qur'an that prevented it. Their strategy was to argue that certain restrictions on women's rights were imposed by social custom, not religion.[113] When the space for feminist voices is so restricted, it may be tactical to use reference points close to people's reality but interpret them more progressively to achieve incremental change. British journalist Natasha Walters, who travelled to Saudi Arabia in 2005, found that progressive women referenced the freedoms available to women in the Qur'an to push for change. A young woman activist told her: 'The rights that we want to exercise are not invented by the west. They are the rights that were exercised by women in the time of the Prophet, economic and religious and political rights that are given to us by our religion.'[114]

PLANET PATRIARCHY

How far does the pendulum swing?

Despite being a class issue, the driving ban became emblematic of the evils faced by all Saudi women. As far back as 1990, forty-seven professional Saudi women drove cars in a protest against the ban on their driving. They were dismissed from their jobs, and their families were threatened. They were publicly shamed: their names were read out in mosques and printed on flyers. An activist remembers that 'people were told to do everything they could—it was an open invitation to kill them'.[115] MBS lifted the ban in 2017, but at the same time many of the women who had campaigned for the ban to be lifted, among them Loujain al-Hathloul, were arrested, thrown into prison, tortured, sexually abused and, when released from prison in 2021, faced travel bans and were forbidden from talking to the media. Al-Hathloul could, however, use social media as long as she did not speak about her experience of prison. In effect, al-Hathloul entered a prison without physical walls, a fate that befalls many human rights activists.

MBS's reforms were implemented alongside the brutal repression of liberals and those on the religious right. This suggests both implicitly and explicitly that demands for change from below will not be tolerated, that the new women-friendly policies are not an expression of greater democracy but simply a gift from the powers that be. In any case, as Nadia, a human rights dissident, points out, factors such as the cost of car ownership and the higher costs of insurance and driving lessons for women, as well as their conservative families, remain a disincentive.[116] Only 2 per cent of Saudi women have been issued a driving licence as of 2020.[117] As a *New York Times* journalist observed, these reforms are not meant to unsettle men: 'The government will no longer legally force men to keep the women of their household under heightened control—but it won't force men to emancipate women, either.'¹¹⁸ Lina al-Hathloul, Loujain's sister, sees MBS's 'reforms' as 'a new packaging of the repression, before the repression was packaged as religion'.¹¹⁹ Lina says that Loujain was treated well during her first detention in 2014 and was arrested several times after that, but it was only with detention under MBS that she suffered badly.

All reports suggest that women are no longer forced to wear the *abaya* or the veil unless they are in a holy place. In March 2018, MBS said that 'the decision is entirely left for women to decide what type of decent and respectful attire she chooses to wear'.¹²⁰ However, Manahel al-Otaibi, a fitness instructor and blogger, was arrested in November 2022 under the kingdom's draconian Anti-Cybercrime Law for posting pictures on her private Instagram account of herself without an *abaya* and for campaigning for the end of guardianship laws. While the *mutawa* have been defanged, they have been replaced by state security. This lack of certainty, of wrong-footing people about the actual law, seems to be a common feature of dictatorial regimes. Loujain's travel ban officially ended in November 2023, but the kingdom still refuses to provide her permission to travel. The same is true for her whole family, even though they have never formally been banned from travel. It is impossible to challenge something so arbitrary.¹²¹ Al-Otaibi has been detained since November 2022. She 'was disappeared' between November 2023 and April 2024, when she contacted her family and told them she had been beaten so badly by the authorities that her leg had broken, but she was not allowed medical visits. She was also abused by fellow prisoners.¹²² She was secretly sentenced to eleven years in prison in January 2024 for terrorism offences.¹²³

The 2022 Personal Status Law (PSL), dubbed the disobedience laws by activists, reputedly ended the guardianship system, which infantilised women by forbidding them from doing anything without the permission of a male relative (even a son) or travelling without a male companion. But again, the hype eclipsed the reality. Women can now travel unaccompanied, study, apply for their own passports without permission from a male relative, but they still have to seek permission to marry. Women are expected to 'obey' their husbands. Amnesty International reports that '[i]t also makes women's financial support from their husbands during marriage conditional on wives "submit[ing]" themselves to their husbands. Such provisions place women at risk of exploitation and abuse, including marital rape, which Saudi law does not criminalize.'[124] While the disobedience laws are still in place, Lina al-Hathloul points out, the system remains substantially unchanged.[125] Safeguards introduced by the PSL, such as obtaining the consent of a woman to her proposed marriage, do not include guidance as to how that consent will be obtained. Marriage of girls under eighteen is forbidden but again undermined by the proviso that 'the court may permit the marriage of a man and woman under the age of eighteen in cases where they have reached puberty and their "interest" in the marriage is verified'. Entrenched inequalities between men and women in divorce rights, child custody, financial support and inheritance have not been reversed.[126]

Another pernicious institution is the *dar al-reaya*, the misleadingly named 'care homes', set up for the 'protection' of women, where minors up to the age of thirty (another example of the infantilisation of women) are sent when escaping domestic violence or for committing acts of moral indecency (extramarital sexual relations), delinquency or political dissidence. The conditions are so appalling that they act as a form of deterrence for women seeking refuge. The British-based Saudi human rights group ALQST reports that women's prisons are preferable to the care homes—four women who were being transferred from prison attempted suicide to avoid the transfer.[127] One father used the threat of sending his daughter to a 'care home' to persuade her to accept his marriage proposal. The percentage of Saudi girls and women held in state-run care facilities is, not surprisingly, very small. In 2016, the last time figures were released, 233 girls and women—out of a population of over 13 million women—were held in seven facilities across the kingdom.[128] Once inside, they are locked up until a male guardian, often the same person abusing them, agrees that they can leave; or until a woman agrees to marry and has a new guardian. Those who resist reconciliation can be punished with regular floggings and solitary confinement until they concede.[129] Loujain al-Hathloul was politicised by her stay in one such care home when she realised that there were women whose lives were more scarred by violence than the driving ban. When she came out, she worked with others in an unsuccessful attempt to set up a refuge, called Aminah.[130] Aminah was intended to be a place of real shelter that women could leave without male permission. They did not get official approval and were later arrested.[131]

With the male guardianship system still mostly in place, women often become 'prisoners' in their own homes, a place that is both a 'woman's grave and a man's paradise'. In 2024, using the hashtag #HomeDetainees, women's rights activists launched an online campaign to which they received a substantial response despite evidence that anonymity can no longer be guaranteed on social media. At one point, the internet had provided women anonymous access to the public square to enable them to make various demands for their rights—a kind of digital *abaya* that provided a cover for freedom of movement and expression. Yahya Assiri, founder of ALQST,[132] strongly believes that it was access to the internet in 1999/2000 that was a turning point for Saudi activists, enabling them to speak freely in a way that they could not in real life. However, since 2019, when it was revealed that the Saudi government had paid Twitter (now X) staff to expose the identities of activists tweeting anonymously,[133] even this route has been blocked off. The last refuge for a critique of Saudi society is novels—fiction is the only veil that can be safely drawn on reality. Al-Rasheed reports that '[o]ne Saudi novelist told me that she can discuss daring topics in her novels without being harassed, as there is no law in the country against fiction, while real mobilisation and organisation around women's rights bring about greater risks'.[134]

The Basic Law of Governance refers to the role of the family as the 'nucleus of Saudi society' and requires the state to strengthen the bonds that hold the family together and to preserve its Arab and Islamic values.[135] When the overriding mission is to keep the family together, and women are required to 'obey' men, domestic violence almost by definition cannot exist. A law criminalising domestic violence, nonetheless, was passed in Saudi Arabia in 2013. The text defines domestic abuse as 'all forms of exploitation, or bodily, psychological, or sexual abuse, or threat of it, committed by one person against another, including if [that person] has authority, power, or responsibility, or [if there is] a family, support, sponsorship, guardianship, or living dependency relationship between the two [individuals]'.[136] The definition includes neglect. However, no particular department of the government is charged with the duty of investigation apart from an unspecified 'competent' agency. As always, the figures for domestic violence are hard to estimate. Saudi Arabia's National Family Protection Programme estimates that 35 per cent of Saudi women have experienced violence, yet the head of Saudi Arabia's Human Rights Commission said that of the 1,059 cases referred to Saudi courts in 2017 involving violence against women, only fifty-nine were for domestic violence.[137] The law sets the penalty for domestic abuse at between one month and one year in prison and/or a fine of between 5,000 ($1,333) and 50,000 ($13,330) Saudi riyals.[138] Again, no figures are available for the number of men sentenced to prison or the number of fines issued. FGM, the ultimate method of men's control over women's sexuality, is also practised in Saudi Arabia. Almost 20 per cent of women self-reported FGM in a sample survey carried out in 2017.[139] There is no specific law against it.[140] The laws on rape are such that a woman is likely to be sentenced for fornication and adultery, a fate that befalls many migrant women workers, some of whom are executed.

At the intersection of class

What is interesting in the Saudi context is a kind of universalism of oppression where women of all classes have had their freedoms curtailed by a literalist version of Islam. Women in the royal family have no more freedom to marry than those of other classes and must accept their fate as one of many wives. Princess Sultana observes that

> [t]he poorest bedouin have only to erect four tents and provide simple fare. For these reasons, you find many of the richest and the poorest Muslims with four wives. It is only the middle-class Saudi who has to find contentment with one woman, for it is impossible for him to find the funds to provide middle-class standards for four separate families.[141]

Women may have the privileges afforded by wealth, but they live in a gilded cage. Wealth allowed them to travel abroad and exercise freedom of dress and mingling of sexes, but before the travel ban was lifted, even the women in the wealthy Bin Laden family had to seek permission from their husbands. If they wanted to go shopping abroad, they would lie to their husbands and say they had a medical appointment.[142] They could also buy passports and letters of permission on the black market. It was easy to adopt another identity because an immigration official would never dare ask a woman to unveil.[143] Many women dissidents come from the privileged classes, says Lina al-Hathloul, who defines 'privilege' as not so much about wealth as having 'supportive' families who are not seen by the government as a threat.[144] Though they will still be punished, the punishment will be lighter. Women without families to champion them are picked off.

In her memoir, Princess Sultana says that '[t]he authority of the Saudi male is unlimited',[145] and much of her story describes the manipulations and wiles that women had to employ to exercise some power over their lives and the terrible punishments that were meted out when caught. At the same time, at her sister's wedding in the early 1970s, many of the royal women carried small jewelled flasks in their handbags and would go to the bathroom, giggling, to take a small sip of alcohol, even though it was strictly forbidden.[146] CBL describes Saudi princesses without anything to do, living in grand homes with swimming pools and armies of servants but heavily drugged on anti-depressants. There was even a lesbian party circuit that gave women the chance to find love.[147]

The 'armies of servants', of course, were predominantly made up of migrant workers who were not just the poorest but also most powerless, whose status was just a cut above slavery, which had only been abolished in 1962. The widely documented contempt with which domestics were treated appears to be a hangover from this period. Saudi Arabia's reliance on domestic workers is the highest in the world, with domestic work representing 28 per cent of all employment according to an International Labour Organization report in 2021.[148] Not surprisingly, these workers have very few protections. They face being exploited not only by their Saudi employers but also the recruitment agencies before they get to their final destination. The operation of the *kafala* (sponsorship) system that prevents workers from changing employers without their permission leaves them vulnerable to violence and exploitation. Saudi Arabia has now eliminated the need for 'no objection certificates' for all migrant workers bar domestic workers, meaning that migrants will no longer be required to obtain their employers' consent to leave or change jobs.[149] The 'legal' requirements stipulate a maximum working day of fifteen hours and a possible negotiated one day off a week, a ninety-hour week, which hardly amounts to good working conditions.[150] Women who work mainly as cooks, cleaners and carers of children and elderly within the home are also at risk of being raped by their employers and executed for adultery. Of the thirty-one women executed between 2010 and 2021, twenty-three were foreign nationals, and over half of this number were domestic workers (42 per cent of total executions but only 6 to 7 per cent of the Saudi population). These figures are viewed as an underestimate and do not include a number of suicides and disappearances.[151]

Localising the Saudi workforce has been a stated aim of the government since 1985, but the policy has had limited success, progressing in fits and starts to various triggers. At that time, there were not enough educated Saudis to fill the skilled jobs and not enough Saudis interested in menial work.[152] Although the number of educated Saudis has since increased dramatically and quotas are in place, the country is still heavily reliant on foreign labour, which constitutes 51.2 per cent of the total labour market and 77.4 per cent of the private sector.[153] When the feminisation of the workplace began in 2011 and intensified in 2016 as part of MBS's plans for the diversification of the Saudi economy, namely Vision 2030, the aim was to increase the numbers of women in employment from 18 per cent to 30 per cent in 2030, a target that was reached by 2022. As well as employers being attracted by cheaper female labour, this was made possible by the number of vacancies created during the COVID-19 pandemic when foreign workers returned to their home countries. Encouraging more women to enter the workplace necessarily means that domestic workers still need to be 'imported'. In fact, the number of domestic workers has increased. This is one of the contradictions between the Saudisation policy and feminisation policy of the workforce. While patriarchy requires women to bear the burden of reproductive labour, the capitalist system ensures that this burden is passed on to a less powerful group of women to keep its middle- and upper-class women quiescent. Nearly 4 million migrants are domestic workers in Saudi Arabia, most of them women.

Even though the poverty rate in Saudi Arabia is 13 per cent today, in which women-headed households are disproportionately represented, Maryam Aldossari, Saudi dissident and academic, believes that Saudi women will not take up domestic work 'given the predominant social abuse of household workers and the lack of a system to protect them'. She also believes that Saudi households will not be willing to recruit Saudis as domestic workers for privacy reasons, as 'we are a very closed society' and 'having foreign helpers is better suited, as they are easily managed'.[154] While Saudisation of labour reduces male unemployment, feminisation has the opposite effect. The threat to male jobs from more women in work became a particular concern after the Arab Spring, when youth unemployment was one of the drivers of political instability. 'There persists a prevalent belief among Saudi men,' says Aldossari, 'that they are experiencing reverse discrimination. They perceive women as receiving preferential treatment and view them as unqualified for the opportunities granted—an idea deeply rooted in their reluctance to share power and resources.'[155]

The increasing presence of women in the workplace has highlighted the contradictions of rapid modernisation being imposed on a conservative culture from above. Tribal, religious and patriarchal norms intersect in ways that enforce conservative dress codes, modest behaviour and even a preference for gender segregation at work to feel safe from sexual harassment, even though there is no longer a legal requirement for gender segregation. Working in low-paid sectors and having to negotiate conservative social expectations of women's presence in the public sphere adds to the precarity of women's employment.[156] However, in terms of numbers, women's employment has been one of the few successes of MBS's Vision 2030, having now surpassed the 30 per cent target. While the blurb suggests that women's involvement contributes to economic growth, cultural transformation and sustainable development and helps Saudi Arabia meet the fifth Sustainable Development Goal on gender equality, the real reasons are mired in the hype—a combination of putting clear water between the monarchy and the religious authorities and convincing the West that MBS is sincere about modernisation.

Vision 2030 aims to attract foreign investment and tourism by making Saudi Arabia a 'vibrant society' offering cultural, entertainment and sporting events, which will also help the kingdom expand its non-oil-based revenue.[157] Between 2014 and 2016, there was a drastic reduction in oil revenue, creating a budget deficit that led to cuts in wages, energy subsidies and the imposition of a sales tax for the first time in 2018.[158] There is conflicting information about the level of Saudi oil reserves, possibly because a key strategy, under US guidance, has been to artificially lower oil production to maintain high prices. Saudi reserves, last assessed in 2016, may be enough to last 221 years on the basis of its current consumption, not including net exports. The international pressure to phase out fossil fuels in response to global heating may also be a factor. Less publicised goals of Vision 2030 include the privatisation of the government sector and services such as health and education, reducing the proportion of public sector jobs from 60 to 20 per cent and cutting pay and increasing taxation. Salaries in the private sector are on average 60 per cent lower than in the government sector. All of this has had an adverse impact on the poor and middle class, so much so that more than 1 million people migrated from Saudi Arabia in 2016, the year in which these proposals were announced. The outflow was not stemmed even though MBS introduced bonus payments for public sector employees and a Citizen Account Programme to disburse money to families in need.[159]

Under Vision 2030, MBS plans to shift from religious nationalism to a more secular-sounding 'Saudi First' approach to unify the country, although this new vision 'creates real and fictional enemies both inside the country (e.g. the Muslim Brotherhood, foreign workers, and the Islamic State) and outside (e.g. Iran and Yemen's Houthi rebels)'.[160] Given that the annual Haj to Mecca and Medina will continue to be important to the world's Muslim community, Saudi Arabia cannot ditch its religious credentials anytime soon and will continue its complicated dance between opposing forces, remaining the 'cradle of Islam' while adopting a 'moderate Islam' ideology.[161]

The diaspora calls for democracy

The brutal killing in 2018 of the dissident Saudi journalist Jamal Khashoggi, who advocated for democracy and had once been close to the Saudi royal family, has cast a pall on Saudi dissidents abroad. The long arm of the state is a frightening prospect, and a state with powerful friends in the West can act with impunity. Despite widespread condemnation of the killing, the West continues to do business with Saudi Arabia. All the dissidents I interviewed for this chapter have developed strategies or justifications for their publicly critical stance on Saudi Arabia. Dissidents abroad are manipulated by the targeting of the two soft centres of every human being: personal safety, and the safety of their family at home. Many have been disowned by their families or have deliberately cut ties. Nadia, who uses only her first name for safety, says: 'If you leave the country and start talking publicly, your family can get fired from the jobs, they can even go to prison.'[162] Others cling to straws, such as their cases having been so widely publicised that the Saudi government would not dare to eliminate them after the fiasco in public relations caused by the killing of Khashoggi. Loujain's family opted to pull strings behind the scenes, but when they discovered she had been tortured, they felt that their silence had enabled it and so went public. Some in the diaspora believe that once they are citizens of their adoptive country, they will be safe. But US citizenship did not stop Saad Ibrahim Almadi from being imprisoned for a year for posting tweets critical of the government in 2021 when he returned to Saudi Arabia. And now he is facing a travel ban that prevents him from returning to the US.[163]

The main demand from the Saudi dissidents is for democracy and constitutional monarchy in Saudi Arabia. They are very clear that they do not want Western assistance in their fight for democracy; they just want the West 'to stop arming, supporting, financing, protecting these dictatorships'.[164] This was the call made by speaker after speaker at the Quest for Democracy conference held in Washington in May 2024. One of the speakers thought that the 'revolution' in Tunisia in 2011 was partly brought about by Tunisians in the diaspora.[165] This theory is lent some credence by the fact that emigrants were given eighteen seats (out of 217) in the October 2011 elections for the Constituent Assembly tasked with drafting a new constitution.[166] This is the hope that keeps the Saudi dissidents going. The signs are not promising, though: a draft penal code currently being considered

> criminalizes the rights to freedom of expression, thought and religion and fails to protect the right to freedom of peaceful assembly. It criminalizes 'illegitimate' consensual sexual relations, homosexuality and abortion and fails to protect women and girls from gender-based violence. The draft also codifies use of the death penalty as one of the primary punishments and continues to permit corporal punishments such as flogging.[167]

When I asked Abdullah Alaoudh, one of the organisers of the conference, what he thought of the Saudi women's agenda, he agreed with most of their demands and said that 'focusing on [the] democratic issue can solve problems of equality'.[168] There appears to be a widespread view that democracy will deliver for women. But that has not been the experience of mature democracies. Al-Rasheed too believes that 'women's real emancipation and equality' will come through participatory democracy but warns that an essentially conservative society could produce negative results for women.[169] It is widely recognised that MBS's top-down liberalisations have not permeated the depths of Saudi society. There is no knowing the extent of the Saudi clergy's reservations towards these changes, which they are afraid to articulate for fear of facing brutal repression from MBS. However, if these forces were given greater influence in a democracy, women's rights would suffer a setback. Al-Rasheed further nuances her position by declaring that 'real change will come only when the economy cannot function without them [women]'. Aldossari believes that 'while democracy may serve as an initial step in addressing patriarchy, it alone is insufficient to eradicate it entirely. True progress requires a generational shift in education and mindset, where men recognise women as equals in the workplace and beyond, not exceptions to the norm.'[170] Alaoudh was a 'little hesitant around the ... anti-men sentiments among a minority' of women.[171] However, on the women's panel in Quest for Democracy, Lina al-Hathloul talked about the male allies without whom her activism would not have been possible; for her, the main enemy was not men but state-orchestrated gender-based violence. There was a defensiveness about Saudi men being seen as brutal or patriarchal. When an entire society is crushed by an authoritarian government, it is tactically necessary for women to seek the support of men for their rights and maintain a single focus in an existential struggle for survival.

RAQQA TO RIYADH

If MBS's economic gamble of switching investment from oil to tourism—as represented by the billions of petrodollars invested in Vision 2030—pays off, the monarchy is likely to remain entrenched for the foreseeable future. Any gains that women may make from this new economic strategy will be incidental: patriarchal and religious values will be set aside only as far as it is strictly necessary for the success of Vision 2030. Meanwhile, women are being disappeared into prisons, homes or forced into exile abroad. The near total in-country absence of public spaces for feminist and democratic activism will put the burden of change on to the diaspora of Saudi dissidents, who depend on the government of their adoptive countries, especially powerful ones like the UK or the US, to lobby Saudi Arabia for change. While the US sells billions of dollars of arms to Saudi Arabia,[172] its largest customer, it is unlikely to exert meaningful pressure on Saudi Arabia to improve its human rights record. If the global move away from fossil fuels is successful, and Saudi Arabia loses its importance as a major trading partner, if there is an economic collapse, then a dissident diaspora may come into its own. However, there are many ifs to surmount before Saudi dissidents can weaken patriarchal and authoritarian systems in their homeland.

3

RUSSIA

WE WILL GET UP OFF OUR KNEES

Rahila Gupta

It is 4 am when Anna Zobnina, aged fifteen, stumbles out of bed to clean the church in readiness for the 6 am mass. It is her first day in a religious community she joined in her quest for meaning, for spirituality—a nunnery splintered from the Russian Orthodox Church (ROC) and run by a man. It is 1993 in St Petersburg. She is cleaning the altar when one of the senior nuns spots her and scolds her. The altar is the holiest of holy places. No woman is allowed to step on it. The way to the altar for a woman is a long and arduous one. She is likely to reach it at the end of her life, if her body allows it, as she progresses up the ranks and attains the state of angelhood, a sex-less and woman-free space. Every step is marked by the growing length of a piece of fabric attached to her headgear, like a mantilla. At the first initiation, she is given a robe, but there are several more steps indicated by an ever-lengthening mantilla. It can become so long that older nuns have to wrap it around their arm to avoid tripping—a perfect metaphor for the obstacles that lie in the path of women aiming to get to the top.

Anna, now a radical feminist, lives in Scotland and runs the European Network of Migrant Women. She is contextualising the scandal of Pussy Riot's 'punk prayer' protest against Putin in 2012 on the altar at the Cathedral of Christ the Saviour in Moscow in the minds of the faithful. 'That's why it was such a massive statement—genius what they did—location, moment in history. It was personal for me. These girls at the altar. I would have been one of them.'[1] We are talking via Skype during the first COVID lockdown in 2020. She looks tired and dishevelled by the pressures of running an organisation remotely during the pandemic but is enlivened by her stories of corruption at the nunnery. The song 'Punk Prayer' is a plea to the Virgin Mary to banish Putin,[2] a refrain that begins and ends it, neatly making the point that the ROC is very much part of his brand. The lyrics are not particularly offensive unless describing shit as holy offends. 'Shit', Anna explains, is a reference to the black limos coming to church, exposing corruption and power. In any case, they did not get around to singing the whole song, which is six minutes long, because they were on the altar for only forty to fifty seconds before the security guards nabbed them.

The history of this cathedral, a famous landmark that shouts out Moscow to tourists, encapsulates Russia's troubled history with religion. The original was demolished by Stalin in 1931, with the space to have been used to build a Palace of the Soviets, a grand plan that was abandoned because of the Second World War. Permission to rebuild the cathedral was given in 1990, and the building was completed in 2000. The halls are rented out to mafia men and politicians for functions such as weddings and birthdays. 'A good bribe,' says Anna. 'I have no doubt that there would have been strip tease shows and women dancing in these parties. To have a party in this church for oligarchs would be a matter of status. It's huge, it's like a mini-city, function rooms, altar.'³ Only 7 per cent of the cathedral is used for religious purposes,⁴ an irrefutably imbalanced relationship between mammon and messiah.

Three members of Pussy Riot were sentenced to two years' imprisonment for 'hooliganism motivated by religious hatred'.⁵ Unsurprisingly, religious and conservative Russians have nothing but disdain for them. The Cossacks, known for their vigilante violence and policing of Russia's return to conservative values, beat Pussy Riot up when they protested at the Sochi Games in 2014.⁶ More surprisingly, the women could not rely on support from Russian feminists, because they were divided about the effectiveness and content of Pussy Riot's protests. Some feminists argued that their lyrics were violent, sexist and often objectified women, such as their glorification of the role of the dominatrix and asking feminists to give Russia a whipping. Demands that sexists should be killed were seen to go against the feminist principle of non-violence.⁷ At their very first protest in Red Square in 2011, before the infamous stunt in the cathedral went viral, they sang about Putin wetting his pants and likened the ROC to a hard penis, directly addressing the Russian president's cult of masculinity, which was both embedded in the Orthodox Church and had been honed with religious fervour. Some condemned them for their 'adolescent shock tactics' and felt that their actions were designed to impress the men in the art group Voina with which they had been connected before Pussy Riot.⁸

This vignette raises the themes this chapter will illuminate: how messiah, mammon, mafia and *muzhik* (the construction of a new Russian man, like Putin) have intersected to renew misogyny in the post-Soviet period. For reasons of space, this chapter focuses mainly on European Russia. The trajectory of the nine Muslim-majority republics like Tatarstan and Bashkortostan, seven of which are known collectively as the North Caucasus, has been quite different and is touched upon only briefly. The construction of a Russian national identity is a joint 'Christian' project between Putin and the ROC in a bid to set out a distinct path from the rest of the world and create a break from its own atheist and secular past without reference to its Muslim constituencies. It rests on traditional family values as defined by the church and the regime; it is enforced by vigilantes, pro-Kremlin youth groups and the oligarchs that fund it. The invasions of Ukraine in 2014 and 2022, including the annexation of Crimea, are part of the project of building a greater Russia, folding neighbouring countries into its embrace, by force if necessary, and carried out, to a significant extent, by a private army, the Wagner group, made up of thugs and led by a thug, Yevgeny Prigozhin, until his assassination by the Russian state in August 2023.

Central to the project of masculinity—and patriarchy—is the remoulding of the family by restoring power and control to the father. A case in 2018 involving three women, the Khachaturyan sisters, who were imprisoned after attacking their abusive, Orthodox Christian father with pepper spray, a knife and a hammer following years of physical, sexual and verbal abuse, exemplified Russian attitudes to women.[9] The country was immediately divided. An online petition for their release gathered more than a million signatures.[10] Members of the father's family toured TV studios in a public spat with the daughters and their mother. Were the sisters out to steal their father's money, as their aunts alleged? Or had they acted out of self-defence, as their mother believed? The national debate that followed provides some indicators of where Russia stands on the issue of violence against women. A defensive battle is being fought by feminists in Russia to overturn the decriminalisation of domestic violence in a law that was passed in 2017 and has allowed perpetrators to behave with impunity. At the same time, Orthodox priests appear on

RUSSIA

TV lamenting the attack on the Russian family and laying the blame on Western values and globalisation.

How did we get here?

This chapter will focus on the role of patriarchy in Russia after the fall of the Soviet Union, delving into two key points of its twentieth-century history—the early years following the 1917 revolution until the advent of Stalin and the collapse of the Soviet system in 1991, the effects of which are still rippling through Russian society. The entrenchment of patriarchy in Russia today is so extensive that the gains for women in the first decade following the 1917 revolution seem like a chimera and beg the question of how deep rooted change must be in order for it to be long lasting. The material impact of the First World War on the Soviet economy and the ideological limitations of conceptualising women's unequal status within the framework of capitalism alone without an understanding of patriarchy may have contributed to its impermanence. However, this period has not been erased from historical memory but rewritten selectively to suit modern agendas. Both Putin and his feminist detractors define themselves politically by reference to this period and its ideological baggage, either repudiating it as in the case of Putin or embracing it with qualifications.

The 'feminist' achievements of the 1917 revolution seem almost unbelievable given the years of repression and regression that followed under Stalin and his successors. It is also staggering that a revolutionary overhaul of the whole system was being attempted while the First World War was raging, followed by a devastating civil war in which a number of anti-Bolshevik forces, including White Russians and Cossacks, supported by British forces and Allied support, fought against the newly formed government, exacerbating the enormous economic hardship and the huge loss of lives suffered during the war. The women's march on International Women's Day (IWD) in 1917, which sparked the February revolution (according to the calendar that was used in Russia), demanding bread, combined with an industrial lockout in the Putilov metalworks, led to a general strike and invasion of the centre of St Petersburg.[11]

While there had been a history of women active in the nihilist movement, the Narodnik movement (mobilising the peasantry against the tsars), the labour movement and women's organisations, misogyny was rife. To make the point, Sheila Rowbotham, a feminist historian, cites a number of Russian proverbs, such as 'A wife isn't a jug—she won't crack if you hit her a few times.'[12] She reports that, in peasant families, the bride's father presented the groom-to-be with a whip that hung over the marital bed as a reminder of the need to keep a wife in check. In the cities, prostitution was often an economic refuge for poor women—with the blessings of the church because it believed that it protected other women from sexual harassment. Women workers were sacked if found to be pregnant, so they often hid their pregnancy until the last minute, sometimes giving birth on the factory floor.[13]

Within a week of the provisional government being formed, a conference organised by Alexandra Kollontai, People's Commissar for Social Welfare, led to maternity benefits and the prohibition of night-time working for pregnant and breastfeeding mothers, as well as time off for breastfeeding mothers and a host of other benefits. The revolution introduced the principle of equality. A women's department in the Central Committee of the Bolshevik Party, the Zhenotdel, was set up by Alexandra Kollontai and Inessa Armand, Bolshevik activists, in 1919. Under their pressure, the right to abortion was introduced. Lenin's thinking on abortion was advanced for those times. He supported the right to abortion but not for the 'petty bourgeois' reason that an unwanted child would be condemned to a terrible life.[14] Within the framework of Lenin's assertion that '[t]he proletariat cannot achieve complete liberty until it has won complete liberty for women',[15] very similar to what Abdullah Öcalan was to proclaim many years later, much attention was paid to how to revolutionise the domestic sphere until 1930 when the Zhenotdel was dissolved.

Ahead of the rest of the world, the revolutionary government introduced a genuinely progressive set of laws, including: the right to abortion at any stage of pregnancy; the right to a simplified divorce at the request of either partner; the right to alimony once a marriage had ended; the recognition of all children as legitimate regardless of whether they were born in or out of wedlock; the reframing of marriage as a secular contract between two people; the legalisation of same-sex marriage; the decriminalisation of homosexuality; cohabiting couples given the same rights as married couples; and transgender people being allowed to serve in the army.[16] Furthermore, for single mothers, where the father could not be identified, often all the men named by the woman as possible fathers were ordered to pay support.[17]

Many of these laws did not penetrate the Muslim regions of Russia, even though the Muslim reformist movements in Türkiye, Iran and Afghanistan were pushing for women's emancipation. It was because the Soviet Union was seen as an imperial power that these changes were resisted—'the family became a sphere that needed to be protected from "foreign" interference, while Islamic and customary marriage and family practices came to be valued as crucial components of "national" identity'. The Soviet secret police reported that these initiatives were seen as a Russian attempt to destroy Islam. So great was the resistance that 2,000 women were killed, their bodies mutilated and desecrated, for cooperating with the Soviet Union's unveiling campaign in Uzbekistan between 1927 and 1929. The Soviet Union did not use the woman question to justify their rule as the Europeans did in their colonies in the Middle East and North Africa and as they continue to do in places like Afghanistan.[18] Some have argued that this was Stalin's attack on Islamic clerics in order to break down the fabric of Soviet Asian society and make the Asian republics submit to his first five-year plan.[19] Today, Putin and Patriarch Kirill too take refuge in the notion that the Russian family is a bastion of Russian culture against the depredations of Westernisation and globalisation.

There is an interesting story of how patriarchy had tried to assert itself under the new regime. In 1918, the Petrograd Council of Trade Unions declared that the only way to deal with growing unemployment was to fire the women. The Petrograd Council rejected this proposal for not respecting the principle of equality under which decisions to hire and fire should be made on the basis of which individual workers are most in need of work—a criterion bound to overwhelmingly benefit single women with children.[20]

Abolish the family

'Abolish the family' was the slogan that drove the collectivisation of domestic chores such as cooking and childcare by the establishment of canteens, laundries and crèches in the expectation that institutional intervention would overturn the private imbalance of power. Trotsky acknowledged that a lack of resources meant that such facilities were not universally available, '[t]he family could not be "abolished"; it had to be replaced. The real liberation of women was unattainable on the basis of "collectivised scarcity".'[21] The Bolshevik view of the family as a drag on women's ability to participate in the public sphere was driven by the imperatives of the revolution and not by a patriarchal analysis of the family as a site of oppression for women. Certainly, there was no acknowledgement of male violence. However, attempts to abolish or replace the family, if they had been successful, would have gone a long way to liberating women. The Bolsheviks were aware that of the facilities for women that were available, the standards were poor. Trotsky went on to argue that

> [u]nless there is actual equality of husband and wife in the family, in a normal sense as well as in the conditions of life, we cannot speak seriously of their equality in social work or even in politics. As long as woman is chained to her housework, the care of the family, the cooking and sewing, all her chances of participation in social and political life are cut down to the extreme.[22]

This echoed Lenin's point that women can only be emancipated through work. When Engels spoke about patriarchy, he preferred to use class-based concepts to convey the unequal relations between men and women in marriage: 'In the family, he is the bourgeois; the wife represents the proletariat.'[23] Trotsky even proposed architectural innovation to enable communal living. The need to have women onside in support of the revolution and the building of the dictatorship of the proletariat runs through many of the writings and speeches by Trotsky and Lenin, especially Lenin. That women represented half the population had not escaped anyone's attention when they argued that the proletariat could not be a successful revolutionary force without women signing up to the struggle. So the wooing of women was both transactional and a principled recognition that equality would not be achieved unless women were released from the drudgery of housework.

Capitalism was postulated as the central reason for women's secondary status, their oppression and even their 'household bondage'. Neither Lenin nor Trotsky articulated these oppressions as deriving from a patriarchal system, although the concept would have been available to them through Engels' writings such as *The Origin of the Family*. Lenin blamed capitalism for the weakness in women's rights—'wherever the power of capital is preserved, the men retain their privileges'.[24] However, work in a socialist state did not turn out to be the emancipatory utopia these leaders had expected it to be. While the Soviet Union achieved the world's highest rates of women's participation in the workforce—90 per cent by the 1980s—women were also lumbered with the burden of domestic and reproductive labour, a double burden. Neither the economic resources nor the ideological commitment was strong enough to prove Lenin's point that women would be emancipated by work if all domestic duties had been effectively collectivised.

In Lenin's conversations with Clara Zetkin, a German communist and advocate for women's rights, he upbraided her for not using her authority to stop German communist women focusing on 'sex problems and the forms of marriage':

> I ask you, is this the time to keep working women busy for months at a stretch with such questions as how to love or be loved, how to woo or be wooed? ... Nowadays all the thoughts of communist women, of working women, should be centred on the proletarian revolution, which will lay the foundation, among other things, for the necessary revision of material and sexual relations.[25]

Lenin was firmly against 'separate organisations of communist women! She who is a communist belongs as a member to the party, just as he who is a communist.'[26] Lenin's critique of the pamphlet that Inessa Armand was drafting was typically shortsighted in that he could see her preoccupation with sexuality only as a bourgeois problem:

> I advise you to throw out altogether §3—the 'demand (women's) for freedom of love'. That is not really a proletarian but a bourgeois demand. After all, what do you understand by that phrase? What can be understood by it? 1. Freedom from material (financial) calculations in affairs of love? 2. The same, from material worries? 3. From religious prejudices? 4. From prohibitions by Papa, etc.? 5.

RUSSIA

From the prejudices of 'society'? 6. From the narrow circumstances of one's environment (peasant or petty bourgeois or bourgeois intellectual)? 7. From the fetters of the law, the courts and the police? 8. From the serious element in love? 9. From childbirth? 10. Freedom of adultery? Etc.[27]

After Lenin's death in 1924, attempts were made to put the economic case for dispersing private chores into the public sphere by economists who calculated the inefficiencies of individual women spending hours on domestic work. Rowbotham writes that '[i]t could be argued that the emancipation of women from the family was economically necessary if the material preconditions for socialism were to be created'.[28] An economic argument to back up an ideological case is always doubly effective and not just under capitalism. However, the ideological climate shifted to justify Stalin's new economic priorities. His first five-year plan, which focused on rapid industrialisation to ensure that Russia caught up with the developed nations of the world, created an inexhaustible demand for women workers. The effect of the First World War, the civil war and the revolution was to alter the male/female ratio to such an extent that in 1926 there were only 71 million men to almost 76 million women.[29] Stalin's reliance on women in the workforce was also a pragmatic solution to the shortage of men. The consequence of women joining the workforce was a falling birth rate and a growing number of 'unsupervised' children, which placed demands on state social services that the bureaucracy did not have the resources to meet. Tough new child support legislation was introduced to force fathers to do more for their children, and couples were encouraged to stay together.[30] Stalin promoted a narrative of the glorious family for the same reason that this narrative is popular under capitalism. The superwoman image of turbocharged productivity outside the home and reproduction inside the home was carefully cultivated during Stalin's time.[31]

By the 1930s, the traditional family was back. Free love advocated by women like Kollontai was seen as 'bourgeois', the ultimate term of abuse in the communist lexicon, a perversion of communist morality. The dismissive attitude towards sexuality revealed by Lenin in his conversations with Zetkin was couched in terms of revolutionary priorities but hid an unacknowledged puritanism that resurfaced under Stalin when *Pravda* denounced 'free love' and a 'disorderly sex life' as poisoning family life and disrupting marriage. Homosexuality was criminalised. Legal abortions were banned; 'illegitimate' children no longer had a right to financial support. Divorce was made more difficult. The withering away of the family became as distant a dream as the withering away of the state. Trotsky rued the fact that 'the leaders are forcing people to glue together again the shell of the broken family, and not only that but to consider it, under threat of extreme penalties, the sacred nucleus of triumphant socialism'.[32] With the coming of the Second World War and anxieties about falling population rates, women were encouraged to have large families. In 1944, the Soviet government created the Order of Maternal Glory, which had three categories: the first went to women with nine children or more, while the third class was awarded to women with seven children,[33] a practice that continued until 1991, with over 5 million recipients of the award. Not so surprisingly, it was restored in 2022 as anxiety grew about the impact of the 'special operation' in Ukraine on population growth and the loss of 1 million lives during the COVID pandemic.[34]

Along with better healthcare, improved life expectancy, the post-war baby boom and the awards system, population numbers returned to their pre-war level in 1955, the same year that the government reintroduced abortion rights.[35] This was earlier than in most other countries, but the previous commitment to true emancipation was nowhere in view. Divorce was made easier.

Women had the right to work, and implicitly the right to education to skill them up for the job market, with the necessary scaffolding to facilitate employment, such as extensive support around pregnancy and childcare, part-time working hours and parental leave—but this was a shadow of the bright future facing them in 1917.

While individual freedom for women was never part of the Soviet project, which was geared up to setting women free to work for the state, Anna Adrianiva, a Russian academic, suggests that we must not overlook its progressive aspects.[36] Women constituted over 50 per cent of the workforce in the Soviet period, working at jobs that were predominantly in poorly paid sectors. There was some state recognition that they were also lumbered with childcare and housework, so factories received subsidies to provide daycare and, in some cases, shopping services and household goods to ease the burden of managing a household. Adrianiva makes an interesting distinction about patriarchy in the Soviet Union—she argues that while men may have been sexist and traditional, they did not have real patriarchal power, which, according to her, depends on property ownership, a classic Marxist position. The state had patriarchal power, and men and women were equally, but differently, dependent on—and exploited by—the state.[37]

When Gorbachev came to power in 1985, he cut back state subsidies in response to the deteriorating economic situation. With fewer jobs available, women were the first to go as the state did not enforce sex discrimination laws, which banned laying off women workers on grounds of sex alone.[38] The contradiction between needing women to work and to produce a workforce seemed to be irreconcilable, though this did not stop Soviet policy from trying to tackle this contradiction in different ways. Setting aside the revolutionary zeal for the emancipation of women in the first decade of the revolution, the USSR spent the next sixty years manipulating birth rates and its abortion and divorce policy to adjust to the labour demands of the economy[39]—a clear example of the central planning mechanism of a socialist economy relying on patriarchal control of women's bodies for its success.

Violence against women—the linchpin of patriarchy

In Soviet times, there was no recognition of domestic violence per se, as it was often categorised as hooliganism or rape in marriage. Better statistics were kept in relation to prostitution, including a breakdown of demand for these services by profession, and much time and government energy went into combatting it, although it was not conceptualised as violence against women. There was no critique of violence as a resource of masculinity; revolutionary violence was acclaimed from Marx to Fanon as the only resource for the disempowered.

The Bolshevik approach to prostitution bore some similarity to the abolitionist model today, as their slogan 'struggle against prostitution not prostitutes' suggests. Lenin railed against those who condemned prostitution from a religious stance without understanding the poverty that drove women to prostitution.[40] So brothel keepers and pimps faced criminal sentences but not the women themselves, along the lines of the Nordic Model that has been adopted by a number of countries today.[41] Kollontai also argued against the criminalisation of prostituted women, saying that the only difference between prostitution and marriage is that in one, a woman sold herself to many men on a temporary basis rather than to one man on a permanent basis.[42] However, this progressive analysis did not translate into action on the ground, especially in the early days of the Soviet Union, which were characterised by confusion after all the tsarist-era laws were revoked. Kollontai described the chaos in a speech to the heads of Women's

Regional Departments: 'In some areas the police still help to round up prostitutes just as in the old days. In other places, brothels exist quite openly ... And there are yet other areas where prostitutes are considered criminals and thrown into forced labour camps.'[43] Prostitution was viewed as a capitalist phenomenon driven by poverty and social inequality. The closest Kollontai came to recognising the role of patriarchy was when she said that prostitution 'strengthens the inequality of the relationships between the sexes'.[44] While Kollontai conceptualised prostitution as a form of violence, she did not see it as male violence against women: 'Prostitution is terrible because it is an act of violence by the woman upon herself in the name of material gain.'[45]

Prostitution was variously dubbed the 'institution of corrupt love', 'love trade', 'venal love' and a 'social anomaly', with the women often referred to as 'walking women'.[46] In the difficult economic years before the mid-1920s, fewer workers went to 'street women', but a 1925 survey showed an increase in demand across all trades, with 78 per cent of printers, the wealthiest category of workers, becoming punters. Much effort was put into tackling demand on the ground. In 1918, one of the regional soviets in Petrograd introduced a fine of 1,000 roubles, one month's forced labour and naming and shaming of punters in the local newspapers. Men found using prostituted women would lose their Communist Party membership, limiting their access to various social and economic benefits. The dilemma facing the authorities was that a significant number of punters were workers; taking action against them would destroy the myths about the moral character of the new Soviet man and that prostitution did not exist under socialism.

Measures to combat unemployment and homelessness and the provision of health services for prostituted women were introduced in the early 1920s.[47] However, the police continued to raid brothels and arrest women, contrary to the more progressive policies being developed at regional government level, an example of the chaos that Kollontai referred to. Just as more funding became available in 1927 and extra beds in shelters were being provided, the arrival of Stalin changed the political context, and the shelters turned into semi-prisons; the tussle between the rehabilitative and punitive trends continued with re-education losing out to the forced labour so central to Stalin's great industrial leap forward.[48] Prostitution was banned by Stalin, and the issue received little further attention until 1987, when Gorbachev decriminalised it but made it an administrative offence subject to a fine of up to 100 roubles payable by the women.[49] The new perspective, propagated by the press, was that women who took to prostitution liked fine clothes and an easy lifestyle and only had themselves to blame.[50] Prostitution thrives under Putin, as we shall see.

No comprehensive statistics on domestic violence are available for the Soviet Union. 'In view of official gender equality and the new model of the Soviet family based on true communist morals',[51] to acknowledge the existence of domestic violence would be to admit the failure of the revolution. Alcoholism and poverty, rather than patriarchy, were considered the primary drivers of domestic violence. Many perpetrators were dealt with under the laws available for hooliganism, which were easier to apply with lower evidential standards. For the Soviet state, the family was part of the public sphere, 'a microcosm of socialist society',[52] so violence within the family was seen as a form of public disorder. Anecdotal stories of violence and letters of complaint from women published in women's magazines and the high rates of spousal murders, figures for which are available, indicate that formal equality was no remedy for domestic violence. However, even figures for spousal murders are muddied by the fact that some were categorised as hooliganism. The statistics on murders motivated by 'jealousy and domestic quarrel', which are available from

1956 to 1990, are extremely high, peaking at nearly 15,000 in 1980, which represented almost 70 per cent of all homicides.[53]

The unravelling of the USSR

Much has been written about the era of glasnost and perestroika under Gorbachev, so much so that these Russian words have entered the English language. However, the new liberalism did not extend to women. Gorbachev's *mea culpa* on behalf of the state was no great feminist manifesto. A little-known consequence of the market liberalisation and freedom of expression that followed perestroika was that the market was flooded with pornography.[54] This 'freedom of expression' did not quite extend to Russian academics, who were cautioned by the KGB about the content of their speeches even as they found greater freedom to attend conferences abroad. One woman academic reports that they were encouraged to say that they were 'returning to Lenin',[55] apparently a fashion under Gorbachev. Gorbachev bemoaned the state's lack of attention to the needs of women as mothers and homemakers and blamed the problems with youth on the inability of Soviet women to create a good family atmosphere. He saw this as a failure of the Soviet Union's

> sincere and politically justified desire to make women equal with men in everything. That is why we are now holding heated debates in the press, in public organizations, at work and at home, about the question of what we should do to make it possible for women to return to their purely womanly mission.[56]

The alcoholism of Russian men was laid at the door of women too. Under the Soviet Union, government policy flipflopped between banning alcohol and lifting the ban to boost government income, but the problem was exacerbated by domestic brewing carried out illegally regardless of government policy.[57]

The flipside of the critique of women for inadequately performing their traditional roles was a glorification of them as mothers and wives. On IWD in 1991, Boris Yeltsin thanked 'all of you, dear women, for your great endurance, for your trust and support, and for your work, for the fact that you do not lose your optimism and remain feminine and beautiful'.

The first autonomous conference held by women in 1991 was dominated by an interest in training women to acquire entrepreneurial skills in the newly emerging market economy because business was seen, under perestroika, as the solution to unemployment.[58] Between 1990 and 1995, women lost 7 million jobs, while men lost 1 to 2 million. By all accounts, prostitution increased.[59] Those countries that were furthest along the path to capitalism had the greatest unemployment among women. Factory closures, unemployment and particularly loss of women's jobs were common to all post-communist societies across Eastern Europe—a feature of the neoliberal patriarchal paradigm.

The Soviet Women's Committee (SWC), a Stalin-era organisation, was given seventy-five seats by Gorbachev in his Congress of People's Deputies. The SWC built links with international organisations and emphasised world peace but did not have much to say on women's issues in the USSR. The head of the committee, Valentina Tereshkova, an ex-cosmonaut, stated that 'Soviet women do in fact enjoy full equal rights. Female equality is stressed and guaranteed. Motherhood is regarded in our country as women's greatest social function. The state values motherhood and helps women to raise children.'[60] The organisation was essentially a mouthpiece of the government but broke away from it in 1990 and was replaced by the Union of Russia's Women (URW). What the new openness did was allow women the space to critique their oppression and the failure of formal equality under the Soviet Union to solve the 'woman question'.[61] During the 1990s, URW organised a political bloc, Women of Russia, which managed to get twenty-one women elected to the Duma. They denied being a feminist group, possibly to avoid bad press, but they did stand against pornography and violence. They mostly campaigned for the restoration of the childcare facilities and women-friendly services that had flourished in the early days of the revolution.

In the immediate aftermath of the fall of the Soviet Union, there was a flowering of autonomous women's organisations, working across a range of issues with varying understandings of women's rights and feminist activism, reminiscent of a similar eruption in El Salvador after the civil war ended with the signing of the Peace Accords in 1992. By 1994, 300 organisations had registered with the Russian Ministry of Justice, and there were many more operating without registration.[62] There was no tradition of civil society organising, no pre-existing networks, a declining welfare state, no economic infrastructure to support social movements and the continued presence of Soviet-era institutions.[63] Valerie Sperling, who has written extensively about women in Russia, outlines the number of changes that took place in the 1990s. Institutional establishment and disestablishment made it even harder for the women's movement to make progress: the dismantling of the USSR; Yeltsin's dissolution and subsequent shelling of the Russian Supreme Soviet in September and October 1993; the creation of a women's party and its entry to the new Russian parliament in December 1993; followed by new elections in 1995 and the failure of the women's party. There was a perpetual search for new allies and a constant struggle to negotiate each new system.[64] The most significant instance of women's influence as a group on the Russian Supreme Soviet was when they managed to defeat a bill on the second reading in 1992 that would have made the family the sole subject of rights, whereby only a family (not an individual) could own an apartment, a plot of land and so on. Women were concerned that this would mean that if the right to decide the issue of having a child belongs to both spouses, the husband could prevent the wife from having an abortion or conversely from having a child. The new openings in Russia's formal political institutions had created channels through which women's movement activists were able to mobilise successfully in order to block legislation.

Rather than mass protest, the 1990s were marked by seminars and conferences and service provision to women escaping violence. It was a kind of truncated feminism bearing the psychological scars of the Soviet era. Sperling believes that feminism in 1990s Russia was a liberal feminism, framed around freedom of choice and equality of opportunity. Women wanting to assert their femininity, as a rebellion against the uniformity of dress imposed by the absence of consumer goods in the Soviet Union—a regressive step from a feminist perspective—paradoxically came to be seen as a gesture of liberation. Women felt that the focus on women's rights was not appropriate in post-Soviet conditions, partly because men and women had been equally oppressed by the Soviet state. Despite all these hangovers from the Soviet era, between 1992 and 1995 all strands of the Russian women's movement could sign up to the framework of 'equal rights and equal opportunities'. Given the negative connotations associated with feminism in the Soviet Union, the language and ideology of feminism was not available to women. In the post-Soviet period, feminism came to be seen as an aggressive, man-hating, lesbian separatist movement imported from the West, a serious slur in Russia.

For collective action to be possible, it is not enough to experience discrimination as a group but to be able to join the dots, to frame it, so that it can transform consciousness. The concept of democracy was initially seen as a positive framing for women's fight for equality reflected in the title of the first autonomous women's conference in 1991, 'Democracy without Women Is No

Democracy', until democracy itself got mired in corruption under Yeltsin. The botched transition from communism to capitalism was not a truly democratic one. Yeltsin had been voted in as Russian president while Russia was still a Soviet republic. The power of the state was like a pendulum, swinging from an omnipresent, all-powerful presence to a diminution too far in the neoliberal '90s before swinging back, under Putin, to capricious power. Power was handed to Putin by Yeltsin. The plunder of state assets by ex-Communist Party officials that had started under Yeltsin combined with inefficiency and corruption in the '90s led to GDP falling by 40 per cent in 1999; hyperinflation wiped out personal savings.

It was not just the public domain that needed to be reconstructed when the transition to a market economy took place in Russia. It has been argued in relation to Eastern Europe that the creation of civil society and a market economy entailed the construction of a man's world and the consequent domestication and marketing of women, which drew on pre-existing traditional concepts of gender that were largely accepted by both sexes.[65] According to this view, men and women were dissatisfied with their roles under communism not because of any perceived inequalities but because the system did not allow them to fulfil their traditional gender roles, that is, women could not be good wives because they had to work outside the home. The transition also created more unemployment for women, which returned them to their domesticated roles. There was a transformation in the relationship between the public and the private spheres that had 'fundamental implications for gender identity, encoding within it new dimensions of inferiority and superiority'.[66] Like everywhere else, Russia also suffered from a gender-based earnings gap. Before perestroika, women's average pay was 70 per cent of men's, but by 1994 it was only 40 per cent. Sexist attitudes were ingrained despite the wider range of jobs that were open to

Soviet women than in the West. Sperling relates an amusing anecdote about a Moscow mayor handing out computers to male employees and irons to female employees as rewards for their work in 1994.[67] Sexual harassment had got worse, particularly for young women in danger of being raped by potential or current employers. With jobs for women being increasingly hard to get, the drum of family values was being beaten louder and louder, an agenda that found favour with and was reinforced by the ROC in the 1990s, when religious forces raised their head above the parapet once again.

Mesmerism of the messiah

With the collapse of the Soviet Union and the repudiation of communism, a new unifying Russian identity was needed, one that was provided by the ROC. Yeltsin, who took part in religious rituals on TV and passed controversial legislation that confirmed the pre-eminent status of the ROC,[68] handed the baton to Putin to support his project of remaking Russian identity. Pussy Riot's protest against the church, the state and the family, therefore, was a torpedo aimed straight at the heart of Putin's grand design. While the Russian constitution is nominally secular, the space provided for the ROC vis-à-vis state and society is commodious. The convergence of church and state grew so complete that at points in the trial of Pussy Riot, it was hard to know whether the case was built on canonical law or secular law.[69] The media coverage focused on the schism between the secular and the sacred in Russian society, but Sperling argues that it was 'feminism that lay silently at the centre of the case'.[70] In response to this case, in 2013, Putin introduced a blasphemy law, an amendment to the criminal law whereby anyone convicted of offending religious feelings could be fined substantial sums or face a prison sentence of up to three years.[71]

RUSSIA

This is a far cry from the days of the Soviet Union, when churches were destroyed or repurposed as warehouses and even museums to atheism as part of Stalin's crass interpretation of Lenin's critique of organised religion. But Lenin had cautioned against offending religious feelings, recommending education to bring about change, constructing unity rather than division, an instruction ignored by Stalin. Even at the height of persecution, the results of the 1937 census, which were suppressed for many years, revealed that over 56 per cent of the population were believers.[72] It was Lenin's belief that '[t]he deepest source of religious prejudice is poverty and ignorance; and that is the evil we have to combat'.[73] In 1961, Yuri Gagarin, the Soviet cosmonaut who became the first man to travel into space, was reported by state media to have said 'I travelled into space but I didn't see God there.' In contrast, in 2016, a blogger who wrote 'There is no God' was arrested and tried. The judge said: 'No one in their right mind would write anything against Orthodox Christianity and the Russian Orthodox Church.'[74] Yet the hegemonic position occupied by the ROC is a political gift from Putin given the low degree of religiosity of the Russian population. While the number of people who identified as Orthodox Christian more than doubled from 31 per cent in 1991 to 72 per cent in 2008, this did not correspond with the number of people regularly attending church, which, according to surveys, ranged from 2 to 7 per cent.[75] The women I interviewed, those who lived through the Soviet period and those born after it, confirm anecdotally that religious observance is minimal. However, religious beliefs provided a clear demarcation from Marxism–Leninism that fitted well with Putin's agenda of creating a proud, pre-revolutionary Russian identity. The figure of Kirill, patriarch of the ROC since 2009 and an ex-KGB agent and close friend of Putin, seems to encapsulate in his muscular propagation of religion all the forces of Russian society and state that conspire against women's freedoms. His business interests stretch to playing the stock market, the oil business, metals trading and cars. He hosts his own television programme called the 'Pastor's Word'.[76]

Orthodox activists are zealous in the pursuit of those seen to be mocking their faith. Artworks in an exhibition entitled 'Careful, Religion!' in 2003 were spray painted and ripped apart. Those responsible were charged with vandalism but acquitted, unlike the women from Pussy Riot, each of whom was sentenced to two years in prison. The Duma then demanded a criminal investigation into the exhibition's organisers for 'fomenting national and religious discord', with art 'experts' deeming the exhibition 'blasphemous'.[77] One of these Orthodox groups, which went by the name of God's Will, was disbanded in 2019. In a surprising turnaround, the leader of the group, Dmitry Enteo, who had worked closely with leading church leaders, entered into a relationship with Maria Alyokhina, a member of Pussy Riot.[78] There have been other violent actions opposing sexual education in schools, demanding a ban on abortions and obstructing scientific lectures held on university premises.

Another Orthodox activist, Andrei Kormukhin, father of nine, leads a pro-life group called the Forty Forties with a membership of 10,000, including senior Orthodox clergy, and campaigned successfully against a bill on domestic violence introduced by Oksana Pushkina, one of seventy-three women in the 450-seat Duma. He wrote an open letter to Putin denouncing the bill because it would destroy the family, arguing that men were mostly violent when drunk and needed to be given a chance to sober up and ask for forgiveness; a family could not survive without its breadwinner. The group organises protests and mass vigils. Football hooligans and neo-Nazis have joined some of their more extreme actions in defence of religion.[79] Kormukhin has gone on to form the Family Party, which derives some of its ideas from a medieval priest who postulated that the father was the head of the family. The ideal man is a defender of the faith, the fatherland and the weak.[80] In the Russian Orthodox tradition, the family is seen as a 'small church', and any interference with the family unit in terms of recriminalising domestic violence would be seen as a restriction on religious rights. Some priests are worried that harsher laws on domestic violence could lead to the break-up of the family, with Russian children left to 'homosexuals' to bring them up.[81]

Unlike in El Salvador, where the primacy of the Catholic Church has been challenged by new Evangelical movements, the proximity of Kirill to Putin has ensured that rival non-Russian Orthodox churches are dissuaded by extra surveillance and legislation that requires a cumbersome registration process. The Russian state provides security and official vehicles to Kirill but not to other religious leaders, and the ROC has been the main beneficiary of presidential grants ostensibly designed to reduce NGO dependence on foreign funding.[82] There is a stark difference between the pre-eminent position of the ROC and Islam in the Muslim republics, where any expression of religion is equated with Islamic fundamentalism and quashed. Anna Tuktasheva, who researched the intersection between religion, gender and public health in one of the Muslim republics, said: 'I don't know how to talk [to Muslims] about women's rights or Islamic feminism because their basic rights are under attack.'[83] She points to the paradox that Muslims were relatively freer to practise their religion in Soviet times, even though they could only practise it in the privacy of their homes, whereas under Putin, a campaign to release Muslims incarcerated due to state repression or to save their endangered languages could lead to prison. Women could not wear the hijab in public in the USSR until the decade of freedom in the 1990s and early 2000s. In 2015, the Russian Supreme Court upheld the ban on hijabs in schools.[84] Tuktasheva believes that 'the Muslim republics became collateral damage of the Chechen war' in terms of suspension of the human rights of the population. Increased religiosity was also a response to state discrimination.

In 2011, when parliamentary elections were widely seen to have been engineered in favour of Putin, there was much protest. Surprisingly, Kirill was among those voices, even if he wasn't the loudest. He supported the 'lawful negative reaction' to corruption but made sure to moderate his anger in recognition of the church's dependence on the government's good will.[85] Putin's strategy to head off the protests was brutal repression, on the one hand, and pandering to the church's agenda of traditional family values on the other, usually asserted by trampling on the rights of women and sexual minorities. He criminalised 'gay propaganda' in 2013. Sperling describes this symbiotic relationship as one in which 'the Church provided an ideology and a constituency for Putin, and, in exchange for its support, the Church had gained access and influence in the policy sphere on such issues as abortion, gay rights, religious education in schools'.[86] The law banned the distribution or expression of information that portrayed non-traditional sexual relationships in a positive light or equated them in value with heterosexual relationships. Duma deputy Elena Mizulina explained that they did not even use the word homosexual in the text of the law as doing so might inadvertently act as propaganda.[87]

The militancy and muscularity of the ROC are clear in its support for Russian imperialist adventures. In 2014, when Russian-backed separatists in Donbas, Eastern Ukraine, seized government buildings, the ROC and Russia's private sector organised assistance to sustain the rebels. Church buildings were used to store ammunition, and fighters received blessings from priests.[88] The war in Ukraine has the full blessings of the ROC, and any pretence at state and church being separate entities appears to have been abandoned. Kirill has been fully supportive of Putin's invasion and occupation of Crimea and Ukraine as part of the project to restore Russia to its previous imperial glory. Pope Francis reprimanded him, saying that 'the patriarch cannot transform himself into Putin's altar boy'.[89]

Cracks have, however, started appearing at lower levels of the ROC, with priests who have begun to lose their faith in Putin and taken part in pro-democracy protests, specifically one in 2019, when dozens of priests were arrested. Over 200 priests signed a letter that appealed to the Orthodox faith of the judges and condemned the cruelty and repressiveness of the judicial proceedings. Apparently, this was the first time the church had participated in a collective action without authorisation from above, and it was roundly rebuked for doing so.[90]

Muzhik/Patsan—the New Russian Man

Putin's desire to build a new Russian empire on the ashes of the old Soviet Union was fuelled by testosterone and patriarchal values. It is Stalin, not Lenin, not Marxist ideology that Putin praises for wartime leadership and stewardship of Soviet industry. He appears to be in line with the public mood on this, with 52 per cent in 2016 agreeing that Stalin's rule was 'probably' or 'definitely' a good thing.[91] Opinion polls confirm that most Russians are nostalgic for the return of the Soviet Union, particularly its welfare benefits and workers' rights, though not its repudiation of human rights. Kirill too has emphasised the positive aspects of Stalin's rule. He is reputed to have said: 'Whoever does not regret the break-up of the Soviet Union has no heart. But whoever wishes its return in its previous form has no head.'[92]

The hypermasculine persona cultivated by Putin, especially in his semi-naked pictures riding on horseback, is a signifier of the new Russia, so close is the identification between the two. The persona of the *muzhik*, which referred to an ignorant peasant in

Soviet times, acquired a positive gloss in the post-Soviet era as a signifier of 'real', tough manhood, valorised through songs, advertisements and movies.[93] Svetlana Stephenson disagrees with the characterisation of Putin as a *muzhik*, arguing that Putin 'performs a different form of masculinity, an urban street masculinity of *patsan* (a lad)'.[94] Sperling says that 'Putin—given his career trajectory and his lifestyle preferences for avoiding alcohol and embracing physical fitness—was well suited to be framed as a macho strongman who could reverse Russia's waning power and oversee the country's resurgence.'[95] His time with the KGB in his early career and, later, as head of the FSB, which also has a reputation for brutality, further underscores this version of masculinity. While Stalin was positioned as the father of the nation, Putin was the lover or the 'stud of the people'.[96] Putin's misogyny is so extreme as to see rape as evidence of masculinity: believing he was off-mic at a meeting with the Israeli prime minister, he sent his regards to President Moshe Katsav, praising him as a 'mighty man' because '[h]e raped ten women—I would never have expected this from him. He surprised us all—we all envy him!'[97]

The man on horseback dominates not just women but also nature. It is precisely this image that Pussy Riot subverted in their anti-Putin lyrics, although feminist scholars have questioned the effectiveness of reinforcing patriarchal stereotypes by describing Putin as weak and unmanly. The Pussy Riot campaign brought feminism to the forefront of Russian popular consciousness in a mostly negative way, confirming the conservative view of feminists as angry, aggressive lesbians. But it 'changed the tactical palette that the women's movement had used until that time'. It marked a shift from the closed doors of academia, seminars and conferences that characterised feminist activity in the 1990s into a more public and openly defiant presence on the streets.[98]

Pussy Riot also point out how masculinity runs through Putin's use of language. He uses the word 'condoms' to describe the opposition's white ribbons—the symbolic colour of the political opposition—meaning that those who do not agree with him are just protections for a 'limp dick'.[99] Wives of the men on board the sinking submarine *Kursk*, a national catastrophe, in 2000, were labelled whores by Putin for demanding that their husbands be rescued.[100] Masculinity is framed as heterosexual. Gay rights and same-sex marriage are seen as an attack on the Russian identity. An important constituent of the hyper-masculine, heteronormative image is the presence of conventionally attractive women doing obeisance to Putin. A *Happy Birthday, Mr Putin!* calendar produced by women student journalists of Moscow University for his birthday in 2010 underscored his masculine image. Each month of the year was illustrated by a photo of a scantily clad woman, accompanied by a slogan heavy with double-entendres. For example, on the February page, a woman in leopard print lingerie asks 'Vladimir Vladimirovich, how about the third time?' in reference to him potentially making a third bid for the presidency in 2012.[101] Popular songs with titles like 'I Want to Be Your Konni', the name of Putin's dog, accompanied by videos in which women are shown to be pining for the attentions of Putin, appeared on social media in 2012.[102] He represented the kind of clean-living, responsible man who might take care of his family, just like he takes charge of the state, a model of masculinity that women, who had long faced the 'double burden' of full-time work and domestic care duties, might have yearned for.[103] It was not just women getting into the act. Two African migrants living in Russia produced a rap number 'I Go Hard Like Vladimir Putin' in 2014,[104] where 'hard' carries a sexual connotation or masculine toughness or a conservative, hard-working ethic, all variations on the theme of masculinity. A surprising homage given Russia's reputation for racism, which the singers insist is a thing of the past.

In the chaos that followed the collapse of the Soviet Union, young men looking for an identity they could take pride in were attracted by the hyper-masculine model offered by the football hooligan, an identity some politicians promoted. On the far right, politicians 'began to court these young men, laying on free transport to away games, paying members to work as bodyguards or street muscle, and even offering the occasional well-paid role as a party official'.[105] However, the outbreak of savage violence at the UEFA European Championship in Marseille in 2016, which was glorified by a Russian rapper and by the deputy chair of the Duma, brought adverse headlines across the world and soon brought state patronage to an end. The hooligans felt betrayed when they lost the support of a government that had encouraged them from the mid-1990s onwards. Many of the erstwhile football hooligans joined far-right extremists who go on attack missions against immigrants and those attending hip-hop concerts, as well as 'white wagon' attacks in which they wear surgical masks, board trains and attack anyone of a non-Slavic descent.

Another group of pro-Putin young men from the poorer regions, Nashi, was set up by Kremlin operator Vladislav Surkov in 2005 as a counterforce to be mobilised against any pro-democracy demonstrations and as a buffer against the kinds of uprisings, like the Orange Revolution, that had taken place in Ukraine. The extent to which the revolution in Ukraine became a turning point in the psychology of Russian leaders and the population at large is underestimated in the West. Nashi became known as Putin's private army.[106] At its height, it was heavily funded by the state and boasted a membership of more than 100,000 people. Its task was to protect Russia's sovereignty, bolster Putin, inculcate patriotism among the youth and promote Russian modernisation.[107] In 2005, Nashi organised a camp for young people attended by 5,000 and organised a mass wedding of two dozen couples in support of the Kremlin's baby-production agenda, sending them off on their wedding night without condoms. Eventually, this annual camp attracted 15,000 youths each year.[108]

RUSSIA

Alongside Nashi were at least two other pro-Kremlin youth groups, Stal and Molodaia Gvardiia Edinoi Rossii (Young Guard of United Russia). Stal tended to operate in a grey area, legally speaking, using bully boy tactics to shut down illegal drug dens, for example. All these groups traded on misogyny to frame their messages, including the smaller anti-Kremlin groups that also came into being.[109] Although women formed around half the membership of these groups, they did very little to challenge sexism. One Nashi woman said she would not marry a man who refused to serve in the army: if he couldn't protect his country, she couldn't expect him to protect her.[110] Women in the anti-Kremlin groups who started a campaign, 'Girls against the Draft', also traded on concepts of masculinity in arguing against conscription, saying that only men who voluntarily joined the professional army were worthy of respect.[111] Nashi became defunct in 2013 after it was unable to counter the mass, spontaneous protests by Russians against the 2011 elections, widely seen to be manipulated, which some scholars have argued points to the inauthenticity of Nashi.[112]

Offshoots of Nashi that carried on its aggressive tactics, such as Khryushi Protiv (Pigs Don't Agree), a movement against expired produce in grocery stores, and StopKham, a movement against lawlessness and privilege, also came into being. These groups, which use violence to deal with relatively minor issues such as cars flouting parking rules, highlight the paradox of Russia: an aggressive state when it comes to Chechnya or Ukraine or political dissidents but unwilling or unable to implement laws in daily life to regulate car parking or ensure the regular payment of salaries. In 1996, Yeltsin issued a decree mandating penalties for bureaucrats who failed to implement presidential decrees, which only highlighted the weakness of the state.[113] The founder of StopKham, Dmitry Chuganov, was a member of Nashi and described it as a way to 'meet beautiful girls'.[114]

The way in which criminality bleeds into the construction of masculinity of Russian men is demonstrated by Marina Yusupova, who has written extensively on this subject: 'Post-Soviet Russian masculinities are in a state of complex power relations with criminal values and hierarchies.'[115] She found that the men she interviewed resorted to prison slang when talking specifically about their understanding of masculinity even though they had never been to prison. The use of prison slang or *fenya* and references to criminal codes of behaviour as signifiers of masculinity seems widespread, even touching Putin himself. His use of colourful language is possibly a leftover from the days of his youth in St Petersburg spent with his wrestling coach who had served twenty years in prison for rape and other crimes.[116] Less surprising is Prigozhin's use of prison slang, given his early criminal history. Interestingly, it requires no explanation for Russian audiences steeped in the culture of *vory v zakone* (thieves' law). This kind of masculinity is represented in someone who stands by his word, is tough, aggressive, sexist, homophobic and does not squeal on someone to the authorities. Acceptance and internalisation of the criminal culture's hierarches and values contribute to the hegemonic masculinity to which Russian men aspire.[117]

A prime example of this was Prigozhin, who embodied an almost caricatured version of criminal masculinity that came into view as the war of aggression against Ukraine persisted. As a petty criminal in the 1980s, among his many muggings, there is a story of him squeezing a lone woman's neck till she nearly lost consciousness while he and his friends robbed her of her purse and jewellery. During the Ukraine war, a video went viral showing Prigozhin standing by as a defector from Wagner, the company of mercenaries he had built, is battered to death with a sledgehammer, saying, 'A dog's death for a dog.'[118] This is the kind of toxic masculinity that permeates the Putin administration. Recruiting hardened criminals serving time in prison to fight in Ukraine seems almost the next logical step in this context. A billboard in Ekaterinburg, Ural, advertised the Wagner group with the words: 'Motherland, Honour, Blood, Bravery. WAGNER'.[119] Every single one of those words encapsulates a particular kind of masculinity, holding terror for women and campaigning fodder for feminists.

The state is the biggest gang in town[120]

There is an old saying in Russia that '[e]very country has a mafia but only in Russia does the mafia have a country'. 'Bratva', the Russian word for mafia, translates as brotherhood, an essentially patriarchal body, regardless of whether there are women in leadership roles. The international characterisation of Russia as a mafia state undoes the work that Putin has put in to build a proud national identity. Putin's links with organised crime are well documented, particularly with the Izmaylovo organised crime group. The group had joined forces with the FSB, successor to the KGB, both home to Putin before he entered politics, to form a murder squad that worked on getting rid of the competition. Once Putin became president, the Izmaylovo family became untouchable. There is a 'systemic entanglement' between criminal networks, the police and the state. Stephenson outlines the interdependencies in a 'reciprocal assimilation between state and organized crime'.[121] Many criminals aspire to state office itself and gradually turn illegal businesses into legitimate ones. For example, protection rackets metamorphose into private security companies either run by the gangs themselves or taken over by the FSB or the police. Having acquired a kind of legitimacy, they do not necessarily let go of the hoodlums who carried out their killings and intimidation but control them at arms-length via intermediaries.[122]

Putin's biographer, Artyom Kruglov, writes a blog on Putin's connections with the mafia that has been banned in Russia by what he describes as a mafia-controlled court.[123] Alexei Navalny's Anti-Corruption Foundation published an investigation in 2015 tracing the links between the Attorney General and the wives of imprisoned mafia bosses.[124] Navalny died in mysterious circumstances in a Russian jail in 2024. Alexander Litvinenko, ex-FSB officer who specialised in organised crime, accused Putin of drug trafficking and money laundering and died in the UK after being poisoned by the Russian state.[125] Litvinenko had broken the *omertà*, the Sicilian code of secrecy. Putin is allegedly worth $40 billion dollars, double the wealth of the king of Saudi Arabia, which would make him the richest man in Russia.[126] The US embassy cables leaked by WikiLeaks reveal that Russia has 'metastasised' into a 'virtual mafia state', whose activities include arms trafficking, kickbacks and extortion, suitcases full of money, secret offshore accounts and personal enrichment of officials, oligarchs and criminals, where bribery alone in the years up to 2010 amounted to $300 billion per annum.[127] José 'Pepe' Grinda Gonzalez, a Spanish prosecutor and expert on organised crime in Russia, describes Russia as a mafia state because it is impossible to differentiate the activities of the government from those of organised crime groups. The groups are used by the government to carry out nefarious activities that the government could not legitimately be seen to be involved in, such as keeping the oligarchs in check by killing them.[128]

Apart from actual traceable connections to criminal gangs, it has been argued that the state under Putin displays the traits of a mafia organisation: '[A]bsolute hierarchical loyalty, a disconnect between official titles and real influence (for example, key figures in Russia operate without formal government status), extreme secrecy in decision-making, and a special "honor code" outside the law that prizes reprisals against "traitors" and violence against competitors.'[129] Prigozhin was a prime example of someone without an official state title but apparently unlimited power.

Behind Prigozhin stood a long line of thugs with one foot in the underworld and one foot above ground who learnt, especially after Putin came to power, to grow their own semi-criminal enterprises to exactly that point where they were not going to pose a threat to Putin. Those who did not learn, like Prigozhin, met an untimely death. Mafia states are characterised by the presence of kinship networks in control of the finances and political power, although in the Russian context it was a fictive brotherhood forged by shared criminality and codes of honour and loyalty. According to Hungarian political scientist Bálint Magyar, mafia states are a particular kind of authoritarian state that came into being in post-communist states where 'public interests are permanently subordinated to private interests'.[130] There is no escape from these networks save through death or ejection. These closed groups pose a particular problem for women seeking relief or escape from domestic violence. Women may be at the heart of nurturing and perpetuating these networks, but their power is derived from their male connections.

Like the Italian mafia, the Russian mafia is very religious, as demonstrated by their ROC crosses and those who still have tattoos. Gangsters like Vladimir Barsukov used their substantial fortune to support the church and buy respectability.[131] There are a number of Russian oligarchs who support and fund the ROC in its fight for family values and against homosexuality. There are also pragmatic reasons for their support: the network of religious contacts has the power to hand out lucrative government contracts to God-fearing oligarchs.[132] If we needed a concrete example of how mammon, messiah and militarism conspire to work against women's rights, we need look no further than oligarch Konstantin Malofeyev, who owns ultra-conservative Tsargrad TV, which has furiously opposed any new legislation on domestic violence. He has funded the annexation of Crimea and the wars in Ukraine, calling Russia's aggression a 'holy war', and is deputy head of the Worldwide Russian People's Council, an organisation run by Kirill.[133] This web of male-dominated interests is so confident of its place in society that it does not even hide the connections. The visibility makes it no easier to unpick.

The crushing effect of patriarchy under Putin

Putin began his reign as a dubious democrat and evolved into a dictator who has manipulated the rules to remain in power for life, using the dictator's playbook to crush dissent by identifying it as the work of 'foreign agents' and bringing in legislation to criminalise the opposition and close down avenues of funding. A series of GONGOs (government funded organisations) apparently promoting women's rights and human rights were set up. One of them, the Council of the All-Russian Women's Forum, which was formed in 2008, promoted Russian Orthodoxy, family values and friendship with the authorities.[134] Other familiar ways of drawing the subversive sting of feminist critique was to promote faux versions of feminism. On the centenary of the Russian revolution, on IWD 2017, Fem Fest organised an event in Moscow in which glamorous 'actionistas' called for peace and unity with a plea to set aside concerns about inequality and rape—an example of the worldwide corporatisation of feminism that even had Russia in its clutches. It was an insult to the memory of the revolution and feminism everywhere. It invited writers of erotica to read from their work as if to underscore the idea of feminism as light and fluffy. Women's rights activists were outraged that the Moscow authorities had given these fake feminist actions permission to go ahead while they were not allowed to organise rallies in support of victims of violence or against unequal wages.[135] More radical women's groups had to frame their activities under 'maternalism' or traditional gender norms in order to survive.[136] Putin starved groups that did not sing from his hymn sheet of government funding or put restrictions on any foreign funding they might have raised.

The feminist flowering of the 1990s was crushed by a number of tractors. One of them was the new national focus on terrorism in the wake of the Moscow theatre siege[137] and the Beslan school massacre in 2002 and 2004 respectively.[138] Chechen separatism provided an excuse for a growing authoritarianism and an aggressively masculine governmental stance. Within this toxic scheme, feminist actions were tolerated as so many fleas to be shaken off unless their actions mocked Putin's masculinity or their demands were seen by the ROC to be an abomination. The absence of women-friendly laws is an example of the complete disregard towards women in Russia. While we know that such legislation can stand side by side with the most brutal violence against women, it still provides a yardstick by which to measure the extent to which the country's lawmakers have yielded to demands for action on this issue. In Russia, there is no legislation that defines or criminalises domestic violence. In 2017, the Duma downgraded 'battery within the family', defined as beating of a spouse or children, from a criminal offence to an administrative one in which incidents resulting in bruises or bleeding but not broken bones would simply attract a fine, community service or a brief prison sentence unless the offence was committed more than once a year.[139] Two women, lawmakers Olga Batalina and Elena Mizulina, authored and advocated for this. When women vote against their own interests, it is a sign of how deeply embedded patriarchy is in the system. Official statistics for the incidence of domestic violence put it at one in five women, which is lower than in many Western countries where police forces have become more sensitised to the issue. From anecdotal evidence of women being treated with disbelief or mockery when they report violence, it is quite likely that reporting rates are low. Alena Popova, who campaigned against these changes, believes that feminism is seen as a Western import that is 'ruining a unique Russian way of life'.¹⁴⁰

This is very much in keeping with the new ideological turn under Putin, who has sought refuge and pride, like other authoritarian populists, in national culture and traditional values to put clear water between Russia and the West and Russia and its immediate past. Any call to tradition is implicitly and explicitly a reinforcement of the most egregious patriarchal values. These values are pinned to women's aprons. While Putin is popular with some sections of the Russian population for his economic policy and military might, his reinforcement of gender stereotypes is also popular. A midsummer holiday was established to celebrate the nuclear, heterosexual 'Day of Family, Love, and Loyalty'.¹⁴¹ Yet, in reality there is a long tradition of single motherhood, dating back to Soviet times when large numbers of men died in the Second World War or were imprisoned in the gulags and there were high rates of divorce as a result of alcoholism and violence from men.¹⁴² Single women rely on their mothers for childcare, and 'family' mainly encapsulates the bonds between women and children.¹⁴³

The sex ratio of men to women throughout the twentieth century favoured women, particularly after the Second World War, when large numbers of men died. In 1946, there were seventy-five men to every 100 women,¹⁴⁴ a disproportionate ratio that continued into 2021, with eighty-six men to 100 women.¹⁴⁵ In 2006, Putin introduced economic incentives to boost population growth, a generous $10,000 lump sum payment to women who had a second or subsequent child, known as 'maternity capital', which they could spend as they wished on education, housing or retirement. This has been buttressed by increases in pre-natal care, childcare, parental leave, child allowance and homecare.¹⁴⁶ Maria Mies believes that women responded to the double burden of childcare and housework and working outside the home by refusing to have more children, by going on an informal 'birthstrike'.[147] An unsurprising concomitant of these policies was more restricted access to abortion: 'Putin's regime replaced the idea of women's equality with the idea of the state's protection of motherhood.'[148] This reinforcement of patriarchal values to deflect attention from inequality generally and the democratic deficit can also be seen in the strengthening of anti-abortion laws in El Salvador in the 1990s.

In a speech to the Duma in 2023, the Russian health minister criticised women who prioritised their education and careers above childbearing and supported a ban on abortion in private clinics, where 20 per cent of abortions are carried out.[149] Before the Ukraine war, the Health Ministry had always faced off the ROC on the question of abortion, arguing that a ban would mean more women getting abortions illegally, at risk to themselves, while women seeing government doctors for an abortion might be persuaded not to go through with it. Rather than recognising that the population of Russia is declining because of the more than 1 million excess deaths caused by COVID, the thousands dead in the Ukraine war and an exodus of draft dodgers, the focus is on restricting abortion rights.[150] The Foundation for Social and Cultural Initiatives, headed by the wife of Dmitry Medvedev, the former president/prime minister, which organises the annual anti-abortion campaign 'Give Me Life', frames abortion as infanticide, a moral and ideological issue, and not one about demographics.[151] Russian nationalists see contraception as a Western plot to weaken Russia and frame both contraception and abortion as national security issues.[152]

With this conservative turn towards the family, prostitution is hardly likely to receive an empathetic, non-victim-blaming state response. Although Putin boasts that Russian prostitutes are 'the best in the world', prostitution remains illegal in Russia today.[153] Between 1 and 3 million women are currently estimated to be working in the sex industry in Russia. More and more women have moved from the street to apartments, using the internet to find their clients. According to a special report for the BBC: 'The women are generally older (in St. Petersburg, the average age is 32), and a whopping 90 percent are mothers.'[154] The Ukraine war has affected the sex industry too. It has led to a drop in demand, which has encouraged women to reduce fees, compromise on health and safety and engage in dangerous, unprotected sexual activity, often with aggressive men who have returned from the front and feel an entitlement to their bodies in exchange for their patriotic services to the country. As the pro-family and 'protection of the fatherland' rhetoric was ratcheted up at the start of the war in Ukraine, the police crackdown on prostituted women increased.[155] While the fines levied are relatively small, the women fear a criminal record. Their illegal status allows police to harass and beat them up, especially transgender women under the harsh new anti-LGBT laws.[156]

As part of a protectionist, paternalist policy, women were historically excluded from 456 occupations in thirty-eight industries. In 2021, the Russian government shortened the list of occupations that were unavailable for women to 100 occupations in twenty-one industries. Oksana Pushkina, deputy chair of the State Duma Committee on Family, Women and Children, called for the abolition of even the new list, arguing that it 'ignores scientific and technological progress and rather protects well-paid jobs for men', which women had long suspected.[157]

Given this context, what is the space available for feminist action? Women's organisations felt an ambivalence towards the state. The formal equality in the Soviet Union, the constitutional guarantees of sexual equality, had not really transformed women's lives, but women did not want to lose the few rights they were granted under the law, nor did they want the very poor levels of social security withdrawn. Linda Racioppi and

RUSSIA

Katherine O'Sullivan See, who have researched women's activism in Russia extensively, found that

> there is a powerful sense among the women activists we interviewed that women's mobilisation in Russia must have as a primary goal the liberation of women from state control, as an experience distinct from but related to that of their male compatriots. It is a compelling motivator for movement building, but it is also fraught with insecurity.[158]

By 2000, there were several thousand NGOs, a large proportion of which were women's groups, led by women, employing nearly 2 million people and benefitting 30 million, nearly 20 per cent of the Russian population.[159] The organisations did not all claim to be feminist, partly because feminism itself was tainted by its association with the Soviet Union and therefore had to be rejected even though the Soviet Union had itself rejected feminism as a 'bourgeois' ideology and had striven for a kind of formal equality that did not do much to further the cause of women.

Two surveys of women's crisis centres that supported women facing domestic and sexual violence, one in 1999, before Putin became president, and the second in 2008/9, found that the centres played an important role in visibilising violence against women as an issue in Russia. The number of women killed annually has remained at nearly the same level as in Soviet times. In 2016, 64,400 acts of domestic violence against women were reported. In 2017, the figures dropped to half that following the decriminalisation of domestic violence when 'minor' battery became an administrative offence.[160] Interestingly, unlike in the UK, where economic abuse as a form of domestic violence was recognised much later, it was central to the work of most centres in Russia from the start because of the economic insecurity caused by the post-Soviet neoliberal regime and the consequent falling away of social services. In the early 2000s, these centres were mostly autonomous and not state funded. But by the end of Putin's second presidential term in 2008, there were few foreign institutional resources for the women's crisis centres to rely on. A 2006 anti-NGO law introduced greater monitoring of foreign funding and bureaucratic reporting requirements.[161] The centres were less likely to identify as feminist, but they all saw themselves as advocating women's rights, although they had become mostly service based as opposed to the earlier model, which included service plus politically transformative work. Half the centres had moved from a women-only space into a gender-neutral space dealing also with the rehabilitation of male perpetrators. The earlier feminist focus on women escaping male violence shifted to anyone who might face violence as a result of family dynamics, although women still remained the focus and they provided counselling for everybody, regardless of their gender.[162]

At the end of Putin's first decade as Russian leader, proposed restrictions on abortion rights and the award of an art prize to a convicted rapist acted as triggers for feminist activism, followed by the Pussy Riot performances. The proposed abortion law would have required the signature of a married woman's husband to approve her abortion, allowed doctors to refuse to perform abortions and restricted second-trimester abortions to those who had medical reasons or in cases of rape.[163] A woman had to wait two to seven days, depending on the stage of pregnancy, in case she changed her mind. Women pushed back against these proposed changes, and only two were adopted nationally: giving doctors the right to follow their conscience and a reduction in the waiting period to forty-eight hours. In 2012, the number of social reasons that allowed a woman to seek an abortion between weeks twelve and twenty-two—which included divorce, unemployment or low income—was cut down to one: rape. A government official even stated that ads for the adoption of animals was a propaganda tool of the child-free movement, persuading people to get dogs rather than children.¹⁶⁴

Despite the mushrooming of women's NGOs, the noughties are generally represented as a dead period as far as feminist action is concerned.¹⁶⁵ However, the weakness of the feminist movement is contested. Vanya Mark Solovey, a grassroots feminist who was involved in the movement for ten years before moving to Germany and transitioning, is keen to counter the commonly held view that only loud and visible protest presents a challenge to the state and argues that through their innumerable discussion groups, feminists were 'doing the fundamental work of challenging power as it is woven into the very tissue of social reality'.¹⁶⁶ He also places the start of the contemporary feminist movement to IWD 2006 rather than 2010 as other scholars have done, when a group of forty people demonstrated outside the Kremlin. Six women in pink balaclavas climbed the portico of a large shopping centre, perhaps foreshadowing Pussy Riot, and hung a banner shaped like a giant pair of panties, which declared: 'Flowers Today—Shackles Every Day?'¹⁶⁷ Other activists handed out leaflets that explained the revolutionary origins of IWD, not a day for handing out flowers to women to thank them for their work as mothers and caregivers.

Solovey does not believe that actions aimed at the state, what he calls 'contentious politics', should be a primary marker of the state of feminism in Russia. He describes the challenges of actions against the state. Whereas marches and rallies required authorisation, which was often withheld, single-person pickets did not require permission. Activists would therefore organise individual pickets standing at some distance from each other along the same street holding protest signs, or picketing queues in which protestors lined up with their placards and each would stand for a limited amount of time until the next person took their turn. The authorities wised up to this innovative attempt to bypass the laws and cracked down on it.¹⁶⁸ Solovey interviewed a number of feminists in Moscow, St Petersburg and two regional cities of Voronezh and Tomsk, who are active online and offline, in loose networks of individuals and organisations that dissolve and re-form. He argued that the role they played in awareness raising, in redefining the boundaries of feminism and creating a more widespread social acceptance of feminist ideas has created an environment in which a singer with feminist views like Manizha was chosen to represent Russia at the Eurovision Song Contest in 2021. She stands up for LGBTI rights, women's reproductive rights, is critical of sexist beauty standards and has launched an alarm-button app for women facing domestic violence.

The other difference between feminism in '90s Russia and the contemporary movement is that it has moved from academia and closed conference halls to online forums that sometimes extend beyond Russia to Russian-speaking areas, including ex-colonies like Ukraine and the diaspora of dissidents who have left Russia. There is a concerted attempt to connect with the general population. A non-exhaustive list of online feminist resources ran to twenty-eight pages in 2010. To justify his picture of Russian feminism as vibrant, Solovey believes that a list would be impossible to compile in 2020 given the vast number of resources:

> In 15 years, feminism in Russia has traveled from near-total media erasure to center stage on federal TV. From a non-issue only existing in public space as a joke and a stereotype, it has grown to occupy a highly contested, yet also highly visible place in the Russian political, social, and cultural landscape.¹⁶⁹

He takes issue with feminists who undervalue their online activism as destructive squabbles or 'doing nothing' because it does not amount to 'real action', such as street protests, or is not as useful as working with women escaping domestic or sexual violence.¹⁷⁰

RUSSIA

Feminist demonstrations that did not directly challenge the state were largely unaffected, unlike the draconian state reaction to Pussy Riot, whose lyrics were an affront to Putin, the state and religion. There were widespread actions against the watering down of the domestic violence offences in 2017, reinforced by outrage at the arrest of the Khachaturyan sisters in 2018, which included street rallies, online actions, blogs and theatre productions, some of it organised by a No to Violence website (Nasilieu. net), with women lawyers and women's rights advocates attempting to amend the bill, unsuccessfully to date. Until feminist protests against the 2022 extension of war in Ukraine, which were harshly dealt with, the patriarchy under Putin was more challenged by the campaign for LGBT rights than feminist demands. In 2016, two women faced charges of extremism for inciting hatred of men, and in 2021 a woman was charged with 'distributing pornography' and 'gay propaganda' for cartoons she published on social media.[171] In 2013, Putin banned gay pride rallies and dissemination of information about gay lifestyles to minors. In 2022, Putin signed off a new law restricting the promotion of 'LGBT propaganda', effectively outlawing any public expression of LGBT behaviour or lifestyle.[172] This affected books in libraries and bookshops, and all references to same-sex relationships were cut from TV and radio. In 2023, the government banned gender change, including surgery, passports in the new gender identity and the international LGBT movement as an extremist organisation, although no such organisation exists. It is too early to say what the impact of this law will be, but legal experts are advising members of the community to hide their sexual identity in public to avoid prosecution as an activist.[173] While this aggressive policing of 'deviant' sexualities could be interpreted as patriarchy in the ascendant, this excessive state reaction is also a sign of how beleaguered it feels.

The belief that military aggression is the ultimate form of patriarchy led to the setting-up of an online forum, the Feminist

Anti-War Resistance (FAR), within weeks of the invasion of Ukraine in February 2022. Women who oppose the war with Ukraine theorise a direct link with domestic violence: 'It is a fundamental idea behind Russian anti-war feminism that any act of violence begets more violence on a larger scale,' Liliya Vezhevatova, a FAR activist from Siberia now living in Armenia, explains. They oppose international calls for an immediate ceasefire and negotiated settlement because they argue that just as official restrictions on domestic abusers are ineffective, Ukraine cannot rely on UN interventions and peace treaties for protection. Putin exhibits classic abusive behaviour, perceiving peaceful intentions as signs of weakness. In this view, a peace treaty would leave Ukrainians living in occupied territories vulnerable to oppression, just as a woman remains vulnerable to her abusive husband when the policeman leaves the scene of the crime.[174]

FAR claimed a membership of nearly 2,000 activists across Russia in the first year, organising a number of demonstrations until the authorities cracked down and many activists left Russia. While the online Telegram group has nearly 40,000 members, only 200 activists are reportedly left behind in Russia. In the first ten weeks of the war, over 15,000 protestors were arrested, 40 per cent of whom were women. When they could no longer gather publicly, FAR members moved on to more creative forms of protests like erecting 1,500 crosses in Russian cities to remind people of the ongoing war. In August 2022, they poured red dye into the waters of the largest military memorial in Moscow to signify the blood of Ukrainians. 'Until the war, the Russian authorities didn't take feminism seriously,' says Vezhevatova.[175] As mentioned earlier, apart from some high-profile cases, feminists were generally spared jail sentences. It was after the 'success' of the anti-war movement that, in April 2023, a bill was introduced in the Duma calling for feminism to be banned on the grounds of it being an 'extremist' ideology. Oleg Matveychev, deputy chairman of the State Duma Committee on Information Policy, Information Technologies and Communications, who drafted the bill, accuses feminists of being against the Ukrainian war and for abortion and childlessness, which subverts Russia's demographic policies.[176] So far, it has not made it on to the statute books.

Conclusion

One of Putin's slogans is reputed to be 'Russia rising from its knees',[177] a change of posture made partly possible by standing on the prostrate bodies of women. It relies not only on imperialist adventures to swallow up independent states like Ukraine but boldly trumpets patriarchal, anti-democratic and Orthodox Christian values as signifiers of a proud Russian identity not to be confused with the weak moral fibre of the West. Groups of men who stand outside state regulation with the patronage, sometimes unacknowledged, of figures like Putin or Kirill, use bully boy tactics to shape the values of Russian society or reach the parts the state cannot. Religious values are enforced violently by ROC activists, but there is a veil drawn over their connections with the highest levels of the establishment. The centrality of family to Putin, to the Orthodox Church, to a mafia state, to masculinity with the father as head of the family and guardian of morality and traditional values, reinforced through legislation and religious activists, all interlock to form a straitjacket from which only Houdini might escape, not your average woman.

Within such a toxic framework, women are fighting a rearguard battle, keeping their horizons low and their hopes high. The key galvanising moments in the history of Russian feminism in the twenty-first century can be counted on the fingers of one hand: Pussy Riot; the protests against proposed restrictions to abortion rights in 2011; widespread protests against the proposed decriminalisation of domestic violence in 2016, which resurfaced in campaigns supporting the Khachaturyan sisters; and the grassroots online flash mob under the hashtag #IAmNotAfraidToSpeak drawing attention to sexual violence, also in 2016.

The full-scale invasion of Ukraine in February 2022 feels like a watershed moment for many progressives in Russia. For Adrianiva, it is a profoundly depressing moment because it represents a victory of the conservative forces that had been tussling with progressive forces for the upper hand until that point. While protest against the state was always risky, now the right to protest has been criminalised, which produces a chilling effect on activism. When safety has to be prioritised over connection, the space for feminism becomes too narrow.[178] FAR is fully aware that Telegram groups and green ribbons, symbols of the resistance, are not going to overthrow Putin, but it provides psychological sustenance to those who oppose the war and know by the ubiquity of the ribbons that they are not alone. Online groups strengthening their feminist identities and sharpening their ideological knives may yet prove to be a mass movement in waiting to rise up when the context is auspicious.

4

CHINA

I ASK FOR THE SWIFTEST HORSE

Beatrix Campbell

A young woman watches the 1998 Disney animation *Mulan*, based on a story that has been told in China for nearly 2,000 years. Mulan's marriage prospects are doomed, and when war is declared she decides to enlist instead of her father, a renowned soldier, now aging and frail. But she is a woman, and so she disguises herself, wears his armour and takes his sword. She becomes a great fighter and vanquishes the evil enemy. In the written version, published around the sixth century, Mulan is asked what she desires: 'I've no need for the post of a gentleman official, / I ask for the swiftest horse, / To carry me back to my hometown.'

Back in her family, she relinquishes her combat livery, and amid her surprised and awed comrades becomes a lady again in her family, her filial duty celebrated. The tale ends: 'The buck bounds here and there, / Whilst the doe has narrow eyes. / But when the two hares run side by side, / How can you tell the female from the male?'

PLANET PATRIARCHY

The young woman watching Mulan is Yinyin, an engineer who works for a large corporation. She had been inspired by Mulan's valour and victory: 'I remember thinking, though, that she didn't get any help, and, though there is a brief moment when she is able to relish her bravery for herself, it was always in the service of others.'[1]

Mulan's courage is motivated by filial loyalty, a system of generational debt that is still invoked in twenty-first-century China as if it were a law of nature. 'I don't think I believed in filial piety so much as I feared the consequences,' says Yinyin:

> My own mother, I felt, was making use of me. I think society colludes in that: every adult seems to have a vested interest in keeping a little slave, and freely admits their greed—they expect a return to come from children. To me there is nothing warm or honourable about this family system.

She is not alone: a mantra among young Chinese feminists is 'serve the people = sacrifice' and 'forget the people—be yourself'. To Yinyin's dismay, however, filial loyalty and patriarchy have become the battle hymn of twenty-first-century China. In 2023, President Xi Jinping's homily to the All-China Women's Federation (ACWF)—a servant of the Communist Party of China (CPC)—was to foster 'traditional Chinese virtues' and 'family values' in the service of 'national rejuvenation'.[2]

The mythic Mulan was again recruited in the People's Republic's pre-Disney gallery of female warriors. 'Gender work' was manifest in the emergence in the 1960s of the gleaming iconography of the Iron Girls, heroines of public manual labour mounting pylons and tractors, wielding spades or rifles, tilling and hewing and harvesting—above all, being strong. Historian Wang Zheng argues that they were not merely subaltern subjects; on the contrary, they had once been 'absent from cultural representations of China's drive for modernity', but now they were empowered.[3]

CHINA

Then the post-Mao state—Yinyin's time—recoiled at the concept of the Iron Girls: the concept was 'mocked mercilessly'[4] as an affront to nature in a 'manmade' backlash against socialism, feminism and assertive women generally.[5] The Iron Girls remain, however, a staunch if shadowy legend, lingering as a strangely resilient sensibility about women's stamina and self-discovery.

China's embrace of capitalism at the end of the 1970s, hailed as 'socialism with Chinese characteristics', is code for an authoritarian, state-sponsored patriarchal state capitalism that ruled by controlling women's reproductive rights, expropriating their labour, relying on their remittances to their rural families, denying their land rights, refusing them the right to their autonomous political agency as women—by relentless repression and violence. Its patriarchal polity did not die; it re-armed.

In the beginning

This chapter explores an extraordinary flowering of women's politics at the end of the twentieth century, experienced as both thrilling and dangerous, that was met by violent repression in the twenty-first century and the dissolution of NGOs and academic centres, some of which had been inspired by the 1995 United Nations Women's Conference in Beijing.

In China, gender equality had been a promise of the communist revolution that created the People's Republic of China (PRC) in 1949. The revolution repudiated Confucian patriarchy, China's dominant ideology that had transcended dynasties, empires and revolutions, that venerated tradition, deference, order and respect for elders. But by the end of the century, China's 'paramount leaders' resurrected Confucius in the name of law, order, tradition, hierarchy, male supremacy—and in the name of a 'harmonious society'. It was an eerie, troubling invocation of the distant past to frame the future. Their invocation of ancient lore exemplified what historians Eric Hobsbawm and Terence Ranger meant by 'the invention of tradition': an attempt to structure social life as unchanging and invariant, by 'the sanction of precedent and continuity' to promote a future. But the peculiarity of 'invented tradition', they warn, is that the imagined continuity is 'largely factitious'.[6]

What did tradition mean in China? It meant foot-binding; domestic confinement; baby towers, structures where abandoned infants could be left;[7] and femicide. Women were 'like slaves, the subjects of commercial transactions,' writes Japanese historian Noboru Niida.[8] 'Few societies in history prescribed for women a more lowly status or treated them in a more routinely brutal way than traditional Confucian China.' Thus begins Kay Ann Johnson's book *Women, the Family and Peasant Revolution in China* (1983),[9] a pioneering analysis of the communist revolution and its often ambivalent engagement with the Confucian ideology that had bequeathed a thoroughly patriarchal lore of life, the notion of yin and yang: female *yin*, dark, cold, negative, deathly; and male *yang*, light, celestial, warm and positive. Women were to obey men, demonstrate submission and self-effacement. She ends with a prescient caution: 'Unreformed family structures and attitudes coupled with a seemingly desperate programme for population control may again threaten an unknown number of female lives in China.'[10]

The feudal principles, deeply embedded in everyday life, were to be rejected by the extraordinary radicalism of the revolution, above all for poor women. One of the communist government's first new laws was the 1950 Marriage Law of the PRC, which aimed to release women from extreme patriarchal bondage and end concubinage. The government legislated for free marriage, monogamy and equal rights between men and women. These measures were inseparable from land reform in that they enabled women to acquire a share of land and 'become creators of family wealth'.[11] That they were adopted was testament to women's political pressure and the role of the ACWF as an educator and advocate in the villages, often in the face of deep and sometimes brutal resistance.

In 1954, China's constitution proclaimed that '[w]omen in the People's Republic of China enjoy equal rights with men in all spheres of life, political, economic, cultural and social, and family life'. But in 1980, following the death of the People's Republic's 'founding father', Mao Zedong, its new 'paramount leaders', notably Deng Xiaoping, embarked on the Four Modernisations: reform of agriculture, industry, defence and science and technology to increase both productivity and popular consumption. But not to end patriarchy. Nor to encourage democracy. This period has come to be known as the transition. After modernisation bred mass protests against wild inequalities—quelled by the military violence at Tiananmen Square in 1989—the party invoked the Confucian idea of a 'harmonious society'.[12]

Johnson was right. A rhetorical ruse masked what we call socialist patriarchy. How did that happen? This chapter explores the context and consequences of the ferocious imposition of a one-child policy and the injection of capitalism, marketisation of agriculture and manufacturing and the rehabilitation of patriarchal Confucian family values.

The Four Modernisations

Millions of young rural women locked in patriarchal custom made their way to the cities where they encountered freedoms and 'new forms of sexual oppression',[13] the modernisation of patriarchy. This was expressed not only in social structures but in strategic nuances and contingencies of political language, specifically terms such as 'feminism' and 'class'—the former denounced as Western and bourgeois, the latter erased by the post-Mao partnership between the state and capitalism that jettisoned class as a category of exploitation.

China would in some ways resemble the modernised patriarchy of the 'Asian tigers', its neighbours, typically South Korea, Japan and Hong Kong. All of them would be characterised by the profound political separation of production from social reproduction—the structural feature of patriarchy: 'growth first' policies, supported by strong neoliberal states (or dictatorships) with weak welfare systems that depended on patriarchal family culture, and the unpaid labour of women, to manage the reproduction of everyday life. Violence was always available to the CPC against political challenge from within and without the party, in the not uncommon social movements, strikes and protests that culminated in Tiananmen Square. The 1995 UN Conference on Women in Beijing had a dramatic impact until its implications, particularly on men's violence against women, were quelled.[14]

While the Four Modernisations invited capitalist interventions in new special economic zones, with irresistible economic and infrastructural inducements provided by the state, it pulled out of thousands of state-owned enterprises and the social welfare system that went with them that were irreducibly vital to women's emancipation. The ethic of the Four Modernisations was flagged in a foundational challenge to official egalitarianism in March 1978, when the party announced women's place in the new order: women 'need to work hard and study, but they have to spend a considerable portion of their time tending to housework and children'.[15] What was the meaning of *but*? That three-letter word signified a redistribution of resources away from women; there was no expectation that men, or society generally, would share responsibility for social reproduction.

This patriarchal regression—the first of several—was made explicit at the fourth national congress of the ACWF a few months later, in September 1978. The federation had been dissolved during the Cultural Revolution: one of its leaders, Kang Keqing, was placed under house arrest, and Dong Bian, the heroically inventive editor of the federation's magazine *Women of China*, was dismissed.[16]

Kang Keqing had been sold to a landlord when she was one month old and treated as a slave until she escaped, joined the Red Army, cut her hair, carried a rifle and became a renowned fighter. She was taught to read by future military leader Zhu De, her husband-to-be, and together they participated in the gruelling Long March in 1935. After the 1949 revolution, she was a women's federation leader. Now elderly and rehabilitated, Kang Keqing and Dong Bian appeared at the re-convened ACWF's congress, where the CPC central committee once again reminded the federation of its subaltern *raison d'être*: to mobilise women for the party, for the state, for production and for the care of everyone.

'Conservative retreat'

Feminists in the CPC 'made tremendous efforts' to institutionalise gender equality, but inequality found new forms.[17] 'A new cohort of Chinese feminists' emerged and engaged in transnational dialogue that changed the feminist paradigm in China by insisting on the theory of 'gender' as a political system.[18] But China expert Phyllis Andors tracked the regression: 'Any lingering doubts about the shift in policy towards women were dispelled' when the women's congress was informed that women should bring their traditional support skills to the service of industry and the home.[19] This was nothing less than a 'conservative' blow to the party's earlier 'goals of female emancipation' and the current 'politics of women's liberation'.[20] Sociologist Yige Dong echoes the verdict that the transition was manifestly gendered: women's paid employment sank, and social services were re-located to municipalities, privatised or abandoned.[21]

The proponent of the transition, Deng Xiaoping, was an audacious veteran of the revolutionary movement who became a 'paramount leader' following the deluge of Mao's capricious and cruel Cultural Revolution, which pilloried the country's intellectuals and closed down its education system for a decade. Deng had spent time in the young, war-torn Soviet Union, when the Bolsheviks launched a tactical experiment, the New Economic Policy, a mixed economy of public and private enterprise, to inspire productivity.

Contrary to expectations, and contrary to Marxist theory, which anticipated socialism as a response to capitalism's contradictions, the great communist revolutions of the twentieth century occurred first in Russia and then China, in exhausted, impoverished pre-capitalist peasant societies. Deng had long believed that Marxist theory predicated communism on material abundance. The task, he explained, was to get rich, 'to develop productive forces ... steadily improve the life of the people and create the material conditions for the advent of communist society. There can be no communism with pauperism.'[22] To which women might have added—had they been consulted—that there can be no communism with patriarchy.

China's enticing re-invention in the 1980s enabled foreign corporations to flee the industrial world's terrain of organised labour movements and social welfare systems to which it was obliged—through taxation—to contribute, and to maximally exploit and control a vast Chinese workforce that was disciplined but politically disorganised. The rush to the East was not like the violent conquest of Africa, the Americas or Asia; it was orderly and invited, it was premised not on gold but the treasure of millions of desperate, hungry, literate—more or less—workers. It was a 'vision of a socialist modernity' in all but name, undisturbed by egalitarian—not to mention feminist—priorities.[23] The state's withdrawal from 'social protection', from what we could call social responsibility,[24] was nothing less than redistribution away from women and children. Almost a third of pre-schools were closed between 1997 and 2006, and most of the rest were privatised. Labour force participation among young mothers of children under two years old declined from 89 per cent in 1990 to 56 per cent in 2005 and from 91 per cent to 71 per cent among mothers of children under six years old.[25] Men's labour market participation, 97 per cent, was unchanged by the transition, or by fatherhood.[26]

Irreconcilable class, regional, rural/urban, generation and gender differences transformed a gap into a crevasse. China became one of the most unequal societies in the world, where 'soaring popular protests' were met by 'severe repression' and violence.[27] How did it get there? This chapter addresses the convergence of the notorious one-child policy and the impact of the 'Four Modernisations'.

Frisson of delight

'Socialism with Chinese characteristics' was the landscape in which Yinyin was raised, where in the early 1980s little children serenaded an experiment unique in human history—and, in its impact on girls, a paradox. American anthropologist Susan Greenhalgh remembers feeling 'a frisson of delight' when she witnessed a troupe of children singing 'one child is the very best, one child is the very best!' on the streets of the southern city of Zhangzhou. Yinyin is a beneficiary of the serenading children's anthem.

China's one-child-per-couple policy was the greatest paradox of patriarchy: millions of girls were abandoned or died, female foetuses were aborted; and millions of living girls were assured that they were as good as boys. But always there, in the air, was the knowledge that *socially* boys were preferred. Yinyin was aware of her mother's disappointment: 'I had the feeling that I was second best.' Yinyin sensed it in her mother's laments: 'My mum would say, "I only have you. My friend has a son, but I only have you."'

Yinyin was always reminded of a girl's responsibility to excel, 'to be outstanding when the male equivalent only had to be mediocre'. By contrast, another young professional woman tells me that 'the one-child policy was a good thing for women: because in my generation we were the only children, so the family invested everything in the daughters'. She tells me about a saying that 'people born after one-child policy are little emperors or little princesses, that we are selfish. I think it's kind of true—that we are more self-centred than women before us. City girls like me have more opportunities than other generations, and that's to do with one-child policy.'

But ultimately, women of this generation discovered they were not the favoured ones. 'You can imagine a single daughter who was treated as a princess from day one, who had high expectations of herself, enjoyed two generations of family resources, received an excellent education and performed superbly through her school career,' says Prof. Wang Zheng, 'but then encounters blatant discrimination when she graduates.' That is the moment when they discover 'this world is dominated by men'.[28]

Yinyin exemplifies the existential crisis for girls:

> In school I fulfilled the expectations of a son, I was a good student, I was very good, but when I graduated suddenly there was talk of marriage. I was extremely ashamed—I thought that just happened in the countryside, not in the city, and not to me. My pride prevented me from telling people, I was angry, I lashed out emotionally, I became a difficult person—it was mostly anger, and a bit of snobbery. I wanted my class privilege to protect me from this thing. I closed myself off, I lost friends, I was so angry. I later discovered that my school friends they were in similar situations. We didn't think to admit our situation to each other.

CHINA

At school, she had been very clever and diligent, yet there was always the shadow of boys: 'It was important to me to compete against boys. When I was young, I felt I had to compete for my survival. I didn't like being inferior.'

This generation of young women belong to a unique cohort born of that one-child policy, 'one of the largest and most controversial social engineering projects in human history'.[29] It was conceived during the uncertain conjuncture following the death of Chairman Mao.[30] When Mao died in 1976, illiteracy was down to 25 per cent from 80 per cent in 1949. After the PRC was created, the living standards, health and employment of millions of people radically improved, but his reign was lashed by devastating consequences—famine induced by the Great Leap Forward and then the chaos and destructive purges of the Cultural Revolution.

Mao's mercurial political experiments left a failing economy, starvation, collapsed institutions and professionals and intellectuals whose fate had been disgrace or death. And patriarchy. In his wake, the communist leadership addressed the havoc left by Mao, contemplated a new constitution, invited capitalist investment, restored rural 'household responsibility' to invigorate agriculture, re-instated the institutions, resumed mass education and invested in science and infrastructure. Central to this medley of 'reform' was the imposition of drastic control over the birth rate in 1980: China's 916,395,000 people were soon to be 1 billion when the government imposed one child per family, even though by 1979 China's birth rate had already fallen from an average of 5.8 children per woman to 2.7 per woman.[31]

Though the 'beautiful dream' may have enriched the life of the infant chorus witnessed by Greenhalgh, millions of others were wrenched by its draconian implementation.[32] This unprecedented mass intrusion upon women's bodies had been designed and implemented by the male political elite who had no inkling of or interest in the policy's impact on women's physical and sexual autonomy, or its effects in a culture characterised by a 'strict patrilineality, patriarchy and patrilocality system. In such a system, men were dominant in wealth inheritance, living arrangements, family line continuity and intrahousehold power structure.'[33]

In 1950, despite decades of war, there were more men than women in China, with 52 per cent males and 48 per cent females.[34] When the one-child policy was enforced, the deadly impact of patriarchy on population was already well known.

In 1990, there were 50 million 'missing women'. In 1992, welfare economist Amartya Sen, the first Asian to win the Nobel Prize in Economics, calculated that there were 100 million missing women in the world, figures that 'tell us, quietly, a terrible story of inequality and neglect leading to the excess mortality of women'.[35]

Greenhalgh prized open the secret 'black box' of the policy's genesis. It originated in the protected, elite milieu of defence and rocket—not social—science.[36] At the end of the 1970s, these men had declared a crisis—population—and proposed a solution: immediate mass birth control. The scholars involved were forbidden to research the gender dimension.[37]

Apocalypse

The belief that the world was over-populated, that it would not be able to feed itself, became an apocalyptic dread in the 1960s and 1970s. In 1974, the United Nations Population Conference in Bucharest anticipated fearful recommendations for tough birth control campaigns, backed by an international financial elite. But China 'delivered a blistering attack on the super-powers for their plundering of the poor countries' while complaining that the 'Third World' was over-populated.[38]

A torrent of resolutions challenged the population control agenda, together with robust lobbying by women's organisations internationally. An alternative to forced control over women's bodies coalesced in a plan of action recommending parents' right to determine the size of their families,[39] the promotion of contraception and, in particular, gender equality.[40] The following year, the United Nations declared 1975–85 as the Decade of Women. Feminism was becoming, if not the zeitgeist exactly, if not hegemonic exactly, then certainly a politics that had to be addressed. For feminists, the priority was women's autonomy, control over their own bodies. But that was not the priority in Delhi or Washington—or, soon, in Beijing.

A small group of Marxist 'humanist' scholars with close ties to peasant communities warned that the one-child policy would produce a 4–2–1 structure—one child, two working adults and four elderly parents—that could only be achieved by 'brute coercion'.[41] The strategy changed the terms of China's sexual contract: women's sexual autonomy was rescinded, and implementation fell to the ACWF, which had always been steered by the party leadership.[42] Since 1949, there had been 'no women's movement if we define it as a social movement, outside of government control,' commented Chinese historian Wang Zheng.[43]

But the federation was also more than the creation of the state: its vast grassroots organisation placed it among women, among their sorrows, their needs and their ambitions. During the period known as the Great Leap Forward between 1958 and 1961, it inspired the organisation of hundreds of thousands of cafeterias and childcare centres.[44]

Later, many of its cadres lamented the chaos and cruelty of the Cultural Revolution in the 1960s; the women's federation was abolished, and in 1968, Women's Liberation Movements burgeoning in the US and Europe were condemned as bourgeois.[45] However, by the 1980s, the ACWF had been re-instated, and it became more assertive, urging women to embrace the 'four selfs': 'self-respect, self-confidence, self-improvement and self-reliance'.[46] It opposed coercion to enforce the one-child policy,[47] especially in the countryside, where the policy was compromised by the long history of preference for sons, families' need of children as part of their labour force and patrilocal marriage, in which the couple settles in the husband's home and community. The ACWF condemned son preference and the ancient—and ongoing—practice of female infanticide and woman abuse.[48] Its own research found that many women and girls had been distraught or harmed by the policy.[49] But it was sacrosanct, and the ACWF was recruited as a key agent of implementation.

Lisa Rofel's book on three generations of women employed in a silk-weaving factory describes the birth control office, run by a young woman named Li Hua, a kind of fertility auditor, who maintained a forensic inventory of the hundreds of women workers on marital status, age, types of birth control used, numbers of abortions or adoptions, menstruation patterns and relationship compatibility. It was Li Hua from whom workers sought permission to marry. She calculated the likely birth rate if women married early or later and the number of generations produced within a hundred years. All of it women's responsibility: 'Women's bodies serve as threshold figures for the national body.'[50]

The contours of these women's intimate and social universe, so intensely mapped, measured and interrupted, thoroughly unsettled the assumed naturalness of bodies and birth. Li Hua embodied the hand of the state, yet she wove control over hundreds of women's bodies with threads of concern and care.

What is a woman?

Tactical manoeuvres to recuperate women's relative political autonomy appear throughout the entire history of the PRC. ACWF activists had to promote their interests within a 'treacherous political environment' that obliged them to improvise codes, to calculate what to say—and what not to say or do, or be.

Not only feminism but the meaning of *feminine*, what it meant to be a woman, was contested throughout the PRC's history. Gail Hershatter, a great historian of China, insists that its 'modern history is not comprehensible without close attention to women's labor and Woman as a flexible symbol of social problems, national humiliation, and political transformation'. She calls this ideological endeavour the 'symbolic work performed by gender itself'.

The post-Mao state from the iconic, egalitarian Iron Girls. They were 'mocked mercilessly' as an affront to nature,[51] as masculinised women, fake boys and even 'mutant'.[52] Elite men's visceral protest appeared as a 'manmade' backlash against socialism, feminism and against assertive women generally.[53] The post-Mao paramount leaders' epitaph to the Iron Girls was to control women's bodies and to invite foreign capital to invest in their hyper-exploitation. Then they bludgeoned feminist protests and weaponised Confucian tradition to tame women—not so much to restore 'home' and 'family' and domesticity as their exclusive habitat, not to evict them from the labour force, but to renew 'the work of gender' to naturalise the sexual division of labour, to restore 'feminine' duty and repair the calamitous consequences of the one-child policy for women, men and social reproduction generally.

Popular culture was not always susceptible to the paramount leaders' worldview—television and cinema attracted huge audiences for lavish costume dramas, lifestyle shows and films exploring the hazards and heroism of women's everyday lives: *Her Story* about single parenthood, a young mother finding solidarity in neighbours and friends; *Like a Rolling Stone*, a sixty-year-old working-class woman quits horrible, thankless family life and finds 'freedom' in her campervan adventure; and *YOLO*, a surprisingly big hit about a glum, overweight, unlikeable woman who gets a job, joins a boxing club, gets fit enough for a real fight—she doesn't win, but she finds herself and feels like a winner as she strides off, alone, into a wintry sunset. It seemed that the Iron Girls remained a spectral memoir that lingered as a strangely resilient sensibility about women's stamina and self-discovery. If the stamina of the Iron Girls was disparaged, in *YOLO* it was relished.

An events organiser born in Beijing, Cecilia (her pseudonym), recalls that

> when I was young, I was sometimes picked on and called names for being a tomboy by a few boys in my class: to these provocations I usually responded with my fists. I've definitely noticed the feminisation of women, especially in advertisements—emaciated and trying to replicate the 'loli' look (from the Japanese genre 'lolicon', which is a portmanteau of the 'Lolita complex'). East Asian men's preference for women who are 'white, young, and thin' seems unparalleled.[54]

Millions of people, mostly women, were also viewing what came to be known as 'big heroine dramas', opulent, ravishing series about dynastic combat, with huge casts of exquisite, mincing, Machiavellian femininity, fearless, flying, killing, navigating the ascent to peak concubinage as the emperor's chosen one. Variously interpreted as quasi-feminist histories or lean-in neoliberalism,[55] the spine of these lavish dramas was always gender and power—while patriarchy was an un-concept in official discourse, it infused popular culture.

Not one child, but no child

The synergy between the one-child policy and the dissolution of China's welfare state had created the predicted demographic crisis: the elderly would comprise a quarter of the population by 2030. Millions of girls had been denied the opportunity to live, by infanticide, neglect, abandonment and sex-selective abortion. In 2015, couples were allowed to have two children, later increased to three in 2022.

Why embark on such a draconian strategy? By 2000, the birth rate had fallen below the society's replacement level, the number of babies that must be born to maintain the population. It had caused great anguish and encouraged corruption, and a decline in the birth rate would still have happened with the less restrictive 'later, longer, fewer' policy of the 1970s.[56]

What it certainly achieved was a perverse patriarchal dividend. Falling fertility was not unique—it was a global phenomenon—but the consequences for the most patriarchal modern economies were different and dire.[57] China was left with a care crisis at both ends of the life span: in the countryside, children who were 'left behinds' when their parents went to work in the cities were underdeveloped, undernourished and undereducated, cared for by elders in villages without access to a welfare state.

An ACWF survey found that only 21 per cent of women said they wanted a second child, still less a third, citing prohibitive housing and healthcare costs, and the responsibilities of caring not only for a child but their elderly parents. The reckless synergy of procreation control, emaciated social services and pervasive patriarchal culture had not only skewed the gender demographic, it also accelerated childlessness among young women.

Before marketisation, female labour force participation in China was 84 per cent compared with the Organisation for Economic Co-operation and Development average of 61 per cent. Thereafter, it sank steadily to its lowest at 60 per cent by 2023.[58] China's gender pay gap had been one of the lowest in the world but rose instantly and became higher than the global average: women's earnings fell to 71 per cent of men's, across all ages and educational levels.[59] In the international equality league, China fell to a new low, 102, between Greece and Malaysia.[60] Chinese researchers Guangye He and Xiaogang Wu are unequivocal: 'marketisation' is the main driver of the increase in gender pay inequality.[61] The gap is 'smallest in government and public institutions', but it soared rapidly in the 2000s in the private sector, where 80 per cent of urban workers are employed.[62] Nearly 20 per cent of job advertisements for the civil service in 2018 were outright sexist: they called for 'men only, or men preferred' or 'suitable for men'. More than half of jobs advertised by the Ministry of Public Security specified 'men only'. Many job ads required women to be married with children.[63]

It was in the context of women's declining relative earnings and labour force participation, loss of rural property rights, weak political representation and the prevalence of sexism and men's violence that in 2021 the State Council launched a ten-year National Programme for Women's Development 2021–30.[64] It hoped gender equality would become 'more deeply rooted in the hearts of the people'[65]—polite recognition that China's collective political-psyche remained patriarchal.

Yinyin explains that she had expected, during her student days, to get married—her education was expected to work as a kind of dowry, a gift to her husband: 'My parents' expectation was typical: they wanted a girl to have a good education because it would be a good accessory to her husband's career.' But she hated the expectation that 'my husband would be more successful than me. I would just be a background to his success.' She finds it puzzling—'so many women I know work hard and then at home they work hard, too, and they concede authority to their husbands'.

Cecilia reckons that

> among my classmates, about half have been married and divorced—often within about a year. It seems they realise pretty fast, really, how terrible the men are—verbal violence and cheating. An older generation would have put up with it—saving face is so important in China. And they realise that getting into a relationship with a man will negatively affect their career prospects. Relationships aren't a priority among my straight friends. Romantic love is not a very popular thing in China. And after COVID people are fed up, and many don't want to have children.[66]

China was learning that many women were finding ways to resist patriarchy if not in the political realm then in their personal strategies—not least mutiny against marriage and motherhood: 44 per cent of young, unmarried urban women aged between eighteen and twenty-five do not intend to marry, according to a Young Communist League Survey.[67]

Patriarchy's comeuppance

Yinyin is heterosexual and has relationships with men, but she will not marry or become a mother: 'I experience a lot of guilt—because I was born for a harder life.' She has a high income, she often works abroad, her parents' deaths have freed her from the fate of a Chinese daughter: 'I feel released. My mother often guilt-tripped me—she conveyed a sense that life had left her behind and marriage didn't give her a better life.' At the same time, the decision not to marry leaves her feeling 'odd, dislocated, part of me feels a bit at a loss'.

A friend at her school became very successful, 'but she has pinged a post thanking her father and her husband. I can't imagine her husband thanking his mother or his wife.' She could never discuss that, though, because China's full-bodied hierarchical culture meant that this woman's success placed her 'out of my league. I could not presume to be her friend. Social hierarchy in China is a bit like South Korea or Singapore.'

In the 2020s, the 'paramount' patriarchs had their comeuppance: betrothed in a doomed marriage of 'socialism with Chinese characteristics' and President Xi Jinping's concept of statecraft, a 'second integration', wedded to the country's ancient Confucian 'cultural and civilisational soil'.[68]

Worlds of work

Agriculture

By the 2050s, China's landscape will likely no longer look like the patchwork of small farms that at the beginning of the century were scattered across the country, seemingly vast, but becoming too small to feed its 1.4 billion people. Industrial food production will cage billions of cows and chickens, circulated through milking sheds and shelves for egg-laying chickens, where bird corpses will be collected by robots, with pigs housed in pig 'skyscrapers', multi-story piggeries that will contain the animals, feed them and convert their waste into fertiliser.

After the 1949 revolution, collectivisation of farming transformed the lives of impoverished peasants, the majority of China's population, and especially of women. China met its growing demand for food largely through its own agricultural production,[69] despite volcanic politics and limited natural resources. Crop yields steadily increased, albeit interrupted by the famine caused by Mao's Great Leap Forward in the 1950s and the chaos of the Cultural Revolution in the 1960s. The Four Modernisations seeded another country: within four decades, the rural majority became an urban majority. At the beginning of the twenty-first century, Chinese agriculture was still based on family farming, small scale—on average around 2.5 acres. 'Household responsibility' was restored to encourage private initiative and a free market in food, and modernisation brought huge state investment in research and development. In the longer term, it was unsustainable: unprecedented urbanisation and degradation of the environment—reduction of the water table and pollution above and below ground—provoked the state to invest in energy, water conservation, food storage, soil rehabilitation and environmental protection.[70]

The Mao-era rural workers—60 per cent female—had no social welfare entitlement. Worse, China's *hukou* household registration system—dividing the population into two classes, rural and urban—was designed to restrict internal migration by limiting their access to public services. Post-Mao, urban capitalism was released from an obligation to contribute to the costs of living. Professor Rachel Murphy argues that the 'structures that prevent children from accompanying their migrant parents to the cities depress employers' and municipal governments' costs in competitive globalising markets'.[71] Initially, men's mass migration left village women in a 'patriarchal trap', disconnected from decision-making, economically and psychologically dependent on absent migrant husbands.[72] According to the ACWF, in 2016 there were 61 million left-behind children, 47 million women and 45 million elders.[73] In the twenty-first century, a third of China's labour force never makes it through high school. Despite its tech-savvy reputation, China ranks below similar 'middle-income' countries whose development is compromised by failure to invest enough in human capital, such as South Africa, Türkiye and Mexico.[74] And like these countries, the deep class cleavage between rural and urban workers is rendered a chasm by the gender gap. Though the government has intervened to raise rural incomes, notably with the Targeted Poverty Alleviation programme from 2013, rural households' per capita disposable income is 40 per cent of that of urban households.[75]

Women bore responsibility not only for farming but everything else—household labour, childcare and eldercare. They endured 'psychological stress and sexual repression' in their relationships, and the anxieties of separation and abandonment were endured by both sexes.[76] Women's longer life expectancy often left them contemplating their 'lonely sunsets'.[77] Children are legally required to support elders, a 'national legal stipulation',[78] and three-quarters of rural elders are entirely supported by their families. However, there is a perceived generational transformation: while women once calculated that appeasement secured married tranquillity, younger wage-earning women became less tolerant of their workload and husbands going out drinking and playing Mahjong.[79]

Domestic life became more conflicted, then, at the very moment when President Xi's response to the declining population placed women at the fulcrum of halcyon happy families propaganda and 'a new culture of marriage and childbearing'.[80] Children faced 'a generational debt for them to repay, through diligence in their studies,' writes Murphy, whose pioneering research on the impact on children of the great migration confirmed that children had not been consulted and 'many recalled feeling unable to speak as they watched their parents packing to leave'.[81] Patriarchal tradition was also palpable in the obligation to save up towards sons' housing and wedding costs, while their obligation to daughters ended with their education.[82] Migration had contradictory effects on women, whose circulation back and forth brought back to the village expectations, aspirations and money.[83] Delia Davin, a chronicler of rural women's lives in China, comments that 'no one individual has complete autonomy within the family-based society of rural China, but some certainly gain increased independence'. Sometimes one form of authority was exchanged for another: in factory dormitories, there was a strict curfew, and women shared a room with eight or ten others, with their employers exercising strict financial control by remitting their pay to their families.[84] Yet migration also disrupted 'the day to day functioning of the family power structures in which authority is conveyed by age and sex'.[85]

Women began to deal with village officials directly, and they were 'pushed into contact with the modern world', with banks and post offices, which proved an empowering experience for young women 'who formerly met few strangers and were closely controlled by senior family members'. Back in the village, life was depleted, peopled by the left-behind who bore the gendered and generational consequences: loss, loneliness and longing, interrupted by the brief comings and goings of villagers employed in the cities. In the twenty-first century, then, farming in China is mainly carried out by what Chinese sociologist Yuqin Huang calls the 'greying' and 'feminization' of the agricultural work force.[86] So who, asks Huang, will be farming in ten years' time?

Manufacturing

Although the promotion of women's engagement in waged work and the principle of equal pay were fundamental principles of Marxist egalitarianism, there was no consensus on the meanings of work, home, ownership, inside and outside, day and night, intimate and public. Hershatter's vivid, encyclopaedic history of elderly rural women's memories of everyday life in Shaanxi reports that when machine-made cloth was 'scarce and rationed', women 'spun by moonlight ... we made shoe soles, twisted thread and treated nighttime like day'.[87] Hershatter argues that 'needlework encapsulates the memories of an entire epoch'.[88] This 'home' work followed the women everywhere, to political meetings and the fields.[89] But it did not change the meaning of 'work', it did not travel to 'house' and 'home', and in a system in which wages were based on points, domestic labour attracted no points, and therefore no pay. Hershatter writes that the 'inner' realm was rendered 'inarticulable', and so 'large parts of women's daily existence'—and their contribution to the private and public economy—'went missing, unavailable to be addressed, even by themselves'.[90]

Post-Mao, the mass journey from farm to factory became from farm and factory to office, where women worked as 'business service personnel' for the 'lowest recorded average earnings'. China exploded the pro-capitalist theory that 'companies should determine wage levels based on a worker's productivity'. The opposite happened. And private enterprises 'did not feel bound by official equality policies'.[91] Everywhere in the world, 'guru masculinity' located the guru in the firm, not the family, or the society, where they depended on state-sponsored infrastructure and the growing precariat, among whom, in the early 2000s, only 12.5 per cent had signed contracts, only 48 per cent were paid regularly, 68 per cent had no weekly day of rest and 54 per cent were never paid for overtime.[92]

PLANET PATRIARCHY

Labour laws and lawbreakers

Confronted by great protest, capitalist patriarchs revealed themselves to be enthusiastic lawbreakers when workers mobilised against employers' refusal to sign contracts, pay wages or social insurance. By 2008, only 50 per cent of enterprises had signed labour contracts. The private sector was the main culprit: fewer than 20 per cent of workers were employed in the state sector; migrants were up to 40 per cent of the urban labour force, more than half of them women, and they had no entitlement to social welfare, health and education.[93]

The Chinese economic miracle enlisted millions of women (and, of course, men) in electronics factories producing cheap commodities, but above all, the phones and screens available everywhere, the iconic signifiers of modernity. They endure pitiless payment regimes, routine bullying and sexual harassment, fearful that protest would force them out. Like male migrants, they were housed in makeshift shanties on the edges of the cities or warehoused in crammed, curfewed dormitories.

Foxconn—the world's largest electronics manufacturer, notably for Apple—exemplifies the labour process of the China miracle. It employs 1.3 million people in China. The king of 'free market' capitalist innovation was in fact the beneficiary of government munificence. Located in the inland Henan city of Zhengzhou, it makes half of the world's iPhones in a vast factory complex, including dormitory blocks for thousands of migrant workers, built on corn and wheat fields; roads were laid with $600 million donated by the provincial government.[94] But no childcare. Sociologist Yige Dong points out that in Zhengzhou, mothers often opt for 'a seasonal gig'—informal, insecure status—to take advantage of 'peak demand' factory seasons and the overtime strategically 'hoarded' by the employers. They work as unpaid providers of care and domestic labour in patriarchal households and as seasonal paid labour for patriarchal employers.[95]

CHINA

In 2020, women and men in Chengdu, making iPhone watches and iPads, organised protests against the failure to pay wages—also known as 'pay theft'—by Foxconn's illegally outsourced contractors and recruitment brokers.[96] The company denied responsibility—these workers weren't Foxconn workers, they were outsourced.

Zhu Xiaomei had worked in the Hitachi metal factory in Guangzhou since she was a teenager: 'Back then, most workers were from rural areas, and we felt content just to earn more than our contemporaries down on the farm.' And yet, in this highly politicised society, '[w]hen our rights were violated, we didn't know what to do or who to turn to'.[97] And when she organised for social insurance premiums, she was put under surveillance and then sacked for organising an independent union.[98]

Xiaoguwei Island, formerly home to eleven rural villages, was annexed in 2003 to build ten universities for 200,000 students—the Guangzhou Higher Education Mega Centre. Hundreds of women who had lost their farms and their homes worked as campus cleaners. Then their employment entitlements were lost in the transfer to another contractor. They went on strike, supported by students, the workers' centre and finally by a government officer and even a local union official. They won.[99] In 2012, Panyu Migrant Workers' Centre and a labour law firm helped sanitation workers gain long-overdue insurance payments. They won.[100] Guangzhou relies on 40,000 street cleaners, who in 2013 went on strike; rubbish piled up in the streets when the People's Congress held its annual meeting.[101] Embarrassed, the contractor paid up. Two years later, Panyu Migrant Workers' Centre staff were arrested, and the centre was closed down.[102] Legal advice centres had become intolerable.

Politics of time

It is a patriarchal impulse everywhere to control women's time and movement. In China, an extreme manifestation of the politics of time was advocated by its capitalist kings: tech tycoon, Jack Ma, co-founder of the online marketplace, Alibaba, defended the ubiquitous 996 regime—9 am to 9 pm, 6 days, for both women and men.[103] JD.com e-commerce giant boss Richard Liu described opponents of 996 as 'slackers'. They were answered by a wave of outrage against this patriarchal paradigm within the tech world,[104] and among millennials generally, which found expression in apocalyptic warnings—a Weibo contributor protested that 'a 996 schedule' would mean 'no one will have children'. It was also manifest in what was known as the 'lying flat' phenomenon, which mean retreating from the toxic pressures of intense competition and exploitation, rising unemployment and highs costs of living.[105] This informal existential movement alarmed the party leadership enough for President Xi to make pronouncements on 'common prosperity' while stating '[i]t is necessary to prevent the stagnation of the social class, unblock the channels for upward social mobility, create opportunities for more people to become rich, and form an environment for improvement in which everyone participates'. Legal action against excessive exploitation also reached the Supreme Court, which in 2021 ruled against companies.[106] But it was not evident that the government was ready yet to outlaw 996 and what *Financial Times* journalist—later British Labour MP—Yuan Yang described as regimes of 'servitude'.

Politics and publics transformed: Beijing 1995

'Most people don't talk about politics,' says Yinyin, 'and a lot of people think democracy is useless because they haven't seen how it works. It may be an illusion of choice. We have online communities but we don't have common goals because we can't imagine what they would be.' Cecilia, hitherto an active netizen, is cautious about networking online—apart from her work life—

because she doesn't want to be identified. These young women find themselves far away from the moment in 1995 when China hosted the Fourth UN Conference on Women that ignited an unexpected flare of feminist activism and academic research: it consolidated transnational links—and resources—that proved to be vital to the expansion of resources for a feminist renaissance in China.

The UN event was midwife to a new generation of feminists, and it excited veterans of the media and the academy: at the time, Professor Wei Pu commented that 'many issues that have troubled me for decades in my life were answered for me by this conference', and *China Women's Newspaper* journalist Yuan Feng stressed its impact on women's politics and politics generally in civil society; it was a call to 'intellectuals to act and do something'.[107] The impact of Beijing 1995 was unexpected and unprecedented. It buried the earlier refusal to recognise not only the problem of domestic violence itself but also, most importantly, that it is always political, that it 'challenges and reframes established distinctions, not only between what is and is not violent,' argue the political theorists Elizabeth Frazer and Kimberly Hutchings, but between 'what is and is not justifiable, and between what is and is not political'.

Feminist theories of violence challenge not only contradictory 'common sense' ideas about violence as passionate, manly incontinence, a response to provocation, or state-sanctioned militarism but also the way that domestic violence impeaches the reputations of both victims and perpetrators. In China, recognition of it, therefore, was perceived as reputational damage for China. When journalist Zingjuan Wang suggested a panel on domestic violence at the UN conference, the ACWF turned her down.[108] Reporting on this 'dark side' of China was prohibited. Wang had set up the Women's Research Institute in 1988 and a Women's Hotline in 1992: although its focus was employment and political participation, women living with violence were calling in desperation. The

ACWF was a resource for women, and often for their troubles, but its capacity was compromised by its mandate: 'boasting' the country's accomplishments, not women's suffering.[109]

However, the UN conference was globally decisive: for the first time, a clear statement of principle about the role of violence in the subjugation of women. This was a time when many women lived the drama of collective self-discovery—always the esprit of feminist consciousness-raising—when violence and abuse of their bodies became speakable. In the context of backlash, it reprised the renaissance of feminism, self-help services dealing with rape and intimate partner violence, public protests, legal challenges to companies and governments and the long march of feminism into the institutions—including a new cohort of younger officials in the ACWF who had no experience of the CPC's internal suppression of feminists.

There was a discursive shift from 'equality' to 'gender' that Wang Zheng and Ying Zhang suggest allowed Chinese feminism to distance itself from the socialist patriarchy's definition of women's liberation. The conference propelled the feminist critique of sexual domination on to the global political agenda. Hillary Clinton's speech declaring that 'women's rights are human rights and human rights are women's rights' was regarded as a watershed. The inclusion of violence in the Beijing Declaration and Platform for Action was thoroughly radical, a breakthrough. Pioneering feminist lawyer Guo Jianmei, who helped draft the 1992 Law on the Protection of the Rights and Interests of Women of the PRC, recalled the Beijing conference as feeling like 'a warm current. I instantly felt that I had found my home.'[110] The law in China was 'the Sleeping Beauty', it seemed, awakened by the kiss of feminism and the noise of thousands of women—until Xi's counter-revolution tried to put her to sleep again.

Frazer and Hutchings suggest that 'when a global authority like the UN' acts upon violence as a manifestation of gender relations, it is important. It 'opens up rather than settles the validity of feminist analysis'.¹¹¹ The naming, far from fixing women as victims,¹¹² released radical political resistance to male domination and the authority of the party and the state. The naming of men's violence against women was the vector of multiple challenges to the socialist equality paradigm and to men's impunity generally.¹¹³ Recognition affirmed feminism's insistence on the 'irreducibly political nature of the concept and theory of violence' in feminism,¹¹⁴ and, most challenging, it threatened the sovereignty of the CPC's secular gods. Beijing 1995 generated collaboration inside and outside the official system—this was huge and unusual: the women's federation had 90,000 paid officials, it had massive networks and alliances with autonomous NGOs and community movements that began to address the violence endured by an estimated 40 per cent of China's women. A surge of activism reached far into the rural hinterlands. The ACWF set up a hotline after the first-ever quantitative research found that more than half of men admitted perpetrating physical or sexual intimate partner violence.¹¹⁵

In 2004, the marriage law was updated to specifically prohibit domestic violence. It was rarely enforced, until a landmark case brought by a well-known American teacher, Kim Lee, in 2013. She went to China on a trade union education mission, married charismatic Li Yang and together they were celebrated for their intensive English-language training camps, 'Crazy English', before the Beijing Olympics. Yang was the charismatic 'Elvis of English, perhaps the world's only language teacher known to bring students to tears of excitement.'¹¹⁶ Then Lee did something rare, 'she decided to go public' about her wealthy and famous husband's violence. A year later, somewhat protected by her American status, she triumphed—for herself, her daughters and for the rule of law—when a Beijing court granted her a divorce, a protection order and (modest) compensation.¹¹⁷ 'We've been waiting for this for a long time,' said the human rights lawyer Guo Jianmei.[118]

In 2012, forlorn-looking young women paraded along Beijing's great Qianmen Street—a celebrated shopping and eating hub—their wedding dresses and their faces splattered with theatrical blood. It was 14 February, and they announced that the date was not only V for Valentine's Day but also V for Victory over Violence Day. 'Love is not an excuse for domestic violence,' they said. Among the onlookers, a man commented that he had only become aware of the problem after the case against Li Yang.[119] Ten years later, China was again roused when a woman identified as Xie also went public—she posted on Weibo after her husband, He Zhongyang, attacked her in 2014 and left her hospitalised, and near death. Outside court, he dragged her to a hotel and beat her for hours. A hotel worker called the police, and he was prosecuted and jailed.[120] It was these women's rare decisions to share their stories that challenged China's violence discourse and kept men's violence in the public mind.

Sleeping Beauty

But by the 2020s, the activist infrastructure had been eviscerated. Jianmei dedicated herself to the provision of free legal advice for thousands of vulnerable women. A direct legacy of the conference was her Women's Legal Research and Service Centre in Beijing University's Law School. It was all too much; in 2016, it was closed down.[121] Undaunted, Jianmei set up the Zhongze Women's Legal Counselling Service Centre. It, too, was shut down by the government in 2024. Jianmei and her team then set up an independent practice, Qianqian Law Firm, that incorporated a commitment to free legal advice as well as litigation.

But the state declared 'categorical' opposition to workers' independent organisations. NGOs endured 'constant harassment, surveillance and repression'.[122] Jianmei's advocacy was of the greatest importance in exposing the political lacunae: the spaces between rights and real life. Qianqian represented thousands of women, pro bono, against rural cooperatives depriving them and their children of land rights.[123] But it was action on domestic violence that exposed the unyielding resistance of the party state security system to autonomous advocacy.

Anthropologist Tiantian Zheng unearthed hidden political treasure when she delved into court records that were opened to the public online from 2010. The records showed that women were expected to appease men's violence. In the courts, women's testimony was overwhelmed by the presumption of family harmony and women's duty to maintain it, to be the shock-absorbers of marriage and thereby keep men's violence safely tucked up in the home and off the streets.[124] It was not long before court verdicts were 'systematically removed from open access by the Chinese state, in part because of research such as this'.[125]

'We would rather demolish 10 temples'

The ACWF, so important after the Beijing conference, now became complicit in collective denial: one of its officials told Tiantian Zheng that '[w]e would rather demolish 10 temples than destroy one marriage'.[126] Scepticism about women's experience was rehabilitated, men's violence normalised and women's experience rendered 'unremarkable and uninterpretable'.[127] Foreign funding of NGOs was targeted, and in 2017 the government required NGOs to register with the Ministry of Public Security and forbade endangerment of 'societal public interest', that is, the status quo. 'The main issue is the NGO,' notes Wang Zheng, 'you are not supposed to organize on your own. In this sense, the state is not singling out feminist activists; there is an overall policy against NGOs. The state fears that a large influential organization will come into existence and become a rival of the Communist Party.'[128] The regulations effectively 'shuttered NGO activity'. Chinese society was reminded that foreign capital was welcome when it invested in the exploitation of women. It was not welcome when it invested in NGOs supporting their autonomy and assertiveness.

The Panyu Migrant Workers' Service Centre in Guangdong province was shut down in 2016. The centre took its case to the International Labour Organisation (ILO) in 2017, which criticised the staff's detentions and the government's failure to allow workers the right to form unions or participate in legitimate strikes or demonstrations.[129] International disgust—including the ILO's disapproval—did not disrupt the regime's crusade. The Beijing Yirenpeng Centre (BYC),[130] rated as one of the best legal advice services in the country in 2013, was also shut down. In 2013, BYC had supported a woman, Cao Ju, who successfully sued a training institute in Beijing for only recruiting male candidates.[131] BYC also represented a woman whose successful job application had been rescinded after a medical check found that she had hepatitis B, a common condition in China. BYC then took on companies and contractors who were banning workers with hepatitis B, got their grievances into the courts and broadcast the issues by enlisting witty performance art to publicise the issues. For a time, they were successful.

BYC founder Lu Jun explains the strategic importance of litigation: '[T]he police do not allow people to express their demands through assemblies, demonstrations, strikes, and so on, and there is no opposition party or independent parliamentarians to assert these rights in the legislature.' Legal proceedings, often heard in public, 'are conducted in accordance with rules set by the authorities themselves'.[132] BYC extended its reach to include *hukou* registration and women's and gay rights.[133] Its caseload was huge. But in 2013, 'the state's violent repression came without warning'. Between then and 2019, staff were jailed and offices were repeatedly searched until they were shut down. NGO anti-discrimination work became 'increasingly impossible'. Jun lived in hope that their collective wisdom would live on, and one day 'there will be a more splendid blossoming of a rights movement'.[134] But that day seemed to be far off. China labour movement expert Eli Friedman reckoned that while in 2010 'we may have imagined the possibility of gradual reform opening more space', by the 2020s the landscape was bleak, the 'promising tendrils' of social movements had been uprooted and there were 'no prospects for further institutional reform'.[135]

The Feminist Five: jailed for 'picking quarrels'

The Feminist Five stories are case studies of the vivacity and creativity of the relatively small networks of China's feminists in the face of the cruelty and mammoth resources—in personnel, time, intelligence gathering—of the patriarchal 'political security' state. Seemingly immune to irony, Xi was about to host a United Nations women's summit in New York in 2015 to mark the great 1995 Beijing conference when a group of young women, who became known as the Feminist Five, were jailed for 'picking quarrels and provoking trouble'. They had been planning to post stickers on public transport against sexual harassment.

The coincidence—and the state's excess of zeal—provoked national and global protests, and even Joe Biden, then vice president and later president of the United States, tweeted a plea to China's leaders to show respect for women's rights and for the Feminist Five.[136] The ACWF was not always a government accomplice: 'Oftentimes, the branch of public security will do something that the All-China Women's Federation hates,' comments Wang Zheng, and this was one of those moments. 'The ACWF's leading bodies were very incensed about the detention of the Feminist Five.'[137] The ACWF had, after all, enjoyed working with a young generation of activists.

Following international protests, the Feminist Five were released after spending thirty-seven days in jail, where they were subjected to gross, humiliating interrogation and threats to themselves and their families.[138] When they were arrested, a supportive petition was launched from Sun Yat-sen University, where one of the five, Zheng Churan, had studied. Managers were ordered to 'deeply penetrate student and classroom circles, investigate and do educational and dissuasive work'.[139] Zhejiang University postgraduate student Zhu Xixi received an unexpected phone call from a security agent in March 2015. She made her excuses, ended the call and went into hiding for a week or so—like feminists in several other cities. Her crime: offering to hide a box of International Women's Day stickers against sexual harassment. She was already an experienced activist—in 2011, she was involved in a protest against mandatory civil service gynaecological examinations.

In the absence of institutional room for manoeuvre, the women created street performance art: they donned large paper underpants with a large red cross across the crotch and argued that the examinations were sexist and contravened anti-discrimination laws. When she returned to her university, she was summonsed for questioning by her Communist Party advisor—all students have one—and then a security agent appeared with a pile of stickers and leaflets taken from a local women's centre, where she had volunteered. Security agents and advisors were questioning most students who had participated in any feminist activity over the last few years. She went into hiding again for a few days. On her return, she was warned that she would be expelled if she failed to cooperate. In 2017, her university was criticised for being 'too weak in their political work'.[140]

The Feminist Five were not merely detained; some were shackled by the ankles, chained to a hospital bed, denied medication for chronic conditions, interrogated by men who threatened rape; their connections to NGOs prompted allegations that they were spies for foreign states; and their partners and parents, too, were menaced.[141] Their phones were tracked, and some of their relatives were put under house arrest.[142] They were endlessly arrested and released; they lost friends, jobs, apartments and their health. They did not stop. But their activism depended on fearless mettle, and the internet.[143]

Toilet humour

The Feminist Five organised a protest in 2012 that, typically, was modest, local, cheeky and tech savvy—images that were appreciated by a huge, if subterranean, community of grievance and a large diaspora and networks of tourist travellers that ensured global online attention. It was the Occupy Men's Toilets protest. China was not alone—it rated as average for toilet provision among middle-income countries, alongside Mexico, Mongolia, Morocco and Mozambique.[144] Social provision of safe sanitation has always been a global feminist issue—urban women's freedom of movement in the cities is contingent on being within reach of a place to 'relieve' and clean themselves.

In China, open defecation was common. Households also used 'chamber pots' that had to be emptied into big containers outside—and then cleaned by women—on the way to being processed as fertiliser for agriculture.[145] Following mass migration between 1990 and 2008, there was a massive rise in open defecation. The toilets crisis exposed different spatial and temporal needs and risks for men and women, who needed an estimated three times more time and space than men. Public toilet blocks continued to display 'masculinist public bathroom design', offering only urinals, no toilets or facilities for menstruation.[146] This, then, was the context for the Occupy Toilets protest, initiated by one of the Feminist Five, Li Maizi, a lesbian and an ingenious political improviser: women queued at a Guangzhou public toilet with banners saying 'love women, starting with convenience' and 'the more convenience the more sexual equality'. She was warned by the police not to leave Beijing for two weeks.[147] When she was jailed in 2015 with the other Feminist Five activists, she was mocked for being a lesbian, an ungrateful daughter and accused of being a spy for 'foreign sources'.[148]

Apparently coincidentally, four years later, in 2019, President Xi announced a 'toilet revolution'. There was no acknowledgement of a debt to the feminists. It was instead, perhaps, an exemplar of the government's gimlet-eyed attention to everything, both to monitor the population and contemplate their grievances. The toilet reform became a longed-for and impressive triumph of central planning and digitalisation. (But in the wake of the COVID strictures and economic turndown also the subject of some dismay about extravagance and white elephant-ism: the digital system enabled users to track every public toilet in the country.)[149]

#MeToo

In 2018, #MeToo hit China when a student accused an eminent professor of sexual harassment. Other students came forward—it seemed the professor had a reputation—and he was dismissed.[150] #MeToo trended on social media, and after a woman known as Liu Li successfully sued her former boss Liu Meng, the civil law was clarified.[151] That same year, a twenty-seven-year-old screenwriter, Zhou Xiaoxuan, using the name Xianzi, posted online about her experiences of sexual harassment by a popular TV host Zhu Jun. She had reported his abuse to the police, who urged her to keep it to herself, and thus began a dispiriting journey to court in 2020. Although some women succeeded in calling abusers to account, she was defeated.[152] #MeToo exemplified the excitement of collective self-discovery and the excruciating perils of the 'political' in China: state scrutiny made general online activism vulnerable to sudden death by relentless censorship. Undaunted, emoji resistance continued—#MeToo appeared as a rice bowl and a bunny (*mi* Chinese for rice bowl, and *tu* for bunny).[153]

But feminist protest was up against the ubiquitous, intimate, visceral impact of the Xi 'security' regime that was encapsulated in the 'Safe China' mission launched in 2013. Scholars Susan Trevaskes and Delia Lin analysed the movements of the 'ideological dial' and state systems to 'widen the aperture of what the party now deems risky or capable of inducing social disorder: national security risks can reside in the political, economic, military, ideological, cultural, and social realms'.[154] So, the security regime reckoned China had to be saved from the people, from itself. Security specialist Dahlia Peterson says this data system enables the party-state to fully visualise 'people, places, things, events, and organizations', to monitor their needs, movements and behaviour.[155] In short: political and 'moral governance' that penetrates anything, anyone, anywhere.

At the October 2022 CPC congress, Xi launched his project for national 'rejuvenation', unity and security. The party's 'leadership core', headed by Xi himself, was to be protected by 'more proactive' and specialised disciplinary personnel to 'further strengthen political loyalty'.[156] He secured his appointment for a third presidential term—presumably he had something on anyone, or everyone. He had cracked down on dissent—notably feminism—and 'eviscerated what little civil society there was'.[157] Civil society was where women's activism mobilised against men's violence, and inequality in the workplace and the housing market was where they expressed themselves in embryonic independent labour unions and NGOs, developed alliances with the ACWF, advanced legal strategies and improvised the networks and the poignant artistry of their public performances that sparkled on international social media. If anyone doubted the pitiless consequences of 'political security' for feminism—online, offline, organised and disorganised—they were disabused in June 2024 when independent journalist Sophia Huang Xueqin was sentenced to five years' jail for 'inciting subversion of state power'. Her crime? Helping to launch #MeToo in China and organising a survey among women journalists, 80 per cent of whom reported experiencing sexual harassment.[158]

'We've got the worst of capitalism and the worst of socialism,' says Cecilia. 'We have to pay a lot of taxes, but social welfare barely exists; we have to work very long hours, we can't form unions, they exist but they are controlled by the employers.' And bizarrely, in a state purportedly dedicated to Marxism, 'when some students tried to form a book club reading Marxism, it got closed down'. And Yinyin reckons that

> [e]veryone knows they are under surveillance. And if you post critical things you can see that it has been censored when there is no engagement with you. So we invent funny ways to circumvent censorship, there a lot of codes, but it is getting harder. Now we are talking more offline, it is easier.

Unsafe, insecure and unrepresented

Feminist scholar Anne Phillips insists that political representation, that is, presence, is the necessary though not sufficient condition for feminism—and women's interests—to discover themselves, thrive and inhabit the institutions.[159] In 2023, the UN Committee on the Elimination of Discrimination against Women found that in China, though low, women's representation had increased, yet women were only 26.54 per cent of deputies to the Fourteenth National People's Congress. Since October 2022, there had been no women at the executive level.[160] In 2023, the all-male party leadership announced 'full-throated embrace of traditional gender norms' at the five-yearly congress of the women's federation. This time by omission.[161] The man from the politburo, Xi's confidant Ding Xuexiang, 'notably omitted a phrase about male–female equality that has been a fixture of leaders' addresses to the Women's Congress for decades'. He did not repeat the ritual endorsement of the party's commitment to 'ensuring gender equality in legal rights or economic opportunity'.[162] The ACWF's new leadership was granted an audience with Xi Jinping, who urged them to uphold the party leadership's authority, to 'promote family and social harmony', to tell 'good stories about family traditions', to keep children in order by strengthening guidance on 'marriage, childbearing and family'.[163] The ACWF had already obliged by 'promoting the Looking for the Most Beautiful Family campaign' to promote the traditional family as a 'new social norm of socialist family civilisation'.[164]

Xi told them that since the beginning of his reign in 2012, he had been urging the ACWF to ensure that women support the state by being 'good wives and mothers'. The CPC central committee had strengthened its 'overall leadership over the cause of women's advancement,' he said.[165] So, women's fate had been determined by men, not women. Having discarded the Iron Girls iconography of equality, having invited foreign capital to commit hyper-exploitation of its people and then bludgeoned women's protests, the paramount party leaders catalysed tradition and capitalism to tame women—not to confine them to 'home' and 'family' and domesticity, nor to evict them from the labour force, but to renew 'the work of gender', to naturalise the sexual division of labour and repair the consequences of the one-child policy for social reproduction. Modernity, then, was modelled not on 'socialism with Chinese characteristics' but male domination with Chinese characteristics—the one-party state did not destroy patriarchy; it renewed it.

5

SOUTH AFRICA

WHITE CAPITALIST MEN GOT WHAT THEY WANTED

Beatrix Campbell

An elderly couple walk out of prison gates in February 1990, hand in hand, handsome and elegant, witnessed by millions of viewers across the world. It was not a royal wedding—though they were African aristocracy—but the gracious reunion of global icons: Winnie Madikizela Mandela and her husband Nelson Mandela, whose lives had been ruined by apartheid, the worst regime of extreme racist and sexual sadism prevailing at the end of the twentieth century. Nelson was the serene hero of the anti-apartheid movement, who, with his comrades, had been locked away after a notorious 'treason trial' and only released after twenty-seven years. Winnie, too, had been jailed, but, unlike her husband, she had been tortured and then banished and eternally harassed; spies penetrated every nook and cranny of her life.

Now they walked into the sun together for the first time in twenty-seven years, as agents of apartheid's destruction. The radiance of that moment cannot be exaggerated: apartheid was a history of trauma, of white hands and the white gaze that scoped the black bodies upon whom they depended, that left no black body or home or community safe from surveillance and savagery.

Gandhi Baai's family was part of the Madikizela dynasty, and she became a senior member of the post-apartheid government after living in the exiled diaspora with her parents; she remembers watching 'that historic moment on television, such a powerful symbol of resilience and the long-awaited dawn of a new South Africa'.[1] But Winnie was denigrated and humiliated, her achievements minimised and her reputation compromised. In the Baai household, like millions of others, however, Winnie Mandela, remained

> an icon of resistance in her own right. My parents would often speak of her strength, beauty and unwavering commitment. In the darkest days, when Mandela's voice was silenced behind prison walls, it was Winnie who kept the flame burning. She was not only his wife but a fierce advocate for freedom, deeply rooted in the community and a symbol of black pride. Her home in Soweto was known as parliament because that is where the community would go whenever they needed assistance with anything. Even as Mandela's release signalled a new chapter, the contributions of women like Winnie, who had kept the struggle alive, were an integral part of the narrative.[2]

After South Africa's first democratic election in 1994, the African National Congress (ANC) formed the government and began to pass 'transformational statutes that re-moralised the legal system', promoted the 'resumption of human dignity' and promised to address the hellish consequences of apartheid.[3] It 'served as a model for constitutional revival' within and beyond Africa.[4] On 10 December 1996, Nelson Mandela, the country's first black president, appeared in Sharpeville, the site of a never-forgotten massacre in 1960 that changed South Africa forever. That day,

SOUTH AFRICA

US-made fighter jets swooped over an unarmed crowd protesting against racist pass laws; the police opened fire, killing at least ninety-one people and injuring hundreds more. Now Mandela announced: 'By our presence here today we solemnly honour the pledge we made to ourselves and to the world, that South Africa will redeem herself ... Those who sought their own freedom in the domination of others were doomed to ignominious failure.'

With these words, he signed and commended to his bloodied society one of the most ethical and egalitarian constitutions in the world, the antithesis of 300 years of its history.[5] Its first chapter commits the country to human dignity, the achievement of equality and the advancement of human rights and freedoms; Section 9 prohibits discrimination on the grounds of race, gender, sex, pregnancy, marital status, ethnic or social origin, colour, sexual orientation, age, disability, religion, conscience, belief, culture, language and birth. Did male domination die? The answer to this question begins with Albie Sachs, a lawyer who had been exiled, and together with fellow exile Kader Asmal[6] began almost a decade earlier to draft what became the constitution signed by Mandela in 1996.[7] Sachs later acknowledged that enduring 'poverty, gender violence and corruption' had exposed the limits of constitutionalism, and in particular that

> [o]ne of the few profoundly non-racial institutions in South Africa is patriarchy. Among the multiple chauvinisms that abound in our country, the male version rears itself with special and equal vigour in all communities. Indeed, it is so firmly rooted that it is frequently given a cultural halo and identified with the customs and personality of the different communities.[8]

This chapter takes up Sachs' critique: it explores the dimensions of patriarchy that rendered women's consent always contingent, trapped 'between the violence of white rule and the violence of patriarchal masculinity'.[9] The transition itself ensured the safety of white economic power and the spatial legacy of apartheid—notably the shack settlements that are still home to millions of citizens, and the political neglect of 'social reproduction', that is, the basic services that make life liveable.

This was exemplified by the growing significance of constitutional law in South African society, as illustrated by:

- State capture—the fraudulent seizure of state assets and manipulation by unaccountable cliques of powerful men that was condemned by the Office of the Public Protector, a creation of the constitution.[10] Equality duties became a strategic focus of prodigious legal activism on behalf of black women, in particular, in diverse and complex contexts.
- Homes and housing—a typically complicated case followed the emergence three decades after the end of apartheid of warnings painted on houses in black townships: 'this house is not for sale'. Women were insisting on their rights to family homes that men had been enabled to claim—and sometimes sell without their knowledge—by post-apartheid legislation.[11] Lawyers representing black women successfully invoked the constitution against both customary law on primogeniture in inheritance and the impact of post-apartheid laws that had fetishised private property against other forms of tenure. The effect had been to commodify a 'collective good' and to favour male ownership of a family resource.[12] The constitution was also invoked against the state's failures to implement socio-economic duties in housing and utilities provision, which had a disproportionate impact on black women.[13]
- HIV/AIDs—during the global pandemic, women challenged the government's refusal to extend free treatment to mothers and new-born babies. President Thabo Mbeki imposed an unfounded dogma that HIV/AIDs was not caused by sexual transmission but by poverty. Six million people were infected

in South Africa; death awaited incalculable numbers from the disease, as well as social ostracism and violence. In 1998, the government estimated that annually 70,000 new-borns were infected around birth—a 30 per cent transmission rate—half of whom could have been protected by medication. Thousands of babies lay buried in unmarked graves.[14] It was the government's refusal to roll-out freely available, potent medicine and counselling to pregnant mothers and their infants that motivated a coalition of HIV/AIDs campaigners and human rights and children's organisations to take legal action. The Constitutional Court not only vindicated social and economic—including health and housing—rights[15] but also established a conceptual framework for proactive enforcement of those rights.[16]

Collective nightmare

The Constitutional Court was the antithesis of the apartheid era that codified the impossible dream of a 'white man's country', a nightmare of cruelty and containment, pillage and rape that gifted ludicrously excessive wealth and power to an elite corps of gold and diamond businessmen. The pre-apartheid colonial project had not been extermination but hyper-exploitation that demanded presence, to dig for gold, diamonds, coal and copper across the Rand and to care for white families, their children and their homes. The diamond and gold rush of the 1880s empowered and enriched the men known as the Randlords, exemplified by maverick Britons, parliamentarian Cecil Rhodes and London diamond dealer Ernest Oppenheimer. They were dedicated imperialists who were to shape the new Union of South Africa, where 'whiteness' was 'enshrined as a constitutional principle'.[17]

It was when pass laws—in operation since the eighteenth century to control the movement of slaves, and later to restrict miners—were stiffened and extended to women in the 1950s that they met unprecedented and daring protest by mothers in defiance of police officers, politicians and the men of their own anti-apartheid parties. Their mobilisation of fearless, disciplined mass resistance was met by violence and incarceration.[18] It was followed by a mass canvass of black Africans that yielded the Freedom Charter, adopted at a huge Congress of the People in 1955: the state reacted with more arrests and the 'treason trial', which led to the leaders' incarceration and exile and mass mobilisations against apartheid. Thus began South Africa's liberation movement, and its struggle to engage global attention.[19]

Gandhi Baai's father was a scholar and a preacher:

> I remember my father would always use his platform on the pulpit to preach on the atrocities of apartheid in the various cities we lived in the USA and UK. What I always found interesting is how people in the 'house of the lord' would suddenly walk out of church when my father would spread the awareness of the evils of apartheid.

Her family felt that '[b]eing part of the ANC or the broader liberation struggle was not just a choice; it was a moral obligation. For many, the oppression we all endured left little room for neutrality. There was a deep responsibility to fight for the people, our dignity, and our future.'

In South Africa, waves of opposition—sometimes unsettling the exiled ANC leadership—blazed among schoolchildren, the Black Consciousness Movement and new social movements, including women's activism, that, in the context of the banning of the ANC, coalesced in the United Democratic Front (UDF) and the international boycott campaigns. By the 1980s, the white corporate magnates had divined that the end was nigh: the country was besieged within by violent industrial conflict and mass mobilisations and by international sanctions and condemnation. Corporations shifted their headquarters abroad, squirrelled money away and finally recognised that they were going to have to do business with the enemy.[20]

SOUTH AFRICA

How the transition was framed: patriarchal cabals

A small clique sponsored private talks between ANC exiles, business leaders and politicians. In 1989, Anglo American Corporation's chairman and dynastic patriarch, Harry Oppenheimer, laid down the terms at the World Economic Forum in Davos: the ruling white minority (himself included) would only accept a post-apartheid state if their capitalist economy and private property rights were assured.[21]

A dozen years earlier, Oppenheimer had hosted Milton Friedman, the intellectual guru of unencumbered capitalism—neoliberalism—who gushed over his 'magnificent estate' and collection of 'priceless original paintings by all of the great artists in the world'.[22] Contrary to the evidence and the international consensus, Friedman concluded that South Africa was a model of freedom and enlightenment.[23] Shortly after his departure, South Africa combusted,[24] and the UN Security Council reaffirmed that apartheid was 'a crime against the conscience and dignity of mankind that seriously disturbs international peace and security'.[25] Friedman had been wrong, of course, but his ghost lived on in the country's transition twenty years later.

How would the ANC, backed by a global diaspora of South African exiles, reconcile social justice with the white elite's rapacious capitalism and neoliberal ideology? Economists Sam Ashman, Ben Fine—an active participant in the ANC's socio-economic research at the time—and Susan Newman describe the outcome: a historic compromise 'premised upon the achievement of political equality whilst leaving the structure and functioning of the economy intact'.[26]

Delving into the ANC archives, veteran economists Vishnu Padayachee and Robert van Niekerk deliver a vivid and forensic analysis of what came to be known as the ANC's neoliberal turn in the early 1990s, hatched by a treasury-based Growth, Employment and Redistribution (GEAR) programme, formulated by bankers, promoted by the 'late apartheid state' and, in the ANC, by future finance minister Trevor Manuel.[27] It 'cast a pall on the emancipatory social democratic policy project' that had been at the heart of the ANC for decades and found form in the early 1990s in a detailed programme formulated by the ANC's Macro Economic Research Group made up of local and international experts, including Fine, and commissioned by Mandela himself.[28] It was ditched, without explanation or discussion, and instead the neoliberal GEAR framed the future. 'There was no debate!' recalls Fine.[29] A commitment by the Department of Economic Policy, a transitional unit in the government, to distribute policy documents to the ANC branches, to encourage mass engagement, 'stopped, bang, just like that,' said Fine.

The introduction of GEAR caused 'immense disquiet in the mass democratic movement'.[30] But decisions were shielded by the repetition of an authoritarian diktat—'non-negotiable'—by the sainted Mandela, and his successor, the gentlemanly but brittle Thabo Mbeki, who, commented Fine, 'was absolutely committed to creating a black capitalist class'.

Where were the women?

Women's movements during the transition were simultaneously significant, busy, organised and yet politically weak. 'It was very difficult for South African women to overcome ANC resistance to feminism,' says political scientist Shireen Hassim.[31] The early 1980s was an exceptional time when 'women's organisations shaped and were shaped by the political vision of feminism,' explains Hassim, but that did not endure: the UDF (the national anti-apartheid front) 'dominated strategic decision-making, and women's organisations lost their capacity for independent political action'.[32]

Women's political subordination bled into the new South Africa. Despite the beautiful constitution, the country became one of the most unequal and violent societies in the world, characterised by the black capitalism of the Mbeki era and the 'kleptocratic, predatory capitalism of the (ruinous) Zuma era'.[33]

In the beginning

The covert talks began when Consolidated Gold Fields, one of the country's big five corporations, sponsored secret meetings with exiled ANC leaders. Harry Oppenheimer hosted gatherings with Mandela and some leading ANC men, insurance magnate Douw Steyn and the Development Bank of South Africa. It would not be unusual, or inappropriate, for adversaries to meet, to negotiate a national transition. But more significant is who was excluded. The head of ANC intelligence, Ronnie Kasrils, later a government minister, recalled that the secret 'night-time shenanigans' had not been revealed to the party's collective leadership or their allies.[34] It was 'our Faustian moment' that left the post-apartheid regime with 'no way of finding solutions' to redress the 'dire plight of the masses of our people' or their 'anguished protests'.[35]

Jay Naidoo, an ANC and trade union leader, later a government minister, complained that a cabal, '[i]n complete secrecy', engineered the destruction of 'the entire social consensus' between the anti-apartheid movement 'and the majority of citizens'.[36] International support for 'a democratic, non-racial, non-sexist' and united nation had never been higher—but the adversary was stupendously rich and 'distinguished by a cult of alpha male leadership, cronyism between firms, banks and government'.[37]

Oligarchs embraced newly released Nelson Mandela with lavish hospitality. He became a regular guest at Oppenheimer's palatial residence, where, with magisterial confidence, Oppenheimer's wife, the brisk mistress of their celebrated hospitality, insisted that Mandela, well known as an elegant, fastidious sharp-dresser, stop wearing his 'silly shirts'—his famously favoured 'Madiba shirts'.[38] Who did she think she was? And who did she think *he* was? Had she not noticed his regal aura and his beautifully tailored suits when he was on trial three decades earlier? Had she not remembered Winnie Madikizela Mandela's elegance, 'drop-dead gorgeous and the epitome of fashion',[39] that announced an African woman's grace and confidence? Had she not noticed her milieu's noxious whiteness? This Oppenheimer vignette illuminates the complacency of this class that never really lost power, that flourished during the twenty-seven years of Mandela's purgatory and now, upon his release and saintly global stardom, extended lavish hospitality that was much appreciated. After all, during his imprisonment he had not been able to earn a rand.

The other 'excluded' were women, the hugely significant but subaltern presence in the anti-apartheid movement; they had most to gain from the ANC's long-standing support for a social democratic welfare state, especially housing, social services and health; they had been a key, instigating presence in the mass community movements that were the social base of the ANC and the UDF but became invisible and ignored in the elite-level negotiations; ultimately, they were 'most disconnected from the state' and therefore from policy-making. They were vocal and vulnerable to the state's failure to deliver adequate social welfare but, in time, were often perceived almost as 'enemies' of the state.[40]

At the beginning of the '90s, when the ANC was unbanned, the UDF was fatefully disbanded, and women's voices were marginalised or unheard in the negotiations. The ANC was 'not an easy ally for South African feminism', comments the sympathetic but critical Hassim; indeed, 'for much of its history it disavowed feminism'.[41] But at the end of the 1980s, feminists successfully convinced the ANC that the emancipation of women could not be subsumed to the national project and could not be limited to inclusive representation but had to be 'addressed in its own right'.[42] However, by the 1990s, women's interests—as women— tended to be reduced to inclusion, but not policy-making generally—they were notably absent from the design of GEAR and the ANC's capitulation to privatisation generally, and in particular to the private healthcare sector.[43]

Zelda Holtzman was at school in the 1970s when 'a close friend was shot and killed'. She was recruited to the ANC and during the 1980s believed in the irreducible importance of 'a mass movement, for the working class, and poor communities to have a direct say—the basis for people power'. But in the 1990s she doubted the rhetorical rush of the *new* South Africa: 'From apartheid and racial oppression to the "rainbow" nation and truth and reconciliation didn't make sense. What were we reconciling with if we had not recovered our land?'

The Black Consciousness Movement led by Steve Biko had been about black people's collective self-discovery. It 'was about self-worth,' Holtzman said, but with the transition, 'it ended too soon'. Holtzman, later a police and security expert in the new dispensation, remembered that '[p]eople stopped talking about socialism and before we knew it the leadership was adopting a neoliberal plan in the name of inviting investment'. Baai, who had returned to South Africa from exile and worked as communications chief for the government, says she 'only realised later, a little late in the day, that GEAR was a neoliberal agenda, and that South Africa would never truly become a social democracy'.

GEAR had been endorsed by Mandela himself (and his successor Mbeki) despite its dismal implications for millions of poor people in general and women in particular. The GEAR neoliberal growth model failed to revitalise the South African economy: capital flowed away to London, and confronted by enduring pauperisation, social policy was conceived as 'assistance for the poor' rather than eradication of poverty.[44] White capitalist patriarchy was safe. It had participated in the villainy of apartheid but impunity beckoned—'at the end of the day, there was a "crime" but no punishment'.[45]

Corruption

Corruption is a feminist issue. Feminist theory clarifies the ways that corruption nests in neoliberal systems and their informal, fraternal 'old boy' networks,[46] often fortified by private militias, that capture the state and diminish the opportunities for political challenge.[47] With the end of apartheid in sight, South Africa was love-bombed by the arms industry, one of the most corrupt—and patriarchal—industrial networks on the planet in which corruption was pathological, embedded and 'systemic'.[48]

During the 1990s, an arms deal was signed involving warships, submarines and fighter aircraft—and huge bribes—even though defence reviews repeatedly acknowledged that there were no external enemies, and the greatest threats to the country's security were mass poverty and violence: unemployment hit 39 per cent in the 1990s (highest among women and young people).[49] The deal provoked 'unmitigated indignation' in parliament and civil society.[50] ANC MP Andrew Feinstein accused the government of spending £6 billion on weapons that it didn't need—and subsequently hardly used—when 6 million of its people were living with—and dying from—HIV/AIDs.[51] South Africa had the highest rate of HIV/AIDS infection on the continent, most of them women. The deal was condemned by Winnie Mandela, greatly concerned by infant mortality and women's health,[52] and the housing minister, ANC veteran Joe Slovo, who protested that a modest portion of the cost would immediately subsidise housing for more than a million people.[53]

By the end of the 1990s, public discontent roared—corruption and patriarchy were becoming the marque of South Africa. The deal had been promoted by Mbeki, and one of its beneficiaries was Jacob Zuma, a maverick ANC politician whose upward trajectory defied multiple encounters with the criminal courts and judicial denunciations. Mbeki dismissed Zuma in 2005 after his financial aide, Schabir Shaik, was jailed for making corrupt arms deal-related payments to Zuma. Zuma, however, was acquitted. He was on trial again, for rape, in 2006, and again he was acquitted. In 2007, he was supported by a left coalition in the ANC that ousted Mbeki,[54] and in 2009 he was elected president. By then, no one could be unaware of the contradictions between the constitutional codes of conduct and the reign of the arms dealers, racketeers, alleged rapists and 'tenderpreneurs'—individuals or businesses using political contacts to gain contracts, facilitated, in turn, by a cruelly ironic initiative: the Black Economic Empowerment (BEE) programme. The BEE was designed not to emancipate the millions of black people impoverished by apartheid but to create a black business elite. Zuma's travails escalated in 2009 when journalists reported on his lavish family home—a veritable campus—in a remote village in Nkandla, in KwaZulu–Natal, constructed at great public expense.[55]

State capture

A key feature of the constitution, one of the 'integrity institutions' created to ensure compliance, was called into service—the Office of the Public Protector.[56] Zuma had appointed Thuli Madonsela to be the public protector. Both of them were veterans of the anti-apartheid struggle: Madonsela was a serene, scrupulous lawyer, exiled during her schooldays, a member of the ANC and the UDF; Zuma was an ANC exile, a swashbuckling populist, the embodiment of the 'big man syndrome'. She would be his nemesis. The argument here is not that their sex defined their behaviour, but that patriarchal privilege was at stake in their confrontation. In 2012, she was asked to investigate his

Nkandla homestead, and in 2013 she concluded that Zuma had lied about 'unconscionable, excessive expenditure' and 'misappropriation of public funds'. Officials in *all* the ministries involved should be reprimanded for the 'appalling' abuse of state funds. He resisted her right to call him to account: he was the president! Zuma pre-figured Donald Trump's presidential defiance of the US constitution, public officials and the criminal and civil courts. Like Trump, Zuma invoked his *personal* credentials against the *impersonal* Office of the Public Protector. In an epochal moment on 31 March 2016, Zuma was condemned in the Constitutional Court—built beside Johannesburg's notorious apartheid prison, with material hauled from that terrifying place to be re-incarnated as the bricks of justice. The court denounced him: he had broken his oath to uphold the constitution, in contrast to the public protector, 'one of the true crusaders and champions of anti-corruption and clean governance'.[57]

Madonsela's final great work, *State Capture*, concerned Zuma and the three Gupta brothers—known as the Zuptas. Her investigation began in March 2016.[58] In April, the Gupta family abruptly evacuated their ostentatious compound in Johannesburg and re-located to Dubai.[59] The public protector exposed the Zuptas' capture of publicly owned state enterprises, of tax-avoidance, offshore accounts, shell companies, money laundering and the role of international management consultancies, all of which eluded public scrutiny.[60] Her report was followed-up by the Zondo Commission, which concluded that the Zuptas had helped 'themselves to the money and assets of the people of South Africa',[61] supported by a vicious circle of criminal sabotage by men who were, in effect, holding the country to ransom.[62] When Zuma was arrested on 29 June 2021 for refusing to give evidence, his consiglieri instantly mobilised: truckers blocked the country's strategic 'food and fuel' highways, factories and warehouses were set alight, billions of rands were ripped out of the economy; more than 350 people lost their lives, 30,000 stores were looted, malls were damaged and 50,000 informal traders—the most precarious—lost business.

Violent democracy

The Zuma era was a political watershed.[63] In effect, Zuma had perpetrated a 'silent coup',[64] and corruption was 'mocking the Constitution's grand promises'.[65] At the end of Zuma's reign, inequalities were greater than at the beginning. This was the context in which South Africa emerged as a 'violent democracy'. Before the transition, South Africa had experienced a decade of intense violence, by the state, by strikers and protestors, by gangs, by men against women. Now armed gangs stole anything that could be removed: overhead wiring, rail track, materials ranging from coal to cement, and forced the abandonment of construction projects, costing the country billions of rands.[66] Murder became a political method. The Global Initiative against Transnational Crime calculated that the main cause of almost 2,000 assassinations between 2000 and 2021 was politically motivated, organised crime. Sociologist Karl von Holdt, an anti-apartheid and trade union activist, explains that violence was embedded in the country's history and that South Africa had now 'transitioned to violent democracy'. We would add that since corruption and violence are resources for masculinity,[67] South Africa had become a violent, patriarchal democracy.

'Safe to rape'

What was Jacob Zuma *thinking* in 2005, when, uninvited, he entered his home's spare room and the bed where a young family friend, Fezekile Ntsukela Kuzwayo, was lying, and entered her body and ejaculated? He had known her throughout her childhood, and to her he was 'uncle'. She was thirty-one, a lesbian, an

HIV/AIDS and ANC activist and held the polygamous Zuma, who was more than twice her age, in awe.[68]

They both knew about HIV/AIDS because everyone did: Kuzwayo was HIV-positive, and Zuma had been head of the National AIDS Council and head of the Moral Regeneration Movement founded in 2002.[69] Zuma's shamelessly monarchical menace was scaffolded by his dynastic Zulu authority and a praetorian guard of enforcers; his vaunted affability was the smile on the face of the tiger; he coveted power and women, invoking 'tradition' to justify polygamy. Ah, he loved women, he'd say, but the watchword among women was 'watch out, Zuma's about'. She called another ANC veteran, the military leader Kasrils, who had known Fezekile and her father, who advised her to report him. Zuma's trial in 2006 became a defining event in the renewal of South African patriarchy.

Rape doesn't just happen in the red mist of men's minds; it is decided. But Zuma's defence claimed he had been provoked by what she was wearing before she retired to bed—a kanga.[70] (Kanga is the ubiquitous African cotton fabric, around 1.5 metres long, that women wrap around themselves—or use to cover furniture or carry babies.)[71] He represented the kanga as a lure, to which he was obliged to respond by tradition, 'for cultural reasons'.[72] What culture? Zuma didn't explain; he didn't need to: everyone understood that he meant custom and patriarchy, a spontaneous combustion without will. He 'cast the complainant as a seducer'.[73] But why, the prosecutor wondered, would she, an HIV-positive lesbian in a country with one of the world's highest rates of infection, want sex with this old man, and why would he have failed to wear a condom—evidently, confirmation of South Africa's failure to reform sexual practice. He didn't deny thinking about HIV, that was why, he said, he showered after the event—a comment that the judge thought was risible: 'I do not even want to comment.'[74]

SOUTH AFRICA

During the trial, the woman's fate was sealed when the judge allowed her life history to be quarried by defence counsel, who forced her to share details of childhood sexual abuse, when no one was held accountable. It was not his character or sexual history as a womanising polygamous man but hers that the defence catalogued and criticised, day after day. It was worse, apparently, to accuse than to abuse. If she did not know this before, the accuser was certainly reminded of it by the ANC women who turned up at the court, dancing, to back Zuma. 'They were the storm troopers of patriarchy.'[75]

Zuma was acquitted. The trial had rehearsed what can be called rape-thought: that women are to blame, and men don't have to explain their thinking, because rape is held to be unbidden. But rape, like violence generally, is never *un*thought. Contrary to myth and some postmodern hypotheses that caution that women are becoming fixed in a victimised identity,[76] women who have been raped rarely speak of it, usually only reluctantly, still less fashion an identity out of it; nor do they routinely mobilise witch hunts[77] and '*resentment*, the moralizing revenge of the powerless.'[78] Judith Lewis Herman, the great American therapist and theorist, cautions that sexual assault 'is a formative in the lives of countless women', that it is repeatedly unearthed and 'just as repeatedly buried'.[79] It provokes such controversy that 'it periodically becomes anathema'.[80]

The conduct of the trial modelled the treatment of women and perpetrators just about anywhere. Zuma's acquittal exposed 'a deep cleavage' in South Africa about sexuality, about women, men, power, consent and desire that had already roused an angry intervention by President Mbeki at the end of the 1990s when rapes reported to the police were already soaring.[81] The statistics had inevitably been unreliable: before 1994, the police operated as the militarised agents of apartheid, three-quarters of police stations were located in white neighbourhoods[82] and the police collected no data in the rural 'homelands'.[83] Mbeki leapt to the defence of the police and the reputation of the nation. How much rape was there in South Africa, really, Mbeki demanded.[84]

But new rape research challenged his scepticism.[85] In a 1999 South African Medical Research Council (MRC) study of pregnant township teenagers, almost all 'described assault as a regular feature of their sexual relationships'.[86] A decade later, an MRC survey of 1,738 men, 70 per cent of them under the age of thirty, delivered a scalding result: 27 per cent admitted they had committed rape.[87] Scepticism was also at odds with the interventions by ANC leaders, by both Nelson Mandela and Winnie Mandela, when former gold miner Moses Sithole was convicted of murder and rape following a marathon trial in 1997.[88] Around the same time, a group of young men were convicted after terrorising and raping women living in township shacks: some of the young men would guard the door while others looted and attacked women and children.[89] This long-running case eventually reached the Constitutional Court, which acknowledged its debt to feminist theory and held all the conspirators culpable.[90]

Mbeki's expectation that rapes would decline was apparently vindicated after the police introduced crime reduction targets in 2010: reported rapes did, indeed, drop. But the targets appeared to have had 'a perverse effect', commented Lisa Vetten, researcher and former police advisor: cases were not recorded, and victims were turned away.[91] Target-culture revealed neither the prevalence nor the outcomes but merely the way police are 'measuring what counts, rather than counting what can't be measured'.[92]

Zuma's acquittal excited misogynist wrath: he embarked on a roadshow to broadcast his popularity, and his allies represented him as the victim of a rich 'Lucifer'.[93] That is, the poor accuser who'd had to live in a 'safe house' during the trial. In 2010, his ambitious ally Julius Malema, the future leader of a breakaway party, the Economic Freedom Fighters, told a student audience that 'when a woman didn't enjoy it she leaves early in the morning. Those who have a nice time will wait until the sun comes out, request breakfast and ask for taxi money.'[94] Sonke Gender Justice, the national campaign for equality and against violence against women, successfully sued him. He was ordered to apologise and pay compensation to a women's shelter. In 2014, Zuma's deputy defence minister, Kebby Maphatsoe, accused ANC veteran Kasrils of being the 'devil' behind 'Lucifer', the woman.[95] Reluctantly, Kasrils sued for defamation (successfully) and in 2016 donated his compensation to the woman.[96] Zuma's ANC chorus was challenged by other voices, too: a woman who had been in the ANC's military wing spoke out: 'I was told to avoid Zuma in the Eighties, specifically because—and I quote—"he couldn't keep his hands off women". And one of the shocking things about the rape trial was that we all bloody knew that.'[97]

'... That something is patriarchy'

The trial provoked a reckoning with the country's history, including the ANC, about who was entitled to criticise, who qualified as an authentic citizen and what the government was doing—or not doing—about the persistence of men's violence.[98] Leading ANC feminists launched the Progressive Women's League, and women's organisations came together to form the One in Nine Campaign.[99] Colleen Lowe Morna, a member of the ANC and the South African Commission on Gender Equality, called out Zuma's promiscuous and polygamous behaviour as 'self-evidently sexist and patriarchal. There is no other word for it.'[100]

After Zuma's election as president in 2009, when he was conspicuously socialising with the rich Gupta brothers, ANC women presented their plan for legislation to ensure 50–50 representation in all sectors, at all levels, and proclaimed loudly that 'the culture remains an overarchingly patriarchal one and that has yet to be broken', which had devastating effects on women, said Angie Motshekga, the women's league president.¹⁰¹ Now, South African diplomat Mavivi Myakayaka-Manzini made public her court order against her husband, Manala Manzini, a former post-apartheid security chief. She accused him of beating her up in front of their child. 'Senior members of the ANC were involved in the matter, but there is no record of Manzini ever having been disciplined,' commented the *Mail and Guardian*, South Africa's premier newspaper.¹⁰² Shireen Hassim draws attention to a seeming paradox: the ANC 'remains the party most committed to gender equality on the African continent', and yet, women 'time and time again have retreated, defeated, and re-grouped'.¹⁰³ In 2021, Myakayaka-Manzini acknowledged, sadly, '[t]he women who led us in the past, they did this through tears. We need those tears at the moment.' In the past, feminists had been accused of being divisive, but equality remained 'an add-on', when what was needed was 'a thoroughgoing gender perspective in whatever we do or say'.¹⁰⁴

After the Zuma trial, celebrated South African writers Mmatshilo Motsei, Redi Tlhabi and Pumla Gqola decided to tell the story of Zuma's accuser, Fezekile Ntsukela Kuzwayo—hitherto anonymised—who had been forced to flee to Holland after her home had been burned down following the trial 'to a chorus of calls to "burn the bitch"'.¹⁰⁵ 'Something makes it acceptable for millions to get raped on a regular basis,' wrote Gqola: 'That something is patriarchy.' Why does rape happen, she asks, and 'what's rape got to do with race?'¹⁰⁶ To which she replies, 'the simple answer is: everything'. She detonates conventional wisdoms about rape culture and race and locates the thinking about the rape of black women in the history of slavery and the 'pornography of Empire'. The idea of 'race as way of seeing, defining, experiencing and ordering the world,' she writes, is the 'history of slavery, colonialism and race science', the same fevered ideologies of 'white supremacy that constructed the stereotype of the Black man as rapist, created the stereotype of Black woman as hypersexual and therefore impossible to rape'. A clue comes from the descriptions of life in the Cape's Slave Lodge—the 'shameless fortress of human misery' where contemporary narratives described female slaves as 'lascivious creatures ... intemperate wretches'.[107] However, 'making Black women *impossible* to rape does not mean making them *safe* from rape,' warns Gqola: 'It means quite the opposite: that Black women are safe to rape, that raping them does not count as harm. And is therefore permissible.'[108] And inevitable. Elizabeth Thornberry, a historian of pre- and postcolonial South Africa, places the Zuma trial in the space between 'who has the right to consent to—or refuse—sex' and who has 'the legitimate right to exercise political power'.[109] Colonial rule was mediated through traditional, tribal authority, which 'justified both familial control of female sexuality and chiefly power'. Consent, then, was always contingent, trapped 'between the violence of white rule and the violence of patriarchal masculinity'.[110]

During the apartheid era, women who were raided and arrested were always at risk of rape: prisoners were tortured and sexually brutalised. In the women's prison, now a museum, located on what is now known as Constitution Hill in Johannesburg, visitors are guided to equipment of torture and to the row of dark metre-wide cells, furnished with only a bucket and an iron ring attached to the wall. The bucket would hold water, urine, faeces and bloody menstrual cloths. Breakfast and dinner would be placed on the bucket. A generation of anti-apartheid activists were locked up here, including Albertina Sisulu and Winnie Mandela, fond comrades whose husbands were their professional and political partners and prisoners.[111] During a tour of the prison, the guide quietly confides that Winnie was subjected to 'everything'.

The experience of such suffering does not come easily to the lips of the survivors. Dori Laub, psychoanalyst and founder of an archive of Holocaust survivors' testimony, describes contradictory imperatives interred in silence as both 'sanctuary and defeat'.[112] South Africa's Truth and Reconciliation Commission (TRC) learned how patriarchal contempt hushed women who had been raped; they were generally 'afraid and ashamed' of their 'dangerous' experience.[113] The TRC and its report, 'the nearest thing South Africa has to an official history',[114] had been encouraged by the Witwatersrand Gender Research Project to bring gender-awareness to the history of apartheid.[115] But the TRC interpreted gender as referring to women, not men, not cultural systems, not patriarchy. The outcome was a single chapter on women in its five-volume output.[116] Women witnesses tended to appear as secondary victims to speak about their relatives' suffering, not their own; few felt able to describe their experience of punishment and torture *as women*, and even fewer could share their experiences of sexual violence in the liberation movements. A former combatant recalled men saying, 'we rape women who need to be disciplined (those women who behave like snobs)'.[117] Thenjiwe Mtintso, an activist born in Soweto who had been jailed, tortured and exiled, and later became an ambassador for the ANC government, thought that some male comrades seemed 'dented somehow', and their experiences surfaced in 'aggression. And then they hate women.'[118]

Years later, she revealed how women officers in the ANC's paramilitary wing, uMkhonto we Sizwe, had been both treasured and threatened, 'we were like a rare species. We were heroines.' But that did not stop men, who 'would, you know, put themselves forward'. When one man threatened to rape her, she pointed her pistol at him: 'I said you are not going to do it because I am going to shoot you.' She never reported him. Former commander Wellington Sejake, in his evidence to the TRC, confirmed women's experience: sexual abuse of young women recruits and soldiers' wives was widespread, he said, and when he protested, he was removed from his post.[119] A decade after the TRC, the Zuma trial roused buried narratives—'I kept silent,' said one former

SOUTH AFRICA

combatant: 'When I was violated by the soldiers who were part of this grand and righteous struggle, I said nothing. In exile the movement, the ANC, was everything, it was family ... Abuse is among those things that will always haunt many women.'[120] But it was not the TRC, nor even the Zuma trial, but the international #MeToo movement that in 2017 convinced a former Pan African Congress (PAC) volunteer, Sibongile 'Promise' Khumalo, to disclose what had happened to her as a Soweto teenager in exile, and to other young women. 'I thought I would take this to my grave,' she said. PAC president Potlako Leballo had used a roster of women soldiers to clean his house, and some of them were also abused by him: 'I became one of them.' She didn't report him; 'you wouldn't,' she said, 'you couldn't'.[121]

Gqola insists that rape is a crime of power, and 'in all societies all men can access patriarchal power'. Anticipating objections that not all men rape, she is adamant: 'patriarchal siege' targets those who are 'safe to violate: mostly women, girls and boys'. Women and children are expected to manage their own safety, she says, and it makes little difference what they do, where they go or with whom. One night in 2013, black teenager Anene Booysen did the 'right thing' when she joined friends—her brother's classmates—for a drink and asked one of them to walk her home in Bredasdorp, in the Western Cape. She was found in the morning, barely alive, but was able to whisper a name to her foster mother. She died later that day. Doctors reported that she could not have lived because her small intestine had been pulled out of her, probably grabbed by a hand reaching through her vagina; she had been beaten all over her body, and her genitalia had been cut.[122]

Diepsloot

Distinguished medical journalist Mia Malan's desk high up in a tower block faces a lush Johannesburg panorama. On the walls are celebrated front pages of her reportage at the *Mail and Guardian* and behind her a large portrait of a suburban landscape—not the kind of sedate, leafy, hushed, gated enclave where Jo'burg's middle class live but bustling dawn in Diepsloot—Afrikaans for deep ditch—a crowded township 34 kilometres away.

Encouraged by a solitary centre for women suffering rape and violence, Green Door, Malan, celebrated for her challenging HIV/AIDS coverage, arrived in Diepsloot after a gruesome incident. Malan spoke to everyone around and heard that rape 'was just everywhere'. She described glowing morning light, just after 6 am, one day in October 2013 when '[t]hose with jobs are on their way to work; most people are hanging around doing nothing, whispering about death'.[123] Off that road, behind the shacks, alleys lead to a labyrinth of thousands of huts where thousands of people, the brave, weary, dutiful and the dangerous, are entering the day. Two toilet cabins, one with a red door inscribed with graffiti saying, 'Look After Me', are the location where, she writes, '[t]wo tiny, mutilated bodies had been found—they were stuffed head-first into a blocked public toilet. The four little feet and legs that stuck out were tied together with plastic, and bodily fluids poured from the corpses, which had started to decompose.'

They were cousins, three-year-old Zandile and two-year-old Yonelisa: they had been playing outside the shack where they lived with their mothers, grandmother, great-grandmother, aunt and five-year-old cousin. Then they disappeared. Frantic searches yielded nothing until four days after their disappearance: '[A] crowd of people are banging on the door of Sisanda and Thokozani Mali's one-room tin shack. "You need to come to the toilets! Quickly!" a voice shouts.'[124] Zandile and Yonelisa had been raped and strangled. A year later, the perpetrator, twenty-eight-year-old Ntokozo Hadebe, who lived nearby, showed only remorseless anger during his trial.

SOUTH AFRICA

Malan believes that health, safety and inequalities are political choices.[125] She is a veteran of reportage on trauma, pandemics and death: 'I was used to speaking to rape victims, but writing this story was the first time it got to me—I was starting to cry.' Diepsloot was formed in 1995 when thousands of people were temporarily relocated from a squatter camp. The 2011 census recorded around 140,000 people (residents reckon there are perhaps a quarter of a million now) living in 62,000 households, half of them in improvised backyard dwellings, a third of them headed by women, a third without electricity and more than 80 per cent without piped water inside. Poverty does not cause rape, but a local police officer told Malan that '[i]t's easy to rape in a place of chaos, easy to drag kids and women into a shack and rape them and hide them away in the mess of Diepsloot. It's easy for criminals to disappear in this congestion.'[126]

Diepsloot's neighbour, Steyn City, is its glittering mirror image: a millionaire's playground, with its own lagoon, golf course, schools and palatial mansions, built by the late financial services billionaire Douw Steyn, one of South Africa's richest men. Steyn repudiated allegations that this gated city was a kind of class apartheid with the rejoinder that Diepsloot benefitted from construction jobs. Evidently a few shack dwellers could help build Steyn City but not live in it. Everything about this proximity, and the lives and deaths of Zandile and Yonelisa, seemed to be a screaming epitaph for a country re-born in 1994.[127]

Planning a visit to Diepsloot, our black hosts insisted on a security driver: it wouldn't be safe for two women, not to mention white women, to wander about. Green Door is a small space attached to a little house belonging to the shelter's founder, Brown Lekekela, one of the thousands of people who arrived in Diepsloot in the 1990s looking in vain for a job. He volunteered for an HIV/AIDS advice centre, going door to door with material on how to live with HIV/AIDS and how to avoid it, and delivering condoms. 'We found women who said "no I will be beaten if I have a condom ... he will rape me ..." We weren't educated about violence or financial abuse,' he recalls.[128] 'This is a society where men can do anything they like to a woman or a child.'

Eventually, in frustration, he decided that women needed refuge, so he made space in his own yard. Women can't stay long, but Green Door provides advice, support and respite.[129] Green Door joined pioneering attempts to engage Diepsloot men in thinking about gender and sexual violence, predicated on the principle that masculinities are social constructs that can change.[130] It proved to be both revelatory and dispiriting. It was not that these men's poverty rendered them unavailable or reluctant—similar research among rural men who were similarly disadvantaged yielded evidence of positive change in men's relationship to alcohol, violence, sexual entitlement and women.[131] But Diepsloot was dense with difficulty. Here people were not 'looking forward to life; people have abandoned their dreams'.[132] Finding venues for the workshops was tough—there was little neutral social space, only taverns or churches—women resisted the former, men resisted the latter. So, they bought gazebos. Over time, participants' attitudes and behaviour scarcely altered— defeated, it seemed, by the men's fiercely patriarchal fortifications amid the intractable hazards of everyday life and by the absence of a positive political culture.

'Do something!'

Rape is a crime that has been virtually normalised everywhere. In South Africa, like elsewhere, women's advocate Brenda Madumise-Pajibo complained that 'political rhetoric and policy statements have not resulted in reducing the risks women in this country encounter'.[133] In every hour of every day, five women would be raped, she warned, yet, while terrorism was deemed a threat to national security, and corruption had attracted a national commission of inquiry, '[t]here is no commission to talk about the criminal acts that are visited upon South African women daily and hourly, and no visible attempt to ensure eyewitnesses or those with knowledge of such egregious acts are compelled to come forward'.[134]

In 2019, women confronted President Cyril Ramaphosa and demanded he do something. He acknowledged that the country's women were 'tired of living in fear'. He promised some money for services. It took until 2021 for South Africa to acquire a national helpline connecting women to the 100 shelters across the country, funded by the Ford Foundation. And still fear was in the air the nation's women breathed. Baai has something to say about this; she is a tall, physically strong, fearless and socially powerful professional woman who lives in Johannesburg: she reckons that 'in a room of twenty women, nineteen would have been raped in South Africa. I fear rape every day in this country. I fear for myself. I fear for my daughter.'

Of mines, men and murder

Rustenburg is the global hub of the Bushveld platinum metals complex—the largest in the world and operated by some of the richest conglomerates—home to 500,000 residents, mostly poor, living with insecurity, debt, disease, high unemployment, high crime, polluted water, prostitution and random violence. Forty-five per cent live in informal shack settlements—massively more than South Africa's national average—where a mere 20 per cent have access to water inside the home.[135]

What's this to do with patriarchy? The answer is: everything. The mining hub is a patriarchal paradigm, a place defined by power axes between capital and labour, between men and women, by the ways that some women are deemed other, exiled from recognition and representation as women.[136] And by violence.[137] In 2012, striking miners were massacred at Marikana—thirty-four were killed and almost 300 injured when armed police, sanctioned at government level, opened fire. Paulina Masuhlo, a bustling ANC councillor and community organiser, died after being hit by a rubber bullet a month later while she was merely waiting with a group, including her best friend and fellow activist Primrose Sonti, to meet some women supporters.

Marikana had previously been regarded as merely a mine inhabited by men, not as a community, a complex web of power, bonds and dependence; Marikana had been defined by men's right to earn a wage, to be represented, to manage and control the means of organisation—and by not doing the things they required women to do. The shacks sit in walking distance from the shafts—their proximity 'collapses the distinction between home and work,' says South African scholar Asanda Benya; women look after men, they 'reproduce mine labour at no cost to capital'.[138] Their lives are 'dictated by men and the mines'.[139] Yet they are unseen and unheeded. The story of mining, then, is as much the story of women as men and metals, of patriarchy as much as race, capital, labour and land.

When driving to Marikana from Johannesburg, the landscape begins to change colour, from green to pale slate: fields and trees fade into mighty, grey slag heaps, wafting dust like mist, the debris of platinum shafts dug into farming land in the 1970s. The road turning off to the mine displays bright billboards announcing corporate pride in innovation and modernity, leading finally to the familiar architecture of mining—conveyor belts, wheels and chimneys. The entrance to the mine meets an eerie, silent prairie of crowded shacks, washing lines, plastic water kettles and a few wandering goats. It is a scene replicated in scores of informal settlements that have expanded around Rustenburg, where in the rainy season sewage erupts and roads become toxic mud. Arbitrary violence 'rules the lives of those who live in informal settlements' amid the 'symbolic violence' of the indigent living conditions across the platinum belt.[140] These are unprotected and unstewarded places, policed by vigilantes, where justice is often 'violent retribution'.[141] Residents are reminded daily of where power lies: in men and in the 'cathedrals of commerce' looming over their homes, 'patchworks of rusting corrugated iron tacked on to frames of timber torn from local trees'.[142]

The landscape of patriarchy

Before platinum, diamonds and gold were the lure that attracted the immense foreign investment in South Africa, inspired by the charismatic, buccaneering British imperialist Cecil Rhodes, described by South Africa's great novelist Olive Schreiner, a feminist and anti-capitalist, who was both entranced and appalled by him, as 'a white politician through and through' in a political culture that was exclusively 'the business of men'.[143] He was the pioneer of the patriarchal, racial capitalist axis identified by the economists Ben Fine and Zavareh Rustomjee as the Minerals Energy Complex (MEC)[144] that treated the black labour force as expendable, infinitely sourced by dispossessed African 'homelands'.[145] There, the 'left-behind women' were the indispensable and unrewarded resource for social reproduction—the work of care, farming and food, and the production of human life itself, in separate racialised spheres.

For a century, companies—now global conglomerates—treated hundreds of thousands of men as if they were itinerants or visitors, 'sojourners', paid below-subsistence wages, moving between crammed company hostels and the faraway homelands to which they returned—or were repatriated if they were sick or dying from the industrial diseases contracted in the mines. There they were replenished by women before returning to work or nursed through their days of dying.

'Racial capitalism' was cruelly exposed by the Marikana massacre.[146] The polarised landscape was renewed in the twenty-first century by what the economist Sam Ashman ascribes as the grim persistence of 'apartheid spatial economic geographies' and the governing ANC's endorsement of neoliberal economic policy, which had not increased funding for diversification of industry. On the contrary, banking and the corporations became even more concentrated (and profitable), and imports, financial services and household debt soared (indebtedness was one of the causes of the 2012 strike by the Marikana miners).[147]

Democracy did not inaugurate a new dialogue between companies and communities and between women and men. The booming post-apartheid platinum belt performed corporate social irresponsibility, an absent and 'dysfunctional' state that 'retreated from the provision of security as a public good'.[148] Having withdrawn, the government pinned hopes on 'collective bargaining' between workers and employers.[149] But the long history of labour movements should have been a caution: for a century, the focus of 'collective bargaining' between businessmen and labouring men just about everywhere prioritised men's money but rarely addressed *communal* wellbeing.[150] Patriarchal—not collective—bargaining was the tradition upon which the government now relied. The immediate prelude to the Marikana massacre was some miners' bid for a new approach to pay that challenged both Lonmin and the National Union of Mineworkers (NUM)—for a living wage/family wage that could help meet their debts and support their dependants.

Lonmin—formed in Britain in 1909—wouldn't talk to them. Nor would the NUM.[151] Thousands of miners ultimately joined a strike that quickly became violent and attracted corporate and state killer instincts. That summer, Marikana became a septic crisis for the ANC government and finally a catharsis about everything that wasn't working. On 16 August 2012, the ghosts of apartheid atrocities, the massacres at Sharpeville in 1960 and Soweto in 1976, swooped over Marikana when armed police ambushed the thousands of miners who had gathered around a 'koppie', a red rock hill beside the mine. 'The hill' is the place in South African tradition where men gather, 'where men become men', comments filmmaker Rehad Desai, who made two searing documentaries about the strike and its aftermath.[152] The women had been supporting the men, bringing them food, but the hill was 'a site of deep-seated patriarchy'. At meetings, women would have to sit separately from the men, on the floor; they weren't given a platform, though they were 'in many ways the most consistent voice' for the community. 'But the men did not share the hill.'[153]

The police had been called in by panicky Lonmin managers,[154] backed by a government minister and, ironically, by Ramaphosa, an embodiment of South Africa's contradictions: founder of the NUM in 1982, an ANC leader, participant in the transition negotiations and, at the time of the strike, a millionaire.[155] The police were mandated to use maximum force.

'Enough! Now!'

Lonmin was confronted by another adversary: the Marikana women. Among them were two great friends, both ANC activists, councillor Paulina Masuhlo and Primrose Sonti, who worked in a Lonmin store. On 16 August, Sonti was at home following the news on television when scenes of horror suddenly brought her to her feet: 'I saw the crowd, the police, the horses, the dogs, and then we saw the barbed wire being rolled out, and I said to myself "enough!" I called the women and said "enough, now! Let's stand up as the women of this community."' She raced out of her house, blowing the whistle she kept around her neck, calling women to the emergency. As they began to march on Lonmin, they heard that men were being shot at the koppie. 'It was very terrible. We didn't sleep that night, we were crying,' recalls Sonti.[156] 'Oh the massacre, I will never forget it for the rest of my life, never.'[157]

Between August and September, forty-four people were killed—during the ambush, thirty-four were shot, many of them in the back or the head.[158] Scholars researching the catastrophe discovered bloody stains in the crannies around the koppie, all that remained of fleeing strikers.[159] The Farlam Commission of Inquiry exonerated the politicians but recommended that the police actions be investigated.[160]

After another marathon strike in 2014—the longest in South Africa's history—Lonmin conceded significant pay rises and, at last, a promise to build up to 400 housing units a year. But it didn't deliver. The women had lived in hope that they could wake from the bad dream of life in a scrapyard of improvised dwellings, where they neatly arranged utensils and a little furniture, where they spent their days working, gathering wood and water and taking care of men. The crisis exposed the hidden complications of workers' survival strategies. Men leave their rural homelands, go to the cities or the mines, find a second wife, have second families. The women raise the communities.

Mining communities are typically starved of access to safe water while the mining industry consumes and discharges vast quantities, sterilising or polluting the land and leaving women 'primarily responsible for the provisioning of safe water supplies for their families'. Many of these women had left their rural communities, and having, therefore, lost access to their families' land and farming upon which they had relied, found themselves 'with little choice but to sell their bodies' in return for access to a roof, a bed, money.[161] Often this was in the knowledge that the man has another woman, a wife and children, to maintain back in the homeland.[162]

Most women arriving in mining communities are migrants, all of them looking for jobs, and so, comments Sonti, 'most of them depend on providing housework or sex for men. They don't feel good about it, they don't feel nice, but they can't do otherwise, they feel they have to get a boyfriend so they can send money home, to their children. It's very bad.' After the massacre, women's grief was compounded by the collision of two worlds—widows and children in the settlements and the widows and children left behind in the homelands.

A month after the massacre, Sonti and councillor Paulina Masuhlo stood with a small group of Marikana women who had formed Sikhala Sonke—'we cry together'—waiting to meet women's groups offering solidarity. 'Then the Hippos came,' said Sonti. The Hippos were a historic shock: they were armoured hulks, blast-proof vehicles that had been mobilised against black people during the apartheid era.[163] 'And then there were rubber bullets, they shot Paulina,' said Sonti. Masuhlo, her great friend and comrade, died in hospital on 19 September. Her death was an epitaph, killed by a 'former liberation movement reborn as an oligarchy' that was 'driven by self-serving elites that will stop at nothing'[164]—including firing rubber bullets at a huddle of women—wrote journalist Mandy de Waal.[165] The women, supported by the Centre for Applied Legal Studies and the Socio-Economic Rights Institute (SERI), which provides free legal advice, representation, redress and research, campaigned to expose the failure to prosecute anyone responsible for the massacre, to seek redress for the survivors and their families, and to secure political recognition of the mine as 'a workplace rooted in the community', not 'a space that is inhabited by men only'.[166]

Opportunity—above and below ground

Lonmin employed around 20,000 miners at Marikana. Men had won extra income to live outside mining compounds, but that didn't enhance communities' living space; it merely increased the sprawl of informal settlements.¹⁶⁷ Yet it could all have been so different had the company, the union and the municipality honoured—or even contemplated—compliance with a legal duty imposed on mining corporations in 2002: this required them to devise Social and Labour Plans, to create healthy—and sexually safe—liveable locales for children, women and men, in collaboration with local government and communities—including women—as a condition of their licence to operate.¹⁶⁸

It was also in 2002 that a Mining Charter introduced a 10 per cent quota for women in mining, within five years, crucially, as a condition of their licence—sought by women who had few other sources of income than cleaning and prostitution. They would undergo rigorous training before joining an underground team. Academic Asanda Benya became one of them. She had learned that for the men, descending in cages, then through shafts and gates helped to leave their fears behind. But fresh fears awaited the women who were squashed in the cages, bumping against the walls, cold wind whistling from the ventilation shaft and, in the darkness, men's hands grabbing women's breasts. Sexual harassment makes the mine 'figuratively and literally a violent space'. To survive, said Benya,¹⁶⁹ women have to learn to 'bargain with patriarchy', to navigate 'spaces that cast them as outsiders and invaders'.¹⁷⁰

In Lonmin's Social and Labour Plan of 2006, approved by the government, the company pledged to provide 5,500 houses, improve water provision and sanitation and employ more women.¹⁷¹ By 2012, only 544 of 2,658 government units promised to Marikana had been built.¹⁷² Between 2007 and 2010, Lonmin attracted massive investment by the International Finance Corporation (IFC), a member of the World Bank Group¹⁷³ that promised to invest in 'large-scale community and local economic development'.¹⁷⁴ But the number of people living in shacks doubled between 2006 and 2011.¹⁷⁵ Lonmin built merely three houses out of the 5,500 it had promised, and it converted only sixty out of 114 hostels. Lonmin did not lose its licence. Before the strike, the company was pleading corporate poverty, but SERI discovered that between 2007 and 2011 Lonmin had paid $607 million in dividends to shareholders.[176] Sonti searched her memory—even though she was a deeply embedded community activist, the Social and Labour Plan was never introduced to community negotiations—'no, unfortunately not, we had no idea about it, I cannot lie, even the words are far from me'.

In 2015, it was the women, supported by the Centre for Applied Legal Studies at Witwatersrand University, SERI and pro bono human rights lawyers, who called Lonmin and the IFC to account in a formal complaint to the Office of the Compliance Advisor Ombudsman (CAO) about housing, water infrastructure and the participation of women in mining.[177] In 2023, the CAO acknowledged—after failed mediation—corporate failure to comply. By then, Lonmin had escaped—in 2019, it made $100 million profit, but this was not to be invested in its mining communities, said Lonmin: it was being saved for takeover by the South African gold colossus Sibanye-Stillwater.[178] Lonmin told shareholders that they would not get 'anything out of' the Marikana social plan.[179] Nor did the people of Marikana.

Lonmin and the IFC were not unusual—Andries Bezuidenhout and Sakhela Buhlungu found that mining companies across the Rustenburg belt were doing what they had always done: they 'insulated and isolated' themselves from regulation and accountability. 'A staggering range' of policy and planning documents fluttered around public and private offices, to no effect.[180] In their forensic analysis of South Africa's MEC before and after apartheid, Ashman and Fine argue that the MEC made huge profits and internationalised its investments 'whilst 37 per cent of the population do not even have a bank account'. Nothing, not legal duty, not shame, had made any difference to corporate behaviour.

PLANET PATRIARCHY

In 2024, Sonti lamented that service deliveries were no better in Marikana, homes still depended on water from mine—not municipal—tanks and shackland was growing; 'some miners are moving with their families back to shacks,' she said, as they couldn't afford living away. The company hostel conversions were too small and too expensive, and she reckoned that 'if you want a house you have to build it yourself'. In the 2020s, she herself was raising pigs in a community farming project beside the mine—supported by voluntary contributions. And what of the women, I asked her. They were still having to trek back and forth to the mine's water tanks with their cans, still living in shacks, she said, and still 'forced to work and ... forced ...' her voice fades.

Life and death in bad buildings

In the early 2000s, women fleeing violence found shelter in Number 80 Albert Square, known as the Usindiso building in Johannesburg's Central Business District. In 2023, Number 80 became a tomb, a monument to that history. It had been a bureaucratic atrocity—the Department of Non-European Affairs' pass office during the apartheid era. 'This building was where black bodies entered the urban migrant labour system,' commented Johannesburg architect Heather Dodd.[181]

Two decades later, this place of safety for women had been taken over by men, some with guns, some trafficking girls. People desperately seeking a home had occupied every corner and every stairwell, paying rent to gangsters. On 31 August 2023, it was a building where seventy-seven black bodies burned to death and hundreds were left homeless.

A place of safety for women had been rendered a place of danger and death by the synergy of two patriarchal cultures—criminals who ran the buildings and public officials who harassed and persecuted poor women living in abandoned 'bad buildings' trying to make a living in the ever-expanding informal economy.

SOUTH AFRICA

Such was the municipal culture of class contempt that women and their families who survived the fire were relocated to a field of 2.5-metre metal shacks, with no toilet, no running water, one window and one door. The survivors were obliged to cook outside. When it rained, the sheds were saturated. The fire was the worst of many breaking out among the hundreds of derelict and so-called 'bad buildings' in the centre of the city, the glowering legacy of corporate white flight and disinvestment. Spatial racism had consigned black residents to the edge of the city and the post-apartheid municipality to resolve a housing crisis in the centre of the city.[182]

In the early 2000s, the women's shelter was part of a 'holistic housing strategy' to rejuvenate the area,[183] turn office towers into homes around newly built flats and a school that occupied—and transformed—a former factory. But after 2010, commitment faded, and then 'the men arrived', explained human rights activist Andy Chinnah, who mobilised support for the fire survivors.[184] 'They overpowered the women' and claimed rents from hundreds of new residents crowded in improvised spaces without water or electricity. The authorities sporadically raided the buildings, but they didn't consult the residents, assess their needs, plan their relocation or initiate redevelopment. When the emergency services arrived on the night of the fire, they found blocked entrances and no functioning fire extinguishers or fire hydrants. By morning, the neighbourhood soundscape—children coming and going to school, singing and shouting, street traders, homeless people recycling whatever they could find—became silent. Corpses were laid out on the road, below charred walls and broken windows. The head teacher of the happily busy school nearby recalled that 'a lot of our children live in social housing here, and after the fire they had to walk past the bodies'.[185]

At the beginning of 2024, huddles of survivors gathered at the Usindiso commission of inquiry into the fire, where they heard

Johannesburg's fire chief acknowledge that fire safety compliance was not enforced because it was a 'hijacked building' whose owners could not be identified. But, in fact, the owner was the City of Johannesburg. A city councillor claimed he had organised meetings about the building—yet he had never actually been inside. Former fire chief Wynand Engelbrecht insisted in his angry testimony that 'accountability and responsibility are long forgotten twins'; there was 'no such thing as a hijacked building, as if that disqualifies the owner from responsibility: it is owned or abandoned. This building was abandoned by the city.' SERI, one of the organisations representing survivors at the inquiry, launched a torrent of legal cases against the owners of 'bad buildings'—including the city itself—as well as the courts for failing to honour the constitutional right to access housing or basic services.[186] SERI was accused of thwarting evictions that the city deemed necessary to enable redevelopment. How did this happen?[187] Post-apartheid, thousands of poor people found refuge in derelict buildings.

Angela Rivers, general manager of the Property Owners and Managers Association, is an expert on 'bad buildings'—her mission is to secure their transformation: 'I'd turn every one of them into housing. No evictions without alternatives.'[188] She, too, is regarded as an enemy of the municipality. She explains that these buildings are an important but particularly risky resource for women: '80 per cent of small traders are women-owned businesses, they are out of the formal market, and if they can't afford a flat they go into a "hijacked" building. There they will be abused. There is very little protection for women.' A life-long Johannesburg resident, she never walks around the city; she only drives, with the doors and windows locked. Rivers keeps her eye out for 'bad buildings' that should be rehabilitated: 'If they are not managed properly, people can literally go in with a gun and start collecting rent.'

SOUTH AFRICA

Home—a metal container

Thobeka Biyela attends the commission every day. After the fire, she and other survivors were relocated to the rows of about 130 metal containers planted on a bare patch of land in the industrial edge of Johannesburg, called Denver, once designated as a pound for police vehicles. Biyela lives in one of these cans, with her husband and children. It is as if they are cargo, living dead. Biyela brings to the hearings a little girl whom she had gathered up after discovering that the child's mother died in the fire and 'she was staying with five men'. That, she decided, was not acceptable. 'Life was better before the fire,' she said.[189] For four years, she had a rented a room among hundreds of residents in 80 Albert Street, with her husband and children, a bed and bits of furniture: 'We were not struggling, we had a shop.' Now she is struggling. 'Everything was lost in the fire.' She lost her husband, too—he was taken away after his passport, and, therefore, his right to remain, was destroyed. She lost her means of making a living, too.

Sphiwe Ngcobo was thirty-eight years old when she lost her two-year-old daughter, and her livelihood as a night-time vendor selling food and cigarettes: 'I was working in the street when I heard screams from inside the building, then I heard "fire!" "fire!" I tried to reach my room, but it was too difficult. I tried another entrance, it was the same. I tried and tried.'[190] The fire fighters refused entry. 'Then I heard one of my friends shouting, "here is your child", my six-year-old son.' She found her husband, too; he had been injured in the fire, 'other guys were supporting him, he could not stand up'. But her daughter had been left inside. Her brother fought his way back into the building, returned holding her child and rushed her to an ambulance where she was given oxygen. 'But the ambulance people said, "sorry, you've lost your baby". That was the most terrible time.' She becomes silent, staring ahead.

She insisted that the baby be taken to hospital with her injured husband. 'They said "the ambulance cannot wait".' Again, she is silent. She is among the survivors who were relocated to Denver who attend the inquiry daily; she takes an empty lunch box with her to keep some of the snack that is provided to take home for supper. 'I can't work. I'm begging. We had a car, but we had to sell it, and borrow more money, to cover the funeral expenses.'

Kenneth Sihle owns a car and works as a logistics clerk in a dispatch office. His rent in the city became too much, and in 2019 he moved into 80 Albert Square with his family. On 31 August,

> I came home, there was load-shedding in the vicinity so there was no electricity, I ate whatever I found in the fridge and went to bed. During the night there was a crash, smoke and flames, when I opened my door smoke flew into my room, I ran to get my clothes and the guy next door ran into the room carrying a baby. He wanted to throw her out of the window, I said 'no, no, no'.[191]

They raced around, finding only locked doors: 'I realised I wouldn't make it. I saw my man again, he couldn't breathe, so he got out of the window and I followed him—I held on to the satellite dish but it came off the wall.' He crashed to the ground on his back: '[T]wo guys came to me and said "brother you are injured, we saw you come down". I couldn't walk. They lifted me up and took me to a tree. We could hear screams inside the building and then they'd go quiet. We'd realise, they'd gone.'

After he recovered in hospital, he found another building where he pays rent. He'd bought that room in Albert Square and felt happy until criminals and drug dealers began to move in— 'every morning you could hear screams of people getting robbed of their phones and wallets at gunpoint or knives; there were drugs and prostitution'. Residents' efforts to get organised were defeated: 'I was born during the apartheid era, in Kwa-Zula-Natal,' he said, 'my wife and kids are there. I send them money every month and I see them twice or four times a year.' After the end of apartheid, '[w]e were rejoicing, there was a new South Africa and the promise of a good life. But that's only in dreams—it didn't happen. I'd voted ANC, but I stopped after Zuma.'

In May 2024, the inquiry chairperson, retired Constitutional Court Judge Sisi Khampepe, announced her conclusion: though the desperate living conditions exacerbated the outcome, the City of Johannesburg 'must bear the responsibility, in part, for what ultimately became the tragedy of the 31 August 2023 fire'. In August, survivors—many still homeless—and relatives launched a class action against the city.[192] The residents' dreams expired when they found themselves in 80 Albert Square, a death zone.

Conclusion

The radiant dawn of democracy beckoned by Winnie Madikizela Mandela and Nelson Mandela that day in February 1990 swirled into a storm. How could it be otherwise? Nelson had been stuck in a cloistered community of comrades, imprisoned but not unsafe; Winnie had been imprisoned, tortured, released into banishment and betrayal—her public and private world invaded by spies. She had lived amid the renewal of resistance by successive generations who created the Black Consciousness Movement and the UDF. But community action and joyous cultural revival were up against endemic rapacity and violence.

Winnie's household was populated by notorious groups of boys and men, the Mandela United Football Club—ostensibly to protect her and be protected. Yet they were emblematic of the cult of violence that suffocated South Africa. Undoubtedly, she needed protection—but could she not have been guarded by a platoon of women rather than thugs? 'That wasn't thinkable,' commented former post-apartheid police chief Zelda Holtzman. But the football club was not only wildly violent; it was run by apartheid agents: this was hardly unusual—during the Northern Ireland armed conflict, boys and young men involved in petty crime were routinely enlisted by the security services to inform on their communities; British security forces penetrated the very core of the republican movement's security system and coordinated assassinations.[193] So it was in South Africa. Holtzman describes the 1980s as 'South Africa's *intifada*',[194] and Winnie lent herself to that emerging movement, '[b]ut there was a shocking level of infiltration, and agent provocateurs'. Her life was penetrated by men and violence and espionage, her reputation damaged by degenerate *fin de siècle* apartheid. The Mandelas' marriage didn't survive—although she was with Mandela as his life ebbed away.

So much had been achieved, and there was so much to celebrate, yet, like the marriage, the equality ethic didn't survive either, and peaceful transition was always a mirage, blown away by the global economic and political forces that never really lost power and now incubated patriarchal violent democracy.

6

ICELAND

PARADISE?

Beatrix Campbell

Iceland is one of the world's smallest nations. It is top of the global gender equality league and a beacon to women everywhere. Is this because Iceland is small, where everyone knows everyone, law-abiding, nice, fun-loving and peaceful?

Hardly—two of the world's smallest states, the Vatican and Monaco, are rich, conservative and patriarchal. Is there something about the landscape—an Arctic-Atlantic island cleaved strategically between America and Euro-Asia, mountainous, volcanic, bleak but warmed by spectacular hot springs—that incubates cooperation? It belongs to the Nordic community of typically social democratic nations that for more than half a century pioneered social and sexual solidarity, and yet Iceland is an anomaly—conservative parties have almost always been in government.[1] Is that, therefore, a sign of hope, that even in seemingly inhospitable circumstances, patriarchy can be overcome?

PLANET PATRIARCHY

This chapter explores the themes of this book through the prism of two defining movements that emerged in Iceland in the 1970s: women's liberation and neoliberal capitalism. Icelandic feminism has audaciously challenged intimate and institutional relations of domination, and simultaneously a men's movement promoting neoliberal economics and politics has reconfigured the country's key industries and institutions—fishing and banking—and created new means of male domination. Iceland, therefore, has been hailed as a herald of both gender equality and feminism and its antithesis, a myth of Viking heroism imprinted on a surge of unfettered capitalism.

Is Iceland, then, a model of promiscuous feminism supping with the devil, 'leaning in' and helping capitalism to be more productive?[2] On the contrary, these defining movements are contemporary and incompatible with each other and in different and contradictory ways hegemonic. The feminist movement was a response to patriarchal capitalism, and the men's movement a response to social democracy and labourism. Feminism repudiated patriarchy. Neoliberalism assumed it. Icelandic patriarchy is simultaneously resisted and robust: men's intimate violence and sexual abuse of women and children—and the impunity they attract—is not much better than its Nordic and European neighbours, and corporate patriarchy is undaunted.

The 1970s was a decade of economic and political turbulence: Iceland's productivity fell, inflation rose to a scary 50 per cent and class conflict was intense. Iceland was not alone—there was a global oil crisis, economies were volatile and Keynesian social settlements following the Second World War were being unsettled. Women's liberation was for equality and social justice, for universal shared childcare, for sexual safety and freedom from men's violence; neoliberalism advanced a revival of classical, capitalist political economy untethered by sissy social responsibility or social justice, equality or democracy; it was global, a political project that became hegemonic, yielding inequalities generally, year on year, culminating in unprecedented global economic crises.

Icelandic feminists, animated by the international Women's Liberation Movement and the UN declaration of the Decade of Women 1975–85, organised an unprecedented event. A national strike in October 1975 engaged an astonishing 90 per cent of women. The women mobilised a mass movement across Iceland's diverse civil society that affirmed direct, participant democracy, working in networks and neighbourhoods, improvising services and systems to address inequality and oppression. They had roots but no institutional power. But the men's modus operandi depended on proximity to power: it was cloistered and clubby—they were fellows who lunched together, who captured the conservative political elite and created the conditions that reinstated male domination of Iceland's political economy.

The women advanced an ethos that would be acclaimed internationally as the Icelandic *esprit*; the men were hailed as an incarnation of Viking bravado,[3] who transformed a small country that half a century earlier was, per capita, one of Europe's poorest into one of the richest. Except that it wasn't: it was one of the most indebted. The corps of marauding Vikings had, in fact, bounced Iceland into conspicuous consumption, debt and corruption, followed by bankruptcy. That, too, attracted a problematic, essentialist interpretation—women as safe, men as risk-takers—that obscured the political logic of neoliberal capitalism.[4]

The women's movement

Women's activism in Iceland began in the nineteenth century, following the country's transition from colonial domination by Denmark and rural servitude towards home rule.[5] In 1907, the Iceland Women's Rights Association was formed; in 1908, women won the right to vote in local elections; the Working

Women's Association was formed in 1914; and in 1920 all women secured the right to vote and hold office. In Iceland, more than 90 per cent of employees are union members, half of them in the Icelandic Confederation of Labour (Alþýðusamband Íslands, ASÍ).[6] The labour movement is the largest mass membership movement in Iceland.

The international renaissance of feminism began in the 1960s amid a global surge of radical social movements. In Denmark and Iceland, women's liberation in 1970 took the name Redstockings, from the New York Redstockings, founded a year earlier. The international *elan* of women's liberation found expression in the 1975 UN Decade of Women.

Working on the UN initiative, Iceland's main women's organisations organised a congress in June 1975 at which a women's strike was proposed to show the irreducible importance of women's work, paid and unpaid, and to support women's reproductive rights. After much internal debate, the proposed 'strike' metamorphosed into 'a day off' to maximise engagement among women of all ages, classes and political inclinations and to accommodate women outside the labour movement, or who were worried about being sacked for going on strike. They circulated thousands of leaflets and stickers and posted 50,000 letters explaining the strike, which was publicised as Women's Day Off—saturation coverage in a population of only 217,979 in 1975. They lobbied the national press and got their music played and their voices heard on the national broadcast media.

Around fifty years later, some of the organisers met me for coffee in a Reykjavik café to recall that day.[7] They described the team as 'driven, interesting, warm, close', who paid attention to each other, disagreed sometimes, but held on to friendship and the mantra 'you have to dare to discuss'. Their agenda comprised themes that none of the political parties addressed: childcare, violence, rape, incest, the environment, unequal pay, unequal representation. For example, despite the massive scale and significance of the labour movement, and women's presence therein, none of the national pay negotiators were women.

The employers' organisation opposed the strike. The labour confederation supported it. By 24 October 1975, everyone knew about the Women's Day Off. The organisers' commitment to consensus expressed a confidence in crafting a radical representation of women's work, paid and unpaid, as vital to the national economy and social wellbeing, yet challenging the experience of motherhood as a kind of solitary confinement sanctified by patriarchal sentimentality, a tradition of maternalism that venerated a separate sphere, where women were unpaid and unacknowledged. They wanted recognition of the labours of love and women's contribution to everything. That day, 'old women, young women, women who'd never been to a meeting—across all political lines,' they said, joined 'the biggest demonstration ever seen in Iceland!' The day aimed to show how much women mattered: '[W]e were saying society can't function without us. So, we can stop society, we can stop the wheels. It was a big thing to do, to tell that to the men.'

An estimated 90 per cent of Iceland's women went on strike—from fishers to typesetters, bank clerks, care staff, teachers, flight attendants, bakers and homemakers, women from all walks of life. One of those women was still a girl when she joined the demonstration: 'I was there with my childhood friend, we took our mothers on the ferry. I still get goosebumps just thinking about it.'

The women didn't do any housework that day, and in those workplaces that remained open, the fathers took the kids to work. Kitchens smouldered with burned sausages and toast. People who were small children recall standing amid a forest of women's knees; schoolgirls taking their mothers' and grandmothers' hands.

Guðrún Jónsdóttir was twenty-one years old, a student, a mother:

> I went alone, it was my own inner, private journey. I realised that it was a great risk—if we were very few, then women could be punished [they didn't have permission to take the day off, and doing so could be illegal]. I had no idea what would happen. I'd never dreamt of what I found, not in my wildest dreams: it was the biggest demonstration ever! My partner took our daughter to work, he was working in an office. I stood there with 25,000 women. Until then I'd never felt normal, and now at last I felt that my inner struggle was normal. I suddenly felt *normal*.

One of the speakers was her mother's best friend:

> I'd known her all my life, they would sit in the kitchen, talking and smoking—I remember hiding under the table to listen. She was an uneducated woman who'd had five children, and she became active in the labour movement. This ordinary woman was part of my life—I still remember her harsh, whiskey voice. She was the last speaker, she talked from the bottom of her heart, and she was listened to. It was an ordinary women's revolution. It was marvellous. We were so many, unknown. There was no way back. The fantastic solidarity and power—it changed my life forever. I was looking for that movement ... I stood there crying, I knew we would find ways to change things, and I knew that I would be part of that change.

Did that day of collective self-discovery and beautiful politics become more than a blissful memory, was the magic moment and collective spirit of the nation's women enough to transform its politics? These are the questions that animate this chapter; the first part tracks what the men's movement did next, and the second part follows the feminist movement and its impact.

The men's movement

Across a political crevasse, a group of ambitious men—right wing, patriarchal and well connected—captured Iceland's elite, its ruling Independence Party and ultimately the government. The insurgents penetrated Iceland's banking system and the international financial sector, 'one of the few bastions of virtually uncontested masculine privilege remaining in the aftermath of feminism',[8] and by the end of the century they were cheered as miracle-workers. They also brought the country to its knees in 2008 when the collapse of Iceland's banks led to the worst economic crisis anywhere, after which they were denounced as destructive, corrupt and, again, thoroughly patriarchal. Hannes Hólmsteinn Gissurarson, a political scientist and their leading theorist, remembers the women's strike in 1975: his mother, a strong feminist, he tells me, 'participated and my sisters, too; everybody thought it was good. It was like a national celebration.'[9] He recognised its resonance among women, but he offers his own sentimental reinterpretation and repudiation of its radical implications.

It was and it wasn't a celebration—women remembered it as the *jouissance* of collective self-discovery, of protest, of being present in something about them but big and so much bigger than themselves, for affirming their importance and for demanding recognition and redistribution—it was a psychic and political revolution. But Gissurarson simultaneously offered benediction and disrespect. 'I thought it was good,' he told me, but when I asked what he learned from it, he replied, 'I didn't learn from it.' He rejects the concept of the gender pay gap—'personally I think it is a statistical illusion'. Inequality, he believed, was not about sex discrimination but the different choices men and women make: men and women may be equally well qualified, but they 'rotate', he said, to different occupations and priorities, and the nub of it is that 'the maternal instinct is absent in men', which he attributes to 'natural selection'. The new Vikings' were pro-market, competition, private property and profit; they were anti-egalitarian and anti-socialist, and although they may never have articulated an ideology of male supremacy, they upheld notions of biological determinism, tradition and competition as the lore of life.[10] There was no engagement with sexual difference and dominance, because they were implicit, invisible and natural. In 1972, they aimed 'to rejuvenate' the Independence Party, the largest party in every election since its formation in 1929.

Gissurarson formed the Icelandic Libertarian Alliance and duly invited their hero, Friedrich Hayek, to address them. By the 1980s, the club was ascendant. He insists, however, that there was 'no such thing as a group—we just happened to be friends, who lunched together,' he told me. The chums were part of an international neoliberal insurgency that attracted ardent supporters on the political hard right: in the 1970s, the Chilean dictator Augusto Pinochet, in the UK Margaret Thatcher was a believer and so, too, were the extreme right-wing Republican politicians Barry Goldwater and Ronald Reagan in the United States. Three eminent critics summarise the global project: political economist Will Davies describes the neoliberal state as seeking to organise society around the 'ethos of competitiveness';[11] pioneering urban geographer David Harvey argues that it restores the class power of the global capitalist elite;[12] Andrew Gamble, theorist of Thatcherism, analyses it as a portmanteau ideology that reinvented economic liberalism and strong states.[13]

Gissurarson reckons that this club's ideology was 'a clarion call for the times'. In a sense, he was right. By the 1990s, it had become 'the dominant western ideology'.[14] The chums included a businessman, three future prime ministers and a couple of future Supreme Court judges. The blood of fraternity, thicker than family, flooded Iceland's dominant institutions—Gissurarson's friend Davíð Oddsson, 'a bullying *bon viveur*',[15] became an Independence mayor of Reykjavik in 1982, promoting privatisation, including the sale of its municipal fishing fleet; in 1991, he led a coalition government and reigned as prime minister for the next thirteen years.¹⁶ He was also on the board of Iceland's Central Bank when it collapsed in 2008. These men didn't create so much as capture institutions: privatisation breached the barriers between government and business; they informalised governance and promoted an almost mystical faith in their own economic wizardry that mesmerised the world—before their hubris wrought ruin and pauperised their entire country. By contrast, Icelandic feminism was a social movement that had no institutional power but a large popular base, and its influence challenged and changed patriarchal arrangements.

The new Vikings

Political scientists Silla Sigurgeirsdóttir and Robert Wade, in a coruscating critique of Iceland's conservative politicians, clarify the mystifying (to some of us) tenacity of the country's conservative parties. They describe a 'direct line of descent' from the colonial, 'quasi-feudal power structures of the nineteenth century to those of the modernised Icelandic capitalism of the late twentieth'.¹⁷ Modern and male, power was thoroughly gendered in 'tangled webs of bullying, sycophancy and distrust, permeated with a masculinist culture that celebrated the strength of one's hairy right arm'.¹⁸

Icelanders often say of themselves that everybody knows everybody, and everybody knows where they came from. That certainly encouraged congeniality—but also corruption. It did not inhibit robust class struggle: Iceland figured high on the international scale of industrial conflict in the 1970s, but a 'local oligopoly dominated—and restricted—both the polity and the economy,' argue Sigurgeirsdóttir and Wade. Journalist and political advisor Halla Gunnarsdóttir admits that she—like many outside Iceland—is mystified by the hegemony of gender equality and dominance of the centre right: 'I don't know why it is,' she says, but somehow the image of the chancellor 'is a man, always a man'.[19]

The state-owned banking system was 'effectively run by the dominant parties', both of them conservative, that had reduced citizens to clients: '[O]rdinary people had to go through party functionaries in order to get loans to buy a car, or foreign exchange for travel abroad.'[20] The 'hairy-armed' privatisers rewarded the same elite, and exemplified Janine Wedel's theory of private power usurping the public realm by the 'privatisation of power; the melding of state and private power', and by the players' replacement of the national interest with their own interests.[21] The impact on democracy is catastrophic, says Wedel: '[A]ccountability slips even further away from its citizens.'[22] Rasma Karklins' research on privatisation in post-Soviet Eastern Europe identified grand corruption that transformed public institutions into 'private fiefdoms'.

Advancing a feminist theory of political corruption, Janet Elise Johnson, Þorgerður Einarsdóttir and Gyða Margrét Pétursdóttir suggest that in Iceland the important decisions were being 'arranged through a parallel Byzantine parapolitics of factions and informal groups' that exceeded popular notions of corruption.[23] Decisions of national importance were taken in confidential networks of shadowy 'prerogative regimes' that are one of the ways that male domination is reconstituted in the twenty-first century: 'Policy deciders snake through official and private organisations, creating a loop that is closed to democratic processes.'[24]

This analysis has global resonance: although the percentage of women in Iceland's parliament had risen to around 30 per cent at the time, this representation did not translate into power. Political power shifted from the constitutional state to the 'prerogative regime centered in the confluence of finance and governance', sidelining Iceland's powerful women's movement and rendering the increasing women's presence 'less influential'.[25]

ICELAND

So, critical mass was no guarantee of feminist hegemony. Iceland's banking and fishing industries exemplified the warning that contemporary democracies are outgunned 'by politico-economic elites that are beyond reach or reason'.[26] Iceland's political economy had been captured by men: the banks and thirty-three companies had been privatised, and fishing was in the control of a few conglomerates.[27] President Ólafur Ragnar Grímsson boasted to a City of London dining club in 2005 that Icelanders were 'risk-takers ... daring and aggressive', a modern incarnation of Viking exploration. He ended his speech with a proud declaration: 'You ain't seen nothing yet.' He was not alluding to the looming crash.

In 2008, the three major commercial banks collapsed. When no heads rolled, one of the country's much-loved troubadours, Hörður Torfason, a poet, playwright, songwriter and gay activist, initiated what became the 'pots and pans' revolution—weekly demonstrations in which citizens armed with clanky kitchenware made a lot of noise outside the parliament building. The Social Democrats pulled out of the coalition, and Prime Minister Geir Haarde's government collapsed. After an April 2009 general election, Social Democratic Alliance and the Left-Green Movement formed a new coalition with the Progressive and Liberal Parties, led by Jóhanna Sigurðardóttir—the world's first openly lesbian prime minister.

Politics became enlivened, grassroots initiatives proliferated and there were several referenda. Voters refused to support payment of the banks' foreign debts, and they resisted pension funds being used to pay off the debt. Iceland survived. Voters gave overwhelming support to a long-overdue new constitution. It was not a feminist constitution, but it re-affirmed restoration of the seas to 'the commons'—collective ownership by the people. Despite the government's bravura survival strategy, Halla Gunnarsdóttir reckoned there was a view that it had made too many cuts and at the same time tried to do too much. After another general election in 2013, the centre-right parties recovered and formed another coalition. It refused to honour the referendum. The patriarchy was undaunted.

'None of us really knows what to do'

Jared Bibler, a Wall Street banker, briefly worked in an Icelandic bank and in 2009 joined the small national financial supervisory body in Reykjavik: a colleague gave him a short document sent by the Stock Exchange, saying 'none of us really knows what to do with it'. Bibler read the hieroglyphics and consulted the numbers all the way back to 2004, all of which told the same story: at any sign of a dip, the banks instantly bulk-bought their own shares. The data disclosed an epic scam involving Davið Oddsson, the former prime minister,[28] and the Central Bank, on whose board sat none other than his great friend Professor Gissurarson. Over the next decade, a total of thirty-six 'banksters' were convicted. Prime Minister Geir Haarde was later found guilty of failing to address the looming crisis. Iceland acquired a reputation as the country that locked up bankers.

The Special Investigation Commission appointed to investigate the crisis learned how a chance discovery by a curious investigator, Bibler, exposed a paradigm of patriarchal dominion: businessmen, bankers and politicians relying on informal and personal and professional communications, who at signs of danger merely called friends and relatives instead of holding constitutionally required formal meetings.[29] Ten out of Iceland's sixty-three MPs, including leaders of the Independence Party, were intimately involved and owed millions of euros in debt.[30] Bjarni Benediktsson, later the Independence Party prime minister, was implicated. The regulators suspected that three years after the collapse, the same culture was still active. They were right. The business Vikings never acknowledged culpability. It fell to Social

ICELAND

Democrat Jóhanna Sigurðardóttir's government to steer Iceland through the deluge, to impose harsh cuts while also trying to initiate ambitious reforms. She paid the price: in the 2013 general election, the Independence Party became, again, the biggest party in parliament and abandoned constitutional reform despite a massive public mandate.

In the aftermath of the global banking crisis, the undisclosed wealth of political leaders across Europe and Asia, including Iceland, was being exposed by a consortium of journalists in what became known as the Panama Papers.[31] Prime Minister Sigmundur Gunnlaugsson was palpably shocked in a 2016 television interview when he was questioned about his family's offshore investments. Once again, mass mobilisation in civil society forced his resignation. Still, the party survived, until patriarchal pacts tested public opinion once again. In 2017, his successor, Bjarni Benediktsson—also identified in the Panama Papers and now leader of the Independence Party—led a fragile coalition. This collapsed after it was revealed that he (and others) knew but did not disclose that his father had recommended that an old friend, convicted of years-long child rape, should have his 'honour restored'.[32] After the subsequent October 2017 general election, Left-Green leader Katrín Jakobsdóttir became prime minister. Benediktsson became finance minister in her coalition. Political resurrection beckoned in 2024 when he briefly became Iceland's prime minister.

Fishy finance

The idea of Iceland is framed by its great sagas—legends of landscape, Northern Lights, volcanos, geysers and glaciers, humans skittering between day-long light and the deepest dark—and fish. But for most of its history, everyday life was not the Viking mythology of piracy and pillage.[33] Its settled people scattered across the coastline were wreathed in poverty; they raised cows and sheep and fished. Conditions resembling serfdom lasted until the end of the nineteenth century.

Iceland's industrial revolution was inaugurated when fishing boats could go fast and far, powered by oil and steam. But their emancipating potential was reserved for men: in her vivid book, *Seawomen of Iceland: Survival on the Edge*, anthropologist Margaret Willson writes that a patriarchal division of labour defined the industrialisation of fishing: it massively increased fishers' capacity to fish but also licensed the containment of women.[34] Big boats needed deep water harbours, and now people who 'had dragged their small rowing boats onto lava-littered shores for centuries' were forced to move—their 'villages became obsolete' and thus began their protracted migration out of coastal communities,[35] and another gendered division of labour in fishing became 'crystallised'.[36]

Iceland was emblematic of geographer Doreen Massey's pioneering theory of the relationship between the spatial and the social: spaces become endowed with fixed identities and interests.[37] Fishing became narrowly understood as 'practices which take place at sea', and thus the sea is misconceived as 'a male domain'.[38] The metaphorical domain did not reflect the sexual division of labour so much as create it.[39] Women and children were recruited to work in the harbours to process fish caught by (mainly) men out at sea. The fishing industry—the catching, processing, production and marketing of sea foods—is reduced to 'capturing fish at sea'.[40] Yet, globally, it is estimated that only a fraction of fishing is performed by men aboard vessels out at sea, while 'women fill 90 per cent of land-based jobs at fisheries'. The industry is 'male-dominated but female intensive,' comments scientist Elena Finkbeiner.[41]

Fishing was also the site of global conflict—the 'cod wars' between Iceland and the UK ended in 1976 with Iceland's triumph: an exclusive zone of 200 nautical miles. It was about much more than fishing—the source of 80 per cent of Iceland's income—and sustainability; it was about nationalism, Iceland's location in Cold War geopolitics and domestic power.[42]

The degradation of intensively harvested fishing grounds everywhere had been graphically exposed by the extreme fate of herring fishing in the 1900s. For more than half a century, Icelandic women had congregated from all over the island in summertime to a seasonal herring hub, Siglufjörður. They gutted and processed the fish, they unionised, earned a lot of money and enjoyed themselves. But all of that came to an abrupt end when herring simply disappeared. They had been fished out. An absolute moratorium was declared in 1969. Nations all over the world were being forced to address sustainability of the seas—at the very moment when the neoliberal vanguard advocated privatisation of fishing rights.

By the end of the twentieth century, the number of vessels was vastly reduced, and it became increasingly difficult for Icelandic women to get (relatively well-paid) employment on the big boats, while men tended to shun (relatively poorly paid) work in fish processing, writes Willson, and furthermore seafaring fishermen were entitled to a share of the value of the catch, but fisherwomen processing the catch were not.[43]

Human–marine relationships re-made: 'all about patriarchy'

The neoliberal caucus in the Independence Party claimed that when property rights and profit were applied to fish stocks or to fishing grounds and to sustainability, 'then the problem spontaneously would be solved by the owners'.[44] Iceland's business 'Vikings' proposed a quick fix: privatisation and the profit motive. The mechanism that became widespread was the Individual Transferable Quota (ITQ)—initially allocated gratis to boat-owners on the basis of historical catches—to regulate and restrict who would be allowed to fish and where. Quotas, introduced in the 1980s, were a form of enclosure.[45] Iceland's Fisheries Management Act of 1990 affirms fish stocks in Icelandic waters as the common property of the Icelandic people[46] and at the same time confirms the quota system to eliminate smaller firms or fishers and, in effect, to enclose fishing grounds.[47]

The system also closed women's access to a resource that had been available to all: 'Quotas have become men's formal property right,' commented fisheries expert Eva Munk-Madsen, 'another patriarchal construction' formalising 'male control of and access to the fisheries'.[48] Women in the coastal communities had not been consulted.[49] Willson is unequivocal: 'Despite Iceland being touted as having the greatest gender equality in the world', what happened to fishing 'is all about patriarchy'. Geographer Becky Mansfield argues that privatisation made nature a kind of property, which became central in 'remaking ecosystems, livelihoods and identities'.[50] The introduction of ITQs activated an exodus from the villages, and waves of lay-offs swept across Iceland's fish-processing factories when the work left the land altogether and was relocated on trawler freezer factories.[51]

Contrary to the belief that the system would democratise the community of owners,[52] anthropologist Evelyn Pinkerton concludes that privatisation only led to concentration of ownership and market power and the separation of producers from the means of production—they lost access to the fishing and to the sea.[53] Pinkerton describes this as a gendered process of 'accumulation by dispossession'.[54] A boat-owner could profit by selling his quota, even though its value had derived not only from him and his boat but also those who made and maintained him and his work—the women, the teachers and the crews whose collective knowledge was embedded in his boat's productivity.[55]

ICELAND

Women driven out

The beating heart of coastal communities' sustainability, the women, had been exiled from the decision-making,[56] and what followed was female migration out of the villages.[57] A few communities found alternatives—tourism and whale-watching—but scores were eviscerated: they lost their schools, their factories and social infrastructure. Those villages that retained a fish-processing plant depended on immigrant women, mainly from Eastern Europe and the Philippines. Within two decades, around 20 per cent of Iceland's hitherto homogenous population came from overseas: they were vital but low paid and disempowered.[58] Those women who got work in fish processing in the cities found themselves in another rigidly gendered labour market. Willson notes that by the end of the twentieth century, the fisherwomen in factories were paid 55 per cent less than fishermen out at sea.[59]

When work left the land altogether, relocated onto trawler freezer factories,[60] followed by fully automated factories and the export of raw fish to other countries to be processed, coastal women lost not only their livelihoods and their collective knowledge but also whatever political power they might have had.[61] The outcome: in 'all levels of society related to fisheries women are rendered invisible'.[62]

The Scramble for Africa

As predicted, the neoliberal revolution had not expanded but diminished ownership and control of fishing: more than 400 companies had simply 'ceased to exist', and three-fifths of jobs in coastal communities disappeared.[63] Merely ten corporations, owned by men, dominated the industry, and two took half the entire profits,[64] only 30 per cent of which reached public coffers.

A classic case is Samherji, Iceland's most powerful fishing company, owned and controlled by three men who are related to each other. Samherji's vessels trawl the seas from the Arctic to Africa, in a twenty-first-century re-enactment of the white 'Scramble for Africa' in the nineteenth century. Around 80 per cent of fish imported by the North comes from the South.[65]

A heroic axis of forensic journalists from Al Jazeera, Iceland's RÚV television company, *Stundin* newspaper and a network of independent financial and legal experts delved into thousands of documents and discovered that Samherji's trawler crews operating off the African coast were being paid from millions of dollars secreted in a Marshall Islands tax haven. Its owners were accused of bribing Namibian politicians—several of whom were later convicted—for access to Namibia's quotas and thus to coastal resources. According to a whistle-blower, they 'leave nothing behind but burnt soil and money in the pockets of a corrupt political elite'.[66]

Samherji denied responsibility for the scam. In 2021, the company told its shareholders that now a massive part of Iceland's population was actively involved in the industry through their investments in pension funds. But people whose savings were invested in pension funds were, precisely, not active participants. 'Fishing lords' and 'codfathers' joined 'banksters' in the lexicon of patriarchs whose project was not 'property-owning democracy' but dominion. Threats to that dominion met focused ferocity. Helgi Seljan, who worked for the TV broadcaster that, together with *Stundin* newspaper and Al Jazeera, broke the story, found that that Samherji had created a crew, known as 'the guerrillas', to target journalists and discredit critics.[67]

Fisheries Minister Svandís Svavarsdóttir, of the Left-Green Movement, gave voice to popular outrage: the nation, she said, viewed the consolidation of fishing quotas in so few hands as 'deeply unjust'.[68] (Her predecessor as fisheries minister was Kristján Þór Júlíusson, a former Samherji managing director.)[69]

ICELAND

The modern patriarchs, 'fishing lords', 'banksters' and 'codfathers', had toppled Iceland from its place near the top of the global clean governance league.[70] Thorvaldur Gylfason, an eminent economist and activist for constitutional reform, commented that although previously 'oligarchy' had not been the typical nomenclature of Iceland's elite, it was now, thanks to 'a more stringent class of journalists and academics than we've ever had'.

Changemakers

After the 1975 strike, one of the changemakers was Vigdís Finnbogadóttir, the artistic director of Reykjavik Theatre Company, who had joined the multitude with her three-year-old daughter and her mother. She recalled listening to the radio that day: 'We heard children playing in the background while the newsreaders read the news. It was a great thing to listen to, knowing that the men had to take care of everything.' She had been a long-time progressive activist in campaigns against the US military presence established during the Second World War[71] and became the first single woman allowed to adopt a child in Iceland; in 1980, she was persuaded by the women's movement to—somewhat reluctantly—stand for election as president, a ceremonial head of state. She won and was re-elected three more times.[72] She reckoned her election could not have happened but for that day in October 1975, out of which grew the Women's List/Women's Alliance that in the 1980s enjoyed some electoral success and by 1987 secured 10 per cent of the parliamentary vote. Another changemaker was Guðrún Jónsdóttir, who had joined the demonstration anxiously alone. She became a coordinator for women's lists in local and national elections.[73]

By 2021, Icelanders joined the handful of nations with equal—or almost equal—parliamentary representation when it elected thirty women to its sixty-three-member parliament.

Left-Green Movement leader Katrín Jakobsdóttir, a feminist and socialist, was re-elected prime minister, 'the first elected head of state who comes from a new breed of Nordic left wing parties that link democratic socialism, environmentalism, feminism and anti-militarism'.[74] Jakobsdóttir's party was a minority, but despite the continued dominance of the right-wing Independence Party, tainted still by corruption, she became enormously popular, apparently the personification of integrity, a sea-green incorruptible whose generous, smart presence signalled the remarkable impact of feminism in the otherwise hostile terrain of prevailing neoliberalism.

Seemingly prosaic legislation showed the profound impact of feminism on popular culture: the country's patriarchal settlement was being shaken in those social and political spaces where women could claim, if not power, then influence—the distribution of domestic labour, childcare provision, incomes and violence. By the end of the twentieth century, Icelandic employment rates for both men and women were among the highest in the world, and in the twenty-first century Iceland came out consistently near or at the top of the World Economic Forum Equality League. But that hid huge gaps: Iceland's welfare state had been under-developed, and, as everywhere, women's incomes were scythed by motherhood—the rate of part-time employment among women was among the highest in the Organisation for Economic Co-operation and Development (OECD).

Labour movement militancy had made great progress in equalising hourly pay rates but not incomes over a year or over a lifetime, nor the sexual division of labour, time and power. Internationally, the patriarchal politics of time and money has always driven the pay differential as a time differential. Historical infrastructural weakness, most importantly childcare, did not match the aim of equal participation in parenting and public life. Icelanders worked long hours; they had more children, but public expenditure on families with children was only half the Nordic average.[75] By the 1990s, there was intense debate, and 'all the parties agreed that steps needed to be taken to make it easier for fathers to take leave,' recalls Ingólfur Gíslason, a sociologist and veteran researcher and advocate of parental leave.[76] In the early 2000s, parenthood resulted in 57 per cent of women but only 19 per cent of men reducing their paid working time. Before the 2000s, under 1 per cent of men took parental leave. Inevitably, the male breadwinner appeared to be undead; parents found themselves 'haunted by the spirit of the male breadwinner'.[77]

At the time, European paternal leave was only two weeks. Like other Nordic societies, Iceland stipulated that fathers must 'use it or lose it'. Now, something more needed to be done. Pressure galvanised among women's organisations, left-wing parties and the unions. 'We'd had a women's party—it was never in government but it had huge influence, and all the political parties had to put more emphasis on equality to stay in the game,' reckoned Berglind Ásgeirsdóttir, an Icelandic diplomat.[78] The centre-right government was confronted by the zeitgeist, and Ásgeirsdóttir, by then the Ministry of Social Affairs secretary general, was appointed to chair a working party.

Ásgeirsdóttir had been involved in women's rights since her student days and a senior civil servant and diplomat since 1979. 'We were all so experienced, we knew the system, we knew how it could be done,' she explained. That was decisive. 'We had decided to go the whole hog,' she said, 'and make a profound change in our society.' The team knew that two weeks' paternal leave would have little or no impact on the sexual division of labour. They had learned that if men lost money, then unlike women, they would not take parental leave. 'We took a drastic step: to make it non-transferable.'

The real challenge now was how paid parental leave would be paid for. Ásgeirsdóttir's working party had an idea: there was a national unemployment insurance fund, to which the employers contributed. 'At that time, Iceland had very little unemployment, and I knew that the fund was growing bigger and bigger,' she said. 'We proposed that a percentage would go into a parental leave fund.' These parents, temporarily out of paid labour, could be legitimate beneficiaries at no additional cost. 'We'd found the money! It was a stroke of genius.' Sociologist Gíslason thought it was 'thrilling, amazing—it was a win-win, it could be done without raising taxes'. The team had found the finance and proposed nine months' paid leave, three for each parent and three shared, at 80 per cent of salaries, and no ceiling: 'There was a lot of debate about that on the committee, the majority thought it would be key because we were trying to change mentality.'

In 2000, Iceland became the first country to legislate for equal paid parental leave for men and women: unlike in other Nordic societies, Iceland's parliament was unanimous in support.[79] The response among men was unexpected and unsurpassed. In the first year, fathers' take up was 82 per cent; by 2004, it was nearly 90 per cent. That 'was a wonderful moment,' said Gíslason. There had never been more Icelandic fathers active in caring for their young children. (After the 2008 crash, the payment was reduced—and so was men's take-up.) For Ásgeirsdóttir, the parental leave revolution was her proudest moment:

> I've been Iceland's ambassador to Russia, ambassador to Paris; I was deputy secretary general of OECD, secretary general of the Nordic Council, but this is really where I felt I'd made an impact. I'd say it was the biggest thing I ever achieved. I don't think I ever realised how big this was.

In time, the notion, not to say the expectation, that men and women generally should share parenting, led to some unexpected negative outcomes. In cases of divorce and separation, the traditionally patriarchal fathers' rights movements in many countries

ICELAND

exploited the idea of equal parenting against mothers who tried to protect themselves and their children from violence and sexual abuse. Iceland was no exception. In evidence to the UN Human Rights Commission in 2022, men's movement advocates were described as being influential in the courts and in the Independence Party, which on several occasions tried (in vain) to introduce legislation to criminalise mothers for withholding children's contact with fathers accused of violence and abuse.[80] They invoked the discredited notion of 'parental alienation', a hypothesis invented in 1985 by American psychologist Richard Gardner, a defender of paedophilia, who claimed that children were being brainwashed by mothers to believe they had been abused in order to resist contact with their fathers.[81]

When Iceland pioneered the rolling-out of a four-and-a-half-day week for public employees, the impact on the domestic division of labour was significant: though still not equal, women spent twenty-two hours a week on care, men seventeen hours.[82]

Equal pay activism had a discernible impact: the gender income-from-work gap dropped from 36 per cent in 2008 to 22 per cent in 2023. (The hourly wage gap between men and women doing equivalent jobs declined 6 per cent to 3.4 per cent.)[83] In 2017, Iceland's parliament became the first in the world to pass legislation requiring employers with over twenty-five workers to prove that they were paying people equally for similar work. It was a measure of the extraordinary consensus that it was introduced by a centre-right minister for social affairs, Þorsteinn Víglundsson.

Body politics—'we know who is hurting who'

And yet, and yet ... another spectre menaced women's well-being and secured men's sovereignty: sexual violence. In Iceland, it was said, every woman seemed to know another woman who had endured rape or assault.[84] Good intentions about equality between the sexes had not interrupted men's violence. Feminists generally expect that violence against women should be made to count as a measure of equality. It had not been until the 1960s and 1970s that the enduring impact of men's sexual violence came to be understood internationally: the pioneering American psychiatrist and feminist activist Judith Lewis Herman wrote that although public knowledge of the impact of violence in traumatic disorders began with the study of First World War combat victims, it was the Women's Liberation Movement in the 1970s that brought recognition that 'the most common post-traumatic disorders are not those of men in war, but of women in civilian life' enduring patriarchal tyrannies.[85] American political philosopher Iris Marion Young identified violence as 'probably the most obvious and visible form of oppression. Members of some groups live with the knowledge that they must fear random, unprovoked attacks on their persons or property. These attacks do not necessarily need a motive but are intended to damage, humiliate, or destroy the person.'[86] Fear, according to Young, is on every woman's horizon. Historically, it has often animated women's support for conservative law and order policies.[87] By the twenty-first century, violence and sexual abuse of women and children is being increasingly identified as a national security threat, a form of gendered terrorism.

Iceland is said to be one of the most peaceful societies on earth: it does not have an army, and its murder rate is low. However, whereas, globally, 38 per cent of female homicides are committed by intimate partners, in Iceland 50 per cent of murders of women are by intimate partners.[88] Experience of intimate partner violence in Nordic countries is high: between 20 and 30 per cent of women across a lifetime.[89] Then Iceland learned something about itself that detonated conventional wisdoms about Icelandic society and about how things come to be known. About a third of Iceland's entire female population participated in a unique study of the impact of trauma on women's health by two epidemiologists, Professors Unnur Anna Valdimarsdóttir and Arna Hauksdóttir, who discovered that 25 per cent had experienced rape or attempted rape, and 40 per cent had experienced physical or sexual violence.[90] 'People had a hard time believing that these are real numbers,' commented Valdimarsdóttir: 'The spontaneous reaction is "40 per cent! No way."' Hauksdóttir added that although Icelandic women had access 'to a lot of things that most of the people living on this Earth don't have ... we still have these numbers'. Hauksdóttir attributed Iceland's numbers both to prevalence and to the ways that knowledge is translated into policy and public awareness.[91]

That consciousness had been spread by Iceland's internationally acclaimed resource for women, Stígamót, an indefatigable, calm, elegant, service for survivors, located in a nondescript Reykjavik office block. 'We map the big patterns,' explains Stígamót's (now retired) spokesperson Guðrún Jónsdóttir, a feminist heroine in Iceland: 'We know who is hurting who.' The centre also confronted the impact of shame: victims, particularly children, 'are experts on secrets in the family,' says Jónsdóttir: '[A] child may be raped every day of her life, but she will say she would rather die than tell.' And so, Stígamót ventured into the education system: 'We go into every school and college, challenging the notion that children can be taught about road safety, healthy food, fire hazards, but not about sexual abuse. We want to reach the children who don't speak but who are suffering.'

She is confident that 'everyone knows that what we know is first hand'. Stígamót is trusted. But still the law is not implemented. Stígamót reports that only 12 per cent of victims of sexual violence press charges, and of these three-quarters are dismissed.

Worldwide, the 'justice gap' is universal. An average of 30 per cent of women are estimated to have experienced sexual abuse and violence. In the United States, for example, fewer than 1 per cent of reported rapes result in conviction, and in the UK only 1.6 per cent of reported rapes result in prosecution.[92] Although reporting of rape since the 1960s has increased, prosecution rates have sunk from 53 to 26 per cent.[93] Conviction rates have declined so much that rape—and in particular childhood rape—is virtually de-criminalised.[94]

Public opinion in Iceland has been alerted by feminism to the correlation between cultures of sexual entitlement and exploitation and was strongly supportive of Sweden's radical reform of the law on sexual exploitation, to target procurers and purchasers rather than prostituted women. In 2007, Iceland adopted the 'Nordic model' by prohibiting purchasing and profiteering rather than prosecuting exploited women. Exploited women continued to contact Stígamót for help—many of them trafficked from overseas. In 2010, Iceland banned strip clubs. Jónsdóttir explains that 'in 2000 Iceland had thirteen strip clubs; around 1,000 foreign women were brought over to work there', and although they could stay for only one month, they were allowed to return, again and again. As 'Iceland's adult male population was around 100,000', that meant 'one imported woman per 1,000 men'. There were suspicions of trafficking and prostitution.

But public opinion and law reform were up against the criminal justice system and the gatekeepers, the police. In 2011, Stígamót confronted police inaction by direct action: 'Operation Big Sister' placed advertisements in the press and on the internet—aided by women exploited in prostitution to get the language and the arrangements right. On the day the ads were published, '[w]ithin an hour we had one hundred calls; we arranged to meet—sometimes we sent the men to the home of the chief of police, others to a grocery market. One girl found her father among them.' The operation alerted the police to these men, 'to show the police how easy it was to find the buyers!'

ICELAND

When the strip clubs were closed down, 'so-called champagne clubs opened up', again using foreign women. 'So we opened our own club and advertised in the press, "women for sale" at Stígamót. Champagne clubs had sued us for criticising them and pointing out that they were selling women just as they did at the strip clubs.' Stígamót invited television cameras to their opening, where men were promised 'all kinds of services—teaching them to knit, chatting lightly about when they'd been raped, reading out Stígamót's reports'.

'We always kept champagne in the fridge to celebrate our successes,' says Jónsdóttir: 'And you have to make fun!' However, the police were unmoved—although the repertoire of men's violence against women may have roused public outrage, it was also sheltered by police misogyny. Joyously theatrical activism was mobilised again by Slutwalk—inspired by Canadian protests against a police officer's advice to women to 'avoid dressing like sluts' that went viral in 2011. Icelandic women's Slutwalk became a regular part of the country's summer calendar: by 2014, it attracted 11,000 women and men, huge for such a small place. It was followed by enthusiastic support in 2017 for the worldwide #MeToo movement.[95]

In 2018, the government's gender equality advisor, Halla Gunnarsdóttir—elected president of one of the country's biggest unions, known as VR, in 2025—took a risk: she planned an international #MeToo conference, to be hosted by Prime Minister Katrín Jakobsdóttir. They were astonished when a galaxy of international speakers arrived—perhaps they were not yet confident about how interested so many feminists were in their achievements in Iceland. The evidence of sexism was an alarming caution to the prevailing view of 'Iceland as the number one in the world, held up as a gender equality utopia,' explained Gunnarsdóttir. 'But we had been thinking "If this is as good as it gets it's not good, is it?"'[96]

PLANET PATRIARCHY

How 'not good' was confirmed by a national catharsis triggered by a group of women who found each other on Facebook and formed Öfgar to campaign against impunity. They identified more than thirty complaints about a celebrated Icelandic musician, and in 2021 they exposed sexual abuse in the national football team—lauded as heroes when Iceland became the smallest country to reach the World Cup finals in 2018. Öfgar had already reported six team members and the dates of their offences, resulting in half of the team being de-selected. This was an emergency: the team couldn't play, the national board resigned, sponsors withdrew and Jakobsdóttir protested publicly that it had taken these allegations to address sexual abuse in football.

Police

In 2014, Sigríður Björk Guðjónsdóttir became Reykjavik's first woman police chief since its origin in 1803, and in 2021 she became Iceland's national police commissioner. She could not have been more unlike any previous police chief. She was democratic and down to earth. Her earlier appointment in Reykjavik attracted scores of complaints from male officers. Police culture had ensured that women, particularly senior women, were isolated both inside and outside the organisation, and instantly, feminists recognised the risk and began to create a social base around her. She recruited specialist expertise in the candid acknowledgement (hitherto unrecognised by her male superiors) that 'I'm a police officer not a criminologist.'[97] She reformed police headquarters: top management had sequestered the fifth floor, the door was never open, the chiefs were serviced entirely by women, and officers were not expected to confer freely with their subordinates. Guðjónsdóttir abolished the fifth floor, opened up the building, recruited more women—within a year, there were more women trainees than men, and by 2020 women constituted 20 per cent of the force.

ICELAND

She focused on the police response to one of the most serious threats to Iceland's endemic problem of violence: men's violence against women and sexual assault. She adopted an alternative model of policing: 'We try to take responsibility from the women; with domestic violence, women are trying to keep everything together, the finances, the children, and we know that there are on average seven incidents before it gets to us. For children the effect is equivalent to living in a war zone.' Intimate partner violence reports to the police tripled, and charges rose by 30 per cent. Instead of delays following a woman's call, with perpetrators typically being bailed out, the new 'twenty-four-hour window' approach, she explains, seizes the time—multi-agency teams work instantly with the woman to make a safety plan, linking up with housing, therapeutic, employment and legal services—thus enabling a woman to envisage another life.

However, rape proved to be more intractable. The criminal justice system was not built to deliver justice to women. What would it mean for women, asks sexual violence researcher Hildur Fjóla Antonsdóttir, to live in a social landscape without risk and danger: to go partying downtown, drinking, letting their hair down and not be worrying about safety?[98] This, she insists, is one of the frontiers for young women who want to be able to engage with life, to have fun and to be safe in society—not sequestered, home alone. Crucially, the system sees these women not as subjects: the victim is only a witness in a process over which she has no control. Antonsdóttir's research confirmed that 'there is no legal relationship between the state and the victim', and even if there was an acknowledgement of her suffering—rare enough—it did not deliver repair. Antonsdóttir advocates a different response, shared by Icelandic feminism, that society and its institutions must address the impact of assault, fear, of fright, sadness or depression in a social landscape that is shadowed by perpetrators' presence. But there is no statutory duty to make space safe, she says, and despite the impact of police chief Guðjónsdóttir's initiatives, the outcomes of cases once they leave the police station and appear in the criminal courts is no better than anywhere else.

In 2021, Stígamót, together with Öfgar and other women's organisations, found a way to do something risky and radical: sue the state. They took Iceland to the European Court of Human Rights (ECHR) for failure to comply with international law to effectively investigate and prosecute violence against women reported to the police.[99]

Feminists had for years been thinking about how to bring cases that could call the state to account and confront the irony that protection of women from men is given to its most patriarchal institutions—the police and criminal justice system. There is 'no justice for the victim,' comments Antonsdóttir, and the perpetrator is given no chance to be changed by justice, 'no opportunity to be a better person'.[100] Human rights lawyer Sigrún Ingibjörg Gísladóttir helped them find a way: they formulated a challenge based on Article 3 of the Istanbul Convention, an international treaty that came into force in 2014, the first legally binding instrument that commits states to proactively prevent violence against women, to protect victims and prosecute perpetrators.[101] They made the case that most rapes—clearly gendered crimes against women—are systematically shut down. They challenged a universal phenomenon: institutional civil disobedience by masculinised criminal justice systems.[102] They selected a group of cases that met the stringent criteria, aware that 90 cent of cases didn't get through the ECHR's first phase to qualify for consideration. Theirs did.

Conclusion

This chapter has encountered a uniquely spirited, adroit and confident feminist movement that since 1975 engaged virtually the entire population of women; that raised women's representation in government; that challenged and changed the patriarchal politics of time and money, paid and unpaid work between women and men; that penetrated the sovereignty of corporate patriarchy by requiring companies to prove equal treatment of women and men; that raised collective awareness of the scale and meaning of men's sexual violence as a strategy of damage and domination; and exposed the impunity wrapped around perpetrators.

That Women's Day Off in 1975 affirmed those who had not been 'located at the centre of cultural power' and yet without whom society could not function.[103] It became emblematic of what was perceived to be the best of Iceland, egalitarian, generous, productive, playful and peaceful. Iceland's feminist prime minister, Katrín Jakobsdóttir, was consistently the country's most popular politician. Her government steered many significant feminist changes in Icelandic society. Icelanders are more cosmopolitan than the country's size and location might suggest: it is strategically located between great powers, and many of the people are widely travelled—spending time abroad. Halla Gunnarsdóttir is one of them, and when she returned to Iceland in 2017 after spending time in London, 'I felt we were more of a society than the UK', and that the impact of feminism on Icelandic culture was striking. 'When I returned I was very pregnant, and yet I was being offered jobs—I could not imagine that happening in the UK, I was aware that there was not a good infrastructure there for pregnant women, whereas in Iceland the employers don't have to bear the costs of pregnancy and parenthood.'

In 2023, every woman who could downed tools in a reprise of the 1975 women's strike/day off—this time, it was bigger than ever. They knew that 'solidarity brings change,' said one of the organisers, Sonja Yr Þorbergsdóttir, president of the public sector workers' federation.[104] 'Not only is Iceland not a paradise for women but there is a backlash—you can't grab it, it is not as clear as in other countries, but we are stagnating and that means that things will go backwards.' They focused on economic equality, violence, unpaid work and the domestic division of labour. They organised task forces to galvanise support for workers of foreign origin—now 20 per cent of the population—for people experiencing different discriminations, any and all organisations and employers. The public sector agreed not to penalise women. 'That created a moral principle among the employers,' she said, and if a private sector employer did not agree, the diverse network of organisers made it clear that 'we would make it known, and we told them "you don't want that kind of bad publicity"'.

Halla Gunnarsdóttir, a young veteran of Icelandic feminism, like many Icelanders, was reminded that day how 'the experience of solidarity is really important, women were having so many conversations that day about their lives, it was a massive opportunity to address what's happening at home, the importance of what they do and how that has to be institutionally recognised'.

Katrín Jakobsdóttir joined the women. By then, however, she had been the leader of the Left-Green minority party in a centre-right government that had been bundled into compromises that dispirited and ultimately diminished her social base. The coalition had endorsed hugely controversial legislation to deny asylum-seekers rights, including access to housing and healthcare, and despite protests pursued illegal deportations. Ultimately, her government could not—would not—breach the country's fundamental neoliberal fortifications, valorised as a manly money-making crusade that commandeered its economic citadels, fishing and banking, that flourished in secrecy, camaraderie and corruption. Its dominance was achieved by destruction and dispossession. As the anthropologist Margaret Willson put it, 'This is all about patriarchy.' It defied disgrace, it didn't die.

Iceland exemplified the heroic impact of feminism and the almost impossible distance between democracy and unaccount-

ICELAND

able, elite economic power.[105] An ugly reminder of its corruption emerged in 2023 after the privatisation of Íslandsbanki,[106] one of the banks that had been nationalised and rescued after the crash in 2008: the Icelandic National Audit Office criticised the coalition's finance minister, Bjarni Benediktsson, for the heavily discounted sale of a 22 per cent stake in the bank. Buyers included none other than his father.[107] Nearly 70 per cent of Icelanders believed the sale had broken the law.[108] But scandal did not disrupt his career—he became prime minister in 2024, albeit briefly: his government collapsed, and after a general election at the end of 2024 his Independence Party and Left-Green ally were swept from the Icelandic parliament. The Left-Greens (who had backed the anti-asylum-seeker bill) were wiped out and fully replaced by the Social Democratic Alliance, now the biggest party in parliament: it had opposed the bill, and—opposed to anti-immigrant populism—formed a new coalition government composed of three parties, all of them led by women.[109] Iceland continued to confound expectations.

And yet, as of 2024, Iceland's male-dominated elites had been 'able to regain formal power because they never really lost informal power'.[110] The unique impact of feminism on the country remained, therefore, up against an impregnable shadow state and neoliberal capitalist political economy, distanced and beyond the reach of democracy, which rendered Iceland not so much a women's paradise as a paradox.

7

ROJAVA

'THE STREET WAS OPEN TO THE WOMEN'

Rahila Gupta

In March 2016, I was standing on the Iraqi Kurdistan side of the River Tigris, at the border with Syria, waiting to cross, my pulse racing because borders produce that kind of reaction in migrants and because, on the other side of the river, a women's revolution was rumoured to be unfolding in a place called Rojava while the rest of Syria was in flames. In that short trip, I was to visit yet another border on International Women's Day when the free women of Rojava—now called the Democratic Autonomous Administration of North and East Syria or DAANES—marched to the border with Türkiye to ululate to their Kurdish sisters still in chains under the Turkish dictator, Recep Erdoğan. These two borders alone point to the fractured nature of the Kurdish people living in the four separate countries of Syria, Iraq, Türkiye and Iran.

Accompanying me to the water's edge was a young Iraqi Kurdish woman, a border control officer, who had asked me about the purpose of my visit. When I said I was going to research a book entitled 'Why Doesn't Patriarchy Die?' (the previous title), she asked me what 'patriarchy' meant. In response to my explanation, she said: 'Good, I hope it dies and never comes back.' I was here because the year before I had attended a conference in London and listened with scepticism as Mehmet Aksoy, a British-Kurdish journalist, filmmaker and activist, extolled the Rojava revolution.[1] Two years later, he was shot dead by ISIS fighters when he travelled to the frontline to film the final battle for the liberation of Raqqa from ISIS by the Kurdish-led Syrian Democratic Forces (SDF). This life of promise, cut short, of male enthusiasm for a feminist revolution and the Kurdish struggle for freedom, provides a glimpse into all that is wondrous and unimaginable about this momentous development.

The other reason for my racing pulse was that my road journey through Iraqi Kurdistan to the Tigris had skirted past smoke plumes, no doubt generated by bombs, and past Mosul, then the stronghold of ISIS in Iraq. My destination in Northern Syria was Qamişlo, the de-facto capital of Rojava, a mere three hours away by road from Raqqa, the de-facto capital of the short-lived ISIS caliphate in Syria. In both cases, in Rojava and Raqqa, although the trajectory was in completely opposite directions, the transformation in the position of women appeared to be dramatic and almost instantaneous in comparison to the slow rate of change in other parts of the world. In this chapter, I want to focus on the factors that made it possible, to try to answer the classic question that preoccupies all activists trying to change a system—why and how do revolutions take place?—being fully aware that there is no single answer, and even several answers do not fully satisfy. When you dig deeper, of course, you find that the ground was being prepared for some time. What was the catalyst? What were the mechanics of change? And once that change had been achieved, how did they encourage and maintain the cultural shift, how did vast sections of the population sign up to a new way of living, thinking and being? Can patriarchy be reinforced or dismantled at speed by a conscious focus on ideological indoctrination? In both Rojava and Raqqa, the ideas that underpinned the new social structures were consciously and systematically reinforced throughout society.

At the border post on the Syrian side, my papers were cleared by a man who spoke English, who took me in to see his boss, the head of border control, who then spent two hours discussing world politics with me. We were served tea by a sixteen-year-old boy. I discovered that all three were paid the same wage. This was not just a gender revolution. I had been raised in a communist household where adult conversations had been elevated by dreams of another world. I never thought I would have the opportunity of witnessing a revolution in my lifetime, especially not after the bottomless consumerism and individualism of the neoliberal West made equal pay sound like a fantasy. I was enthralled. And I hadn't even left the border. Apart from a handful of women in military fatigues and floral scarves in the canteen, I was yet to meet the powerful women, the motor force of the revolution.

The road to Qamişlo was greener than I had expected given the dusty browns of Syria that I had grown familiar with on British television: there were no bombed-out buildings, no smoke plumes, no signs of war, no motorways, no high-rise buildings, no malls, no advertising billboards, all in stark contrast to the more developed, more urbanised, Iraqi Kurdistan. The landscape was curiously featureless: there were no trees, but there were plenty of 'nodding donkeys', which pointed to the concentration of oil wealth—one explanation for the intense international interest in this area. The few billboards that could be seen carried pictures of their martyrs, the men and women who had died in the war against ISIS. The glaring absence of advertising, symbol of capitalist consumption, recalled Cuba. This northernmost strip of Syria, along the border with Türkiye, was home to between 3 and 5 million predominantly Kurdish people with substantial Arab and Christian (Syriac) populations as well as Turkmen and Armenian, Chechen and Circassian minorities. Since then, the demographics and territorial size have changed.

While war was raging across Syria, the Rojava administration had been experimenting with a radical form of direct democracy, attempting to achieve class and race equality and ecological sustainability, with women in the driving seat since 2012. War is the classic moment in which all rights get suspended or eroded. Who thinks about the importance of gender equality, or racial inclusivity, or direct democracy during war? But that is the project the Kurds are developing in Northern Syria. And all they want is to be left in peace to do so. The political vacuum created by the rebellion against Assad in 2011, another front of the 'Arab Spring', gave them that peace initially, but then ISIS attacked. ISIS represented not only an existential threat but an ideological threat to everything Rojava stands for. They had to fight back—in self-defence. Kurdish feminist Dilar Dirik believes that the rise of

> ISIS has accelerated this entire process of people seeing the women's freedom question as the most fundamental problem that needs to be solved. This never started with ISIS and it will not end with ISIS. That is why the women's movement in Kurdistan is so radical because it knows what it is up against and what is the alternative.[2]

We are interested in the role of ideology as a mobilising force for social change. As a sociologist put it: 'Metaphorically, constituents have to be moved from the balcony to the barricades.'[3] Scholars who analyse the anatomy of social movements focus mainly on two aspects: resource mobilisation and programmes for action that arise from structural dislocations. There has not been enough work on the third element, and that is the meaning attributed to the changes in material conditions, the framing, how things are represented or, in Stuart Hall's words, the 'politics of signification'.[4] Under what conditions does the framing help to rally support and inspire action?[5] In Rojava, as we will see, the ideology developed by Abdullah Öcalan, jailed leader of the Kurdistan Workers' Party (Partiya Karkerên Kurdistanê, PKK), emerged out of a history of oppression faced by Kurds dispersed across Syria, Türkiye, Iraq and Iran as a result of the imperial carve-up that took place in the twentieth century, the Sykes–Picot line of 1916;[6] everywhere they have faced discrimination, with perhaps the greatest brutality and attempts to annihilate them having taken place under Saddam Hussein in Iraq and various regimes in Türkiye. Öcalan provided an analysis that made sense of Kurdish history, was culturally resonant and a route out of the wretchedness. The route changed in response to material circumstances: from a revolutionary struggle in the 1980s, underpinned by Marxist–Leninist political theory, to reconstitute the separate bits of Kurdistan into a single, independent nation-state, to a rejection of the state as an oppressive entity, opting instead for a localised form of direct democracy to be practised within the national boundaries of the states in which the Kurds lived.

Land of the Setting Sun

So how did Rojava come into existence? Rojava translates as Western Kurdistan or more poetically as the 'Land of the Setting Sun'. The political freedoms of the Kurds had been heavily restricted by Assad; expressions of Kurdish identity were criminalised, and their demographic density was diluted by Syria's 'Arabisation' policy, in which Arabs were resettled in Kurdish areas. Under the direction of the Democratic Union Party (Partiya Yekîtiya Demokrat, PYD), which was influenced by the ideology of 'democratic confederalism' propounded by Öcalan, across the border in Türkiye, the Syrian Kurds took advantage of the Syrian civil war to set up a secular and ethnically inclusive, genuinely bottom-up democratic system with the emancipation of women as its key goal. The defence forces of Rojava were led to victory against Raqqa by a woman, Rojda Felat, a little reported fact in Western media,[7] with the Syrian Kurds eventually liberating nearly one-third of Syrian territory. Meanwhile, their westernmost canton, Afrin, and other towns along the border have been attacked and occupied by Turkish-backed Syrian rebels and the Turkish army, which relied on remnants of ISIS fighters as mercenaries.[8] The map changed on an almost daily basis until the Turkish invasion and occupation that ate away at the western and northern edges of Rojava in 2018 and 2019. Since then, Rojava's borders have been stable, although instability stalks its future: first at risk from the Assad regime and then, from December 2024, by its replacement, the Islamist HTS (Hay'at Tahrir al-Sham), as well as Türkiye and a number of Middle Eastern countries with their complicated and conflicting agendas.

There is not much research on the position of women prior to the revolution—this in itself is a result of discrimination by successive Syrian governments. 'Research permits' were not issued for field work,[9] and the Kurds were not recognised as a linguistic or ethnic minority, so census data on Kurdish women was not available. Scholars disagree about whether Kurdish women were genuinely more liberated than their Arab sisters because they did not wear veils and because polygyny was not generally practised among Kurds. However, as in many profoundly patriarchal societies, male honour and even national honour was tied to women's sexuality. Any hint of premarital or extramarital sex could end in an 'honour' killing. It is from the radical legislative reform that was carried out in Rojava in 2014 by Kongra Star, the women's umbrella organisation, that we can determine the contours of

Kurdish patriarchal society. Kongra Star was set up only in 2005, although individual women had been politically active for twenty years or more.

The story of Rojava cannot be told without reference to Bakur (the south-eastern Kurdish region of Türkiye), where there was a huge overlap in political sympathies and support for democratic confederalism between Turkish and Syrian Kurds. Political parties were tolerated by Assad as long as they did not call for a Kurdish state or advocate revolution or regime change in Syria. Unlike the Kurds in Iraq or Türkiye, the Syrian Kurds never took up armed struggle against Assad. Their activities were monitored by an intricate network of spies that created such an atmosphere of mutual suspicion that most political parties had a pyramid structure with secret cells of three to five people.

How could such a factionalised polity have been transformed seemingly overnight into a cohesive force capable of running a revolution in such difficult circumstances? The real political foundations had been laid by Öcalan in the eighteen years he lived among the Syrian Kurds. He founded the PKK in Türkiye in 1978 to wage an armed struggle against the state in support of Kurdish self-determination. He fled Türkiye in 1980 after the third military coup and remained in Syria until he was expelled in 1998. In Damascus, the PKK ran an academy where more than 10,000 cadres and supporters were schooled. They were funded by donations from the sizeable Kurdish diaspora, supported by the Palestine Liberation Organization and Assad. It was the cadres who would go from home to home to win over people to the idea of an independent Kurdistan. They lived for the liberation struggle; they had no home or property and renounced family and romantic relationships.[10] Officially, Öcalan's presence was denied, but he was a crucial pawn in the relationship between Syria and Türkiye. Türkiye controlled the water of the Euphrates and used that to exert pressure on Syria over

Öcalan's continued presence, while Syria also used Öcalan to limit Turkish power over them. The PKK drew thousands of Syrian Kurds into its ranks in the 1980s and dominated Syrian Kurdish political parties. Many fought against Türkiye on behalf of the PKK, which suited Assad to such an extent that the Syrian state did not conscript those Kurds into state military service because serving in the PKK was recognised in practice as a substitute.[11] In 1999, Öcalan was arrested in Kenya by the Turkish authorities with the help of the CIA and has been held in isolation on İmralı island ever since.

After 2003, support for the PKK was transferred to the PYD, which identified as a Syrian Kurdish party but adopted the PKK ideology of national liberation and became a member of the Union of Communities in Kurdistan (Koma Civakên Kurdistanê, KCK), an umbrella organisation founded by Öcalan of Kurds from all the four regions. With the exception of the PYD, there were no women in the leadership of the Syrian Kurdish political parties. Dirik, a Kurdish activist, says that 'with the PKK, women started to become active for the first time, and this challenged the patriarchal notions of the people on the ground. Until then, nobody suspected that women were going to do political activism ... especially not Kurdish women because they were very marginalised.'[12] After 2004, when violence broke out between the Kurds and the Arabs at a football game and seventy people were killed by the security forces, repression by the Syrian state intensified. Men suffered brutal punishments, so it was women who did all the organising because they could move around openly.[13] The Kurdish women in Türkiye came to play a central role in the PKK for the same reason as their Kurdish sisters in Syria: men were being imprisoned, tortured and killed, so women started becoming active and joining the PKK in their thousands in the mid-1990s.

In 2011, Rojava, like the rest of Syria, was in ferment, caught up initially in peaceful protests against Assad. One of my interpreters, who was a university student in 2011, used to sneak away from home without permission from her parents, travelling a fair distance to Qamişlo to join the variously themed protests every Friday: 'Freedom Friday', 'Free Children Friday', 'Day of Rage Friday' and so on. When the protests became militarised after being infiltrated by Christian and Muslim radicals, she left, disheartened; the Syrian rebellion across the country was similarly abandoned by advocates of democracy and infiltrated by religious extremists. This is one of the reasons why Rojava did not join the Syrian opposition against Assad. A young woman revolutionary explains: '[M]ost of the Syrian opposition was Islamist, and we couldn't ally with them—a revolution can't come from the mosque.'[14] In 2012, the People's Protection Units (Yekîneyên Parastina Gel, YPG), an armed defence unit, which had been formed after the 2004 football match and riots in Qamişlo, took over the city of Kobanî without resistance from Assad's soldiers.

According to one account,[15] when the protests against Assad began, the Kurds were watching carefully. Within months, they had established illicit self-protection units and commandeered the private armoury of individuals, which included shotguns, pistols and Kalashnikovs. At the same time, they set up people's councils, courts, women's organisations and economic cooperatives on the democratic model proposed by Öcalan. In July 2012, the YPG set up checkpoints around Kobanî city. The people then assembled at the regime's army headquarters and told the soldiers that if they gave up their weapons, their security would be guaranteed. The soldiers realised they had no alternative when they saw the mass of people out there. Assad's regime was preoccupied with the civil war in the South and could not send reinforcements. It was a bloodless revolution.

A German journalist reported:

> In Kobanî, the outer city perimeter was quickly fortified with checkpoints on all major roads (flying the Kurdish flag) and heavily armed

fighters controlling each incoming car. 'We want to prevent any members of the Free Syrian Army, but also regime spies, from entering the city,' said one masked fighter, proudly displaying his newly acquired shotgun. Some of the weapons used by the Kurdish fighters were smuggled into the country via northern Iraq. Other weapons were acquired on the black market or confiscated from Syrian Army and police forces.[16]

Although not one shot was fired, the presence of an armed militia led by PKK-trained cadres established the pre-eminence of the PYD and brought the many political parties that had been active to date to a state of grudging acquiescence. The real bloodshed began when ISIS laid siege to Kobanî in September 2014, a baptism of fire for Rojava's fledgling defence forces, which struggled to keep hold of it. It was at this point that the US-led coalition entered the fray and launched air strikes against ISIS, enabling the Kurds to regain the city by January 2015. The US remained involved until Trump announced the sudden withdrawal of his support in October 2019, believing the fight against ISIS was over, and gave Türkiye carte blanche to invade and occupy parts of Rojava. As evidence grew that ISIS was regrouping and sleeper cells were mounting occasional attacks, a rump of US forces remained to advise DAANES on containing the threat from ISIS. At the time of writing, with the Islamist HTS in place in Damascus, and with the support of Türkiye, Islamist groups, including ISIS, have become emboldened to launch further attacks on Rojava.

The creation of a politicised culture

A politicised culture provided fertile ground for the birth of the revolution. The PKK adopted a time-intensive route, going from house to house in Bakur (South East Türkiye) and Rojava, staying the night and engaging the family members in discussion. Dirik says they 'would talk to the same people for hours, for days, for weeks until they got that person's heart'.[17] My stay in Rojava was hosted by a range of different families who were connected to the women's umbrella organisation Kongra Star through daughters, sisters and mothers who were active in it.[18] I stayed at the apartment of a young woman, Hebun, on the first night. Her mother, Halima, a warm and welcoming woman, had been illiterate before the revolution but learned to read and write Kurdish after 2012. While watching TV, she would delightedly read the captions out loud. Although she'd had an arranged marriage and stayed at home to look after seven children, she was influenced by Öcalan's ideas. She spoke of ending male domination and giving her daughters the freedom to choose their husbands and pursue careers. I asked how she came under his influence when she couldn't read. She said she had participated in political discussions with her husband's friends who used to come to the house. I later found out that 'friends' is the Kurdish equivalent of 'comrades', political cadre who would stay the night engaged in discussion. Literacy was not essential to the spread of ideas.

In her autobiography,[19] Sakine Cansiz, a founding member of the PKK, describes the tactics used in the 'educational work' she carried out with women in the late 1970s in Türkiye, although her primary aim was the creation of a national liberation movement rather than a challenge to patriarchy. She would identify those who seemed most open to her political ideas and those who had authority within their families and invite them to her sessions. Through that person, she would aim to work on the entire family: 'Especially for the women who decided to join the revolutionary work, I wanted to get to know their families and win over the people around them, too. That was part of the plan.'[20] She believed that '[s]ince women were the most oppressed, they also have the best prospects of becoming revolutionaries'.[21] This was a point of view reinforced by Öcalan: 'He thereby bolstered our confidence and our will to fight for our own freedom.' Cansiz herself had to run away from home in order to become a revolutionary.

This method of consciousness raising applied not just in the cities and villages but also in the mountains in Türkiye. According to Dirik, who has interviewed some of the PKK guerrillas,

> the people in the mountainous villages wouldn't open their doors to them sometimes because they were afraid and they didn't know who the PKK were. The women, however, would open the door to them because they were curious to know who these guerrilla women were and why they were talking about women's liberation.

Unlike other political parties, the PKK did not mobilise the urban or rural elite like the tribal leaders or the middle-class bourgeoisie; they preferred to work with marginalised people—the peasants, the workers, the students and the women. One woman guerrilla told Dirik: 'If you go to a house to discuss patriarchy with a housewife and she asks whether she should cook pasta or potatoes today, don't argue with her about patriarchy. Say pasta. You have to go slowly.'[22] What impressed people was the respect accorded to them by the PKK: that they were not doing this for money; that they were sacrificing themselves for their movement; that they didn't have a roof over their heads; that they were eating at other people's houses and sometimes didn't eat for days. According to Dirik, all of these attributes endeared the PKK to the people. For Dirik herself,

> the fact that there is a movement like PKK in our life has shaped my understanding of what womanhood means; it is pluralistic and multifaceted. I see a peace mother, a guerrilla, a parliamentarian, I see my own mother organising demonstrations, I see my younger sister organising actions. You can be married, single or divorced, you can be educated, not educated, young or old, and there is a place for you in this movement as a woman. It's not defining one type of woman. It's the woman's freedom that is the defining factor of the struggle,

not her body and her behaviour. For me, this is something the Middle Eastern women's movement has struggled with: the struggle between modernity and conservatism, secularism and religion, the battle was always the woman's body. The woman's clothes, her body, her behaviour, her speech, her marital status represented your ideology. The Kurdish freedom movement has established that women can be themselves.[23]

At the barrel of a gun

This immersive consciousness-raising work created a stratum of politicised women. But would this have been enough to enable a relatively conservative society with very few women in public life to leap forward to a revolution where a co-presidency rule ensures that every institution is headed by a man and a woman? There are dozens of examples of this level of feminist activism that did not end in a similarly revolutionary society. One of the answers lies with the women's army the Union of Free Women of Kurdistan (Yekitiya Azadiye Jinen Kurdistan, YAJK), which was created by the PKK in Türkiye. By 1993, one-third of the PKK's armed forces were women.[24] In *Revolution in Rojava*, Anja Flach, a German sympathiser who spent some time with YAJK in the mid-1990s in the Qandil Mountains, on the Türkiye–Iraq border, writes that

> [o]ne of YAJK's goals was to overcome the traditional socialization of feudal society that was reproduced in the guerrilla army. There in the mountains, YAJK developed principles of autonomous women's organizing, dual leadership, and the minimum 40 percent participation of women in all areas—principles that now apply to the movement in all four parts of Kurdistan.[25]

Today in Rojava, the figure stands at 50 per cent.

I have often been told by Kurdish activists that I should visit the Qandil Mountains in north-western Iraq where the PKK has its military camps if I want to see a truly non-patriarchal society in operation. This is an implicit recognition that there is still a long way to go in Rojava. However, the point is to see how these ideas play out in the 'real world'. My resistance to the idea on the grounds that no lessons can be learnt from a closed and militarised society like the one in the Qandil Mountains was reinforced by Fréderike Geerdink, a Dutch journalist who spent a year in PKK camps between May 2016 and June 2017.[26] She felt that the presence of fighters in the Qandil camps made it an artificial society in comparison to Rojava, which was truly a non-patriarchal society in operation.

Almost all the women I met in Rojava felt empowered by the presence and success of the YPJ, the women's defence forces. They experienced a new respect from men impressed by women wielding guns. David Graeber, the late anthropologist and supporter of Rojava, makes a similar point, semi-flippantly: 'Well, how do you get rid of patriarchy? Well, making sure all women have access to automatic weapons is one place to start. You really can't push people around if they're armed.'[27] A spokeswoman for Kongra Star pointed to the Ezidi women of Sinjar (Iraq) who were abducted, raped, sold as slaves, killed and brutalised by ISIS as an explanation for why Kurdish women cannot afford to be defenceless.[28] She argued that 'there is a need to rethink the privileged position of non-violence'. For Kurdish women, self-defence goes beyond the use of arms: '[I]t includes the preservation of culture, against an aggressive politics of assimilation and the organisation of the economy, education, politics, social affairs from a women's perspective.'[29] Dirik defines self-defence as 'a complete dedication and responsibility to life. To exist means to resist. And in order to exist meaningfully and freely, one must be politically autonomous.'[30]

There are four protection forces made up of women active in Rojava: the HXP (Hêzên Xweparastinê), a conscripted self-defence force that is part of the military structure; the volunteer-based military women's self-defence forces, the YPJ; the women's civil self-defence forces connected to the communes, the HPC (Hêzên Parastina Civakî), who, in particular, are tasked with intervening in incidents of abuse or violence against women; and the women's security or police force (Asayiş a Jin), which is a salaried role but also recruits volunteers. The Social Contract (Rojava's provisional constitution) redrafted in December 2023 explicitly states that self-defence is both a right and duty for every citizen.[31]

Is achieving gender equality at the barrel of a gun a contradiction in terms, especially as feminists have extensively theorised the link between aggressive masculinity and militarisation? This has exercised feminists nurtured in the pacifist tradition who support peaceful solutions to conflict and cannot accommodate armed struggle by the YPJ even if carried out in self-defence.

A women's revolution

So what has Rojava managed to achieve in the middle of an existential battle with ISIS in the South, Turkish aggression from the North, shortages of essential goods and floods of internally displaced persons (IDPs)? A women's revolution that has brought about astronomical changes in the legal, social and economic position of women; an ethnically inclusive society; and an ecologically sustainable co-op-based economy.

Kongra Star is deeply embedded across Rojava: their structure mirrors the multi-party TEV-DEM (the Movement for a Democratic Society), an umbrella organisation established in Rojava in 2011 that includes all ethnicities and religions and is an exercise in direct grassroots democracy. At the neighbourhood level, TEV-DEM has set up communes ranging in size from seven to 300 families depending on whether they are based in villages or cities. All the members elect a man and a woman under the co-presidentship rule to manage the work and to represent their interests at the next level, the House of the People (Mala Gel), a kind of regional town council that elects members to the city level, which in turn elects members to the cantonal level, which sends members to the overarching People's Council responsible for coordinating all of DAANES. The commune elects members of specialist committees like health, education, services or conflict resolution, which will also be led by co-presidents. Only problems that cannot be resolved at commune level make their way up the structure. The same democratic confederal principles apply to specialist councils that deal with education, health, environment, law, culture, religion, social work, economy and agriculture, youth and welfare. According to Walîda Botî, then president of Kongra Star, the women's umbrella organisation was the first to push for co-leadership. She said that not all the parties were happy with the idea, not even the PYD, the dominant party in DAANES: 'Everywhere you will find co-management, even in the PYD; it was written into the Social Contract.'[32]

The autonomous, parallel women-only structure set up by Kongra Star, with its own committees, alongside TEV-DEM, contributes equally to law and policy-making and has the power of veto over any policies affecting women's rights. All kinds of women have entered the public sphere as a result. Women who could not read or write before the revolution have gone to the academies that have been set up and become educated and empowered. Halima, mentioned earlier, joined the conflict resolution committee that dealt mainly with domestic violence. The very presence of women in the public sphere has transformed how they are seen, and a new respect for women's abilities has permeated every level of society. The existence of this separate structure implies that women's liberation is not to be achieved by equal numbers but by tilting the scales in favour of women in order to achieve a level playing field.[33]

I asked Hediye Yusuf, then co-president of Cizire Canton, the largest of the three cantons that comprised Rojava at that time, about the experience of sharing power with the Arab tribal leader Sheikh Humaydi Daham al-Hadi. Al-Hadi moved from being a supporter of al-Qaeda to embracing Öcalan's ideology, possibly an opportunistic power grab. Yusuf told me that al-Hadi did not think she would be capable of fulfilling her responsibilities, but after two years of working together, he had grudgingly come to accept her as an equal.[34] The 'enforced' practice of sharing power with a woman was in itself a transformative experience for al-Hadi, an example of bringing about ideological change through action in a new democratic structure that was an expression of the ideas of Öcalan as interpreted by the women. Yusuf was quoted in the *New York Times* saying 'Hadi is certainly not a feminist ... but he supports us because we offer a new, functional society that respects everyone, unlike Assad, unlike IS, unlike Erdoğan.' Al-Hadi joked about his new co-dependent relationship—'I didn't ask to share power with a woman,' he said, seated alongside Yusuf. 'They made me do it.'[35]

Amina Omar, then head of the Women's Ministry, handed me a booklet when I asked about their legislative programme. 'Basic Principles and General Provisions for Women' begins with the exhortation: 'Fighting the reactionary authoritarian mentality in the [sic] society is the duty of every individual in the areas of Democratic Self-Administration.' The booklet lists the administration's extensive legislative assault on patriarchal practices: child marriage, forced marriage, dowry and polygamy have been banned; honour killings, violence and discrimination against women have been criminalised; a woman's testimony is equal to a man's; a woman has a right to equal inheritance; marriage contracts will be issued in civil courts; women, regardless of their marital status, have been given the right to custody of their children until the age of fifteen, as compared to Syrian sharia law, which decrees that a divorced woman can only hold on to her sons until the age of nine and girls until the age of eleven so long as she does not remarry. Impressive work when you consider that these laws came into place in January 2014, two years after the Women's Ministry was set up. Allowing women custody of their children, regardless of their marital status, is an extremely daring legal right given how conservative Syrian society is. Of course, reality has yet to catch up with the new laws: Omar said that many of the spaces in their refuges are taken up by young women running away from the wrath of their families because they had become pregnant outside of marriage.[36]

Sharia courts, in which women get a raw deal, have been disbanded in DAANES, but they thrived in other parts of Syria under the control of various Islamists, including ISIS before their defeat, and will probably be implemented by Ahmed al-Sharaa, head of HTS, who has previously declared his intention of introducing sharia law in the new Syria.[37] Although Assad claimed to be committed to secularism,[38] Syria has always had a network of religious courts to deal with personal laws of the various denominations. In Rojava, there is a clear understanding of the need to keep religion out of the public sphere in a way that is even more advanced than the UK, where sharia councils and Muslim arbitration tribunals exist in an uneasy, parallel relationship with state law. DAANES's first Social Contract stated their intention to build a society 'free from ... the intervention of religious authority in public affairs'.[39] Mona Abdsalam of SARA, an organisation that supports women escaping violence and honour crimes, believes that the incidence of violence had halved since the passing of the laws. Margaret Owen, a British human rights lawyer, tells a story she heard when she was in Rojava. When a man is convicted of domestic violence offences, he is put in prison and given gender equality classes. It is only when he appears to have been rehabilitated that he is taken back to his wife—if she agrees to have him back—and the situation is monitored by the commune's conflict resolution committee.

These changes were not without pushback. In the newly liberated areas after the fall of Raqqa in October 2017, where the Arabs are in a majority, there were reports of astonishment among Arab women, having been dressed from head to toe in black under ISIS, at the freedom and apparent equality of Kurdish women, and disquiet among the Arab men. The *Los Angeles Times* quoted a fifty-year-old Arab builder who escaped ISIS and was relieved to find himself in a refugee camp run by the Kurdish defence forces but nonetheless complained that '[t]hey give a lot of rights to women. If I raise my voice at a woman, they might put me in jail.' Some of the men at the camp complained to the authorities but were told: 'We are a democracy here.' The reporter comments that '[i]t's been something of a culture shock for many of the residents who for three years had lived under the crushing religious fundamentalism of Islamic State'.[40] When officials tried to enforce the polygyny ban in Manbij, an Arab-majority town, anger from tribal leaders led to the granting of an exception there.[41] In the interests of democracy, some of the gender equality legislation was ditched. The same pattern was repeated in other Arab-majority areas liberated from ISIS. The original intention of keeping religion out of public affairs also seems to have been watered down—though the revised Social Contract still opposes 'religious fanaticism' and any 'mentality' that is in conflict with its democratic ideals, it also devotes several clauses to ensuring representation of ethnic and religious groups in its governing structures.[42] This is an example of the kinds of tensions and compromises between democracy and patriarchy, where democracy has taken precedence over gender rights, that Rojava hopes to eliminate through intensive education of the people on the goals of the revolution.

However, the Social Contract continues to stipulate the 50 per cent rule for women's representation at every level of the administration and in every region. I asked Berivan Şaredariye, university lecturer and co-president of the Union of Municipalities,[43] how they were able to fulfil this requirement in the Arab-majority areas that had had no previous engagement with Öcalan's ideas. She acknowledged that it had been difficult to recruit Arab women when Raqqa fell in 2017 and other Arab areas were absorbed in 2019, but it was important not to be defeatist: 'No, we should have women, we should prepare them. We should give them training, and they will take a place.' Today, there are many Arab women in the administration, which suggests that, within a matter of years, Rojava's awareness-raising policies have worked.

In addition to the women-friendly policies, they have built a women-only village, Jinwar, where life is designed to be ecologically sustainable and to be lived on the basis of 'women-centered ethics and values'.[44] It includes a herbal medicine centre, a school for children, a women's academy, self-sustaining agricultural projects, thirty houses, arts and crafts workshops and a sewing centre. Despite the huge changes the revolution has brought about, women can still only leave their parental homes after getting married or if they join the YPJ. Jinwar is another alternative for women who do not wish to be married, are escaping violence (whether domestic or the violence of war) or who have been widowed. They hope to build such spaces across the region. It is another example of the freedom that Kurdish women have carved out for themselves to develop the ideas of Öcalan in a direction of their choosing. They were inspired by the example of Umoja,[45] a women-only village established in Kenya in 1990 for homeless survivors of violence and young girls escaping forced marriage. It is also run along democratic principles, and the women survive by selling crafts and jewellery.

What the women's revolution has not resolved is the question of sexuality. Feminist researchers who interviewed Kurdish women activists found that '[a]ccording to all of our respondents, the focus on sexuality in today's society is a side effect of capitalism'.[46] Öcalan's view, that the sexual revolution did not bring freedom for women and was not likely to while relations between men and women were based on domination by one sex, was received favourably by a society with conservative attitudes to sex. It is a view to be found among so-called anti-sex feminists in the West like US lawyer Catharine Mackinnon, who argues that all sexual encounters take place under patriarchy and are therefore bound to replicate the master/slave relationship.[47] A wounded male soldier from the YPG, whom I interviewed while he was still recuperating, echoed Öcalan's words to explain why he had renounced married life.[48] Enforcing celibacy in a mixed fighting force may be a pragmatic approach to policing sexual violence—if all sex is forbidden, there can be no blurring of boundaries between rape and consensual sex. It is also pragmatic because it reassures parents that their daughters' virginity will be protected and so eases recruitment to the YPG and YPJ in a community that frowns on sexual freedoms, especially for women. Across the border in Iraqi Kurdistan, which is much more conservative when it comes to men mixing with women, a commander of the Iraqi army, the Peshmerga, claimed that men and women fighting together in the Iranian Kurdish resistance movement, Komalah, was like mixing 'fire with petrol'.[49]

Celibacy among the party cadre has been enforced with ideological rigour. However, not all those fighting in the YPG and YPJ are necessarily cadres, so rules of celibacy do not apply to them. Each force has devised its own rules. Women fighters may marry, but they will not return to the frontline. Married men are allowed to fight at the frontline and are given leave every ten days to visit their families. This was the only example of institutionalised inequality that I came across. When I put this to a British woman who had joined the YPJ, she said:

> It's a difficult question to answer because you have to remember that we are autonomous. YPJ make their own decision on how to deal with married women and mothers, based on their own ideas not just comparing to what men have. That's the difference between here and Western feminism. Feminists are always comparing themselves with men instead of just thinking about what they want and what's best.[50]

Meredith Tax also looks at the pros and cons of this issue in *A Road Unforeseen*. She quotes Handan Çağlayan, author of *Mothers, Comrades, Goddesses*, who is critical of the PKK taboo on romantic relationships: 'Women are asked to desexualize themselves when entering the public sphere much as they are in other anti-colonial pro-modernization national movements. ... Therefore, the same discourse that enables women to leave their homes by overcoming the *namus* [honour] barrier also establishes a new patriarchal control in the public sphere.'[51] Flach, who had spent time with the PKK women's army, did not see it as problematic. She found it liberating: 'For the first time in my life ... I did not feel like a woman who was available. I felt like a comrade. There was a really wonderful feeling of freedom. That was the culture of the guerrillas, comradeship.' She justified it on the basis of choice. It is possible to be a member of the movement without being a cadre or a *heval* (friend). If you choose to become a *heval*, then special relationships are not allowed; the revolution comes first.[52] Geerdink also speaks of the joy of not being treated like a sex object during her year in the Qandil guerrilla camps in Northern Iraq. She found such true equality between men and women and such a non-hierarchical approach that she sometimes found it hard to identify the commander of the camp because they could be so self-effacing. On the question of sex, if anybody breaks the rules, she said, the couple will be split up, made to write a report, reflect on their actions and participate in extra education classes. The worst punishment would be exclusion from the communal life of the camp for a couple of weeks. For a serious offence like rape or sexual assault, the punishment is prison. However, Geerdink was told by a woman who had been in the force for thirty-five years that she had never come across such incidents. They appear to be truly 'married to the struggle'.[53] There is a level of sexual puritanism that Geerdink finds amusing. She describes how men and women mingle. The men's camp is about 20 metres away from the women's camp. When the men visit the women, the protocol is to stand by the entrance and ask 'Are you ready?' The women would always say 'wait a second' in order to clear away any laundry, even if it is only socks. Once, when they had left a bra hanging, they were mortified. When Geerdink laughed at this after the men had gone and asked why it was such a problem, the women said we want to show them how we think, based on our brains, not our underwear.

Given this ground-zero approach to sex, perhaps it is not so disturbing that same-sex relationships do not appear on anyone's radar. The British YPJ woman mentioned above says that any discussions around sex always erupted in giggling. The assumption was that you had sex only once you were married; sex between women was greeted with incredulity. A 'psychological consultant' based in Qamişlo ran sessions for parents about homosexuality. Promising, I thought. However, her approach was to make them aware of the existence of such a phenomenon, and her solution was to talk young people out of it because it was—and my interpreter had to look the word up in a dictionary—an 'aberration'. When I asked whether this was not likely to make the young person more depressed, she confessed that she hadn't actually come across a homosexual client. For the journalists of JINHA, a women-only newsgathering outfit, there were more pressing concerns than gay rights. Ditto for Omar, the women's minister. However, the question of sexuality goes to the heart of patriarchy. How it is addressed will be central to the anti-patriarchal project.

PLANET PATRIARCHY

The economy

There is a widespread view in DAANES that until the economy is in the hands of the people, operated according to their needs, there will be no democracy. According to Kongra Star,

> with the advent of capitalism and class society, their [women's] role has been limited and unacknowledged and the economy regarded as the sphere of men. In order to break this dominance of the few over the many, of men over women, we need a different type of economy: a communal economy.[54]

I asked Delal Afrin (then head of the Women's Economic Committee) why they thought it was important to set up women-only co-operatives, especially when gender equality was being encouraged across the whole of society:

> The historic imbalance of power cannot simply be corrected by introducing quotas for women or the principle of co-presidentship shared by one man and one woman. The confidence that men and women bring to the job will be different unless the confidence of women is built up through the self-reliance, knowledge building and training they acquire in the setting up of co-operatives. A society that is able to organise an economy where women are given productive roles is the sign of a mature and reflective society. When the economy is not in the control of men, women will be able to express themselves freely.[55]

She reached back into history to explain what happened to women in patriarchal societies. In the Middle East, during Neolithic times, 'the street was open to the women'. But it has since been gradually closed off: 'We think it is necessary for women to organise autonomously so that women get an opportunity for self-discovery and self-love.' I asked if she meant solidarity, to which she replied it was not solidarity but love, to love life, to love their own life, to love the fact of being women.[56]

The goal of DAANES is the construction of a co-operative-based economy with a very small private sector. Private businesses are not forbidden. They are allowed to exist as long as they are environmentally friendly, their activities do not create deprivation and do not counter their principles as laid out in the Social Contract. The private sector must follow rules so that wealth inequality is not deepened. Their goal is to create an economy that is developed by society to meet the needs of society. It is the opposite of a statist economy, says Yusuf, 'because the state impoverishes society by concentrating wealth in the hands of very few people'.[57]

There are many distortions in the economy caused by the war situation, so it is difficult to draw any conclusions on what their eventual economy will look like. Many government servants were receiving a salary from Assad, which contributes to the economy of Rojava. It is estimated that in Cizire Canton up to 60 per cent of central government employees were still being paid at the time of my visit. This was Assad's way of retaining his hold on the region. Most of the women who run SARA were teachers in government schools. Even though the schools had been shut down, their salaries were still being paid by Assad, and they were running Kurdish classes for children, which was prohibited under Assad.

Assad also had his hands on other levers of the economy in DAANES. According to an article first published on the website Kurdishquestion.com in 2017:

> The state remained involved in the oil industry which the councils had no means of managing themselves. They relied on the government's engineers and its maintenance of the industry's infrastructure ... The state remained in charge of the healthcare, water, electricity and education systems for some time and kept operating several other civil institutions including municipality offices in some cities, at times parallel to the new Xweserî (self-administration) institutions that bit by bit made them redundant.[58]

There are very few discernible sources of income for the Rojava administration. No taxes are levied on individuals or businesses, apart from business rates, within Rojava; income from taxes on the export and import of goods dries up whenever the border with Iraqi Kurdistan (the Kurdistan Regional Government, KRG) is closed. Commentators have said that the upside of the closure of borders was that it forced Rojava to become self-sufficient. Under Assad, the refining of oil and the manufacturing of bread had been centralised. Although Rojava was the breadbasket of Syria, there were no bakeries as all the wheat travelled down to Damascus to be made into bread and sent back up. Apart from a short spell, immediately after the revolution, when people went hungry, the co-ops quickly set up bakeries to make bread and gradually achieved self-sufficiency. Although I did not see signs of starvation, people generally live frugal lives, with eggs providing the main source of protein. The shortage (and the cost) of electricity meant that it was mainly available for domestic use in the evenings until 10 or 11 pm. In winter, homes are heated by paraffin heaters, which exude dangerous fumes. Combined with a culture of extensive smoking and closed windows and doors, the pollution is a far cry from the revolution's commitment to ecological sustainability. The very fact that 80 per cent of Syrian oil and gas is under Rojava's control forces a reliance on fossil fuels and ups the stakes; a glittering prize for all predators waiting to pounce.

Alan Semo, the London representative of the PYD, explained that '[h]ealth, education and welfare are organised cooperatively and funded mostly by community contributions and voluntary services by professionals, e.g. a doctor may work half day and charge a symbolic fee to see a patient and work half day voluntarily in a community medical centre'. The war is funded by donations from Kurdish political parties and individuals and military donations from the global coalition against terrorism, which includes the US and the UK. Much of the weaponry comes from the spoils of war, and the fighters are not paid a salary, except for the poorest families, who are compensated to the tune of 45,000 Syrian pounds per month (100,000 Syrian pounds, equivalent to around UK£6 at the time of my visit, is considered a reasonable monthly salary) for the loss of potential earnings by a family member.

When the profit motive does not drive economic development, there is no need to reduce labour costs by encouraging division among the workforce by gender, age, race, ability or any of the other myriad ways that have been devised by capitalism. Harnessing the energies of women equally with those of men has allowed the economy to achieve an amazing degree of self-sufficiency in very difficult circumstances.

Continuous ideological training

Everywhere I went in Rojava, women railed against patriarchy and emphasised the importance of the struggle against it; the idea that 'society cannot be truly free until its women are liberated' was voiced everywhere. Despite the war, great emphasis is placed on the education of the people. Three new universities have been set up; a fourth one had to be closed after the area came under Turkish occupation. Before the revolution, according to Semo,[59] low educational attainment was part of a deliberate strategy by Assad to keep the Kurds down. There was only one university—at Hasakeh, which opened in 2000, so only those Kurds wealthy enough to travel to Syrian cities in the South could get a higher education. Janet Biehl, who travelled to Rojava in 2014, said that after the revolution the need for a new kind of education was paramount: '[E]ducation was crucial to creating the revolutionary culture in which the new institutions could thrive. It is a matter not for children and youths alone but for adults as well, even the elderly.'[60]

There are also academies, centres of 'people's education' that 'have played a crucial role in setting up the new society'.[61] A teacher at one of these academies in Rimelan explained that Öcalan's writings have a central place in the academy's curriculum. He said: 'We want to think freely now, without boundaries, and question everything.'[62] However, disconcertingly I found that there was a tendency to sloganising rather than questioning. Some people argued that levels of education had been so low prior to the revolution that people in Rojava tended to regurgitate their new learning. I noticed this tendency at all levels of society. For example, when I expressed surprise to Yusuf that she had made a conscious decision at the age of eighteen not to get married but to give her life up to the revolution, she said 'the biggest revolution is the one that needs to take place inside'. This emphasis on personal transformation is unusual for revolutionary movements, which normally argue that the focus should be on changing the system, which, in turn, will transform human character. When I later ploughed through some of Öcalan's vast oeuvre, I saw that this is one of his sayings.[63]

Kongra Star also emphasised the centrality of education in shedding the patriarchal mindset in a pamphlet on its structure and work issued in November 2016: 'For the transformation of a system based on dominance to a society based on democracy and equality, education is essential.' Of the five committees on health, the economy, self-defence, education and conflict resolution, they described the goal of the education committees as

> threefold, namely, furthering the education of women, spreading awareness of women's topics in society at large and transforming existing structures of education. The larger objective of the committee of education is to make women wise again, in order to shed the attitudes towards men and women that serve patriarchy. When women regain their 'wiseness', they are able to play an active, positive role for the society and family.

Courses for the general public run from twenty-five days to two and a half months. Of the subjects on offer, history is a central thread. History, according to Öcalan, teaches us that Neolithic civilisation was women-centred, that patriarchy and other systems of domination came into being with the rise of the nation-state. It was his view that '[t]he nation-state has left a trail of blood throughout world history, notably in the Arabization of Syria and the Turkification of Turkey. It relies on social homogenisation through identity formation and its inevitably violent enforcement. By contrast, Democratic Confederalism is grounded in diversity.'[64] Awareness of a historical time when patriarchy did not exist reinforces the possibility that not only is patriarchy man-made but that it can also be overthrown.

An entirely new academic discipline, the science of women or Jineolojî, was theorised by Öcalan as a radical alternative and necessary ideological challenge to patriarchy. 'Jin' is the Kurdish word for women, coming from the same root as 'Jiyan', meaning life. The aim was to reformulate the social sciences from a feminist perspective. While Öcalan laid out the broad principles for this new science, it is Kurdish women who have put flesh on the bones of this framework. The Kongra Star pamphlet states that 'one task of Jineolojî is "the archaeology of women": the identity of women has been put under earth and archaeology of women should dig the identity of women out in the visibility again [sic]'.[65] In that task, it stands on common ground with feminist theory and practice around the world. It has also been described as the science of the women's revolution, which is probably its primary distinction from other feminist theorising.[66]

Jineolojî 'addresses the ideological and societal problems that all women face'.[67] It seeks to challenge '[e]xisting dominant ideologies and power structures such as patriarchy, capitalism, orientalism and the nation-state system', which 'are embedded and reinforced by dominant knowledge production systems'. The privileging of certain kinds of knowledge produces a hierarchy of 'mind over body, human over nature, west over east, north over south, white over black, man over woman ... Jineolojî aims to break down this hierarchy through studying life from the perspective and experiences of women and therefore accepting and adopting a point of view deeply embedded in struggle.' Their focus is not just on women but also men:

> They [i.e. men] have, for example, lost the freedom of emotional expression, as this is not considered masculine. They have not been taught how to do housework, or how to take care of themselves, of the children, of the elderly or the ill. When women's roles in society change, naturally the roles of men must change as well. It is necessary to provide men with the tools to deal with this change and the tools to be able to participate in the new society.[68]

As I have argued elsewhere, 'Jineolojî is a template for action, a solutions-based approach which posits the establishment of democratic confederalism, with women at the centre, as the only way to fight capitalist and patriarchal oppression.'[69]

Alongside Jineolojî and Öcalan's teachings sits another major and totally unexpected influence on the population of Rojava—a love of Bollywood films. My status was vastly enhanced by the fact that I am Indian and, therefore, the soul of Bollywood manifest. I was mobbed by young people wanting to take selfies with me. Bollywood sells the dream of romance to repressed young souls without challenging patriarchal norms or stereotypical gender roles, often criticised in India for undermining the institution of arranged marriages but running counter to everything being taught in Rojava.

Continuous and widespread ideological training is so prioritised that it was carried out with the volunteer army even on the battlefield while the war against Raqqa was raging. According to a journalist writing in the *New Yorker*:

> In a camp outside Kobanî, I attended a graduation ceremony for some five hundred conscripts, who'd just completed basic training.

Most of them were Arabs. When I asked one of the instructors—nearly all of whom were Kurds—what the training entailed, he said, 'We really focus on the mentality, the beliefs, more than the military stuff. Our main objective is to send a new man back to society, and in this way to build a new society.'[70]

Putting Öcalan's ideology into practice

When he set up the PKK to engage in the struggle for the independent nation-state of Kurdistan in 1978, Öcalan's ideas were firmly rooted in Marxism–Leninism. Many Kurdish people who supported the notion of an independent nation-state on the principle that '[t]he Kurds are the world's largest nation without a state' have not necessarily signed up to Öcalan's renunciation of the state as an inherently patriarchal, violent and anti-democratic institution. They accused him of giving up on independence because independence can only be understood within the framework of the state. However, the successful practice of self-administration in Rojava has led many of them to accept Öcalan's critique of the nation-state.

Öcalan's thinking evolved in prison; he read widely, including the feminist works of Judith Butler and Maria Mies, which, alongside his lengthy discussions with Kurdish feminist revolutionaries like Cansiz, are credited with influencing his thinking. Without wanting to diminish the contribution of Öcalan and his Kurdish compatriots to the cause of feminism, it is important to reflect on whether Öcalan's new avatar would have been possible without the theoretical outpourings and extensive activism of second-wave feminism. It is a pleasing cross-fertilisation of ideas. The internationalist outlook of Kurdish feminists is reflected in their knowledge of a range of Western feminist thinkers, a compliment that is not returned. Öcalan adapted the ideas of Murray Bookchin, a social theorist and political philosopher, on libertarian municipalism to develop his theory of democratic confederalism,[71] which is 'based on a radical conception of democracy—one that aims at the dissociation of democracy from nationalism by excluding state and nation from it and considering democracy as an unrestricted and unmediated form of people's sovereignty rather than a form of government'.[72] While Bookchin did not put women at the vanguard of this movement, the model in operation in Rojava seems almost a textbook implementation of the system that Bookchin outlined. For me, after a lifetime of activism in trying to bend the neocolonial British state to the needs of migrant women because our communities were too conservative to accommodate those rights, the idea of relying on community, anti-patriarchal as it may have become, felt like a non-sequitur.

Öcalan went so far as to assert that '[t]o me, women's freedom is more precious than the freedom of the homeland'.[73] This was a much harder journey for his supporters to embark upon, but embark they did; anecdotally, I have heard more reservations about the abandonment of the goal of Kurdistan than I have heard criticisms of the focus on ending patriarchy. In fact, even the critics of Rojava appear to be united in praise of the advances made on gender equality, although some critics, like Dr Lina Khatib of Chatham House, believe it is window dressing in order to attract Western support.[74]

Öcalan's analysis of patriarchy stands equal to that of any feminist, an unprecedented position to be adopted by the male leader of a liberation struggle:

> Woman's biological difference is used as justification for her enslavement. All the work she does is taken for granted and called unworthy 'woman's work'. Her presence in the public sphere is claimed to be prohibited by religion, morally shameful; progressively, she is secluded from all important social activities. As the dominant power of the political, social and economic activities are taken over by the men, the weakness of the women becomes even more institution-

alised. Thus, the idea of a 'weak sex' becomes a shared belief. In fact, society treats woman not merely as a biologically separate sex but almost as a separate race, nation or class—the most oppressed race, nation or class: no race, class or nation is subjected to such systematic slavery as housewifisation.[75]

In his pamphlet on women's revolution, *Liberating Life*, Öcalan argues that feminism can never be totally successful in a capitalist system, that class and race equality in a secular democratic system is part of the struggle for women's liberation. While many feminist movements would agree with this analysis, they are unable to put into practice ideas of race and class equality in a capitalist system. This probably explains the divisions faced by feminism in Western democracies, where it is often derided as a white, middle-class affair that excludes working-class and minority women. As the classic statement issued by the Combahee River Collective of black feminists in 1977 reads: 'We realize that the liberation of all oppressed peoples necessitates the destruction of the political-economic systems of capitalism and imperialism as well as patriarchy.'[76]

The importance of giving minorities a voice has been a central concern of the revolution from the start and has been reconfirmed in the new Social Contract, even though the Arab population is now in a majority in several cantons in the region. Article 29 of the contract guarantees '[f]air representation of all communities in Democratic Autonomous Administration institutions according to the demographics of the cantons'.[77] This is a highly enlightened approach to racial inclusivity. This inclusivity is indicated by the administration dropping the name Rojava because it is a Kurdish word and renaming it the Democratic Autonomous Administration of North and East Syria, although it has become popularly known as Rojava. In terms of class, people are paid the same salary or work for the revolution on a voluntary basis.

It was precisely this inclusivity that attracted the Arab shopkeeper I met in the souk in Qamişlo. He had fled from Raqqa, partly because he was disgusted by ISIS's persecution of religious and ethnic minorities. When I asked about his commitment to the revolution's ideals of gender equality, he robustly disagreed, saying that his wife's place was definitely in the home. He does appear to be in a minority if a 2016 survey carried out by the self-administration is anything to go by. Of over 1,200 people surveyed, around 500 men and 700 women, 85 per cent agreed that women should have equal rights. Almost all the questions relating to improvements in women's status received support from 80 to 90 per cent of the respondents. Interestingly, the question that received the least support—65 per cent, although that is still a substantial majority—related to women's rights after divorce, whether a woman should have custody of the children until they turned fifteen and whether the father should be obliged to pay alimony.[78]

Öcalan believes that 'a movement for woman's freedom should strive for anti-hierarchical and non-statist political formations'.[79] Dirik argues that the rejection of the state as the mechanism by which women's freedoms will be delivered can be put into practice even in a brutal, authoritarian country like Türkiye. In the self-administered Kurdish areas of South East Türkiye, she gives the example of men who want to work in the municipality. They have to enter into a social contract with the women's movement and agree that they will not do anything to harm their partner:

> If the man is found to be beating his wife they will tell him to stop, and if that doesn't work, kick him out of the job and offer the job and salary to his wife. It's not something that is in reaction to the state. It's something that builds its own power from within, without reliance on the state.[80]

However, when the state is led by someone as authoritarian as Recep Tayyip Erdoğan, who has been removing elected Kurdish mayors since the 2016 elections and replacing them with his own agents who promptly reverse all progressive measures,[81] building a parallel system is fraught with the prospect of failure.

The various cantons in Rojava still need to be coordinated, and the economy needs to be overseen, as does their defence strategy. The coordinating bodies have all the outward appearance of a state. Sociologist Nazan Üstündağ believes that the 'state' of Rojava is necessitated by the war situation: 'As a result of war and embargo and the need to present themselves diplomatically at the global stage, as well as represent their cantons internally to people as emerging systems, canton governments often end up performing stateness.'[82] The people running these ministries have not been elected, as this stratum of government sits above and separately from the TEV-DEM/commune structure. Elections that were scheduled for January 2018 had to be postponed because Türkiye invaded Afrin. Omar, then head of the Women's Ministry, explained that she was a member of Kongra Star and that, like other ministers, she was appointed to her post for six months by agreement of the various stakeholders in the highest political body, the People's Democratic Council. Elections that were to be held in June 2024 have been postponed; America signalled its disapproval on the grounds that the conditions for a free and fair election have not been met, and Türkiye threatened another invasion.

TEV-DEM members explained that

> the relationship between the canton government and assemblies is conceived not in terms of representation but in terms of self-defense. In other words, the primary aim is not to achieve the representation of assemblies in the government, although that is automatically the case. Rather assemblies, academies, and communes will be the means by which localities maintain their autonomy against the canton governments, unmake the latter's claims to state-ness, and eventually appropriate their functions, proving them redundant.[83]

Dirik expressed a similar view but went further to say that it would be the women's movement that would hold the 'state' accountable: '[D]irect democracy is guarded by the women's movement. The moment it becomes a state, the moment it gets appropriated by capitalism, the project will fail.' The 'state' in Rojava needs to be understood as an 'administration' with a coordinating role but no power. The power resides with the people. Graeber illustrates this point with an incident he witnessed when visiting Rojava. Local police officers were called to investigate a merchant who was suspected of hoarding sugar. When they said they couldn't do so without clearance from their commanding officers, this caused outrage among the people, who said you work for us not them: 'It seemed a strong matter of principle that anyone with a gun should ultimately be answerable to the bottom-up structures, and not the top down—and if not, there was something terribly wrong.'[84] Graeber believed that '[i]n terms of revolutionary theory, I would say that the case of Rojava is in certain ways unique. What we find is essentially a dual power situation.' On the one hand, there are the ministries, parliament, the higher courts, everything that looks like a government, and on the other hand, there are the bottom-up structures where power flows entirely from the popular assemblies. Graeber observed that '[t]he balance of power between these two institutional structures appears to be fluid and under constant renegotiation'.[85]

Öcalan's body of writing provides an overarching theory that contextualises the oppression of the Kurds by a patriarchal, capitalist state; it has the double attraction of advancing the notion of democratic modernity, shorn of these oppressive structures, plus a kind of blueprint, the self-administration structures of democratic confederalism, of how to get there. By situating this new social model as the continuation of a possibly idealised society harking back to a matrilocal Neolithic culture in Mesopotamia— the cradle of civilisation—Öcalan offers the comforting thought that this revolution is in fact a return to roots.

Rojava's commitment to secularism owes much to Öcalan. He is very clear about the role of religion in the oppression of women. In *Liberating Life*, Öcalan advances his three sexual ruptures theory of women's enslavement and eventual liberation. The first rupture, or turning point, was the rise of patriarchy when Neolithic times ended and 'statist civilisation' arose;[86] the second sexual rupture was the intensification of patriarchy through religious ideology, when '[t]reating women as inferior now became the sacred command of god';[87] and the third rupture is yet to come, the end of patriarchy, or as Öcalan puts it, 'killing the dominant male',[88] which is about reshaping masculinity so that it no longer defines itself in relation to its power over women.

Those who have followed the history of the PKK and Öcalan, through its Stalinist phase when dissenters were assassinated, may be cynical about this new phase in Öcalan's thinking, but we should allow for the possibility of change, especially when those ideas have given birth to a society where 'it's raining women'.[89] While his beliefs that women's subjugation is more damaging to society than class division and that religion is a primary site for women's oppression are refreshing for a male revolutionary, he has an idealised view of Neolithic society's non-patriarchal nature before the rise of the nation-state, especially in the Mesopotamian cradle where Kurdish communities are based. Tax described this aspect of Öcalan's thinking in biblical terms: 'Now Kurdistan, the place of original sin, must become the place where this sin is reversed',[90] which encapsulates my own anxieties about Öcalan harking back to some mythical state when all was well with the world and men and women were equal—Eden before the apple.

In my ten days in Rojava, I was moved from home to home, enabling me to see at first hand the family, the primary site of women's oppression. It did appear to be the case that domestic responsibilities remained overwhelmingly the woman's sphere, although it was hard to judge as I was the guest of the women in the family, so it was they who fetched and carried and prepared the meals. Anecdotally, though, there were plenty of stories of men doing their share of the housework. Omar said that her husband did his share of domestic duties; a young man, Khaleel, who drove the Kongra Star car, said he did his share of the cooking and cleaning. Oddly, this seems to be the last frontier of patriarchy, the double burden that women carried even in the heady days of the revolution in places like the Soviet Union when they were taking on all the jobs conventionally done by men. I say 'oddly' because domestic chores seem like a small loss of privilege in comparison to the loss of status and income from jobs traditionally reserved for men. Is domestic work an encroachment too far into the freedoms of men?

There was also anecdotal evidence of attitudinal change in men. The media centre where I stayed for two nights was run by a couple of men who cooked and cleaned but had done their stint for the revolution as members of the defence forces, the YPG or the Asayiş (police force). Neither of them could speak English, but one of them called me over to show me short films on his mobile phone of him detonating unexploded bombs when he was with the Asayiş. In the background, on the television, a daytime cookery programme was being broadcast, which I discovered was a favourite pastime of his—an unselfconscious pick 'n mix of gendered behaviours.

Critique

There is a world-weary response from feminists who have been around for some time in the face of excitement about yet another band of women freedom fighters who will transform the patriarchal nature of the society from which they have emerged. Nicaragua, El Salvador, Cuba, Nepal, Sri Lanka—to name just a few revolutionary struggles: Where are the women today, and what have they achieved? While a degree of scepticism is healthy, each new movement must be analysed with hope and respect. When I appeared on *Women's Hour*, BBC Radio 4, to talk about my journey to Rojava, I found myself sharing airtime unequally with a discussion of the fictional feminist utopia *Herland*, first published in 1915. It was almost as if the idea of a feminist revolution was so incredible that instead of giving it the time it needed, it was accorded lower status than a work of fiction.

There are certainly disquieting aspects to the gender revolution in Rojava. In the main office of Kongra Star, behind the president's desk, hung a portrait of Öcalan. On the facing wall, in a subordinate position, is a portrait of Cansiz, the woman co-founder of the PKK. I found this order of preference troubling for a women's organisation. The document describing the organisation's work opens with a quote from Öcalan: '[The] [r]evolution that fails to liberate women is not a real revolution, and the organization that cannot organize women is not a real one.' Of course, we should give Öcalan credit as the first 'freedom fighter' or revolutionary leader to place women at the centre of his revolution and to argue that the enslavement of women was the start of all other forms of enslavement. However, this feels like hero worship. Even though portraits of leaders are plastered in official places in many parts of the world, the cult of personality harks back to what happened in places like the Soviet Union. At the same time, there is no doubt that he is a towering figure of our times, a Nelson Mandela of the Kurdish people. While there may be disquiet among feminists that the icon of such a strong women-led movement is a man, it is women who are putting his ideas into practice and taking them in unforeseen directions such as the building of Jinwar, the women-only village.

There is a worryingly essentialist strand to Öcalan's writings on women. While he acknowledges that gender is constructed, he also makes frequent references to '[t]he emotional intelligence of woman that created wonders, that was humane and committed to nature and life'[91] or statements like '[t]he natural consequence of their differing physiques is that woman's emotional intelligence is much stronger than man's is'.[92] Öcalan's solution to the impossibility of equal sexual relations under patriarchy—celibacy—doesn't seem like a solution either, as many religious orders have demonstrated.

Challenges—internal and external

It is a spartan existence. The war economy brings severe hardships: shortages of basic goods, housing, medicines, building materials and machinery. Much of the work of the revolution is being done on little or no wages. People often use the term a 'symbolic' wage to describe the pittance they earn. As Yusuf said, 'the majority of the people are working with their heart for the revolution because they believe in what they're doing'.[93] But for how long can this enthusiasm be sustained? And though it may be true of the revolutionaries, what about the others? At the border, the entry clearance officer who did my paperwork did not resent the young man who served us tea earning as much as him because he worked very hard for it, but he did resent the fact that his salary barely covered the cost of his cigarettes. Disgruntled feelings about salary cropped up a few times. Since then, according to a 2019 report by the Rojava Information Centre (RIC),[94] salaries have improved, citing the case of teachers who earn double that of teachers in Syrian government schools. Access to basic goods, like bread and diesel, is better than in other areas of Syria, but water and electricity supplies have suffered due to Turkish targeting of civilian infrastructure.[95] The material realities highlight the contradictions of the revolution as two internationalists who volunteered in Rojava for a year point out: the aim of developing ecological energy sources versus the immediate need for fossil fuels; the principle of a decentralised democracy versus the need for centralised military decision-making in the fight for self-defence.[96]

RIC, staffed by international volunteers and local Kurdish staff, provides critical and fair commentary on the DAANES administration from a position of sympathy with the aims of the revolution. Their 2019 report recommends development of the commune system as not enough people are participating at commune level, which is the most important unit of their grassroots democracy; that elections should be held more regularly while recognising factors such as the war with ISIS and Turkish aggression that destabilise the situation; that the electoral system needs to be changed. As it currently stands, it 'combines forms of direct and representative democracy in a way which undermines the strengths of each system' so that 'the elected candidates are neither truly "representative" nor directly selected by the people'.[97] The RIC report finds that class and gender inequalities remain, that ecological projects have suffered for a lack of capacity and funding and despite extensive engagement with Arab leaders, tensions between Arabs and Kurds remain because of perceived Arab complicity with ISIS and Türkiye. In the aftermath of Assad's fall, Arabs are defecting to HTS in their hundreds.[98] Of course, that RIC can be critical is itself evidence of a healthy democracy.

Elections have never been held in the Arab-majority areas. In the rest of the region, elections up to municipality level took place in 2015 and 2018. While the co-presidents at municipality level participate in levels further up in the administration at the city level, representatives are nominated through negotiations between various parties. If there is a dispute between different levels of the administration, explains Berivan Şaredariye, like the municipality imposing a tax on the people that they believe is unfair, the dispute is thrashed out in court. The process can take months but ensures that the people are persuaded of the need for a particular proposal. Without consensus, the policy changes will not be imposed.

There is a great deal of disunity among the Kurds. Some support an independent state of Kurdistan carved out of Türkiye, Iran, Iraq and Syria, a long-held nationalist dream, while others have swung behind this new non-ethnically defined self-administration. This lack of unity gives rise to the big conundrum: How can one system satisfy the vast differences in human aspirations? Which aspirations will get priority? And if these aspirations are articulated through a genuinely democratic process, will everybody abide by it?

The borders with Türkiye are closed. Since March 2016, the border with the KRG is intermittently closed, a result of the tangle of mutually conflicting alliances and relationships between the major players in the Middle East, such as Iran and Saudi Arabia, and world powers such as Russia and the United States. the KRG sells its oil to Türkiye, with which it is currently discussing the possibility of setting up a gas pipeline. It supports a brand of nationalist politics where the state, although nominally a democracy, has been captured by the corrupt Barzani clan. As the crossing into Rojava is controlled by the KRG, it may shut the border at whim and not allow travellers, even with permission, to cross over. The haemorrhaging of Rojava's population either through war dead or emigration is also a great source of pain. Additional pressure on meagre resources comes from the number of refugees, technically IDPs, running away from ISIS-controlled areas, Turkish-occupied areas and those parts of Syria where Assad's pushback squeezed jihadis and civilians into ever smaller pockets of land. Rojava has had to accommodate nearly 2 million IDPs (almost half its population of 4 million).

External challenges arise from the continued and entrenched hostility of Türkiye along the northern border. In 2019, Türkiye invaded and occupied Afrin, one of the cantons of Rojava, and other areas along the northern edge. The SDF has been pushed back 30 kilometres from the border, a key demand of Türkiye, an area that was jointly patrolled by Russia and Türkiye. Türkiye is pushing further into Rojava while the world focuses on HTS's plans for a future Syria. HTS is being given the benefit of the doubt by Western media and governments desperate to see an end to Assad's rule, but given its Islamist ideology, its informal alliance with Türkiye and its stated declaration to unite all of Syria, the future of the revolution is at grave risk. The new HTS minister of justice, a former member of al-Nusra (a branch of al-Qaeda), presided over the public executions of two women for 'adultery' and 'prostitution' in 2015.[99] Some of the world's major players have a direct or proxy presence in DAANES: Russia, the US, France and the UK. All these changing allegiances and tensions, which the Rojava administration has tried to balance in its own self-interest, make Rojava's future totally unpredictable.

In relation to the question posed by this book, democratic confederalism is a system that does not rely on patriarchy for its power; in fact, it conceptualises it as an obstruction to their goals of equality and women's freedom. As the area under self-governance expanded to absorb communities without the same history as the Kurds, like the Arabs, DAANES has jettisoned some of its women-friendly policies in favour of democracy, such as giving in to Arab demands to retain polygamy or a religious curriculum in schools. The administration's hopes that intensive education will win them over to new ways of thinking may be scuppered if Arab communities leave in droves to join forces with HTS.

This is the first revolution driven by the understanding that capitalist modernity cannot be dismantled without tackling patriarchy, racism and environmental damage. It is the first in which changing the 'mentality' of the people has been as important as changing the system—a recognition that patriarchy is embedded not only in our institutions but in our psyches. To undo the damage of patriarchy, it has encouraged women to love themselves. It has created the space for women to be inventive and creative in moulding its future direction. It has challenged those of us in the West who are alive to the shortcomings of the state and yet have pursued the safety net provided by the state because there was seemingly no other way out of our patriarchal communities. This flickering flame that promises true freedom and equality for women deserves to be steadied and supported by all progressive forces.

CONCLUSION

Rahila Gupta and Beatrix Campbell

In his poem, 'The Second Coming', written in 1919, a year after the First World War had ended, Yeats observed, 'Things fall apart; the centre cannot hold / Mere anarchy is loosed upon the world,' an observation that perfectly conjures up the second coming of Donald Trump as 'monarch' of what is still the most powerful country in the world. Trump's comeback has been financed by a handful of wealthy white men, most visibly Elon Musk, an example of the accretion of extreme power and wealth enabled by a capitalist system that sees democratic accountability as a chokehold. Arguably this is not a rogue mutation, or as the tech bros would have it, 'not a bug but a feature' of capitalism when allowed to grow unchecked. Trump may be around for only four years, but is Trumpism likely to survive his departure? Extreme inequality and irreversible environmental damage could well lead to an implosion of the current system into something darker rather than something more humane. The reconfiguration of social, political and economic relations that we are seeing play out has spurred academics and commentators to capture this degraded version of capitalism variously as necrocapitalism,[1] disaster capitalism,² surveillance capitalism³ and technofeudalism.⁴ The regression of women's rights in each of these scenarios is writ large.

The exhaustion of democracy

The year 2024 was the year of elections: sixty-four countries went to the polls, representing a combined population of around 49 per cent of the world's voters.⁵ There are now 120 democracies among the 193 member states of the UN, up from forty in 1972. Yet democracy has never been in worse shape. With countries like Syria, Venezuela and Russia on the list, it appears that the very concept of democracy has been etiolated by neoliberalism. Democracy bestowed upon the capitalist West the moral high ground it needed against the rise of communism in the twentieth century until that prospect was extinguished and it began to cut into the ability of capital to grow unhindered. As Timothy Mitchell has observed: 'Neoliberal policies have always been intended to weaken democratic and egalitarian politics by moving control from accountable public representatives to the private forces of the market.'⁶

In the leading democracies of the twenty-first century, there has been a noticeable trend in the rise of leaders who have broken with the consensus between centre-left and centre-right two-party systems. On the left, politicians with radical left agendas like Jeremy Corbyn, Bernie Sanders and Jean-Luc Mélenchon have had unexpected success. However, dangerously populist, right-wing leaders have proven more effective, and the appeal of their agendas often relies on the sacrifice of women's rights. Political leaders like Trump, Marine Le Pen, Narendra Modi and Vladimir Putin, with their deployment of 'machismo as political style, the wall-building and xenophobia, the mythology and race theory, the fantastical promises of national restoration', espouse an 'apocalyptic nationalism'.⁷ This macho nationalism can be

CONCLUSION

seen in Russia, El Salvador and Saudi Arabia, with distinctly masculine characteristics. Startling 'post-national' forces, such as ISIS, are cutting across national borders and transmitting chaos, potentially, into every corner of the world. This is why energetic authoritarian 'solutions' are currently so popular: distraction by war (Russia, Türkiye); ethno-religious 'purification' (India, Hungary, Myanmar); the magnification of presidential powers and the corresponding abandonment of civil rights and the rule of law (the US, China, Rwanda, Venezuela, Thailand, the Philippines and many more).

There are some common patterns that emerge in authoritarian countries, such as the harassment of NGOs (cast as foreign agents) in Russia and China, where they are burdened with bureaucratic reporting restrictions and forced to forego foreign donations. Work on democracy, human rights and women's rights is framed as terrorism by Putin or 'woke culture' by Trump. El Salvador, under Nayib Bukele, refuses to issue statistics on rates of homicide, femicide and disappearances of women, making it impossible to establish a baseline. Laws are deliberately vague; loopholes allow a captive judiciary to do the bidding of the autocrat. In Saudi Arabia, the law of counterterrorism holds that the very questioning of the wisdom of the king or crown prince is an act of terrorism. The concept of *tazir*, a discretionary punishment that can range from a warning to imprisonment, flogging or exile, allows the judiciary free reign.[8]

In South Africa during the Zuma era, Russia, El Salvador and now, astonishingly, the United States, the direction of travel is away from democratic accountability towards a rule of oligarchs, shadow figures and mafia states. Where it is mostly powerful men belonging to a small network of political elites who hover in the shadows, women will have no way of having their rights implemented regardless of what is on the statute books. To what extent is women's position in society compromised by a shadow or mafia state? To what extent is patriarchy central to these kinds of structures? Even in Iceland (see Chapter 6), we see shadowy groupings of elite men exercising power outside the normal channels of government.

Religious fundamentalist forces have also worked hard to erode democracy. It is popularly believed that one of Islam's shortcomings is its antipathy to democracy. It is not just Islam but other religions too that are opposed to it, even religions like Hinduism that are theoretically polytheistic. Rob Reiner's documentary *God & Country* examines the process by which the Christian Evangelical movement began to pour their hopes into Trump, a 'flawed vessel', an unlikely Christian who didn't even put his hand on the Bible when being sworn in as president in January 2025. It became an internet meme/joke that his presidency was not even legitimate. Evangelicals apparently were not that bothered about abortion in the 1970s, 'but through huge funding and smart organisation, abortion was successfully turned into a key religious issue, and the idea began to take shape that democracy itself was an obstacle to God's plans'.[9] In Modi's India, shaped around his political philosophy of Hindutva, an ideology that gives pride of place to Hindus and Hinduism, democracy too is a nuisance; at the same time, elections are held to provide democratic cover to autocratic rule. When Modi claims that he was sent by God to emancipate women, we know we are in trouble.[10] The Russian Orthodox Church and the Catholic and Evangelical movements in El Salvador have enabled and supported regressive policies in relation to women and the LGB and T community. It is not all gloom and doom: there are examples of effective feminist resistance like the one against the Catholic Church in Ireland, which led to ground-breaking gains for women in relation to abortion and divorce.

Those living under authoritarian regimes have not given up on democracy. Saudi activists believe that democracy will deliver the

CONCLUSION

human rights and equality that they are seeking. Madawi al-Rasheed, Saudi feminist and scholar, agrees, but she points out that a democratic system could set back the struggle for women's rights while conservative voices dominate.[11] This can be seen at work in Rojava, North East Syria. Arab populations, who were unfamiliar with the radical ideas of the revolution, demanded that the ban on polygamy be reversed when they came under the sway of the administration after the destruction of the ISIS caliphate. Polygamy was reversed: sex equality was sacrificed in the interests of democracy.

The widespread feeling that the system is broken and something needs to be done found expression in the occupation of squares across the Middle East during the 'Arab Spring', the Indignados in Spain and Occupy London and Wall Street. Just like the pockets of matrilineal societies in existence today carry with them the possibility of alternative ways of living, we need to take account of localised attempts to renew democracy in the brief but significant sparks of the Occupy movements, away from a representative system to a participatory grassroots democracy like the one that is being attempted in Rojava (see Chapter 7) and could be a model for activists everywhere.

The vexed relationship with the state

At the heart of participatory systems is the idea of horizontal power, which eschews the notion of hierarchy and an overarching state. Given that commentators as diverse as Abdullah Öcalan, Friedrich Engels and Angela Saini attribute the rise of male domination to the rise of early states, this relationship is an important one to trace. Whether we live under democratic or authoritarian states, feminists have had to engage with the state no matter what their theoretical perspective might be. It has been noted that paradoxically 'states are at the same time the main violators of human rights and the main guarantors of human rights'.[12] Those experts engaged in theories of the state acknowledge the difficulties of definition. Having surveyed the literature, they suggest the following formulation: '[T]he modern state is, then, an institutional complex claiming sovereignty for itself as the supreme political authority within a defined territory for whose governance it claims and is held responsible.'[13] It has been left to feminist scholars to develop a theory of the patriarchal state. 'I would argue for a conceptualisation of the state as both capitalist and patriarchal,'[14] says Sylvia Walby. To which we would add, racist, as well. 'The state is male in the feminist sense: the law sees and treats women the way men see and treat women,'[15] argues Catharine Mackinnon.

Liberal feminism recognises that the state is dominated by men and masculine interests, but because they see the state as just 'a neutral arbiter between different interest groups',[16] they believe that getting more women into state institutions will rectify the situation. Radical feminists, while believing that the patriarchal state cannot be expected to liberate women unless it is totally dismantled, nonetheless continue to hold the state to account for shortcomings in the laws on violence against women and its failures to implement the laws that are available. Both these perspectives tend to construct men as a homogenous category, while socialist and black feminisms are likely to see the state as shaped by class, race and gender inequalities.[17] Nordic feminists are most likely to have a positive view of the state, or rather the welfare state, as a facilitator or a context for women's political and economic empowerment.[18] Given that the community in traditional Asian and African societies has been the source of much oppression, it leaves minoritised women with no choice but to look to the state for solutions, racist and sexist though it is as an institution. Black women in the UK have found to their dismay that any support from the state in crimi-

CONCLUSION

nalising harmful traditional practices like FGM or forced marriage often results in the state tightening the screws on immigration legislation rather than providing more resources to deal with these issues. Recognising the state as anti-democratic, patriarchal and nationalist, in Rojava they have attempted to do away with the state altogether. There is a layer of governance at the top that plays a coordinating role, but all power and decision-making is theoretically vested in the people. This is an almost impossible solution for feminists to imagine in their own contexts, where they have known no other way to progress their demands except by lobbying the state.

This is why political representation of women has been an important strategy for feminists around the world. Presence in public institutions is the necessary—if insufficient—condition of political progress. Presence matters, argues Anne Phillips, because of what it conveys 'about who does and who does not count as a full member of society'.[19] It is when women organise autonomously and also claim space and create strategic alliances with political parties that their priorities are made to matter. Without collective self-discovery in their own movements, women cannot escape subordinate subjectivity. There is the gender paradox of the Soviet Union in which women achieved substantial equality in employment and education but very little presence in political institutions. Iceland ranks number 1 in the world for gender equality—unusually, Iceland has a vigorous civil society and mass labour movement, with around 90 per cent of workers belonging to trade unions, which are well established in its political economy. Yet women constitute 48 per cent of Iceland's parliament, whereas Rwanda, with the highest number of women in parliament at 61 per cent, stands at twelfth in the Global Gender Gap Report.[20] Providing equal opportunity for women in politics is not like equal opportunity in employment because every woman in government who does not pursue the advancement of women's rights is a wasted opportunity. When Clanci Rosa, a journalist from El Salvador, made a case for more women in government, and I mentioned the example of Margaret Thatcher, she said simply, 'Well I prefer female Marxists to male Marxists.'[21]

Authoritarian states are generally hostile to political activism. Their approach to governance is more likely to be influenced by powerful stakeholders like religious authorities or international trading partners than demands from the people, which are often brutally suppressed. But even in Saudi Arabia, before brutal repression under Mohammed Bin Salman (MBS), both liberal and religious women demanded that the state act on their behalf to restrict the social, religious and familial patriarchy dominant in their society (see Chapter 2). They were aware that the state is patriarchal, and while it may offer them some limited rights, in the long term it would not work in their interest.[22] Extreme repression leaves no room for engagement, forcing an exodus of activists.

Initially, women's demands were not seen as threatening to authoritarian regimes. There was a 'tolerance' of feminist campaigns against domestic violence or restrictions on abortion in Russia, even as ultra-conservatives railed in public about the destruction of the family. Pussy Riot felt the full weight of the state only because their actions directly challenged Putin and his allies, the Russian Orthodox Church. It was when women started campaigning against the invasion of Ukraine in 2022 that they were imprisoned in large numbers and the calls to legislate against feminism as a form of terrorism grew. The same could be said about Saudi Arabia, until MBS assumed power. 'As long as women mobilise to pursue women's demands, they are not seen as a challenge to authoritarian rule,' observed al-Rasheed in 2013.[23] MBS made it clear that the limited reforms he had introduced to enable women to enter the public space were not an expansion of the democratic space. The day he announced the lifting of the ban on women drivers, he imprisoned the women who had been campaigning for it.

CONCLUSION

Conversely, we did not find any correlation between a weak state and a strong feminist movement. Russia, in the decade after the Soviet Union had ended, was a weak state that did not have the infrastructure to enable women to meet, network and make common cause partly because no such infrastructure had existed in the Soviet Union. In El Salvador, women were unable to safely negotiate public spaces when criminal gangs had taken advantage of a weak state to wreak terror in communities. When Bukele came to power and introduced draconian measures to wipe the gangs out, it gave women huge respite from the gangs, but this was partly replaced by harassment from the police and military. The undeniably strong state under Bukele has shrunk the public and civic space to such an extent that the women's movement must make its demands as non-confrontationally as possible. Women who had become used to a culture of consultation under the previous FMLN government are adrift today because Bukele has shut down all channels of communication.[24]

Where welfare states are strong, benefits may provide a better basis than marriage to single mothers, enabling women to move from private to public patriarchy. Walby found that women do better in societies where private patriarchy has been weakened,[25] except in relation to the violence they face. Women's organisations in the UK and elsewhere have made demands of the state from childcare to protection from domestic violence. The state did respond. As Walby has noted, 'there is a degree of autonomy of the political struggle from the material base of patriarchy and of capitalism. This political struggle is important in determining the state's actions.'[26] The winning of suffrage and thereby political citizenship has led the state to be more responsive to women's demands like the passing of women-friendly legislation.[27] On the other hand, Cynthia Enloe argues that wherever women win the vote, the system adapts to ensure that masculinity continues to be privileged in other ways.[28]

PLANET PATRIARCHY

The prospect for change

The fight for equal pay, which began in the nineteenth century and is predicted to take 257 years to be achieved worldwide at the current pace of change,[29] tells us all we need to know about the intransigence of patriarchy. Despite universal laws on equal pay, the gender pay gap is actually increasing.[30] The old notion that unequal education created unequal pay is confounded by the evidence in China and the United States (and elsewhere), where the pay gap widens among workers with college degrees or advanced qualifications to 30 per cent.[31] Although the hourly wage is typically used to measure the gender pay gap, incomes are determined by time and access to other resources. When women's overall labour *income* is counted, nowhere in the world does women's share come close to 50 per cent of men's.[32] Women's labour force participation rates have slipped generally, and significantly so in two of the world's largest countries—in 2023, it stood at 60 per cent in China and 31 per cent in India. The caution that the gender pay gap is only salient in 'developed' economies is not borne out by women's experience of time and money in medium-income or poor economies.

One of the things our research revealed is the extent to which change builds on prevailing tradition, even revolutionary change. Orlando Figes, British historian, observed that 'the "direct democracy" of the Soviets was much closer to the experience of the Russian masses—it was reminiscent of the peasant commune'.[33] In the Middle East, the Kurds had a reputation for being more liberal on women's rights than other communities, which may have made the women's revolution more palatable. They were also used to making decisions collectively through councils made up of male elders and leaders, which the revolution democratised and opened up to women on an equal basis. Ideological mobilisation is more successful when it builds on perceived and con-

CONCLUSION

structed continuities within a belief system. Taking Muslims back to an 'authentic and pure' Islam, as ISIS sought to do, has a particular pull in today's age of inauthenticity and consumerism, of false gods, rampant capitalism and the humiliation of racism experienced by Muslim communities in the West. An article analysing the mechanics of social change uses the peace movement as an example and argues that the reason why it was more successful in Japan and Western Europe than in the US is because people there had direct experience of warfare. In fact, Japan faced nuclear wipe-out in Hiroshima and Nagasaki, while the US had not seen war on its territory for nearly 200 years.[34] The article's author felt that one of the key elements of successful social movements is the extent to which their framing of a particular problem fits with people's experience of it.

The mechanism of change in modern democracies, reformist change not revolutionary change, involves a spectrum of political positions in which the radical fringe has no *locus standi* in relation to the centre where power is concentrated, but their demands are mediated through a range of political groups of varying degrees of radicalism, influencing the next one along, a degree less radical. If the radical fringes are successful in being disruptive, thereby drawing attention to their demands, the establishment is likely to undermine or weaken their disruptive power by making concessions to the more moderate groups. In fact, moderate demands are often ignored by the centre until the radical fringe needs to be enervated. One of the many examples of this process of change is where so-called Islamic feminism situates itself. Afsaneh Najmabadi, an Iranian feminist, believes that '"the piecemeal" approach of "postmodern feminism" enables cooperation around specific issues without making generalized claims for women's equality or women's rights'. Najmabadi says: 'I want to propose that the Islamicist onslaught cannot be resisted by defensibly hanging onto a competing set of foundational truths, but by a willingness to suspend such groundings, and to risk the impurity of pragmatism for the possibility of an often elusive conversation.'[35] What this position often fails to recognise is that any successes it achieves are due to the ground that has been laid by women making a more radical and irrefutable claim for women's rights. What feminists have to assess is whether this piecemeal approach sets back the cause or whether a case can be made for incremental change, especially in the absence of revolutionary change.

There is also the contested question of what constitutes a movement and whether the various disparate groups who define themselves as feminists in many of the countries examined in this book could rightly be seen as a movement. There is no doubt that the Kurdish struggle for self-determination, as seen in Rojava, can be described as a movement. Despite disagreements, it is generally united around the ideas of Öcalan and sets out to implement a grassroots democracy that centres women and young people, respects multi-ethnic communities and ecological sustainability within a co-op-based economy. In Russia, in contrast, the climate of fear, the size of the country, the activism of women in the diaspora and the schisms between 'European' and 'Muslim' Russians contribute to a sense of a fractured community of feminists. However, Ella Rossman, a young Russian activist now living in the diaspora, argues that Russian feminists did constitute a movement despite the huge differences in ideology and regional dispersal because they had shown their capacity to come together on major campaigns around domestic violence and assaults on gay rights, for example. Since the latest invasion of Ukraine in 2022, however, when some feminists took up the anti-war cry, the government managed to sow so much division between feminists by describing the anti-war campaign as the work of foreign agents that there is no longer what she would call a movement.

CONCLUSION

Our takeaways in brief

We learnt that real power often lies outside governance structures in shadowy networks of wealth and corruption dominated by men whether it is an authoritarian state like Russia or a democratic one like Iceland, which means that formal gains in women's rights were often skewered in invisible ways. For all their contradictions, social democratic welfare states have proved to be the most propitious context for feminist political activism, for re-distribution across class, gender and generation. But everywhere this has been cauterised by the contagion of neoliberalism.[36] Yet, despite the turn to right-wing populism and illiberalism, we have been heartened to discover that women find a way to resist, sometimes at great risk to themselves, physically and mentally, in-country or in the diaspora. Donning our activist hats, we found that there was plenty to think about in the variation of transnational feminist approaches that could be applied to our local contexts. For example, the law on domestic violence in El Salvador is so nuanced in its definition of economic abuse that it differentiates between economic and patrimonial categories. Patrimonial refers to the 'wealth' that the woman brings into the marriage and may be appropriated by the husband, a situation regularly faced by women who come from cultures where dowry-giving is common. Reclaiming the dowry may be the only source of independent support for a woman wanting to end a relationship.

The detail raised larger questions implicitly and explicitly of where feminist activism should target its energies. Despite such a progressive law in El Salvador, the situation for women is much worse there than in the UK. How much change can the law deliver? South Africa has an internationally acclaimed progressive constitution proclaiming sex equality as a founding principle and stating that women have a right to freedom from domestic and sexual violence. Yet the country's rates of femicide and rape are higher than the global average. The constitution as a tool to hold the government to account has failed to live up to its initial promise. The post-apartheid government's abandonment of a social democratic programme in favour of neoliberalism has served to defeat egalitarianism. Our investigation into very different contexts also taught us humility and the importance of not being purist in our analysis and tactics. In El Salvador, where abortions are totally criminalised, feminists don't campaign in terms of women's choice or rights to her own body but in terms of the danger to maternal health. In Saudi Arabia, women attack social custom rather than the Qur'an to argue for the expansion of their rights.

We noticed significant gaps in feminist activism especially in influencing the foreign policy of those countries that have significant global influence. US foreign policy in places like Afghanistan or Saudi Arabia has promoted fundamentalist religious forces that have implemented misogynist practices of the kind that would be anathema to American women. Following Sweden in 2014, fifteen countries have officially adopted a feminist foreign policy, including France and Spain, with varying degrees of effectiveness.[37] Climate change campaigners have been particularly successful in shareholder activism to influence companies' sustainability agendas, but feminist activism has been low key. It is also becoming painfully obvious that democracy is essentially incompatible with neoliberalism, so all efforts to reform democracy will run aground under this economic system.

There have been puzzles too, none greater than the showdown between the defence forces of the Rojava women's revolution and ISIS. Rojava was contiguous with ISIS before the 'caliphate' was defeated, two ends of the patriarchal spectrum within touching distance of each other. Whereas the streets of Rojava were filled with colour, be it the red, yellow and green of the flag or the

CONCLUSION

long traditional Kurdish dresses, often glittering with gold thread, black was the only colour in Raqqa, rippling through the throngs of women in full burqas and men carrying the ISIS flag. Where women crowded into commune meetings to have equal say with the men about the decisions that affected their day-to-day life in Rojava, women in Raqqa could be stoned in a public square for adultery, forced to watch beheadings or walk past decapitated heads stuck on spikes at roundabouts.[38] All of life in the ISIS 'caliphate' was a preparation for the afterlife, whereas Rojava's secular revolution is about life on earth; its slogan for women is *Jin, Jiyan, Azadi* (Woman, Life, Freedom)—its aim is to sustain an earth in working order to be handed over responsibly to the next generation. The puzzle is that two such polar opposite societies could emerge from the same soil, same culture, even the same religion, but different ideological framing and mobilisation could provide such different trajectories to histories of hurt and victimisation.

This has been an ambitious book in terms of its scope and worldwide sweep. Every question we have touched upon, be it the state, democracy, capitalism, patriarchy, religion, masculinity or feminism, has entire libraries devoted to them. We have tried to approach these issues as accessibly as possible to try to understand the resilience of patriarchy. We have found that its armour is pierced by women saying no. In that chink lies hope. The Rojava women's revolution has widened that chink and given us a glimpse into another world that is struggling to take breath. As readers and activists, it is up to all of us to bring it into existence wherever we are.

ACKNOWLEDGEMENTS

Our book would not have been possible without the collective wisdom of all those we interviewed and who gave generously of their time, loaned us books and/or opened their address book for us. It is a shame that we could not always honour their wisdom by giving them the space their words required. For that, we might have needed a book for each country.

Some names are pseudonyms or first names only to protect their identity.

UK

Ahmed Abu
Sukhwant Dhaliwal
Liz Kelly
Preethi Manuel
Joan Scanlon
Sandi Toksvig

Saudi Arabia

Abdullah Alaoudh
Maryam Aldossari
Lina Alhathloul
Nadia

Russia

Anna Adrianiva

ACKNOWLEDGEMENTS

Lynne Attwood
Ella Rossman
Svetlana Stephenson
Natasha Tambieva
Anna Tuktasheva
Armorer Wason
Anna Zobnina

El Salvador

Diana Beccera
Maria Candelaria Navas
Deysi Cheyne
Marta Digna Ortiz
Edith Elizondo
Norma Leticia Lobos
Anna Maria Rivera
Morena Herrera
Silvia Juárez
Nubia Lazo
Raúl Martinez
Ainhoya Montoya
Maria Paula
Rafael Peñate
Lorena Portillo
Antonia Recinos
Clanci Rosa
Atiha Sen-Gupta
Carmen Urquilla

China

Delia Davin
Yige Dong
Elizabeth Frazer

ACKNOWLEDGEMENTS

Yinyin
Zong
Zongdan Zhang

South Africa

Sam Ashman
Gandhi Baii
Asanda Benya
Rehad Desai
Nicholas Beveney
Thobeka Biyela
Andy Chinnah
Ben Fine
Shireen Hassim
Karl von Holdt
Zelda Holtzman
Rachel Jewkes
Brown Lekekela
Brenda Madumise-Pajibo
Sphiwe Ngcobo
Candice Pillay
Angela Rivers
Kenneth Sihle
Madikizela Sipelele
Primrose Sonti

Iceland

Hildur Fjóla Antonsdóttir
Berglind Ásgeirsdóttir
Kristín Ástgeirsdottir
Jared Bibler
Sigrún Ingibjörg Gísladótt
Ingólfur Gíslason

ACKNOWLEDGEMENTS

Hannes Hólmsteinn Gissurarson
Sigríður Björk Guðjónsdóttir
Halla Gunarsdóttir
The Group
Valur Ingimundarson
Katrín Jakobsdóttir
Janet Elise Johnson
Guðrún Jónsdóttir
Kristín Jónsdóttir
Elizabeth Prugl
Helgi Seljan
Drífa Snædal
Danfiour Starphediusd
Þórunn Sveinbjarnardóttir
Margaret Willson

Rojava

Nesrin Abdullah
Delal Afrin
Mehmet Aksoy
Nadje Al-Ali
Walîda Botî
Dilar Dirik
Gîven Erzîngen
Anja Flach
Frederike Geerdink
David Graeber
Havin Gunesar
Nuvin Ibrahim
Meike Nack
Amina Omar
Ronahi
Berivan Şaredariye

ACKNOWLEDGEMENTS

Estella Schmidt
Alan Semo
Hediye Yusuf

All the families in Rojava I stayed with

Donors

Our thanks go to the Barry Amiel & Norman Melburn Trust for funding the cost of our travel.

This book was made possible through crowdfunding from individual donors. We are deeply grateful to the following:

Rose Ades
Rukhsana Ahmad
Sally Alexander
Lesley Allan
Sophia Al Maria
Jenifer Armitage
Julia Bard
Juliet Bowbrick
Marion Bowman
Kate Bromwich-Alexandra
Margaret Busby
Duncan Campbell
Hazel Conley
Alix Davis
Ann Day
David Donald
Maria Duggan
Michele Estermann
Sue Finch
Jane Gabriel
Cara Gillespie
Carol Gilligan

ACKNOWLEDGEMENTS

Rayya Ghul
Halla Gunnarsdóttir
Catherine Hall
Jalna Hanmer
Jeremy Hardy
John Harvey
Isabel Hilton
Sandra Horne
Jan Jarvis
E. J. Johnston
Judith Jones
Susanne Kappeler
Liz Kelly
Robert Langford
Gill Lawrence
Annette Lawson
Alison Light
Jordan Lim
Deborah Lincoln
Ruth Lister
Louise Livesey
Kirsty Lowe
Shakila Maan
Nancy MacKeith
John Mann
Margaret Mann
Elizabeth Mansfield
Vicky Marsh
Ehpriya Matharu
John Mellotone
Lucinda Montefiore
Helen Trevillion Moore
Helen Mott
Chitra Nagarajan

ACKNOWLEDGEMENTS

Sara Naudi
Sue O'Sullivan
Frances Orchover
Sue Parrish
Pragna Patel
Ravinder Randhawa
Jacqueline Rose
Joan Scanlon
Sandhya Sharma
Elaine Snaith
Caroline Spry
Mary-Ann Stephenson
Kanta Talukdar
Mridu Thanki
Marianna Tortell
Stephen Trafford
Eva Turner
Harriet Wistrich
Elizabeth Woodcraft
Medora Woods
Kamila Zahno

Beatrix Campbell: Books are always communal, between writers and readers, our sources, supporters and producers, and in such a project as this even more so: thanks to all, and especially my co-author Rahila, and above all to my travelling companion Judith Jones, for everything.

Rahila Gupta: My thanks to my family for their forbearance, my partner Rohan, for absorbing the lessons of this book and keeping the home fires burning, and my daughter, Atiha, who had to live with my unavailability at critical moments. Thanks to Beatrix Campbell for sharing the weight of the question that this book seeks to answer.

NOTES

INTRODUCTION

1. Andrew Harding, 'Gisèle Pelicot: How an Ordinary Woman Shook Attitudes to Rape in France', BBC, 18/12/24, https://www.bbc.co.uk/news/articles/cd75v8eqz44o, accessed 04/02/25.
2. Angela Saini, *The Patriarchs: How Men Came to Rule*, London: Fourth Estate, 2023, p. 248.
3. Stuart Hall, *The Hard Road to Renewal: Thatcherism and the Crisis of the Left*, London: Verso, 1988.
4. Blake Morrison, *Two Sisters*, London: Borough Press, 2023.
5. Quoted in Avery Gordon's *Ghostly Matters: Haunting and the Sociological Imagination*, Minneapolis: University of Minnesota Press, 2008, p. 167.
6. Rahila Gupta, interview with Edith Elizondo via Zoom, 13/06/23.
7. Steven Goldberg, *The Inevitability of Patriarchy*, New York: W. Morrow, 1974.
8. Raewyn Connell, *Masculinities*, Cambridge: Polity Press, 1995, p. 71.
9. Saini, *Patriarchs*, p. 6.
10. Nira Yuval Davis, *Gender and Nation*, London: Sage, 1997, p. 9.
11. Liz Kelly, 'The Conducive Context of Violence against Women and Girls', Discover Society, 01/03/16, https://archive.discoversociety.org/2016/03/01/theorising-violence-against-women-and-girls/, accessed 06/10/24.
12. Raewyn Connell, *Gender: In World Perspective*, 4th edn, Cambridge: Polity Press, 2021.
13. Gayle Rubin, 'The Traffic in Women: Notes on the "Political Economy" of Sex', in Karen Hansen and Ilene Philipson (eds), *Women, Class, and the Feminist Imagination*, Philadelphia: Temple, 1990, pp. 74–113, https://summermeet-

ings2013.wordpress.com/wp-content/uploads/2013/04/rubin-traffic.pdf, accessed 8/6/24.
14. Raewyn Connell, *Gender and Power: Society, the Person and Sexual Politics*, Cambridge: Polity Press, 1987.
15. Sylvia Walby, *Theorising Patriarchy*, Oxford: Blackwell, 1990, p. 177.
16. Timothy Mitchell, 'McJihad: Empire and Islam between the US and Saudi Arabia?', Verso Books, 07/06/17, https://www.versobooks.com/en-gb/blogs/news/3256-mcjihad-empire-and-islam-between-the-us-and-saudi-arabia?, accessed 08/03/2024.
17. Moncef Marzouki speaking at a conference, The Quest for Democracy in Saudi Arabia, Washington, DC, 02/05/24.
18. Maria Alyokhina, *Riot Days*, London: Penguin, 2018, p. 3.
19. Ibid., p. 5.
20. Heather Pringle, 'New Women of the Ice Age', *Discover Magazine*, 19/01/98, https://www.discovermagazine.com/the-sciences/new-women-of-the-ice-age, accessed 24/09/24.
21. Olga Soffer, James M. Adovasio and David C. Hyland, 'The "Venus" Figurines: Textiles, Basketry, Gender, and Status in the Upper Paleolithic', *Current Anthropology* 41, no. 4 (2000), pp. 511–37, https://www.researchgate.net/publication/235979951_The_Venus_Figurines_Textiles_Basketry_Gender_and_Status_in_the_Upper_Paleolithic, accessed 18/09/24.
22. Saini, *Patriarchs*.
23. Ibid., pp. 30–1.
24. Ibid., p. 29.
25. VICE, 'The Land of No Men: Inside Kenya's Women-Only Village', YouTube, 09/09/15, https://www.youtube.com/watch?v=UrnmBLB-UX4&t=107s&ab_channel=VICELife, accessed 03/07/24.
26. Gerda Lerner, *The Creation of Patriarchy*, Oxford: Oxford University Press, 1987.
27. Ibid., p. 46.
28. Sara Horrell and Jane Humphries, 'The Origins and Expansion of the Male Breadwinner Family: The Case of Nineteenth-Century Britain', *International Review for Social History* 42 (1997), pp. 25–64, https://www.cambridge.org/core/journals/international-review-of-social-history/article/origins-and-expansion-of-the-male-breadwinner-family-the-case-of-nineteenthcentury-britain/C5D42E9BA2C056B5BF2CD074A26A2D8A, accessed 10/09/24.

29. Ibid. See also Hilary Land, *The Family Wage*, Liverpool: Liverpool University Press, 1979.
30. See website of the Centre for the Study of the Legacies of British Slavery: https://www.ucl.ac.uk/lbs/, accessed 14/03/25; Catherine Hall 'Gendering Property, Racing Capital', *History Workshop Journal* 78, no. 1 (2014), pp. 22–38, https://academic.oup.com/hwj/article/78/1/22/2907397?login=false, accessed 13/03/25.
31. Heidi I. Hartmann, 'The Unhappy Marriage of Marxism and Feminism: Towards a More Progressive Union', Purdue University, 1979, p. 18, https://web.ics.purdue.edu/~hoganr/SOC%20602/Hartmann_1979.pdf, accessed 05/06/24.
32. Gary Blank, 'Production and Patriarchy in Capitalist Society: A Comparative Review of Hartmann and Young', *Analize: Journal of Gender and Feminist Studies* 2 (2014), p. 3, https://oaji.net/articles/2014/1159-1407945733.pdf, accessed 24/01/23.
33. Barbara Taylor, *Eve and the New Jerusalem: Socialism and Feminism in the Nineteenth Century*, London: Virago, 1983.
34. Susan Pedersen, *Eleanor Rathbone and the Politics of Conscience*, London: Yale University Press, 2004, pp. 214–16.
35. Hartmann, 'Unhappy Marriage of Marxism and Feminism', pp. 19–20.
36. 'Women in Work Index 2023', PwC UK, https://www.pwc.co.uk/services/economics/insights/women-in-work-index/2023.html, accessed 28/06/24.
37. 'Disturbing Rise in Countries Coercing Women into Having More Children, Report Finds', Population Matters, https://populationmatters.org/disturbing-rise-in-countries-coercing-women-into-having-more-children-report-finds/, accessed 02/08/24.
38. Michèle Barrett, *Women's Oppression Today: Problems in Marxist Feminist Analysis*, London: Verso, 1980.
39. 'Deloitte Named a Top 50 Employer for Gender Equality', Deloitte, https://www2.deloitte.com/uk/en/pages/press-releases/articles/deloitte-named-a-top-50-employer-for-gender-equality.html, accessed 24/05/24.
40. Bonnie Chiu, 'Shareholder Activists Advocating for Gender Equality Focus on Tackling Sexual Harassment', *Forbes*, 20/06/21, https://www.forbes.com/sites/bonniechiu/2021/06/20/shareholder-activists-advocating-for-gender-equality-focus-on-tackling-sexual-harassment/?sh=636b67586def, accessed 29/11/23.
41. Nancy Fraser, 'Feminism, Capitalism and the Cunning of History', *New Left*

Review 56 (2009), https://newleftreview.org/issues/ii56/articles/nancy-fraser-feminism-capitalism-and-the-cunning-of-history.pdf, accessed 22/05/24.

42. Rahila Gupta, 'Has Neoliberalism Knocked Feminism Sideways?', openDemocracy 50:50, 4/01/12, https://www.opendemocracy.net/en/5050/has-neoliberalism-knocked-feminism-sideways/, accessed 22/05/24.

43. Sheryl Sandberg, *Lean In: Women, Work and the Will to Lead*, London: W. H. Allen, 2015.

44. Carole Pateman, *The Disorder of Women*, Cambridge: Polity Press, 1989, p. 133.

45. Friedrich Engels, *The Origin of the Family, Private Property and the State*, 4th edn, Stuttgart: n.p., 1892, https://www.marxists.org/archive/marx/works/1884/origin-family/index.htm, accessed 05/10/23.

46. Ibid., p. 39.

47. Carol Hanisch, 'The Personal is Political', 2006, https://webhome.cs.uvic.ca/-mserra/AttachedFiles/PersonalPolitical.pdf, accessed 20/09/24.

48. Tithi Bhattacharya (ed.), *Social Reproduction Theory: Remapping Class, Recentering Oppression*, London: Pluto Press, 2017, p. 1.

49. Susan Himmelweit, 'Can We Afford Not to Care: Prospects and Policy', 2005, https://www.researchgate.net/publication/251266566, accessed 20/09/24.

50. Hilary Land and Susan Himmelweit, 'Who Cares: Who Pays? A Report on the Personalisation of Social Care', London: Unison, 2010.

51. A. Haridasani Gupta, 'Today's Capitalism Is Incompatible with Feminism', *New York Times*, 19/11/20, https://www.nytimes.com/2020/11/19/us/economist-covid-recovery-mariana-mazzucato.html, accessed 04/02/25.

52. Jayati Ghosh, 'Time Poverty and the Poverty of Economics', *METU Studies in Development* 43 (Apr. 2016), p. 4.

53. Sonya Michel and Ito Peng, *Gender, Migration and the Work of Care*, London: Springer, 2017.

54. Fiona Williams, 'Care: Intersections of Scales, Inequalities and Crises', *Current Sociology* 66, no. 4 (2018).

55. Michel and Peng, *Gender, Migration and the Work of Care*.

56. Rahila Gupta, interview with Anna Adrianiva on Zoom, 12/12/23.

57. 'A "Cage Match" between Elon Musk and Mark Zuckerberg May Be No Joke', *New York Times*, 01/07/23, https://www.nytimes.com/2023/07/01/technology/elon-musk-mark-zuckerberg-cage-match.html, accessed 24/10/23.

58. 'Who Is Andrew Tate? The Self-proclaimed Misogynist Influencer', BBC, 23/07/24, https://www.bbc.co.uk/news/uk-64125045, 01/10/24.

59. A YouGov poll found that 27 per cent of young men had a positive opinion of Tate. Matthew Smith, 'How Many Britons Agree with Andrew Tate's Views on Women?', YouGov, 23/05/23, https://yougov.co.uk/society/articles/45735-how-many-britons-agree-andrew-tates-views-women, accessed 01/10/24.
60. Jonathan Griffin, 'Incels: Inside a Dark World of Online Hate', BBC, 13/08/21, https://www.bbc.co.uk/news/blogs-trending-44053828, accessed 30/09/24.
61. Joe Ehrmann, 'The Limits of "Be A Man"', TEDx Baltimore, YouTube, 25/05/17, https://www.youtube.com/watch?v=R17fwmsEocs&ab_channel=eugenedebs, accessed 30/09/25.
62. Raewyn Connell and James W. Messerschmidt, 'Hegemonic Masculinity: Rethinking the Concept', *Gender & Society* 19, no. 6 (December 2005), pp. 829–59 (pp. 840–1).
63. 'The Patriarchy', BBC Radio 4, 19/07/18, https://www.bbc.co.uk/programmes/b0b9z645, accessed 22/07/18.
64. Raewyn Connell, 'The Social Organization of Masculinity', in Connell, *Masculinities*, 2nd edn, London: Routledge, 2005.
65. Svetlana Stephenson, *Gangs of Russia: From the Streets to the Corridors of Power*, Ithaca, NY: Cornell University Press, 2015, p. 5.
66. Valerie Sperling, *Sex, Politics, and Putin: Political Legitimacy in Russia*, Oxford: Oxford University Press, 2015, p. 25.
67. Ibid., p. 28.
68. Interview with Rûken, 09/09/19.
69. Interview, Xezal, 29/07/19, quoted in Nadje Al-Ali and Isabel Kaiser 'Jineolojî and the Kurdish Women's Freedom Movement', *Politics and Gender* 18, no. 1 (2022), https://doi.org/10.1017/S1743923X20000501, accessed 19/01/21.
70. Deniz Kandiyoti, 'Fear and Fury: Women and Post-revolutionary Violence', openDemocracy, 10/01/13, https://www.opendemocracy.net/en/5050/fear-and-fury-women-and-post-revolutionary-violence/, accessed 30/09/24.
71. Quoted in V. Nikolic-Ristanovic, *Social Change, Gender and Violence: Post-communist and War Affected Societies*, Dordrecht: Kluwer, 2002.
72. Linda Gordon, *Heroes of Their Own Lives: The Politics and History of Family Violence*, London: Virago, 1989, p. 4.
73. Elizabeth Frazer and Kimberly Hutchings, 'The Feminist Politics of Naming Violence', *Feminist Theory* 21, no. 2 (2018), https://www.researchgate.net/publication/334306925_The_feminist_politics_of_naming_violence, accessed 20/09/24.

74. Judith Green, 'Looking Back: The Women's Liberation Movement', *Woman's Place UK*, 20/11/09, https://womansplaceuk.org/2019/11/20/looking-back-the-womens-liberation, accessed 20/09/24.
75. UN Secretary-General, 'Ending Violence against Women: From Words to Action', 2006, https://www.unwomen.org/sites/default/files/Headquarters/Media/Publications/UN/en/EnglishStudy.pdf, accessed 20/09/24.
76. Lynnmarie Sardinha et al., 'Global, Regional and National Prevalence Estimates of Physical and Sexual, or Both, Intimate Partner Violence against Women', *The Lancet* 399, no. 10327 (2022), https://www.thelancet.com/journals/lancet/article/PIIS0140-6736(21)02664-7/fulltext, accessed 20/09/24.
77. Rachel Pain, 'Everyday Terrorism: How Fear Works in Domestic Abuse', Scottish Women's Aid, p. 8, https://womensaid.scot/wp-content/uploads/2017/07/EverydayTerrorismReport.pdf, accessed 30/09/24.
78. Ruth Sunderland, 'After the Crash, Iceland's Women Lead the Rescue', *The Guardian*, 22/02/09, https://www.theguardian.com/world/2009/feb/22/iceland-women, accessed 24/01/23.
79. 'One in Four Women Has Been Raped or Sexually Assaulted', University of Iceland, 16/11/18, https://english.hi.is/news/one_in_four_women_has_been_raped_or_sexually_assaulted, accessed 30/09/24.
80. Joan Smith, 'What Do Many Terrorists Have in Common? They Abuse Women', *The Guardian*, 05/08/21, https://www.theguardian.com/commentisfree/2021/aug/05/many-terrorists-abuse-women-research-extremist-attackers-violent-misogyny, accessed 30/09/25.
81. Nata Duvvury et al., 'Intimate Partner Violence: Economic Costs and Implications for Growth and Development', Washington, DC: World Bank, 2013, https://openknowledge.worldbank.org/entities/publication/2b335414-7cf7-5542-ade0-9f62b3221ba3, accessed 04/04/25.
82. Southall Black Sisters is a London-based women's organisation supporting women escaping violence. See Fiona Sheil, 'Investing in Safety', London: Southall Black Sisters, 2024.
83. Interview with Gail Dines, 'FiLiA Meets: Gail Dines', Culture Reframed, podcast, 24/07/18, https://www.filia.org.uk/latest-news/2018/7/24/gail-dines-culture-reframed?rq=pornography, accessed 30/09/24.
84. Brooke M. Beloso, 'Sex, Work, and the Feminist Erasure of Class', *Signs: Journal of Women in Culture and Society* 38, no. 1 (Sept. 2012), https://digitalcommons.butler.edu/cgi/viewcontent.cgi?article=1455&context=facsch_papers, accessed 31/05/24.

85. 'Marital Rape Is Not a Crime in 32 Countries: One of Them Is India', News18, 26/08/21, https://www.news18.com/news/india/marital-rape-is-not-a-crime-in-32-countries-one-of-them-is-india-4130363.html, accessed 09/08/24.
86. Carole Pateman, 'What's Wrong with Prostitution?', *Women's Studies Quarterly* 27, no. 1/2 (Spring–Summer 1999), pp. 53–64, https://www.jstor.org/stable/40003398?read-now=, accessed 09/08/24.
87. Shivam Patel, 'India Struggles with High Rape Cases, Low Convictions Rates', Reuters, 16/08/24, https://www.reuters.com/world/india/indias-struggles-with-high-rape-cases-low-conviction-rates-2024-08-15/#, accessed 30/09/24.
88. 'Number of Police Recorded Rape Offences in England and Wales from 2002/03 to 2023/24', Statista, 30/07/24, https://www.statista.com/statistics/283100/recorded-rape-offences-in-england-and-wales/, accessed 30/09/24.
89. Sam Jones, 'UN Report: South Sudan Allowed Soldiers to Rape Civilians in Civil War', *The Guardian*, 11/03/2016, https://www.theguardian.com/global-development/2016/mar/11/south-sudans-soldiers-allowed-to-rape-civilians-civil-war-says-un-government-torture, accessed 09/08/24.
90. Oxfam International and Harvard Humanitarian Initiative, '"Now, the world is without me": An Investigation of Sexual Violence in the Eastern Democratic Republic of Congo', Oxfam International, 15/04/10, https://oi-files-d8-prod.s3.eu-west-2.amazonaws.com/s3fs-public/file_attachments/DRC-sexual-violence-2010-04_2.pdf, accessed 20/09/24.
91. Cynthia Enloe, *Manoeuvres: The International Politics of Militarizing Women's Lives*, Berkeley: University of California Press, 2000.
92. 'UN Official Calls DR Congo "rape capital of the world"', BBC, 24/04/10, http://news.bbc.co.uk/2/hi/8650112.stm, accessed 20/09/24.
93. Diana Carolina Sierra Becerra, 'Insurgent Butterflies: Gender and Revolution in El Salvador, 1965–2015', PhD thesis, University of Michigan, 2017, pp. 1–2, https://www.academia.edu/34224310/Insurgent_Butterflies_Gender_and_Revolution_in_El_Salvador_1965_2015, accessed 06/03/23.
94. 'López Soto and Others v Venezuela', Tackling Violence against Women, LSE, 2018, https://blogs.lse.ac.uk/vaw/landmark-cases/a-z-of-cases/lopez-soto-and-others-v-venezuela-2018/, accessed 30/09/24.
95. Andy Heintz, 'Secularism Is a Women's Issue: Interview with Marieme Helie-Lucas', Workers Liberty, 04/02/18, https://www.workersliberty.org/story/2018-02-04/secularism-womens-issue-interview-marieme-helie-lucas, accessed 30/09/24.

96. Quoted by Kate Nash, 'The Cultural Politics of Human Rights and Neo-liberalism', https://research.gold.ac.uk/id/eprint/26430/3/Human%20rights%20and%20neo-liberalism%20for%20Journal%20of%20Human%20Rights%20for%20GRO.pdf, p. 1, accessed 13/03/25.
97. Ibid., p. 20.
98. Sperling, *Sex, Politics, and Putin*, p. 14.
99. Catherine Porter, 'French Lawmakers Enshrine Access to Abortion in Constitution', *The New York Times*, 04/03/24, https://www.nytimes.com/2024/03/04/world/europe/france-abortion-rights-constitution.html#:-:text, accessed 07/03/24.
100. Sheryl Sandberg, *Lean In*.
101. A. Haridasani Gupta, 'Today's Capitalism Is Incompatible with Feminism', *New York Times*, 19/11/20.
102. David E. Sanger and Maggie Haberman, 'In Donald Trump's Worldview, America Comes First, and Everybody Else Pays', *The New York Times*, 26/03/16, https://www.nytimes.com/2016/03/27/us/politics/donald-trump-foreign-policy.html?, accessed 13/08/24.
103. Swaminathan S. Anklesaria Aiyar, 'Indian Nationalism and the Historical Fantasy of a Golden Hindu Period', Cato Institute, 21/06/23, https://www.cato.org/policy-analysis/indian-nationalism-historical-fantasy-golden-hindu-period, accessed 13/08/24.
104. Saini, *Patriarchs*, p. 221.
105. Gary Younge talk at 'Darcus Howe, Race Today: Legacies of Resistance' for launch of the commemorative issue of *Race Today*, 03/03/23.

1. EL SALVADOR: THE CURRENCY OF VIOLENCE

1. Maria Abi-Habib and Bryan Avelar, 'El Salvador's New Law on Gangs Raises Censorship Fears', *New York Times*, 06/04/22, https://www.nytimes.com/2022/04/06/world/americas/el-salvador-media-gangs.html, accessed 11/09/23.
2. Randall Thompson, 'Visioning a New Social Imaginary in El Salvador to Prevent Violence against Women', *Journal of Gender-Based Violence* 5, no. 1 (2021), https://www.academia.edu/44882812/Visioning_a_New_Social_Imaginary_in_El_Salvador_to_Prevent_Violence_Against_Women, accessed 30/01/23.
3. Ainhoa Montoya, *The Violence of Democracy: Political Life in Postwar El Salvador*, London: Palgrave Macmillan, 2018.
4. Author interview with Edith Elizondo, 13/06/23.

5. Carlos Martinez, 'Montaña: The Prison Guard Identified as Torturer of Mariona Prison', El Faro, 19/08/24, https://elfaro.net/en/202408/el_salvador/27531/montana-the-prison-guard-identified-as-torturer-of-mariona-prison, accessed 27/08/24.
6. Ibid.
7. Joan Didion, *Salvador*, London: Granta Books, 2006, p. 13.
8. Exchange of WhatsApp texts with Clanci Rosa, Sept. 2023.
9. Interview with Silvia Juárez, 22/08/23.
10. The number of femicides dropped from 271 in 2017 to 232 in 2018; see 'Number of Femicide and Feminicide', Cepal, https://statistics.cepal.org/portal/databank/index.html?lang=en&indicator_id=2780&area_id=, accessed 06/09/23. ORMUSA's figures for 2022 stand at sixty-eight; see 'Violencia feminicida', ORMUSA, https://observatoriodeviolenciaormusa.org/violencia-feminicida/, accessed 06/09/23.
11. Lilian Martínez, 'Four Times as Many Girls as Boys Disappeared in El Salvador', Elsalvador.com, 30/10/21, https://historico.elsalvador.com/historico/895381/ninas-desaparecidos-alerta-angel-fiscalia.html, accessed 06/09/23.
12. Michael Paarlberg, 'The Emerging Gang State in El Salvador', Global Americans, 15/02/2022, https://globalamericans.org/the-emerging-gang-state-in-el-salvador/, accessed 06/09/2023.
13. Víctor Peña and María Luz Nóchez, 'In the Chalchuapa Pit There Is Confusion and Mothers Looking for Their Children', El Faro, 25/08/23, https://elfaro.net/es/202105/el_salvador/25498/En-la-fosa-de-Chalchuapa-hay-confusión-y-madres-que-buscan-a-sus-hijos.htm, accessed 06/09/23.
14. Author interview with Edith Elizondo and Clanci Rosa, 13/06/23, and Carmen Urquilla, 15/06/23.
15. Thomas Boerman, 'The Sociopolitical Context of Violence in El Salvador, Honduras and Guatemala', Immigration Briefings, 23/04/19, https://ssrn.com/abstract=3376374, accessed 25/04/23.
16. 'Celebrate the Day of the Unborn Child', Priests for Life, https://www.priestsforlife.org/annunciation/, accessed 15/09/23.
17. 'El Salvador', CIA World Factbook, https://www.cia.gov/the-world-factbook/countries/el-salvador/#people-and-society, accessed 21/06/2023.
18. Gabriel Labrador, 'How Bukele Crafted a Best-Selling Political Brand?', El Faro, 03/05/22, https://elfaro.net/en/202205/el_salvador/0000026155-how-bukele-crafted-a-best-selling-political-brand?, accessed 12/05/23.

19. 'Does God Support Corrupt Leaders?', El Faro, 21/10/21, https://elfaro.net/en/202110/centroamerica/25804/Does-God-Support-Corrupt-Leaders.htm, accessed 12/04/23.
20. Ibid.
21. Author's follow up interview with Clanci Rosa, 22/08/23.
22. Nina Lakhani, 'Human Rights Officials Call for Pegasus Spyware Ban at El Salvador Hearing', *The Guardian*, 17/03/22, https://www.theguardian.com/world/2022/mar/17/pegasus-spyware-ban-el-salvador-iachr-hearing, accessed 5/09/23.
23. My daughter, Atiha Sen Gupta, acted as my interpreter.
24. Author interviews with Carmen Urquilla, 15/01/23, and Deysi Cheyne, 16/01/23.
25. 'From 14 Families to 8 Business Groups', El Salvador Perspectives, 07/04/06, https://www.elsalvadorperspectives.com/2006/04/from-14-families-to-8-business-groups.html, accessed 24/04/2023.
26. Montoya, *Violence of Democracy*, p. 22.
27. Diana Carolina Sierra Becerra, 'Insurgent Butterflies: Gender and Revolution in El Salvador, 1965–2015', PhD thesis, University of Michigan, 2017, https://www.academia.edu/34224310/Insurgent_Butterflies_Gender_and_Revolution_in_El_Salvador_1965_2015, accessed 06/03/23.
28. I have relied extensively on the research in 'Insurgent Butterflies' for my understanding of the revolutionary movement and the women involved in it.
29. Author interview with Marta Digna Ortiz, 22/08/23.
30. Gary Younge talk at 'Darcus Howe, Race Today: Legacies of Resistance' for the launch of the commemorative issue of *Race Today*, 03/03/23.
31. Carlos Dada, 'The Beatification of Óscar Romero', *The New Yorker*, 21/05/15, https://www.newyorker.com/news/news-desk/the-beatification-of-oscar-romero#:-:text=Romero%20was%20not%20a%20theologian,movement%20born%20of%20Vatican%20II, accessed 06/09/23.
32. Pat Marrin, 'Oscar Romero, "A saint for our times"', Liberation Theology, June 2015, https://liberationtheology.org/oscar-romero-saint-for-our-times/, accessed 29/03/23.
33. Becerra, 'Insurgent Butterflies', p. 226.
34. Ibid., p. 75.
35. Author interview with Nubia Lazo, 23/08/23.
36. Leo Guardado, 'After 50 Years, Liberation Theology is Still Reshaping

Catholicism and Politics', The Conversation, 13/12/22, https://theconversation.com/after-50-years-liberation-theology-is-still-reshaping-catholicism-and-politics-but-what-is-it-186804, accessed 14/03/23.

37. Speech given by Joaquín Villalobos in June 1993; 'Discurso de Joaquín Villalobos en el acto de cierre del Primer Congreso del PRS-ERP', CeDeMA, https://cedema.org/digital_items/3979, accessed 07/09/23.

38. Julie D. Shayne, *The Revolution Question: Feminisms in El Salvador, Chile, and Cuba*, New Brunswick, NJ: Rutgers University Press, 2004, p. 23.

40. Carlos Colorado, 'Romero and Abortion: A Practice to "Castrate the People"', *La Stampa*, 23/04/18, https://www.lastampa.it/vatican-insider/en/2018/04/23/news/romero-and-abortion-a-practice-to-castrate-the-people-1.34008888/, accessed 11/09/23.

41. United Nations Truth Commission, 1993, https://www.usip.org/publications/1992/07/truth-commission-el-salvador, accessed 16/05/23.

42. Noam Chomsky, '1970–1990: The War of Counter-Insurgency in El Salvador', 1992, https://archive.org/details/19701990thewarofcounterinunknown/page/n5/mode/2up, accessed 29/03/23.

43. Becerra, 'Insurgent Butterflies', pp. 25–9.

44. Ibid., pp. 165–6.

45. Ibid., pp. 202–4.

46. Author interview with Deysi Cheyne, 16/06/23.

47. Author follow-up interview with Deysi Cheyne, 18/08/23.

48. Author interview with Raúl Martinez, 23/08/23.

49. Becerra, 'Insurgent Butterflies', p. 150.

50. Ibid., p. 105.

51. Ibid., p. 127.

52. Author interview with Deysi Cheyne, 16/06/23.

53. Beccera, 'Insurgent Butterflies', p. 136.

54. Ibid., p. 144.

55. Author interview with Morena Herrera, 25/08/23.

56. Beccera, 'Insurgent Butterflies', p. 123.

57. Shayne, *Revolution Question*, pp. 36–7.

58. Ibid., p. 85.

59. Christopher Dickey, 'Salvadoran Rebel Intrigue', *The Washington Post*, 26/06/83, https://www.washingtonpost.com/archive/politics/1983/06/27/salvadoran-rebel-intrigue/f70f906c-220f-40e9-b5c9-b5323e408507/, accessed 12/09/23.

60. Becerra, 'Insurgent Butterflies', p. 211.
61. 'Discurso de Joaquín Villalobos en el acto de cierre del Primer Congreso del PRS-ERP'.
62. Becerra, 'Insurgent Butterflies', p. 213.
63. Stephen Offutt, *Blood Entanglements: Evangelicals and Gangs in El Salvador*, Oxford: Oxford University Press, 2023.
64. Margriet Zoethout, 'Enhancing Citizen Security on the Frontline in a Contested Playing Field', 11/12/14, p. 10, https://www.academia.edu/10353304/Enhancing_Citizen_Security_on_the_Frontline_in_a_Contested_Playing_Field_A_Case_Study_of_the_Gang_Truce_in_San_Jos%C3%A9_del_Pino_El_Salvador, accessed 24/03/23.
65. Ibid., p. 47.
66. Ibid., p. 37.
67. Carlos Martínez, Efren Lemus and Óscar Martínez, 'Bukele Government Dismantled Gang Presence in El Salvador', El Faro, 03/02/23, https://elfaro.net/en/202302/el_salvador/26694/Bukele-Government-Dismantled-Gang-Presence-in-El-Salvador.htm, accessed 04/04/23.
68. Thomas W. Ward, *Gangsters without Borders: An Ethnography of a Salvadoran Street Gang*, Oxford: Oxford University Press, 2012, p. 4.
69. Samantha B. Karlin, 'A Conflict Analysis of Gang Violence', 10/04/15, p. 4, https://www.academia.edu/18165057/A_Conflict_Analysis_of_Gang_Violence_in_El_Salvador, accessed 01/02/2023.
70. Óscar Martínez, 'A Brief History of El Salvador, Gangs, the U.S., and The Difficulties of Empathy', New American History Project, https://newamericanstoryproject.org/context/brief-history-of-el-salvador/, accessed 26/04/23.
71. Ibid.
72. University Institute of Public Opinion, *'Seconds in the air': Women Gang-Members and Their Prisons*, San Salvador: n.p., 2010, pp. 318–24, https://uca.edu.sv/iudop/wp-content/uploads/SegIN.pdf, accessed 20/04/23.
73. Boerman, 'Sociopolitical Context of Violence'.
74. Carlos Garcia, 'The Gospel of Man, in Church and Gang', Insight Crime, 15/06/22, https://insightcrime.org/investigations/gangsters-preachers-culture-sexism-ms13/, accessed 28/03/23.
75. *'Seconds in the air'*, pp. 328–9.
76. Floor Keuleers and Natasha Mulenga Hornsby, 'Women in El Salvador's Gang War: Surviving the State of Exception', Reliefweb, 10/08/22, https://reliefweb.

int/report/el-salvador/women-el-salvadors-gang-war-surviving-state-exception, accessed 28/03/23.

77. Broadcast in 2015; see 'Translation: Postcard from San Salvador', Radio Ambulante, https://radioambulante.org/en/translation/translation-postcard-from-san-salvador, accessed 23/03/23.
78. 'El Salvador: Rights Violations against Children in "State of Emergency"', Human Rights Watch, 16/07/24, https://www.hrw.org/news/2024/07/16/el-salvador-rights-violations-against-children-state-emergency, accessed 28/08/24.
79. Ibid., p. 52.
80. Zoom author interview with Silvia Juárez.
81. Julia Zulver and María José Méndez, 'El Salvador's State of Exception Makes Women Collateral Damage', Carnegie Endowment, 04/05/23, https://carnegieendowment.org/2023/05/04/el-salvador-s-state-of-exception-makes-women-collateral-damage-pub-89686, accessed 18/05/23.
82. 'At Least 261 People Have Died in El Salvador's Prisons under Anti-gang Crackdown, Rights Group Says', *The Independent*, 10/07/24, https://www.independent.co.uk/news/nayib-bukele-ap-el-salvador-people-central-american-b2577698.html, accessed 28/08/24.
83. Twitter/X, @nayibbukele, 27/03/23, https://twitter.com/nayibbukele/status/1640469676458164226, accessed 28/03/23.
84. Martínez, Lemus and Martínez, 'Bukele Government Dismantled Gang Presence'.
85. Thomas Dolzall, 'Can El Salvador Sustain Its Rising Defense Expenditures?', Defense and Security Monitor, 23/03/22, https://dsm.forecastinternational.com/wordpress/2022/03/23/can-el-salvador-sustain-its-rising-defense-expenditures/, accessed 23/05/2023.
86. Author interview with Edith Elizondo, 13/06/23.
87. Abigail Parada, 'Government Says It Will "Use" $30 Million from INSAFORP to Finance Territorial Control Plan', elsalvador.com, 15/09/23, https://www.elsalvador.com/noticias/nacional/fondos-plan-control-territorial-insaforp/1090433/2023/, accessed 18/09/23.
88. Cameroonian critical theorist Achille Mbembe defines necropolitics as the 'contemporary forms of subjugation of life to the power of death'.
89. Maria Abi-Habib and Bryan Avelar, 'El Salvador's New Law on Gangs Raises Censorship Fears', *New York Times*, 06/04/22, https://www.nytimes.com/2022/04/06/world/americas/el-salvador-media-gangs.html, accessed 28/04/23.

90. Wilfredo Miranda, 'Mass Trials in Bukele's El Salvador: Legal Reform Will Allow Hearings of up to 900 Prisoners', *El Pais*, https://english.elpais.com/international/2023-07-28/mass-trials-in-bukeles-el-salvador-legal-reform-will-allow-hearings-of-up-to-900-prisoners.html, accessed 13/09/23.
91. *'Seconds in the air'*, p. 73.
92. Ibid., p. 78.
93. 'The MS13 Will Never Be a Gang for Women', Insight Crime, 15/06/22, https://insightcrime.org/investigations/ms13-gang-for-women/, accessed 28/03/23.
94. Garcia, 'Gospel of Man'.
95. Offutt, *Blood Entanglements*.
96. Author conversation with Jaime Iraheta, 27/08/23.
97. Offutt, *Blood Entanglements*.
98. 'Does God Support Corrupt Leaders?'
99. 'El Salvador', CIA World Factbook, https://www.cia.gov/the-world-factbook/countries/el-salvador/, accessed 24/04/23.
100. Author interview with Silvia Juárez, 22/08/23.
101. 'U.S. Relations with El Salvador, Bilateral Relations Fact Sheet', State Department, 01/02/2023, https://www.state.gov/u-s-relations-with-el-salvador/, accessed 02/02/23.
102. J. Hennebry, J. Holliday and M. Moniruzzaman, 'At What Cost? Women Migrant Workers, Remittances and Development', UN Women, January 2017, https://unwomen.org/sites/default/files/Headquarters/Attachments/Sections/Library/Publications/2017/women-migrant-workers-remittances-and-development.pdf, accessed 02/02/23.
103. Becerra, 'Insurgent Butterflies', p. 218.
104. Justus Links, 'The Catastrophe in Turkey', *N+1* (Spring 2023), https://www.nplusonemag.com/issue-45/politics/the-catastrophe-in-turkey/, accessed 05/05/23.
105. 'Poor in El Salvador Face Brunt of Crackdown on Gang Violence as Gov't Suspends Rights, Arrests 6,000+', Democracy Now!, 05/04/22, https://www.democracynow.org/2022/4/5/el_salvador_gang_crackdown_constitutional_rights, accessed 27/04/2023.
106. Shayne, *Revolution Question*, p. 48.
107. Becerra, 'Insurgent Butterflies'.
108. Serena Cosgrove et al., 'Aftermath: Women's Organizations in Postconflict El

Salvador', 2000, https://www.academia.edu/14539408/Aftermath_Womens_Organizations_in_Postconflict_El_Salvador, accessed 23/03/23.
109. Ibid., pp. 10–11.
110. Thompson, 'Visioning a New Social Imaginary in El Salvador', p. 4.
111. Author interview with Silvia Juárez, Zoom, 27/04/23.
112. Evelyn P. Stevens and Ann Pescatello, *Marianismo: The Other Face of Machismo in Latin America*, Pittsburgh, PA: University of Pittsburgh Press, 1973, p. 4.
113. Thompson, 'Visioning a New Social Imaginary in El Salvador', p. 19.
114. Gabriel Labrador, 'How Bukele Crafted a Best-Selling Political Brand', El Faro, 03/05/22, https://elfaro.net/en/202205/el_salvador/0000026155-how-bukele-crafted-a-best-selling-political-brand?, accessed 12/05/23.
115. Author interview with Deysi Cheyne, 16/06/23.
116. Author interview with Silvia Juárez, Zoom, 27/04/23.
117. Zulver and Méndez, 'El Salvador's State of Exception Makes Women Collateral Damage'.
118. Conversations with various activists, Aug. 2023.
119. Author interview with Silvia Juárez, 22/08/23.
120. Interview with Deysi Cheyne, 16/06/23.
121. Ibid.
122. 'Sixth Report on GBV Statistics in El Salvador', Research Institute on Gender-Based Violence, Mar. 2024, https://ri.ufg.edu.sv/jspui/bitstream/11592/9935/2/Sixth%20report%20on%20GBV%20statistics%20in%20El%20Salvador, accessed 07/03/25.
123. Keuleers and Hornsby, 'Women in El Salvador's Gang War'.
124. María Luz Nóchez and Laura Aguirre, 'A Haven for Child Rapists', El Faro, 22/05/20, https://elfaro.net/en/202005/el_salvador/24440/A-Haven-For-Child-Rapists.htm, accessed 14/09/23.
125. Author interview with Norma Letitia Lobos, 22/08/23.
126. Author interview with Silvia Juárez, 22/08/23. 'Masculine abortion' is a literal translation from the Spanish.
127. Edgardo Ayala, '"No" to Sex Education Fuels Early Pregnancies in Central America', Global Issues, 03/08/23, https://www.globalissues.org/news/2023/08/03/34418, accessed 20/09/23.
128. Citizens' Group for the Decriminalization of Abortion, https://agrupacionciudadana.org/agrupacion-ciudadana-por-la-despenalizacion-del-aborto-el-salvador/, accessed 14/09/23.

129. Keuleers and Hornsby, 'Women in El Salvador's Gang War'.
130. Author interview with Morena Herrera, 25/08/23.
131. Author interview with Nubia Lazo, 23/08/23.
132. Ibid.
133. Author interview with Norma Lobos, 22/08/23.
134. Becerra, 'Insurgent Butterflies', p. 217.
135. Author interview with Silvia Juárez, 22/08/23.
136. Sian Taylder, 'The Hour Is Coming, the Hour Is Come: Church and Feminist Theology in Post-revolutionary El Salvador', *Journal of Feminist Theology* 11, no. 1 (2002), p. 58, https://www.academia.edu/57327706/The_Hour_is_Coming_the_Hour_is_Come_Church_and_Feminist_Theology_in_Post_Revolutionary_El_Salvador, accessed 20/06/23.
137. Jocelyn Viterna et al., 'Governance and the Reversal of Women's Rights: The Case of Abortion in El Salvador', in Siwan Anderson, Lori Beaman and Jean-Philippe Platteau (eds), *Towards Gender Equity in Development*, Oxford: Oxford University Press, 2018, https://academic.oup.com/book/26611/chapter/195286495, accessed 22/05/23.
138. Interview with Morena Herrera, Focus 2030, 09/03/2023, https://focus2030.org/3-Questions-to-Morena-Herrera-President-of-the-Citizen-Group-for-the, accessed 15/09/23.
139. Interview with Deysi Cheyne, 16/06/23.
140. Catalina Lobo-Guerrero, 'In El Salvador, "Girls are a problem"', *New York Times*, 02/09/17, https://www.nytimes.com/2017/09/02/opinion/sunday/el-salvador-girls-homicides.html?searchResultPosition=8, accessed 28/04/23.
141. Kristina Zanzinger, S. J. Fernandez and Yanxi Liu, 'Underreported and Unpunished, Femicides in El Salvador Continue', Nacla, 05/03/21, https://nacla.org/news/2021/03/04/femicides-el-salvador-pandemic, accessed 27/04/23.
142. Interview with Deysi Cheyne, 16/06/23.
143. Mark LeVine, 'From Neoliberalism to Necrocapitalism in 20 Years', Al Jazeera, 07/15/20, https://www.aljazeera.com/opinions/2020/7/15/from-neoliberalism-to-necrocapitalism-in-20-years, accessed 06/01/2023.

2. RAQQA TO RIYADH: THE COPY AND THE TEMPLATE

1. 'Saudi Arabia and the Death Penalty: Everything You Need to Know about the Rise in Executions under Mohammed Bin Salman', Reprieve, 31/01/23, https://

reprieve.org/us/2023/01/31/saudi-arabia-and-the-death-penalty-everything-you-need-to-know-about-the-rise-in-executions-under-mohammed-bin-salman/, accessed 03/04/2024.
2. Email exchange with Nadia, Saudi political refugee, 04/04/24.
3. The Islamic State of Iraq and Syria (ISIS) is also known as the Islamic State of Iraq and the Levant (ISIL) and by its Arabic acronym Daesh. In Afghanistan, it is known as Islamic State-Khorasan Province (IS-KP). In Africa, it is Islamic State-West Africa (ISIS-WA), also known as Boko Haram. ISIS is the acronym used throughout this chapter, and the focus is exclusively on the caliphate in Syria and Iraq.
4. 'Islamic Extremist Strategy: Executions', Tony Blair Institute for Global Change, 13/09/18, https://www.institute.global/insights/geopolitics-and-security/islamist-extremist-strategy-executions, accessed 03/04/24.
5. Ibid.
6. Carmen bin Ladin, *The Veiled Kingdom*, London: Virago, 2006, p. 168.
7. Lincoln Clapper, 'Wahhabism, ISIS, and the Saudi Connection', Geopolitical Monitor, 31/01/16, https://www.geopoliticalmonitor.com/wahhabism-isis-and-the-saudi-connection/, accessed 19/03/24.
8. Abubakr al-Shamahi, 'Baghdadi's Purported Audio Message: IS Targets Arab Governments', New Arab, 14/11/14, https://www.newarab.com/news/baghdadis-purported-audio-message-targets-arab-governments, accessed 19/03/24.
9. Since the 1980s, Saudi Arabia has reportedly spent at least $100 billion exporting Wahhabism; see Cameron Glenn, 'Iran v Saudi Arabia: Government & Ideology', United States Institute of Peace, 4/01/16, https://iranprimer.usip.org/blog/2016/jan/04/iran-v-saudi-arabia-government-ideology, accessed 08/03/24.
10. Bin Ladin, *Veiled Kingdom*, p. 169.
11. Andrew Roth and Pjotr Sauer, 'Four Suspects in Moscow Concert Hall Terror Attack Appear in Court', *The Guardian*, 24/03/24, https://www.theguardian.com/world/2024/mar/24/new-islamic-state-videos-back-claim-it-carried-out-moscow-concert-hall-attack, accessed 02/02/24.
12. 'Jihad and Terrorism Threat Monitor', MEMRI, 12/07/22, https://www.memri.org/jttm/article-issue-nine-isis-k-magazine-voice-khurasan-criticizes-saudi-crown-prince-muhammad-bin, accessed 16/04/24.
13. Martin Chulov, 'Isis: The Inside Story', *The Guardian*, 11/12/14, https://www.theguardian.com/world/2014/dec/11/-sp-isis-the-inside-story, accessed 05/04/18.

14. Patrick Cockburn, *The Rise of Islamic State: ISIS and the New Sunni Revolution*, London: Verso, 2015.
15. Mara R. Revkin, 'ISIS' Social Contract', *Foreign Affairs*, 10/01/16, https://www.foreignaffairs.com/articles/syria/2016-01-10/isis-social-contract, accessed 09/04/18.
16. 'Islamic State NHS-Style Hospital Video Posted', BBC, 24/04/15, https://www.bbc.co.uk/news/world-middle-east/32456789, accessed 04/12/24.
17. Samer, *The Raqqa Diaries: Escape from Islamic State*, London: Hutchinson, 2017.
18. Rukmini Callimachi, 'The ISIS Files', *New York Times*, 04/04/18, https://www.nytimes.com/interactive/2018/04/04/world/middleeast/isis-documents-mosul-iraq.html, accessed 08/04/18.
19. Cockburn, *Rise of Islamic State*, p. 49.
20. Timothy Mitchell, 'McJihad: Empire and Islam between the US and Saudi Arabia?', Verso Books, 07/06/17, https://www.versobooks.com/en-gb/blogs/news/3256-mcjihad-empire-and-islam-between-the-us-and-saudi-arabia?, accessed 08/03/24.
21. Ibid.
22. Ibid.
23. Figures from the Saudi Census Portal: https://portal.saudicensus.sa/portal, accessed 08/04/24.
24. John Cantlie, 'If I Were the US President Today', *Dabiq* no. 5, 1436 (Islamic Calendar), p. 38.
25. Susanne Koelbl, *Behind the Kingdom's Veil: Inside the New Saudi Arabia under Crown Prince Mohammed Bin Salman*, trans. Maurice Frank, Coral Gables, FL: Mango Press, 2019.
26. Hugh Kennedy, 'How ISIS Twisted the Meaning of "Caliphate"', *Time*, 11/10/16, http://time.com/4471463/caliphate-history/, accessed 14/06/18.
27. Michael Weiss and Hassan Hassan, 'Why Some Secular Sunnis Support ISIS', Business Insider India, 12/03/15, https://www.businessinsider.in/why-some-secular-sunnis-support-isis/articleshow/46548205.cms, accessed 05/12/24.
28. Joana Cook and Gina Vale, 'From Daesh to "Diaspora": Tracing the Women and Minors of Islamic State', ICSR, https://icsr.info/wp-content/uploads/2018/07/Women-in-ISIS-report_20180719_web.pdf, accessed 24/07/18.
29. Ibid.
30. Hanna Yusuf and Steve Swann, 'Shamima Begum: Lawyer Says Teen Was

"Groomed'", BBC News, 31/05/24, https://www.bbc.co.uk/news/uk-48444604, accessed 11/09/24.

31. Lizzie Dearden, 'How ISIS Attracts Women and Girls from Europe with False Offer of "Empowerment"', *The Independent*, 05/08/17, https://www.independent.co.uk/news/world/europe/isis-jihadi-brides-islamic-state-women-girls-europe-british-radicalisation-recruitment-report-a7878681.html, accessed 26/03/18.

32. Carolyn Hoyle, Alexandra Bradford and Ross Frenett, 'Becoming Mulan? Female Western Migrants to ISIS', Institute for Strategic Dialogue, January 2015, https://www.isdglobal.org/isd-publications/becoming-mulan-female-western-migrants-to-isis/, accessed 09/11/16.

33. Erin Marie Saltman and Melanie Smith, 'Till Martyrdom Do Us Part: Gender and the ISIS Phenomenon', Institute for Strategic Dialogue, 2015, p. 5, https://www.isdglobal.org/wp-content/uploads/2016/02/Till_Martyrdom_Do_Us_Part_Gender_and_the_ISIS_Phenomenon.pdf, accessed 07/11/16.

34. Ibid., p. 9.

35. Hoyle, Bradford and Frenett, 'Becoming Mulan', p. 29.

36. Hoyle, Bradford and Frenett, 'Becoming Mulan', pp. 12–13.

37. Rachel Bryson, 'Female Suicide Bombers May Be New to ISIS But They're No Stranger to Iraq', Tony Blair Institute for Global Change, 12/07/17, https://institute.global/insights/geopolitics-and-security/female-suicide-bombers-may-be-new-isis-theyre-no-stranger-iraq, accessed 26/03/18.

38. Karima Bennoune, *Your Fatwa Does Not Apply Here: Untold Stories from the Fight against Muslim Fundamentalism*, New York: W. W. Norton & Company, 2013, p. 15.

39. Hoyle, Bradford and Frenett, 'Becoming Mulan', p. 23.

40. Umm Sumaiyya al-Muhājirah, 'The Twin Halves of the Muhājirīn', *Dabiq* no. 8, 1436 (Islamic Calendar), p. 35.

41. Hoyle, Bradford and Frenett, 'Becoming Mulan', p. 24.

42. Ben Farmer and Josie Ensor, 'British Jihadi Brides Return Home after Being Widowed or Sent Back by Husbands Preparing Last Stand for ISIL', *The Telegraph*, 22/05/17, http://www.telegraph.co.uk/news/2017/05/22/british-jihadi-brides-returning-home-widowed-sent-home-husbands/, accessed 23/01/18.

43. 'Advice on Ihdād', *Dabiq* no. 13, 1437 (Islamic Calendar), p. 25.

44. Umm Sumayyah al-Muhājirah, 'They Are Not Lawful Spouses for One Another', *Dabiq* no. 10, 1436 (Islamic Calendar), p. 44.

45. Al-Muhājirah, 'Twin Halves of the Muhājirīn', p. 33.
46. Ibid., p. 35.
47. 'Online Briefing on Women's Rights in the Middle East and Afghanistan', ALQST, 21/08/23, https://alqst.org/en/post/online-briefing-on-womens-rights-in-the-middle-east-and-afghanistan, accessed 15/04/24.
48. Dania Akkad, 'Where the Abused Are Abused: Welcome to Saudi Arabia's Shelters for Women and Girls', Middle East Eye, 03/05/22, https://www.middleeasteye.net/big-story/saudi-arabia-women-girls-shelters-where-abused, accessed 29/04/24.
49. Anna Erelle, *In the Skin of a Jihadist: A Young Journalist Enters the ISIS Recruitment Networks*, New York: HarperCollins, 2015, p. 21.
50. Ibid., pp. 3–4.
51. Ibid., pp. 118–119.
52. Jean Sasson, *Princess*, London: Bantam Books, 1993, p. 137.
53. Quoted in Meredith Tax, *A Road Unforeseen: Women Fight the Islamic State*, New York: Bellevue Literary Press, 2016, p. 40.
54. James Reini, 'Q&A: Probing Islamic State's Sex Atrocities with United Nations', Middle East Eye, 27/05/15, http://www.middleeasteye.net/news/qa-probing-islamic-state-s-sex-atrocities-united-nations-1064004421, accessed 20/03/18.
55. Olivia Goldhill, 'This Man Risks His Life Every Day to Rescue Kidnapped Women from Islamic State', *The Telegraph*, 08/07/15, https://www.telegraph.co.uk/women/womens-life/11723360/Islamic-State-Meet-the-man-who-helps-kidnapped-women-escape-horrors.html, accessed 29/03/18.
56. 'Nearly 300,000 Yazidis Remain in Kurdistan Region Camps: Official', Rudaw, 06/12/23, https://www.rudaw.net/english/kurdistan/06122023, accessed 15/05/24.
57. Adam Withnall, 'Isis Releases "Abhorrent" Sex Slaves Pamphlet with 27 Tips for Militants on Taking, Punishing and Raping Female Captives', *The Independent*, 10/12/14, https://www.independent.co.uk/news/world/middle-east/isis-releases-abhorrent-sex-slaves-pamphlet-with-27-tips-for-militants-on-taking-punishing-and-9915913.html, accessed 20/02/18.
58. 'The Revival of Slavery: Before the Hour', *Dabiq* no. 4, 1435 (Islamic Calendar), p. 17.
59. Umm Sumaiyya al-Muhājirah, 'Slave-Girls or Prostitutes', *Dabiq* no. 9, 1436 (Islamic Calendar), pp. 48–9.
60. 'ISIS Computers Full of Porn, Says Former Pentagon Top Spy', Al Arabiya,

14/07/16, http://english.alarabiya.net/en/variety/2016/07/14/ISIS-computers-full-of-porn-says-former-Pentagon-top-spy.html, accessed 28/03/18.
61. Umm Sumaiyya al-Muhājirah 'Two, Three or Four', *Dabiq* no. 12, 1437 (Islamic Calendar), https://clarionproject.org/docs/islamic-state-isis-isil-dabiq-magazine-issue-12-just-terror.pdf, accessed 21/02/18.
63. Charlie Winter (trans.), 'Women of the Islamic State', Quilliam, February 2015, https://therinjfoundation.files.wordpress.com/2015/01/women-of-the-islamic-state3.pdf, accessed 26/03/18.
64. 'Revival of Slavery', p. 17.
65. 'The Murtadd Brotherhood', *Dabiq* no. 14, 1437 (Islamic Calendar), pp. 28–43.
66. Erelle, *In the Skin of a Jihadist*, p. 155.
67. Patrick Cockburn, 'War with ISIS: The Grim Reality of Life under the Islamist Group in Iraq', *The Independent*, 16/05/15, https://www.independent.co.uk/news/world/middle-east/war-with-isis-the-grim-reality-of-life-under-the-islamist-group-in-iraq-10255422.html, accessed 30/03/18.
68. 'Saudi Arabia', US Department of State, https://2009–2017.state.gov/documents/organization/171744.pdf, accessed 09/05/24.
69. Callimachi, 'ISIS Files'.
70. Ibid.
71. Hosam al-Jablawi, 'A Closer Look at the Education System of ISIS', Atlantic Council, 26/04/16, https://www.atlanticcouncil.org/blogs/syriasource/a-closer-look-at-isis-s-educational-system/, accessed 06/04/18.
72. Hassan Hassan, 'The Secret World of ISIS Training Camps: Ruled by Sacred Texts and the Sword', *The Guardian*, 25/01/15, https://www.theguardian.com/world/2015/jan/25/inside-isis-training-camps, accessed 10/04/18.
73. Save the Children Press Release, 06/11/16, https://www.savethechildren.org.uk/news/media-centre/press-releases/over-million-children-living-under-isis-iraq-missed-out-education, accessed 6/4/2018.
74. Hosam al-Jablawi, 'Syria's Conflicting Powers Develop Separate Education Curriculums', Atlantic Council, 23/12/15, http://www.atlanticcouncil.org/blogs/syriasource/syria-s-conflicting-powers-develop-separate-education-curriculums, accessed 09/04/18.
75. Al-Muhājirah, 'Slave-Girls or Prostitutes', pp. 25–6.
76. Clapper, 'Wahhabism, ISIS, and the Saudi Connection'.
77. 'Education System in Saudi Arabia: Overview', Allen Overseas, https://www.allenoverseas.com/blog/education-system-in-saudi-arabia-overview/, accessed 15/04/24.

78. Madawi al-Rasheed, *A Most Masculine State: Gender, Politics, and Religion in Saudi Arabia*, New York: Cambridge University Press, 2013, p. 39.
79. Author Zoom interview with Nadia, 25/03/24.
80. Daban Mohammed, '12,000 ISIS Fighters in Prisons, 39,000 ISIS Relatives, Including Many Iraqis, in Rojava Camps', Channel 8, 13/02/25, https://channel8.com/english/31480, accessed 12/03/25.
81. Anthony Lloyd, 'Killer Isis Brides Rule Al-Hawl Camp with a Rod of Iron', *The Times*, 02/10/19, https://www.thetimes.co.uk/article/killer-isis-brides-rule-al-hawl-camp-with-a-rod-of-iron-j9lkgcg9w, accessed 01/04/20.
82. Guido Steinberg, 'AQAP, ISIS, and Domestic Security in Saudi Arabia', in Joshua Teitelbaum (ed.), *Saudi Arabia, the Gulf, and the New Regional Landscape*, Ramat Gan: Begin-Sadat Center for Strategic Studies, 2017, https://besacenter.org/wp-content/uploads/2017/06/MSPS133.pdf, accessed 04/03/24.
83. Ashley Fantz, 'Who Is Doing What in the Coalition Battle against ISIS', CNN, 17/09/14, https://edition.cnn.com/2014/09/14/world/meast/isis-coalition-nations/, accessed 04/03/24.
84. 'Saudi Arabia and Counterterrorism', Washington, DC: Embassy of Saudi Arabia, Mar. 2019, https://www.saudiembassy.net/sites/default/files/SAUDI%20ARABIA%20AND%20COUNTERTERRORISM.pdf, accessed 17/04/24.
85. Koelbl, *Behind the Kingdom's Veil*, p. 285.
86. 'Saudi Arabia and Counterterrorism', p. 1.
87. 'Saudi Arabia Apologises for Video Labelling Feminism as Extremism', BBC, 13/11/19, https://www.bbc.co.uk/news/world-middle-east-50401311, accessed 04/12/24.
88. 'Jihad and Terrorism Threat Monitor', MEMRI.
89. Muhammad al-Atawneh, 'Is Saudi Arabia a Theocracy? Religion and Governance in Contemporary Saudi Arabia', *Middle Eastern Studies* 45, no. 5 (2009), pp. 721–37.
90. 'Saudi Arabia', US Department of State, https://2009-2017.state.gov/documents/organization/171744.pdf, accessed 09/05/24.
91. 'Saudi Arabia: New Personal Status Law Codifies Discrimination against Women', Amnesty International, 08/03/23, p. 2, https://www.amnesty.org/en/documents/mde23/6431/2023/en/, accessed 10/04/24.
92. Quoted in al-Atawneh, 'Is Saudi Arabia a Theocracy?', p. 721.
93. Ibid., pp. 726–7.
94. Ibid., p. 730.

95. Clapper, 'Wahhabism, ISIS, and the Saudi Connection'.
96. Quoted in Mitchell, 'McJihad'.
97. Antoine Guillemin-Puteaux, 'The Religious Legitimacy of the Saudi State', Cercle Des Chercheurs Sur Le Moyen-Orient, 09/10/18, https://cerclechercheursmoyenorient.wordpress.com/2018/10/09/the-religious-legitimacy-of-the-saudi-state/, accessed 08/03/24.
98. Al-Atawneh, 'Is Saudi Arabia a Theocracy?', p. 733.
99. Bin Ladin, *Veiled Kingdom*, p. 61.
100. Koelbl, *Behind the Kingdom's Veil*, pp. 285–6.
101. Bin Ladin, *Veiled Kingdom*, p. 73.
102. Koelbl, *Behind the Kingdom's Veil*, p. 90.
103. Email exchange with Abdullah Alaoudh, director of Middle East Democracy Center, 20/04/24.
104. Imam Khomeini, *Islam and Revolution*, trans. Hamid Algar, Berkeley: Mizan Press, 1981, p. 202.
105. Bin Ladin, *Veiled Kingdom*, p. 63.
106. Ibid., p. 104.
107. Foreword to Koelbl, *Behind the Kingdom's Veil*, p. 17.
108. Bin Ladin, *Veiled Kingdom*, p. 125.
109. Foreword to Koelbl, *Behind the Kingdom's Veil*, p. 18.
110. Eric Lichtblau and James Risen, '9/11 and the Saudi Connection', The Intercept, 11/09/21, https://theintercept.com/2021/09/11/september-11-saudi-arabia/, accessed 23/04/24.
111. Al-Rasheed, *Most Masculine State*, p. 21.
112. Guillemin-Puteaux, 'Religious Legitimacy of the Saudi State'.
113. Y. Admon, 'Women's Rights in Saudi Arabia: Historic Nomination of Women to Shura Council; Alongside Harsh Action by Regime against Women's Rights Activists', MEMRI, 21/06/13, https://www.memri.org/reports/womens-rights-saudi-arabia-historic-nomination-women-shura-council---alongside-harsh-action#_ednref27, accessed 24/04/24.
114. Natasha Walter, 'Veiled Hopes', *The Guardian*, 05/02/2005, https://www.theguardian.com/world/2005/feb/05/saudiarabia.natashawalter, accessed 18/04/24.
115. Ibid.
116. Author Zoom interview with Nadia, 25/03/24.
117. 'Why Are Saudi Women Still Not Driving?,' Harvard University Report, https://epod.cid.harvard.edu/sites/default/files/2021–12/AlNahda%20Blog_15Sep2021.pdf, accessed 25/04/24.

118. Megan K. Stack, 'The West Is Kidding Itself about Women's Freedom in Saudi Arabia', *New York Times*, 19/08/22, https://www.nytimes.com/2022/08/19/opinion/saudi-arabia-women-rights.html, accessed 14/03/24.
119. Interview with Lina al-Hathloul, 08/04/2024.
120. 'Saudi Arabia: Release Forcibly Disappeared Woman Facing Trial for Supporting Women's Rights Online', Amnesty International, 21/02/24, https://www.amnesty.org/en/latest/news/2024/02/saudi-arabia-release-forcibly-disappeared-woman-facing-trial-for-supporting-womens-rights-online/, accessed 10/04/24.
121. Interview with Lina al-Hathloul, 08/04/2024.
122. 'NGOs Call for Access to Saudi Detainees, as Manahel al-Otaibi Faces Further Abuse', Femena, 26/04/24, https://femena.net/2024/04/26/ngos-call-for-access-to-saudi-detainees-as-manahel-al-otaibi-faces-further-abuse/, accessed 29/04/24.
123. Stephanie Kirchgaessner, 'Saudi Arabia Activist Imprisoned for 11 Years for "Support" of Women's Rights', *The Guardian*, 01/05/24, https://www.theguardian.com/world/2024/may/01/manahel-al-otaibi-saudi-arabia-womens-rights-activist-sentenced-11-years-prison-anti-terrorism-court, accessed 02/05/24.
124. 'Saudi Arabia: Personal Status Law Codifies Discrimination against Women', Amnesty International, 08/03/23, https://www.amnesty.org/en/latest/news/2023/03/saudi-arabia-personal-status-law-codifies-discrimination-against-women/, accessed 10/04/24.
125. Interview with Lina al-Hathloul, 08/04/2024.
126. 'Saudi Arabia: Personal Status Law Codifies Discrimination'.
127. 'Shrouded in Secrecy: Prisons and Detention Centres in Saudi Arabia', ALQST, July 2021, https://www.alqst.org/uploads/Shrouded-in-Secrecy-En.pdf, accessed 02/05/24.
128. Akkad, 'Where the Abused Are Abused'.
129. Ibid.
130. Interview with Lina al-Hathloul, 08/04/2024.
131. Akkad, 'Where the Abused Are Abused'.
132. Yahya Assiri speaking at the Quest for Democracy in Saudi Arabia conference, organised by Middle East Democracy Center in May 2024; see https://www.youtube.com/watch?v=PE5hJms7fro&ab_channel=DemocraticDiwan, accessed 02/05/24.

133. 'Saudi Arabia Recruited Twitter Employees Charged with Spying: US', Al Jazeera, 07/11/19, https://www.aljazeera.com/economy/2019/11/7/saudi-arabia-recruited-twitter-employees-charged-with-spying-us, accessed 02/05/24.
134. Al-Rasheed, *Most Masculine State*, p. 32.
135. 'Saudi Arabia: Personal Status Law Codifies Discrimination', p. 2.
136. 'Saudi Arabia: New Law to Criminalize Domestic Abuse', Human Rights Watch, 03/09/13, https://www.hrw.org/news/2013/09/03/saudi-arabia-new-law-criminalize-domestic-abuse, accessed 10/04/24.
137. 'Saudi Arabia: 10 Reasons Why Women Flee', Human Rights Watch, 30/01/19, https://www.hrw.org/news/2019/01/30/saudi-arabia-10-reasons-why-women-flee, accessed 29/04/24.
138. 'Saudi Arabia: New Law to Criminalize Domestic Abuse'.
139. Abdulrahim A. Rouzi et al., 'Survey on Female Genital Mutilation/Cutting in Jeddah, Saudi Arabia', *BMJ Open* 9, no. 5 (2022), https://bmjopen.bmj.com/content/9/5/e024684, accessed 03/05/24.
140. Hashim H. Almeer et al., 'Female Genital Mutilation in Saudi Arabia: A Systematic Review', *Cureus* 13, no. 11 (2021), https://www.ncbi.nlm.nih.gov/pmc/articles/PMC8649978/#:-:text=FGM%20is%20prevalent%20in%20regions,against%20the%20practice%20of%20FGM, accessed 03/05/24.
141. Sasson, *Princess*, p. 102.
142. Bin Ladin, *Veiled Kingdom*, p. 135.
143. Ibid., p. 90.
144. Interview with Lina al-Hathloul, 08/04/2024.
145. Sasson, *Princess*, p. 29.
146. Ibid., p. 61.
147. Bin Ladin, *Veiled Kingdom*, p. 184.
148. 'Making Decent Work a Reality for Domestic Workers in the Middle East', International Labour Organization, 2021, p. 3, https://webapps.ilo.org/wcmsp5/groups/public/---arabstates/---ro-beirut/documents/publication/wcms_831916.pdf, accessed 03/05/24.
149. Ibid., p. 24.
150. Ibid., p. 11.
151. 'Saudi Arabia and the Death Penalty', p. 17.
152. James Wynbrandt, *A Brief History of Saudi Arabia*, 2nd edn, New York: Facts on File, 2010, p. 252.
153. Quoted by Maryam Aldossari, speech at the conference Quest for Democracy, Washington, DC, 02/05/24.

154. Maryam Aldossari, email, 17/05/24.
155. Maryam Aldossari, email, 19/04/24.
156. Maryam Aldossari and Sara Chaudhry, 'Gendered Precarity in Saudi Arabia: Examining the State Policies and Patriarchal Culture in the Labor Market', *Gender, Work and Organization* 31, no. 6 (2024), https://onlinelibrary.wiley.com/doi/10.1111/gwao.13119, accessed 19/03/24.
157. 'A Vibrant Society', Vision 2030, https://www.vision2030.gov.sa/en/overview/pillars/a-vibrant-society, accessed 05/12/24.
158. Ikran Eum, '"New Women for a New Saudi Arabia?" Gendered Analysis of Saudi Vision 2030 and Women's Reform Policies', *Asian Women* 35, no. 3 (2019), pp. 115–33 (p. 120), http://e-asianwomen.org/_PR/view/?aidx=21116&bidx=1703, accessed 22/03/24.
159. Hana Al-Khamri, 'Vision 2030 and Poverty in Saudi Arabia', Al Jazeera, 23/12/19, https://www.aljazeera.com/opinions/2019/12/23/vision-2030-and-poverty-in-saudi-arabia, accessed 06/05/24.
160. Eum, '"New Women for a New Saudi Arabia?"', p. 5.
161. Ibid., p. 2.
162. Author Zoom interview with Nadia, 25/03/24.
163. Marita Moloney, 'Saad Ibrahim Almadi: Saudi Arabia Releases US Man Jailed over Tweets', BBC, 21/03/23, https://www.bbc.co.uk/news/world-middle-east-65022370, accessed 10/05/24.
164. Interview with Abdullah Alaoudh, 09/04/24.
165. Quest for Democracy, Washington, DC, 02/05/24.
166. Katharina Natter, 'Revolution and Political Transition in Tunisia: A Migration Game Changer?', Migration Policy Institute, 28/05/15, https://www.migrationpolicy.org/article/revolution-and-political-transition-tunisia-migration-game-changer, accessed 12/08/24.
167. 'Saudi Arabia: Repressive Draft Penal Code Shatters Illusions of Progress and Reform', Amnesty International, 13/03/24, https://www.amnesty.org/en/latest/news/2024/03/saudi-arabia-repressive-draft-penal-code-shatters-illusions-of-progress-and-reform/, accessed 12/04/24.
168. Author email exchange with Abdullah Alaoudh.
169. Al-Rasheed, *Most Masculine State*, p. 292.
170. Author email with Maryam Aldossari, 19/04/24.
171. Author email exchange with Abdullah Alaoudh, 13/04/24.
172. 'U.S. Relations with Saudi Arabia', US Department of State, 01/11/23, https://www.state.gov/u-s-relations-with-saudi-arabia/, accessed 16/08/24.

3. RUSSIA: WE WILL GET UP OFF OUR KNEES

1. Author interview with Anna Zobnina on Zoom, 22/05/20.
2. Maria Alyokhina, *Riot Days*, London: Penguin Books, 2018, p. 18.
3. Author interview with Anna Zobnina on Zoom, 22/05/20.
4. Peter Pomerantsev, 'Patriarchy Riot', *London Review of Books*, 16/08/12, https://www.lrb.co.uk/blog/2012/august/patriarchy-riot, accessed 24/01/24.
5. 'All-Girl Punk Band Sentenced to Two Years in Russian Jail: Too Harsh?', *The Week*, 08/01/15, https://theweek.com/articles/472992/allgirl-punk-band-sentenced-two-years-russian-jail-harsh, accessed 26/08/24.
6. Andrew Roth, '4 Things You Need to Know about the Cossacks Fighting Russia's Opposition Groups', *The Washington Post*, 18/05/16, https://www.washingtonpost.com/news/worldviews/wp/2016/05/18/4-things-you-need-to-know-about-the-cossacks-fighting-russias-opposition-groups/, accessed 20/11/20.
7. Valerie Sperling, *Sex, Politics, and Putin: Political Legitimacy in Russia*, Oxford: Oxford University Press, 2015, p. 226.
8. Ibid., p. 238.
9. Matthew Luxmore, 'How the Killing of an Abusive Father Fuelled Russia's Culture Wars', *The Guardian*, 10/03/20, https://www.theguardian.com/world/2020/mar/10/khachaturyan-sisters-killing-of-abusive-father-russia-trial-family-values, accessed 05/12/23.
10. Anish Vij, 'New Evidence Could Save Sisters from Jail after Killing Father', LADbible, 12/08/21, https://www.ladbible.com/news/news-evidence-could-save-sisters-from-jail-after-allegedly-killing-father-20210812, accessed 05/12/23.
11. Mary Buckley, 'Women in the Soviet Union', *Feminist Review* 8 (Summer 1981), pp. 79–106 (p. 81).
12. Sheila Rowbotham, 'Women in Russia before and after the Revolution', Verso Books, 07/11/17, https://www.versobooks.com/en-gb/blogs/news/3202-women-in-russia-before-and-after-the-revolution, accessed 24/07/23.
13. Ibid.
14. V. I. Lenin, *The Emancipation of Women*, n.p.: Resistance Books, 2003, p. 33, https://socialist-alliance.org/sites/default/files/on_the_emancipation_of_women.pdf accessed 26/07/23.
15. Ibid., p. 11.
16. Tim Bay, 'The October Revolution and LGBTQ Struggle', Socialist Revolution,

25/03/16, https://www.socialistrevolution.org/the-october-revolution-and-lgbtq-struggle, accessed 20/07/23.
17. Introduction by Lisa Macdonald to Lenin, *Emancipation of Women*.
18. Adrienne Edgar, 'Bolshevism, Patriarchy, and the Nation: The Soviet "Emancipation" of Muslim Women in Pan-Islamic Perspective', *Slavic Review* 65, no. 2 (Summer 2006), pp. 252–72 (p. 266), https://www.jstor.org/stable/4148592, accessed 24/07/23.
19. Anne McShane, 'Women at the Heart of the Revolution', *Jacobin*, 08/11/19, https://jacobin.com/2019/08/alexandra-kollontai-soviet-womens-rights-revolution-zhenotdel-uzbekistan, accessed 19/08/24.
20. Rowbotham, 'Women in Russia'.
21. Leon Trotsky, 'The Old Family to the New', *Pravda*, 1923 in Lenin, *The Emancipation of Women*, p. 147.
22. Ibid., p. 131.
23. Friedrich Engels, *The Origin of the Family, Private Property and the State*, 4th edn, Stuttgart: n.p., 1892, p. 39, https://www.marxists.org/archive/marx/works/1884/origin-family/index.htm, accessed 12/09/22.
24. V. I. Lenin, 'Speech to a Non-party Working Women's Conference', 1919, in Lenin, *Emancipation of Women*, p. 66.
25. Clara Zetkin, 'My Recollections of Lenin', 1925, in Lenin, *Emancipation of Women*, p. 96.
26. Ibid., p. 101.
27. V. I. Lenin, 'Capitalism & Female Labour', 1913, in Lenin, *Emancipation of Women*, p. 40.
28. Rowbotham, 'Women in Russia', part 1.
29. Ibid., p. 80.
30. Linda Racioppi and Katherine O'Sullivan, 'Organizing Women before and after the Fall: Women's Politics in the Soviet Union and Post-Soviet Russia', *Signs* 20, no. 4 (Summer 1995), pp. 818–50 (p. 823), https://www.jstor.org/stable/3174884, accessed 03/08/23.
31. Ibid., p. 821.
32. Quoted by Rowbotham, 'Women in Russia', part 2.
33. 'Aid for Mothers and Children', Seventeen Moments in Soviet History, https://soviethistory.msu.edu/1943-2/love-and-romance-in-war/love-and-romance-in-war-texts/aid-for-mothers-and-children/, accessed 26/01/24.
34. Uliana Pavlova and Jack Guy, 'Putin Revives Stalin-Era "Mother Heroine"

Award for Women with 10 Children', CNN 18/08/22, https://edition.cnn.com/2022/08/18/europe/putin-mother-heroine-award-decree-intl/index.html, accessed 26/01/24.

35. 'USSR and Russian Populations 1940–1955', Statista, https://www.statista.com/statistics/1260522/soviet-and-russian-population-1940-1950/, accessed 23/08/24.
36. Author interview with Anna Adrianiva on Zoom, 12/12/23.
37. Ibid.
38. 'Neither Jobs nor Justice: State Discrimination against Women in Russia', Human Rights Watch, Refworld, 01/03/95, https://www.refworld.org/reference/countryrep/hrw/1995/en/40359, accessed 26/08/24.
39. Buckley, 'Women in the Soviet Union'.
40. Lenin, *Emancipation of Women*, pp. 35–6.
41. The Nordic Model has been adopted in Sweden, Norway, Iceland, Northern Ireland, Canada, France, Ireland, and Israel.
42. Elizabeth Waters, 'Restructuring the "Woman Question": Perestroika and Prostitution', *Feminist Review* 33, no. 1 (Autumn 1989).
43. Speech by Alexandra Kollontai, 'Prostitution and Ways of Fighting It', 1921, in *Selected Writings of Alexandra Kollontai*, trans. Alix Holt, London: Allison & Busby, 1977, https://www.marxists.org/archive/kollonta/1921/prostitution.htm, accessed 10/01/24.
44. Ibid.
45. Ibid.
46. N. B. Lebina and M. V. Shkarovsky, 'By Whip or by Law?', in *Prostitution in St. Petersburg*, Moscow: Progress Academy, 1994, pp. 132–78, https://a-z.ru/women/texts/lebina2r.htm#, accessed 05/01/24.
47. Ibid.
48. Ibid.
49. Vladimir N. Zakopyrin et al., 'Administrative Offences Legislation in Russia and Abroad: Historical and Legal Genesis', European Proceedings, accessed 26/09/23.
50. Waters, 'Restructuring the "Woman Question"', p. 11.
51. Marianna Muravyeva, 'Bytovukha: Family Violence in Soviet Russia', *Aspasia* 8, no. 1 (March 2014), p. 93, https://www.researchgate.net/publication/263480063_Bytovukha_Family_Violence_in_Soviet_Russia, accessed 12/02/24.
52. Ibid., p. 97.

53. Muravyeva, 'Bytovukha', p. 107.
54. Sperling, *Sex, Politics, and Putin*, p. 65.
55. Ibid., p. 110.
56. Quoted by Racioppi and O'Sullivan, 'Organizing Women before and after the Fall', p. 824.
57. 'How the USSR Fought Alcoholism', Russia Beyond, 01/10/2019, https://www.rbth.com/history/331061-ussr-alcoholism, accessed 05/01/24.
58. Racioppi and O'Sullivan, 'Organizing Women before and after the Fall', pp. 144–5.
59. Introduction by Lisa Macdonald to Lenin, *Emancipation of Women*, p. 16.
60. Racioppi and O'Sullivan, 'Organizing Women before and after the Fall', p. 831.
61. Cynthia Cockburn, 'Democracy without Women Is No Democracy: Soviet Women Hold Their First Autonomous National Conference', *Feminist Review* 39 (Autumn 1991), pp. 141–8 (p. 141).
62. Racioppi and O'Sullivan, 'Organizing Women before and after the Fall', p. 830.
63. Sperling, *Sex, Politics, and Putin*, p. 14.
64. Ibid., p. 140.
65. Peggy Watson, 'Eastern Europe's Silent Revolution: Gender', *Sociology* 27, no. 3 (August 1993), pp. 471–87 (p. 472), https://www.jstor.org/stable/42855234, accessed 03/08/23.
66. Ibid., p. 482.
67. Sperling, *Sex, Politics, and Putin*, p. 74.
68. 'Yeltsin Signs Controversial Religion Bill', CNN, 26/09/97, http://edition.cnn.com/WORLD/9709/26/russia.religion/, accessed 05/02/24.
69. Sperling, *Sex, Politics, and Putin*, p. 279.
70. Ibid., p. 287.
71. Yulia Ponomarev, 'New Law Protecting Religious Feelings Divides Russians', Russia Beyond, 14/06/23, https://www.rbth.com/society/2013/06/14/new_law_protecting_religious_feelings_divides_russians_27089.html, accessed 10/11/23.
72. Felix Corley, 'Believers' Responses to the 1937 and 1939 Soviet Censuses' Religion', *State and Society* 22, no. 4 (1994), p. 407, https://biblicalstudies.org.uk/pdf/rss/22-4_403.pdf, accessed 05/02/24.
73. V. I. Lenin, 'Speech at the First All-Russia Congress of Working Women', 1918, in Lenin, *Emancipation of Women*, pp. 59–60.
74. Marc Bennetts, 'How Russia Fell Back in Love with Stalin', *The New Humanist*,

06/07/2016, https://newhumanist.org.uk/articles/5057/how-russia-fell-back-in-love-with-stalin, accessed 04/10/2023.

75. 'Russians Return to Religion, But Not to Church', Pew Research, Feb. 2014, https://www.pewresearch.org/religion/2014/02/10/russians-return-to-religion-but-not-to-church/, accessed 08/01/24.
76. Binoy Kampmark, 'The Kirill Appointment: Russia's Orthodox Revival', Facts & Arts, 03/02/09, https://www.factsandarts.com/current-affairs/kirill-appointment-russias-orthodox-revival, accessed 09/02/25.
77. Mikhail Ryklin, 'The New Science of Pogromology', https://chtodelat.org/b8-newspapers/12-67/the-new-science-of-pogromology/, accessed 27/09/2023.
78. Lizzie Crocker, 'She's in Pussy Riot, He's on the Far Right: How Maria Alyokhina and Dmitry Enteo Fell in Love', The Daily Beast, 16/10/2017, https://www.thedailybeast.com/shes-in-pussy-riot-hes-on-the-far-right-how-maria-alyokhina-and-dmitry-enteo-fell-in-love, accessed 02/10/23.
79. Luxmore, 'How the Killing of an Abusive Father Fuelled Russia's Culture Wars'.
80. Kathryn Idema, 'Russian Christians Remain Sceptical of the Family Party', CNE, 12/10/23, https://cne.news/article/3736-russian-christians-remain-sceptical-of-family-party, accessed 05/12/23.
81. Kay Rollins, 'Putin's Other War: Domestic Violence, Traditional Values, and Masculinity in Modern Russia', *Harvard International Review*, 03/08/22, https://hir.harvard.edu/putins-other-war/, accessed 03/10/23.
82. 'Putin's Asymmetric Assault on Democracy in Russia and Europe: Implications for U.S. National Security', Senate Foreign Relations Committee, Washington, DC: Government Publishing Office, 2017, https://www.govinfo.gov/content/pkg/CPRT-115SPRT28110/html/CPRT-115SPRT28110.htm, accessed 28/09/23.
83. Author interview with Anna Tuktasheva on Zoom, 24/01/24.
84. 'Russian Supreme Court Upholds Ban on Hijabs in Schools', *The Moscow Times*, 11/02/15, https://www.themoscowtimes.com/2015/02/11/russian-supreme-court-upholds-ban-on-hijabs-in-schools-a43808, accessed 07/02/24.
85. Sophia Kishkovsky, 'Disputed Voting Turns Church, a Kremlin Ally, Into Its Critic', *New York Times*, 29/12/2011, https://www.nytimes.com/2011/12/30/world/europe/russian-orthodox-church-turns-from-kremlin-ally-to-critic.html?ref=hir.harvard.edu, accessed 03/10/23.
86. Sperling, *Sex, Politics, and Putin*, p. 282.
87. Ibid., p. 74.

88. Orysia Lutsevych, 'Agents of the Russian World Proxy Groups in the Contested Neighbourhood', Chatham House, Apr. 2016, https://www.chathamhouse.org/sites/default/files/publications/research/2016-04-14-agents-russian-world-lutsevych.pdf, accessed 13/11/20.
89. Jason Horowitz, 'The Russian Orthodox Leader at the Core of Putin's Ambitions', *New York Times*, 21/05/22, https://www.nytimes.com/2022/05/21/world/europe/kirill-putin-russian-orthodox-church.html, accessed 27/09/23.
90. Marc Bennetts, 'Why Orthodox Christians Are Losing Faith in Putin', Politico, 24/12/19, https://www.politico.eu/article/russian-orthodox-christians-lose-faith-in-vladimir-putin/, accessed 13/11/20.
91. Bennetts, 'How Russia Fell Back in Love with Stalin'.
92. Ibid.
93. Sperling, *Sex, Politics, and Putin*, p. 36.
94. Email exchange with Svetlana Stephenson, 08/07/24.
95. Sperling, *Sex, Politics, and Putin*, p. 4.
96. Ibid., p. 269.
97. Ibid., pp. 188–9.
98. Ibid., p. 215.
99. Alyokhina, *Riot Days*, p. 7.
100. Janet Elise Johnson and Aino Saarinen, 'Twenty-First-Century Feminisms under Repression: Gender Regime Change and the Women's Crisis Center Movement in Russia', *Signs* 38, no. 3 (Spring 2013), pp. 543–67 (p. 547).
101. Sperling, *Sex, Politics, and Putin*, p. 80.
102. Ibid., p. 40.
103. Author interview with Anna Adrianiva on Zoom, 12/12/23.
104. '"Go Hard Like Vladimir Putin": A Hip-Hop Ode to Russia's President', BBC Trending, YouTube, 24/11/14, https://www.youtube.com/watch?v=6AqE_yT1XuM, accessed 07/11/23.
105. Simon Parkin, 'The Rise of Russia's Neo-Nazi Football Hooligans', *The Guardian*, 24/04/2018, https://www.theguardian.com/news/2018/apr/24/russia-neo-nazi-football-hooligans-world-cup, accessed 20/07/2023.
106. Alice Ross and Emma Slater, 'How Russia's Youth Movement Became Putin's Private Army', Bureau of Investigative Journalism, 20/04/12, https://www.thebureauinvestigates.com/stories/2012-04-20/how-russias-youth-movement-became-putins-private-army, accessed 28/09/2023.
107. Sperling, *Sex, Politics, and Putin*, p. 87.

108. Ibid., pp. 151–2.
109. Ibid., p. 83.
110. Ibid., p. 140.
111. Ibid., p. 147.
112. Ibid., p. 163.
113. Ibid., p. 143.
114. Eva Hartog, 'A Kremlin Youth Movement Goes Rogue', *The Moscow Times*, 08/04/2016, https://www.themoscowtimes.com/2016/04/08/a-kremlin-youth-movement-goes-rogue-a52435, accessed 28/09/23.
115. Marina Yusupova, 'Masculinity, Criminality, and Russian Men', n.d., https://eprints.lancs.ac.uk/id/eprint/152915/1/Masculinity_Criminality_and_Russian_Men.pdf, accessed 05/12/2023.
116. Mansur Mirovalev, 'How Putin's Penchant for Jail Jargon Changed Russia', Al Jazeera, 31/05/23, https://www.aljazeera.com/features/2023/5/31/how-putins-penchant-for-jail-jargon-changed-russia, accessed 05/12/23.
117. Yusupova, 'Masculinity, Criminality, and Russian Men', p. 13.
118. Shaun Walker and Pjotr Sauer, 'Yevgeny Prigozhin: The Hotdog Seller Who Rose to the Top of Putin's War Machine', *The Guardian*, 23/08/23, https://www.theguardian.com/world/2023/jan/24/yevgeny-prigozhin-the-hotdog-seller-who-rose-to-the-top-of-putin-war-machine-wagner-group, accessed 25/01/23.
119. Pjotr Sauer, 'Russia's Private Military Contractor Comes Out of the Shadows', *The Guardian*, 07/08/22, https://www.theguardian.com/world/2022/aug/07/russias-private-military-contractor-wagner-comes-out-of-the-shadows-in-ukraine-war, accessed 20/07/23.
120. Mark Galeotti, *The Vory: Russia's Super Mafia*, New Haven: Yale University Press, 2018, p. 213.
121. Svetlana Stephenson, 'It Takes Two to Tango: The State and Organized Crime in Russia', *Current Sociology* 65, no. 3 (2017), pp. 411–26 (p. 412).
122. Ibid.
123. Zarina Zabrisky, 'Pure Poison: Putin's Links to Espionage, Terrorism and Organised Crime', *Byline Times*, 27/08/20, https://bylinetimes.com/2020/08/27/pure-poison-putins-links-to-espionage-terrorism-and-organised-crime/, accessed 05/02/21.
124. 'Russia's Mafia State', Meduza, 01/12/15, https://meduza.io/en/feature/2015/12/01/russia-s-mafia-state, accessed 09/01/25.

125. Luke Harding, *Mafia state: how one reporter an enemy of the brutal new Russia*, London: Guardian Books, 2011, p. 22.
126. Ibid.
127. Ibid., p. 229.
128. Ibid., p. 231.
129. 'The Criminals in the Kremlin', Meduza, 16/06/22, https://meduza.io/en/feature/2022/06/16/the-criminals-in-the-kremlin, accessed 04/12/2023.
130. Quoted by Maria Snegovaya, 'Russia: The Mafia State', Meduza, 17/12/2015, https://meduza.io/en/feature/2015/12/17/opinion-russia-the-mafia-state, accessed 04/12/23.
131. 'Russia: Mob Boss on Trial', OCCRP, 19/05/2009, https://www.occrp.org/en/feature/russia-mob-boss-on-trial, accessed 13/11/20.
132. Leela Jacinto, 'God, Church, Tsar: The World of Russian Oligarch Malofeyev and His Western Associates', France24, 08/04/2022, https://www.france24.com/en/europe/20220408-god-church-tsar-the-world-of-russian-oligarch-malofeyev-and-his-western-associates, accessed 04/10/2023.
133. Alexey Yurtaev, 'Inside the Fight over Russia's Domestic Violence Law', openDemocracy, 17/07/2020, https://www.opendemocracy.net/en/odr/russia-domestic-violence-law/, accessed 21/02/24.
134. Ibid.
135. Nadezhda Azhgikhina, 'In Russia, Are Fake Feminist Groups Back in Action?', *The Nation*, 29/03/17, https://www.thenation.com/article/archive/in-russia-are-fake-feminist-groups-back-in-action/, accessed 1/10/20.
136. Johnson and Saarinen, 'Twenty-First-Century Feminisms under Repression', p. 544.
137. Nick Paton Walsh, 'Elite Forces Storm Moscow Theatre', *The Guardian*, 26/10/2002, https://www.theguardian.com/fromthearchive/story/0,,1929056,00.html, accessed 26/07/23.
138. 'Timeline: The Beslan School Siege', *The Guardian*, 06/09/2004, https://www.theguardian.com/world/2004/sep/06/schoolsworldwide.chechnya, accessed 26/07/23.
139. Shaun Walker, 'Putin Approves Legal Change that Decriminalises Some Domestic Violence', *The Guardian*, 07/02/17, https://www.theguardian.com/world/2017/feb/07/putin-approves-change-to-law-decriminalising-domestic-violence, accessed 20/07/23.
140. Ekaterina Pechenkina, 'Are Feminists Next on Vladimir Putin's List?', Politico,

14/4/23, https://www.politico.com/newsletters/women-rule/2023/04/14/are-feminists-next-on-vladimir-putins-list-00092070, accessed 12/02/24.
141. Sperling, *Sex, Politics, and Putin*, p. 263.
142. In 1923, the divorce rate was 74 per cent. 'Data Analysts on World Divorce Rates: Ranking of Countries from Highest to Lowest Risk of Getting Divorced', ABCD Agency, https://news.cision.com/abcd-agency-ug/r/data-analysts-on-world-divorce-rates--ranking-of-countries-from-highest-to-lowest-risk-of-getting-di,c3747396, accessed 08/01/25.
143. Author interview with Anna Adrianiva on Zoom, 12/12/23.
144. Buckley, 'Women in the Soviet Union', p. 80.
145. 'The Gender Ratio of Russia (2018–2026, Males per 100 Females)', Global Data, https://www.globaldata.com/data-insights/macroeconomic/the-gender-ratio-of-russia-325491, accessed 03/01/24.
146. Janet Elise Johnson, 'Fast-Tracked or Boxed In? Informal Politics, Gender, and Women's Representation in Putin's Russia', *Perspectives on Politics* 14, no. 3 (September 2016), pp. 643–60, http://mlkrook.org/pdf/Johnson_2016.pdf, accessed 16/12/2020.
147. Maria Mies, *Patriarchy and Accumulation on a World Scale: Women in the International Division of Labour*, London: Zed Books, 1986; Kindle edn 2014 (Kindle locations 5112–16).
148. Andrea Chandler quoted in Johnson, 'Fast-Tracked or Boxed In?', p. 646.
149. Dasha Litvinova, 'From Stalin to Putin, Abortion Has Had a Complicated History in Russia', *The Independent*, 27/10/23, https://www.independent.co.uk/news/vladimir-putin-ap-josef-stalin-kaliningrad-soviet-b2436917.html, accessed 08/11/23.
150. '"They need cannon fodder": Concerned about Population Decline but Unwilling to Address Root Causes, Russian Politicians Have Set Their Sights on Citizens' Reproductive Rights', Meduza, 01/11/22, https://meduza.io/en/feature/2022/11/01/they-need-cannon-fodder, accessed 01/12/23.
151. '"Church and state have long since fused together": Why Russian Religious Leaders' Efforts to Restrict Abortion May Soon Succeed', Meduza, 24/07/2023, https://meduza.io/en/feature/2023/07/25/church-and-state-have-long-since-fused-together, accessed 29/11/23.
152. Sperling, *Sex, Politics, and Putin*, p. 253.
153. Chloe Chaplain, 'Vladimir Putin: Russian Prostitutes Are the Best in the World', *Evening Standard*, 18/01/2017, https://www.standard.co.uk/news/

world/vladimir-putin-russian-prostitutes-are-the-best-in-the-world-a3443261.html, accessed 21/02/24.
154. 'The Lives of Russia's Sex Workers Today', Meduza, 09/02/2019, https://meduza.io/en/feature/2019/02/09/the-life-of-russia-s-modern-day-sex-workers, accessed 10/01/24.
155. Michail Danilowicz and Anna Pirogowa, 'For Russian Sex Workers, the Ukraine War Means Higher Risks and Lower Income', WorldCrunch, 02/10/24, https://worldcrunch.com/culture-society/sex-workers-russia-war, accessed 19/01/24.
156. Donna M. Hughes, 'Prostitution in Russia: Does the U.S. State Department Back the Legalization of Prostitution?', *National Review*, 21/11/2002, https://web.archive.org/web/20080603054312/http://www.nationalreview.com/comment/comment-hughes112102.asp, accessed 13/02/24.
157. 'Russian Federation: Government Shortens List of Professions in Which Women's Employment Is Restricted', Library of Congress, 07/10/19, https://www.loc.gov/item/global-legal-monitor/2019-10-07/russian-federation-government-shortens-list-of-professions-in-which-womens-employment-is-restricted, accessed 14/03/25.
158. Racioppi and O'Sullivan, 'Organizing Women before and after the Fall', p. 846.
159. Azhgikhina, 'In Russia, Are Fake Feminist Groups Back in Action?'.
160. 'Number of Violent Crimes Committed against a Family Member in Russia from 2012 to 2021', Statista, https://www.statista.com/statistics/1154893/domestic-violence-crimes-in-russia/, accessed 26/08/24.
161. 'Putin's Crackdown on NGOs', Human Rights Watch, 20/02/08, https://www.hrw.org/news/2008/02/20/putins-crackdown-ngos, accessed 26/06/24.
162. Johnson and Saarinen, 'Twenty-First-Century Feminisms under Repression', p. 560.
163. Sperling, *Sex, Politics, and Putin*, p. 255.
164. '"They need cannon fodder"'.
165. Sperling, *Sex, Politics, and Putin*, p. 48.
166. Vanya Mark Solovey, 'The Contemporary Feminist Movement in Russia: Action, Community, and Difference', PhD thesis, Humboldt University of Berlin, 2021, p. 125.
167. Ibid., p. 10.
168. Ibid., p. 24.
169. Ibid., p. 11.
170. Ibid., p. 93.

171. Ibid., p. 111.
172. 'Putin Signs Law Expanding Russia's Rules against "LGBT Propaganda"', Reuters, 05/12/22, https://www.reuters.com/world/europe/putin-signs-law-expanding-russias-rules-against-lgbt-propaganda-2022-12-05/, accessed 28/09/23.
173. 'Russia Has Banned the So-Called "International LGBT Movement": What Does This Mean for Queer People and Activists Living There?', Meduza, 30/11/23, https://meduza.io/en/cards/russia-has-banned-the-so-called-international-lgbt-movement, accessed 01/12/23.
174. Liubov Tsareva, 'Fighting the Patriarchy in Mother Russia', TruthDig, 08/06/23, https://www.truthdig.com/articles/fighting-the-patriarchy-in-mother-russia/, accessed 15/11/23.
175. Ibid.
176. Pavel Astakhov, 'The State Duma Drafted a Bill Recognizing Feminism as an Extremist Ideology', Absatz, 04/04/23, https://absatz.media/news/31986-v-gosdume-podgotovili-zakonoproekt-o-priznanii-feminizma-ekstremistskoj-ideologiej, accessed 20/07/23.
177. Vladimir Sorokin, 'Vladimir Putin Sits Atop a Crumbling Pyramid of Power', *The Guardian*, 27/02/22, https://www.theguardian.com/commentisfree/2022/feb/27/vladimir-putin-russia-ukraine-power, accessed 05/10/2023.
178. Author interview with Anna Adrianiva on Zoom, 12/12/23.

4. CHINA: I ASK FOR THE SWIFTEST HORSE

1. Interview with the author.
2. Mo Jingxi, 'Xi Calls for Fully Leveraging the Strength of Women', *China Daily*, 31/10/23, https://global.chinadaily.com.cn/a/202310/31/WS653fd8c4a31090682a5eb84c.html, accessed 13/03/25.
3. Wang Zhen, *Finding Women in the State*, Berkeley: University of California Press, 2017.
4. Emily Honig and Gail Hershatter, *Personal Voices: Chinese Women in the 1980s*, Stanford: Stanford University Press, 1988.
5. Ibid.
6. Eric Hobsbawm and Terence Ranger, *The Invention of Tradition*, Cambridge; Cambridge University Press, 2012.
7. 'Fuzhou Baby Tower: The Cruel History behind the Old Photos', Daydaynews, 12/08/21, https://daydaynews.cc/en/history/1625731.html, accessed 14/03/25.

8. Noboru Niida, 'Land Reform and New Marriage Law in China', *The Developing Economies* 2, no. 1 (March 1964), https://www.ide.go.jp/library/English/Publish/Periodicals/De/pdf/64_01_01.pdf?_previewDate_=null&revision=0&viewForce=1, accessed 14/03/25.
9. Kay Ann Johnson, *Women, the Family and Peasant Revolution in China*, Chicago: University of Chicago Press, 1983.
10. Ibid.
11. Noboru Niida, 'Law Reform and New Marriage Law'.
12. Wu Zhong, 'China Yearns for Hu's "Harmonious Society"', *Asia Times*, 11/10/06, https://web.archive.org/web/20061103063705/http://atimes.com/atimes/China/HJ11Ad01.html, accessed 14/03/25.
13. Jude Howell, 'The Struggle for Survival: Prospects for the Women's Federation in Post-Mao China', *World Development* 24, no. 1 (1996), https://lib.icimod.org/record/1445, accessed 14/03/25.
14. This narrative draws heavily on a full account of the Beijing conference legacy in Rangita de Silva de Alwis and Katherine Schroeder, 'The Changing Landscape of Women's Rights Activism in China: The Continued Legacy of the Beijing Conference', *UCLA Women's Law Journal* 28, no. 7 (2021).
15. Phyllis Andors, 'The "Four Modernisations" and Chinese Policy on Women', *Bulletin of Concerned Asian Scholars* 13, no. 2 (1981), pp. 44–5, referring to a statement in Mar. 1978, https://www.tandfonline.com/doi/pdf/10.1080/14672715.1981.10409930, accessed 14/03/25.
16. Wang Zheng, *Finding Women in the State: A Socialist Feminist Revolution in the People's Republic of China, 1949–1964*, Berkeley: University of California Press, 2017.
17. Wang Zheng and Ying Zhang, 'Global Concepts, Local Practices: Chinese Feminism since the Fourth UN Conference on Women', *Feminist Studies* 36, no. 1 (Spring 2010), pp. 40–70.
18. Ibid.
19. Andors, '"Four Modernisations" and Chinese Policy on Women'.
20. Ibid.
21. Yige Dong, 'Spinners or Sitters? Regimes of Social Reproduction and Urban Chinese Workers' Employment Choices', *International Journal of Comparative Sociology* 61, nos. 2–3 (2020), https://doi.org/10.1177/0020715220946074, accessed 14/03/25.
22. Patrick Whiteley, 'The Age of Prosperity Is Upon Us', *China Daily*, 19/10/07,

http://www.chinadaily.com.cn/opinion/2007-10/19/content_6243676.html, accessed 14/03/25.

23. Gail Hershatter, *The Gender of Memory*, Berkeley: University of California Press, 2013.
24. Chris King-Chi Chan, Pun Ngai and Jenny Chan, 'The Role of the State, Labour Policy and Migrant Workers' Struggles in Globalized China', in Paul Bowles and John Harriss (eds), *Globalization and Labour in China and India*, Basingstoke: Palgrave Macmillan, 2010, pp. 45–63.
25. Limin Wang and Jeni Klugman, 'How Women Have Fared in the Labour Market with China's Rise as a Global Economic Power', *Asia and the Pacific Policy Studies* 7, no. 1 (2020), https://onlinelibrary.wiley.com/doi/full/10.1002/app5.293, accessed 14/03/25.
26. Ibid.
27. Chih-Jou Jay Chen, 'A Protest Society Evaluated: Popular Protests in China, 2000–2019', *Mobilisation: An International Journal* 25, no. 5 (2020), pp. 641–60, https://www.researchgate.net/publication/346465380_A_Protest_Society_Evaluated_Popular_Protests_in_China_2000–2019, accessed 14/03/25.
28. Wang Zheng, 'Wang Zheng on Feminism in China', Asia Experts Forum, 23/12/17, https://asiaexpertsforum.org/wang-zheng-feminism-china/, accessed 14/03/25.
29. Yong Cai and Wang Feng, 'The Social and Sociological Consequences of China's One-Child Policy', *Annual Review of Sociology* 47 (2021), pp. 587–606, https://doi.org/10.1146/annurev-soc-090220-032839, accessed 14/03/25.
30. Henry Kissinger recalled a conversation with Mao in 1979 in which Mao, laughing, offered to give the US 10 million women—'we have too many women and they have a way of doing things'. Joking, he added that they would cause trouble in the US. See US Office of the Historian, 'Memorandum of Conversation', 1969–76, https://history.state.gov/historicaldocuments/frus1969-76v18/d12, accessed 14/03/25.
31. Yong Cai and Wang Feng, 'Social and Sociological Consequences of the One-Child Policy'.
32. Susan Greenhalgh, *Just One Child: Science and Policy in Chen's China*, Berkeley: University of California Press, 2008, p. xi.
33. Quanbao Jiang and Cuiling Zhang, 'Recent Sex Ratio at Birth', *British Medical Journal* 6, no. 5 (2021), https://www.ncbi.nlm.nih.gov/pmc/articles/PMC8137222/, accessed 14/03/25.

34. This ratio remained consistent thereafter. See 'Distribution of Total Population in China from 1950 to 2024', Statista, Jan. 2025, https://www.statista.com/statistics/618394/china-population-distribution-by-gender/, accessed 14/03/25.
35. Amartya Sen, 'Missing Women: Social Inequality Outweighs Women's Survival Advantage in Asia and North Africa', *British Medical Journal* 34 (1992), pp. 587–88.
36. Greenhalgh, *Just One Child*, p. 127. Foremost was an eminent cybernetics pioneer, Song Jian, who in 1980 presented to a scientific elite his mathematical population projections—unencumbered by social, ethical or political complications.
37. Greenhalgh, *Just One Child*, p. 235.
38. Michael Carder and Bob Park, 'Bombast in Bucharest: Report on the World Population Conference', *Science for the People* 7, no. 1 (January 1975), pp. 17–19, https://archive.scienceforthepeople.org/vol-7/v7n1/bombast-in-bucharest/, accessed 14/03/25.
39. Ibid.
40. United Nations, 'World Population Conference, August 19–30, 1974, Bucharest, Romania', https://www.un.org/en/conferences/population/bucharest1974, accessed 14/03/25.
41. Greenhalgh, *Just One Child*, pp. 181–3.
42. Wang Zheng, 'The Chinese Socialist Revolution and the Status of Chinese Women', *Chinese Historians* 3, no. 2 (1990), pp. 59–68, https://sites.lsa.umich.edu/wangzheng/wp-content/uploads/sites/948/2021/09/1990WangZ_The-Chinese-Socialist-Revolution-and-the-Status-of-Chinese-Women.pdf, accessed 14/03/25.
43. Ibid., p. 62.
44. Justina Ka Yee Tsui, 'Chinese Women: Active Revolutionaries or Passive Followers? A History of the All China Women's Federation', MA thesis, Montreal, Concordia University, 1998, p. 71, https://spectrum.library.concordia.ca/id/eprint/550/1/MQ39428.pdf, accessed 14/03/25.
45. Ibid.
46. Ibid.
47. Ibid.
48. Ibid.
49. Naihua Zhang, 'The All-China Women's Federation, Chinese Women and the Women's Movement: 1949–1993', PhD Thesis, Michigan State University, 1996, p. 456.

50. Lisa Rofel, *Other Modernities: Gender Yearnings in China after Socialism in China*, Berkeley: University of California Press, 1999, pp. 248–52.
51. Honig and Hershatter, *Personal Voices*.
52. Ibid.
53. Ibid.
54. Interview with the author.
55. Sheryl Sandberg, *Lean In: Women, Work and the Will to Lead*, New York: Knopf, 2013.
56. Stuart Gietel-Basten, Xuehui Han and Yuan Cheng, 'Assessing the Impact of "the One-Child" Policy in China', *PLoS ONE* 14, no. 11 (2019), https://doi.org/10.1371/journal.pone.0220170, accessed 14/03/25.
57. Ibid.
58. 'Female Labour Participation Rate in China 2013–2023', Statista, 04/11/24, https://www.statista.com/statistics/252721/female-labor-force-participation-rate-in-china/, accessed 14/03/25.
59. Wei Bai et al., 'The Gender Gap in China: Insights from a Discrimination Perspective', June 2022, https://www.researchgate.net/publication/361456283, accessed 14/03/25.
60. 'Global Gender Gap Report', World Economic Forum, 2022, p. 9, https://www3.weforum.org/docs/WEF_GGGR_2022.pdf, accessed 14/03/25.
61. Guangye He and Xiaogang Wu, 'Dynamics of the Gender Earnings Inequality in Reform-era Urban China', *Work Employment and Society* 32, no. 4 (2018), https://journals.sagepub.com/doi/10.1177/0950017017746907, accessed 14/03/25.
62. Guangye He and Xiaogang Wu, 'Gender Earnings Inequality in Reform-Era Urban China', Population Studies Centre, University of Michigan, Oct. 2014, https://repository.hkust.edu.hk/ir/bitstream/1783.1-85825/1/GenderEarningsInequalityinReform-EraUrbanChina.pdf, accessed 14/03/25.
63. 'Only Men Need Apply', Human Rights Watch, 23/04/18, https://www.hrw.org/report/2018/04/23/only-men-need-apply/gender-discrimination-job-advertisements-china, accessed 14/03/25.
64. 'Promoting the Development of Women in China: Progress, Challenge and Suggestions', Centre for Gender and Law Studies, Chinese Academy of Social Sciences, 2023, https://www.csosew.org/wp-content/uploads/2023/04/INT_CEDAW_CSS_CHN_52243_E.pdf, accessed 14/03/25.
65. 'Outline of Women's Development in China (2021–2030)', United Nations

Environment Programme and Law and Environment Assistance Programme, 2021, https://leap.unep.org/en/countries/cn/national-legislation/outline-womens-development-china-2021–30, accessed 14/03/25.
66. Interview with the author.
67. Du Xinyu and Fang Yun, '44 % of China's Young Women Don't Plan to Marry, Survey Says', Sixth Tone, 11/10/21, https://www.sixthtone.com/news/1008664, accessed 14/03/25.
68. Zhang Yunlong, 'Report on CPC's "Second Integration" Theory Unlocks Understanding of China', Xinhua, 02/07/23, https://english.news.cn/20230702/073894ef71c0431aabc2976bd07cdd82/c.html, accessed 14/03/25.
69. Jikung Huang and Scott Rozelle, 'China's 40 Years of Agricultural Development and Reform, 1978–2018', in Ross Garnaut, Ligang Song and Cai Fang (eds), *China's 40 Years of Reform and Development 1978–2018*, Canberra: ANU Press, 2018, 10.22459/CYRD.07.2018.24, accessed 14/03/25.
70. Ibid.
71. Nicolas Loubere, 'The Children of China's Great Migration: A Conversation with Rachel Murphy', *Made in China Journal* 5, no. 3 (2020), https://press-files.anu.edu.au/downloads/press/n7964/pdf/22_children_china.pdf, accessed 14/03/25.
72. Liu Lei, 'The Patriarchal Trap: The Village Wives Left Behind amid Chinese Rural–Urban Migration', *SAGE Open* 1, no. 3 (Jan.–Mar. 2023), https://journals.sagepub.com/doi/10.1177/21582440221144245, accessed 14/03/25.
73. Xueqi Qu et al., 'Socio-emotional Challenges and Development of Children Left Behind by Migrant Mothers', *Journal of Global Health* 10, no. 1 (2020), https://pmc.ncbi.nlm.nih.gov/articles/PMC7182358/, accessed 14/03/25.
74. Heather Rahimi, Scott Rozelle and Natalie Hell, 'A Conversation with Scott Rozelle and Natalie Hell on Their New Book, *Invisible China*', Stanford University, Freeman Spogli Institute for International Studies, 2020, https://fsi.stanford.edu/news/new-book-scott-rozelle-and-natalie-hell-invisible-china, accessed 14/03/25.
75. 'Average Per Capita Disposable Income of Urban and Rural Households in China from 1990–2023', Statista, Jan. 2024, https://www.statista.com/statistics/259451/annual-per-capita-disposable-income-of-rural-and-urban-households-in-china/#:-:text=In%202023%2C%20the%20average%20annual%20per%20capita%20disposable,between%20rural%20and%20urban%20households%20is%20still%20large, accessed 14/03/25.

76. Congzhi He and Jingzhong Ye, *Lonely Sunsets: Elderly Left Behind in Rural China*, Beijing: Social Sciences Academic Press, 2008.
77. Ibid.
78. Jingzhong Ye, 'Left-Behind Elderly: Shouldering a Disproportionate Share of Production and Reproduction in Supporting China's Industrial Development', *Journal of Peasant Studies* 44, no. 5 (2016), http://dx.doi.org/10.1080/03066150.2016.1186651, accessed 14/03/25.
79. Yuqin Huang, 'Labour, Leisure, Gender and Generation: The Organisation of "Wan" and the Notion of "Gender Equality" in Contemporary Rural China', in Tamara Jacka and Sally Sargeson (eds), *Women, Gender and Rural Development in China*, Cheltenham: Edward Elgar Publishing, 2011.
80. 'Xi Stresses Organising, Motivating Women to Contribute to China Modernisation', Xinhua, 31/10/23, https://english.news.cn/20231031/2d38b8241a39479cb29a1a7199c52e3b/c.html, accessed 14/03/25.
81. Rachel Murphy, *The Children of China's Great Migration*, Cambridge: Cambridge University Press, 2020.
82. Ibid.
83. Delia Davin, 'Women and Migration in Contemporary China', *China Report* 41, no. 1 (2005), https://doi.org/10.1177/000944550504100102, accessed 14/03/25; see also Delia Davin, 'Gender and Rural–Urban Migration in China', *Urban Development* 4, no. 1 (Feb. 1996), pp. 24–30, https://www.jstor.org/stable/4030354, accessed 14/03/25.
84. Davin, 'Women and Migration in Contemporary China'.
85. Ibid.
86. Juqin Huang, 'From the "Feminization of Agriculture" to the "Aging of Farming Populations": Demographic Transition and Farming in a Central Farming Village', *Local Economy* 27, no. 1 (2012), pp. 19–32.
87. Gail Hershatter, *The Gender of Memory: Rural Women and China's Collective Past*, Berkeley: University of California Press, 2013, p. 191.
88. Ibid.
89. Ibid., p. 192.
90. Ibid.
91. Ichiro Iwasaki and Xinxin Ma, 'Gender Wage Gap in China: A Large Meta-analysis', *Journal for Labour Market Research* 54, no. 17 (2020), https://labourmarketresearch.springeropen.com/articles/10.1186/s12651-020-00279-5, accessed 14/03/25.

92. Iris Zhao and Jenny Cai, 'China Is Considering Making Bosses Pay Workers for "Invisible" Overtime but Is It a Feasible Solution?', ABC News, 25/03/24, https://dyingforaniphone.com/wp-content/uploads/2024/04/2024mar25overtimepayabcnews.pdf, accessed 14/03/25.
93. Eli Friedman and Ching Kwan Lee, 'Remaking the World of Chinese Labour', *British Journal of Industrial Relations* 48, no. 3 (2010), https://doi.org/10.1111/j.1467-8543.2010.00814.x, accessed 14/03/25.
94. Harrison Jacobs, 'Inside "iPhone City", the Massive Chinese Factory Town Where Half of the World's iPhones Are Made', Business Insider, 07/05/18, https://www.businessinsider.com/apple-iphone-factory-foxconn-china-photos-tour-2018-5#spanning-more-than-22-miles-and-dozens-of-buildings-the-business-park-looks-like-any-other-trees-are-everywhere-police-and-security-guards-stand-on-every-street-corner-and-workers-on-break-camp-out-in-the-shade-a-decade-ago-this-area-had-only-dirt-and-fields-of-corn-and-wheat-in-2010-the-government-bought-out-local-farmers-and-the-factory-was-up-and-running-within-the-year-3, accessed 14/03/25.
95. Yige Dong, 'The Dilemma of Foxconn Moms', *Critical Sociology* 49, no. 4 (December 2022), 10.1177/08969205221140927, accessed 14/03/25.
96. 'Foxconn Dispatch Workers Protest Over Owed Wages and Rewards by Foxconn Companies', China Labour Watch, 16/11/20, https://chinalaborwatch.org/foxconn-dispatch-workers-stage-protest-over-owed-wages-and-rewards-by-dispatch-companies/, accessed 14/03/25.
97. 'Sacked Labour Activist Continues to Push for Workers' Trade Unions', China Labour Bulletin, 21/09/15, https://clb.org.hk/en/content/sacked-labour-activist-continues-push-workers'-trade-unions, accessed 14/03/25.
98. Ibid.
99. 'Striking Sanitation in Guangzhou Force Company to Negotiate', China Labour Bulletin, 03/09/14, https://clb.org.hk/en/content/striking-sanitation-workers-guangzhou-force-company-negotiate, accessed 14/03/25.
100. Jacobs, 'Inside iPhone City'.
101. Guo Tin, 'An Oral History of Wang Xingjuan', China Development Brief, 01/05/15., https://chinadevelopmentbrief.org/reports/oral-history-wang-xingjuan/, accessed 14/03/25.
102. 'Chinese Court Gives Panyu Labour Activists Suspended Sentences', Radio Free Asia, 26/09/2016, https://www.rfa.org/english/news/china/labor-sentences-09262016162710.html, accessed 14/03/25.

103. Yuan Yang, 'China and the Anti-996 Campaign', *Financial Times*, 8/05/19, https://www.ft.com/content/6622a42c-7127-11e9-bf5c-6eeb837566c5, accessed 14/03/25.
104. Ibid.
105. Jie Siqui, H. Huiifeng and Brian Peach, 'What Is "Lying Flat", and Why Are Chinese Officials Standing Up to It?', 24/10/21, https://www.scmp.com/economy/china-economy/article/3153362/what-lying-flat-and-why-are-chinese-officials-standing-it, accessed 14/03/25.
106. Zheping Huang, 'China Spells Out How 996 Culture Is Illegal', *Straits Times*, 29/08/21, https://www.taipeitimes.com/News/biz/archives/2021/08/29/2003763388, accessed 14/03/25.
107. Tiantian Zheng, *Violent Intimacy*, London: Bloomsbury, 2022, p. 220.
108. Ibid., p. 216.
109. Ibid., p. 220.
109. Ibid., p. 216.
110. 'Guo Jianmei', Right Livelihood, 2019, https:/rightlivelihood.org/the-change-makers/find-a-laureate/guo-jianmei/, accessed 14/03/25.
111. Elizabeth Frazer and Kimberley Hutchings, 'The Feminist Politics of Naming Violence', *Feminist Theory* 21, no. 2 (2018), pp. 199–216.
112. See Wendy Brown, *States of Injury*, Princeton: Princeton University Press, 1995.
113. Rangita de Silva de Alwis and Katherine Schroeder, 'The Changing Landscape of Women's Rights Activism in China', *UCLA Women's Law Journal* 28 (2001).
114. Frazer and Hutchings, 'Feminist Politics of Naming Violence'.
115. 'A Glimpse into Why Chinese Men Use Violence against Women and Girls', China/United Nations Family Planning Association, 06/12/14, https://china.unfpa.org/en/news/glimpse-why-some-chinese-men-use-violence-against-women-and-girls, accessed 14/03/25.
116. Evan Osnos, 'Crazy English', *The New Yorker*, 21/04/08, https://www.newyorker.com/magazine/2008/04/28/crazy-english, accessed 14/03/25.
117. Didi Kirsten Tatlow, 'In China's Most-Watched Divorce Case, 3 Victories, 1 Defeat', 04/02/13, https://archive.nytimes.com/rendezvous.blogs.nytimes.com/2013/02/04/in-chinas-most-watched-divorce-case-3-victories-1-defeat/, accessed 14/03/25.
118. Ibid.
119. Li Ying, 'Bloody Brides in Abuse Protest', *Global Times*, 14/02/12, https://www.globaltimes.cn/content/695889.shtml, accessed 14/03/25.

120. Jiang Xinyi, 'Her Abuse Was a National Story: Now her Husband Is Going to Prison', Sixth Tone, 31/12/24, https://www.sixthtone.com/news/1016449, accessed 14/03/25.
121. Didi Kirsten Tatlow, 'China Is Said to Force Closing of Women's Legal Aid Centre', *New York Times*, 29/01/16, https://www.nytimes.com/2016/01/30/world/asia/beijing-women-legal-aid-guo-jianmei.html, accessed 14/03/25; see also 'China: Closure of Women's Legal Aid Centre a Blow for Women's Rights and Gender Equality', UN Women of Influence, 02/06/24.
122. Eli Friedman and Ching Kwan Lee, 'Remaking the World of Chinese Labour: A 30-Year Retrospective', *British Journal of Industrial Relations* 48, no. 3 (2010), pp. 507–33.
123. Shihuan Chen, 'For Land's Sake: The Women Fighting to Keep Hold of their Rural Land', *The World of Chinese*, 11/12/22, https://www.theworldofchinese.com/2022/12/for-lands-sake-the-women-fighting-to-keep-hold-of-their-rural-land/, accessed 14/03/25.
124. Tiantian Zheng, *Violent Intimacy: Family Harmony, State Stability and Intimate Partner Violence in Post-socialist China*, London: Bloomsbury, 2023, p. 103.
125. Natalia Antonova, 'Chinese Courts Want Abused Women to Shut Up', *Colombo Gazette*, 28/05/23, https://colombogazette.com/2023/05/28/chinese-courts-want-abused-women-to-shut-up/, accessed 14/03/25.
126. Tiantian Zheng, *Violent Intimacy*, p. 126.
127. Frazer and Hutchings, 'Feminist Politics of Naming Violence'.
128. Wang Zheng, 'Wang Zheng on Feminism in China'.
129. 'Interim Report no. 383', International Labour Organization, 2017, https://normlex.ilo.org/dyn/nrmlx_en/f?p=1000:50001:::::, accessed 14/03/25.
130. Li Jun, 'The Yirenping Experience, Looking Back and Pushing Forward', Made in China, 15/07/21, https://madeinchinajournal.com/2021/07/15/the-yirenping-experience-looking-back-and-pushing-forward/, accessed 14/03/25.
131. Yulanda Wang, 'China's First Workplace Gender Discrimination Case Closes', 19/12/13, https://www.business-humanrights.org/en/latest-news/chinas-first-workplace-gender-discrimination-lawsuit-closes/, accessed 14/03/25.
132. Lu Jun, 'Yirenping Experience'.
133. Ibid.
134. Ibid.
135. Personal communication with the author.
136. Leta Hong Fincher, *Betraying Big Brother*, London: Verso, 2018, p. 2.

137. Wang Zheng, 'Wang Zheng on Feminism in China'.
138. Fincher, *Betraying Big Brother*.
139. Ibid.
140. Ibid., pp. 46–9.
141. Ibid., p. 46.
142. Ibid.
143. Wang Zheng, 'Wang Zheng on Feminism in China'.
144. 'People Practicing Open Defecation (% of Population): China', World Health Organization, World Bank and UNICEF, 2022, https://data.worldbank.org/indicator/SH.STA.ODFC.ZS?locations=CN, accessed 14/03/25.
145. Luo Shiming, 'The Utilisation of Excreta in Chinese Agriculture and the Challenge Ahead', http://www.ecosanres.org/pdf_files/Nanning_PDFs/Eng/Luo%20Shiming%2010_C11rev.pdf, accessed 14/03/25.
146. Qi Liu and Deljana Iossifova, 'Socio-metabolic Practises and Heterogeneous Sanitation Infrastructure in Urbanising China', *Transactions in Planning and Urban Research* 3, nos. 1–3 (December 2023), https://journals.sagepub.com/doi/full/10.1177/27541223231206565, accessed 14/03/25.
147. Derek Mead, 'The Woman Behind China's Occupy Toilet Movement Has Been Canned', Vice, 12/03/12, https://www.vice.com/en/article/the-leader-of-china-s-occupy-men-s-bathroom-movement-has-been-canned/, accessed 14/03/25.
148. Ibid.
149. Sophie Jiayuan Wang, 'China's Toilet Revolution: An Experiment in Top-Down Innovation', Perspectives, Johns Hopkins School of International Studies, 01/04/20, http://www.saisperspectives.com/2020-issue/2020/3/28/chinas-toilet-revolution-an-experiment-in-top-down-innovation, accessed 14/03/25. The programme was less commodious for rural households, who endured forced demolition of old facilities before the construction of new ones and the cost of replacing drainage and bathroom systems—sometimes amounting to two-thirds of an annual income.
150. Amy Hawkins, 'Beijing Professor Sacked over Abuse in Rare Win for #MeToo Movement', Reuters, 12/01/24, https://www.reuters.com/article/world/beijing-professor-dismissed-as-sexual-harassment-allegations-spark-campus-activi-idUSKBN1F10JE/, accessed 14/03/25.
151. Iris Zhao, 'Zhou Xiaoxuan Is at the Forefront of China's MeToo Movement, which Is Slowly Gaining Momentum', ABC, 16/12/20, https://www.abc.net.

au/news/2020-12-17/china-metoo-movement-after-two-years-zhu-jun-xia-oxuan/12973998, accessed 14/03/25.

152. Nectar Gan and Steve George, 'An Intern Took On One of China's Biggest TV Stars in Landmark #MeToo Case: She Lost, but Vowed to Fight On', CNN, 15/09/21, https://edition.cnn.com/2021/09/15/china/xianzi-zhu-jun-sexual-harassment-case-mic-intl-hnk/index.html; Zhou Xiaoxuan complained that the court had decided not to consider corroborative evidence.

153. Jing Zeng, 'From #MeToo to #RiceBunny: How Social Media Users Are Campaigning in China', The Conversation, 06/02/18, https://theconversation.com/from-metoo-to-ricebunny-how-social-media-users-are-campaigning-in-china-90860, accessed 14/03/25.

154. Susan Trevaskes and Delia Lin, 'Integrating Stability Maintenance into Comprehensive Governance: The Burgeoning "Safe China" Behemoth', *Modern China* 50, no. 6 (May 2024), https://www.researchgate.net/publication/381014423_Integrating_Stability_Maintenance_into_Comprehensive_Governance_The_Burgeoning_Safe_China_Behemoth, accessed 14/03/25.

155. Dahlia Peterson, 'AI and the Surveillance State', in William C. Hannas and Huey-Mei Chang (eds), *China, Power and Artificial Intelligence: Perspectives and Challenges*, London: Routledge, 2022, p. 207.

156. 'Xi Delivers Important Speech at CCDI Plenary Session', Xinhua, 10/01/24, https://english.www.gov.cn/news/202401/10/content_WS659dd697c6d0868f4e8e2e74.html, accessed 14/03/25.

157. Ayesha Rascoe and John Ruwitch, 'Xi Jinping Begins Third 5-Year Term, Elevates Several Allies along with Him', NPR, 23/10/22, https://www.npr.org/2022/10/23/1130782443/xi-jinping-begins-third-5-year-term-elevates-several-allies-along-with-him, accessed 14/03/25.

158. 'Malicious Conviction of #MeToo and Labour Activists Shows Beijing's Growing Fear of Dissent', Amnesty International, 2024, https://www.amnesty.org/en/latest/news/2024/06/china-malicious-conviction-of-metoo-and-labour-activists-shows-beijings-growing-fear-of-dissent/, accessed 14/03/25; Frances Mao, '#MeToo Journalist jailed for Five Years', BBC, 14/06/24, https://www.bbc.com/news/articles/c9007v0n05yo, accessed 14/03/25.

159. Anne Phillips, *The Politics of Presence*, Oxford: Clarendon Press, 1995.

160. 'UN Women's Rights Committee Publishes Findings on China, Germany, Iceland, Sao Tome and Principe, Slovakia, Spain, Timor-Leste and Venezuela', UN Committee on the Elimination of Discrimination against Women,

30/05/23, https://www.ohchr.org/en/press-releases/2023/05/un-womens-rights-committee-publishes-findings-china-germany-iceland-sao-tome, accessed 14/03/25.
161. Carl Minzner, 'Beijing's Message to the National Women's Congress: Gender Equality Is Out, Family and Childbirth Are In', Council on Foreign Relations, 26/10/23, https://www.cfr.org/blog/beijings-message-national-womens-congress-gender-equality-out-family-and-childbirth-are, accessed 14/03/25.
162. Ibid.
163. 'Xi Stresses Organizing, Motivating Women to Contribute to Chinese Modernization', China Daily, 31/10/23, http://www.chinadaily.com.cn/a/202310/31/WS65405f10a31090682a5eb9ac.html, accessed 14/03/25.
164. 'Family Happiness and Well-being Campaign', ACFW, 10/07/20, https://www.womenofchina.cn/womenofchina/html1/projects/20041/6095-1.htm, accessed 14/03/25.
165. 'Xi Stresses Organising, Motivating Women'.

5. SOUTH AFRICA: WHITE CAPITALIST MEN GOT WHAT THEY WANTED

1. Interview with the author. See also Shireen Hassim, 'Not Just Nelson Mandela's Wife: Winnie Mandela, Violence and Radicalism in South Africa', *Journal of Southern African Studies* 44 (2018), https://doi.org/10.1080/03057070.2018.1514566, accessed 14/03/25.
2. Interview with the author.
3. Frank I. Michelman, 'Foreword', in R. Dixon and Theunis Robert Roux (eds), *Constitutional Triumphs, Constitutional Disappointments*, Cambridge: Cambridge University Press, 2018.
4. Ibid., p. 2.
5. The constitution was consolidated by the Promotion of Equality and Prevention of Unfair Discrimination Act 2000, which declared that the country 'requires the eradication of social and economic inequalities, especially those that are systemic in nature, which were generated in our history by colonialism, apartheid and patriarchy and which brought pain and suffering to the great majority of our people'. Promotion of Equality and Prevention of Unfair Discrimination Act 4 of 2000, https://justice.gov.za/legislation/acts/2000-004.pdf, accessed 14/03/25.
6. 'Professor Kader Abdul Asmal', South African History Online, https://www.sahistory.org.za/people/professor-kader-abdul-asmal, accessed on 14/03/25.

7. John Jeffrey, 'The Birth of the South African Constitution', Justice Today, Mar. 2016, https://www.justice.gov.za/legislation/constitution/articles/jt-2016-vol02-BirthConstitution.pdf, accessed 14/03/25.
8. Albie Sachs, 'How We Made the Constitution', 18/03/20, https://medium.com/folios-we-the-people/how-we-made-the-constitution-a50d05564f19, accessed 14/03/25.
9. Elizabeth Thornberry, *Colonizing Consent: Rape and Governance in South Africa's Eastern Cape*, Cambridge: Cambridge University Press, 2019, p. 4.
10. 'State of Capture', Johannesburg, Office of the Public Protector, 14/10/16, https://www.gov.za/sites/default/files/gcis_document/201611/stateofcapturereport14october2016_1.pdf, accessed 14/03/25.
11. Some law reforms entrenched the patriarchy already entrenched in customary law: for example, ownership of family homes now required registration in one person's name—typically a man. See 'Women's Equal Rights to Land and Housing', Socio-Economic Rights Institute (SERI), Johannesburg, June 2024, https://www.seri-sa.org/images/SERI_Family_homes_in_South_Africa_Report_FINAL.pdf, accessed 14/03/25; see also Mmatshilo Motsei, *The Kanga and the Kangaroo Court: The Rape Trial of Jacob Zuma*, Auckland Park: Jacana Media, 2007.
12. 'Women's Equal Rights to Land and Housing', SERI, June 2024, pp. 57–8, https://www.seri-sa.org/images/SERI_Family_homes_in_South_Africa_Report_FINAL.pdf, accessed 14/03/25; see also the discussion of a family home as a 'collective good' not just a commodity in 'Shomang v Motsose N.O. and Others (6990/2022) [2022] ZAGPPHC 441; 2022 (5) SA 602 (GP) (24 May 2022)', https://www.saflii.org/za/cases/ZAGPPHC/2022/441.html, accessed 14/03/25.
13. See Marikana massacre, p. xx.
14. 'Minister of Health and Others v Treatment Action Campaign and Others (No 2) (CCT8/02) [2002] ZACC 15; 2002 (5) SA 721 (CC); 2002 (10) BCLR 1033 (CC)', 05/06/02.
15. 'Minister of Health v Treatment Action Campaign (TAC) (2005) 5 SA 721 (CC)', Economic, Social and Cultural Rights-Net, 2006, https://www.escr-net.org/caselaw/2006/minister-health-v-treatment-action-campaign-tac-2002-5-sa-721-cc/, accessed 14/03/25.
16. Ibid.
17. Michael Cardo, *Harry Oppeneimer: Diamonds, Gold and Dynasty*, London:

Jonathan Ball, 2023, p. 33; Ruth First and Ann Scott, *Olive Schreiner: A Biography*, London: Virago, 1980.

18. Shireen Hassim, *The ANC Women's League: Sex, Gender and Politics*, Auckland Park: Jacanda Media, 2014; 'Lilian Masediba Ngoyi', South African History Online, https://www.sahistory.org.za/people/lilian-masediba-ngoyi; 'Women's Resistance to the Pass Laws', South African History Online, https://www.sahistory.org.za/article/womens-resistance-against-pass-laws, accessed 14/03/25.

19. The women's protests against the pass laws were echoed by a simultaneous movement across the Atlantic where black women in Alabama organised the iconic bus boycott, a watershed in civil rights activism: JoAnn Gibson Robinson, *The Montgomery Bus Boycott and the Women Who Started It*, Knoxville: University of Tennessee Press, 1987.

20. Sam Ashman and Ben Fine, 'Neo-liberalism, Varieties of Capitalism, the Shifting Contours of South Africa's Financial system', *Transformation* 81–2 (2013), http://www.transformationjournal.org.za/wp-content/uploads/2017/04/T81_82_Part8.pdf, accessed 14/03/25.

21. Cardo, *Harry Oppenheimer*, p. 477.

22. Ibid.

23. Ibid., p. 478.

24. 'The People Armed, 1984–1990', South African History Online, https://www.sahistory.org.za/article/people-armed-1984-1990, accessed 14/03/25.

25. UN Security Council Resolution 392, http://unscr.com/en/resolutions/392, accessed 14/05/25.

26. Sam Ashman, Ben Fine and Susan Newman, 'Amnesty International? The Nature, Scale and Impact of Capital Flight from South Africa', *Journal of Southern African Studies* 37, no. 1 (2011), pp. 7–25, 10.1080/03057070.2011.555155, accessed 14/03/25; Léonce Ndikumana, Karmen Naido and Adam Aboobaker, 'Capital Flight from South Africa: A Case Study', Political Economy Research Institute, University of Massachusetts, June 2020, https://peri.umass.edu/wp-content/uploads/joomla/images/publication/WP516-SouthAfrica-1-13-21.pdf, accessed 14/03/25.

27. GEAR, 'Growth Employment and Redistribution: A Macroeconomic Strategy', was propelled into the ANC by its finance minister, Trevor Manuel, and formally adopted by the government in 1996: https://www.treasury.gov.za/publications/other/gear/chapters.Pdf, accessed 14/03/25.

28. Vishnu Padayachee and Robert van Niekerk, *Shadow of Liberation: Contestation*

and *Compromise in the Economic and Social Policy of the African National Congress, 1943–1996*, Johannesburg: Wits University Press, 2019, p. 148.
29. Interview with the author.
30. Robert van Niekerk and Vishnu Padayachee, 'The Rise and Fall of a Social Democratic Economic and Social Policy Alternative in the ANC (1990–1996)', *Journal of Contemporary African Studies* 39, no. 2 (2021), p. 10, https://doi.org/10.1080/02589001.2020.1864306, accessed 14/03/25.
31. Shireen Hassim, 'Voices, Hierarchies and Spaces: Reconfiguring the Women's Movement in Democratic South Africa', *Politikon: South African Journal of Political Studies* 32, no. 2 (2005).
32. Ibid., p. 21.
33. Van Niekerk and Padayachee, 'Rise and Fall of a Social Democratic Economic and Social Policy Alternative'.
34. Gillian Hart, *Re-thinking the South African Crisis: Nationalism, Populism, Hegemony*, Athens: University of Georgia Press, 2014, p. 161.
35. Ibid., pp. 160–1.
36. Van Niekerk and Padayachee, 'Rise and Fall of a Social Democratic Economic and Social Policy Alternative'.
37. Ibid.
38. Cardo, *Harry Oppenheimer*, p. 559.
39. Jonny Steinberg, *Winnie & Nelson: Portrait of a Marriage*, London: William Collins, 2023, p. 257.
40. Shireen Hassim, 'Voices, Hierarchies and Spaces: Reconfiguring the Women's Movement in Democratic South Africa', *Politikon: South African Journal of Political Studies* 32, no. 2 (2005), p. 145.
41. Hassim, *ANC Women's League*.
42. Hassim, 'Voices, Hierarches and Spaces', p. 12.
43. Van Niekerk and Padayachee, 'Rise and Fall of a Social Democratic Economic and Social Policy Alternative'.
44. Neva Seidman-Makgetla, 'The Post-apartheid Economy', *Review of African Political Economy* 100 (2004), pp. 263–81, https://www.scienceopen.com/document_file/9c0b26c9-7472-445f-8d1a-1563b847f74e/ScienceOpen/030562404 2000262284.pdf, accessed 14/03/25.
45. Lewis Nkosi, 'The Ideology of Reconciliation', 2016, quoted in Joel M. Modiri, 'Conquest and Constitutionalism: First Thoughts on an Alternative Jurisprudence', *South African Journal on Human Rights* 34, no. 3 (2018), https://doi.org/10.1080/02587203.2018.1550939, accessed 14/03/25.

46. Janet Elise Johnson, Þorgerður Einarsdóttir and Gyða Margrét Pétursdóttir, 'A Feminist Theory of Corruption: Lessons from Iceland', *Politics and Gender* 9 (2013), pp. 174–206, https://rse.hi.is/wp-content/uploads/2017/11/Johnson-Einarsdottir-Petursdottir-2013-feminist-corruption-Iceland.pdf, accessed 14/03/2015.
47. Ibid.
48. Samuel Perlo-Freeman, 'Arms, Corruption and the State: Understanding the Role of Arms Trade Corruption in Power Politics', *The Economics of Peace and Security Journal* 13, no. 2 (2018), https://www.epsjournal.org.uk/index.php/EPSJ/article/view/309/297, accessed 14/03/25.
49. Paul Holden and Andrew Feinstein, 'Submission to the People's Tribunal on Economic Crime', 2017.
50. 'Evidence for the People's Tribunal on Economic Crime', Corruption Watch, 2018, https://corruptiontribunal.org.za/wp-content/uploads/2018/02/1999-Arms-Deal-Submission_CW.pdf, accessed 14/03/25.
51. Paul Holden and Andrew Feinstein, 'Joint Submission to the People's Tribunal', 2017, https://corruptiontribunal.org.za/wp-content/uploads/2018/02/AD1-Joint-Submission-to-the-Peoples-Tribunal-Paul-Holden-and-Andrew-Feinstein-final.pdf, accessed 14/03/25. Researchers also found contributions to various charities associated with political figures, as well as donations delivered to political parties via politicians who did not necessarily benefit personally.
52. 'Winnie Mandela and the Arms Deal', South Africa Broadcasting Corporation, 10/04/18.
53. Holden and Feinstein, 'Submission to the People's Tribunal on Economic Crime'.
54. Mbeki's critics were opposed to his neoliberal economic plan.
55. Mandy Rossouw, 'Zuma's £65m Nkandla Splurge', *Mail and Guardian*, 4/12/09, https://mg.co.za/article/2009-12-04-zumas-r65m-nkandla-splurge/, accessed 14/03/25.
56. See Constitution of the Republic of South Africa 1996, Chapter 9, 'State Institutions Supporting Constitutional Democracy', https://www.gov.za/documents/constitution/constitution-republic-south-africa-1996-chapter-9-state-institutions#182, accessed 14/03/25.
57. Stephen Grootes, 'The Judgement at the End of the Nkandla Road', Daily Maverick, 31/03/16, https://www.dailymaverick.co.za/article/2016-03-31-analysis-the-judgment-at-the-end-of-the-nkandla-road/, accessed 14/03/25.

58. The Catholic Dominican Order and the opposition party, the Democratic Alliance, were joined a month later by a member of the public, see Holden and Feinstein, 'Submission to the People's Tribunal on Economic Crime'.
59. Renée Bonorchis, 'Luxury Cars That Littered Guptas' Yard a Way to Recoup Some Cash', Moneyweb, 21/02/18, https://www.moneyweb.co.za/news/south-africa/luxury-cars-that-littered-guptas-yard-a-way-to-recoup-some-cash/, accessed 14/03/25.
60. 'State of Capture', pp 53–8.
61. See 'Final Reports', Zondo Commission, 2022: https://www.statecapture.org.za/site/information/reports, accessed 14/03/25.
62. Kevin Bloom, 'Introducing the Four Criminal Cartels That Have Brought Eskom and South Africa to Their Knees', Daily Maverick, 27/02/23, https://www.dailymaverick.co.za/article/2023-02-27-introducing-the-four-crime-cartels-that-have-brought-eskom-and-south-africa-to-their-knees/, accessed 14/03/25; Eskom was further disabled by organised theft of coal, cables, copper wiring, just about anything, especially during the electricity outages that became daily events, preventing businesses, schools, homes and traffic lights from operating: they were facilitated by organised criminal fraternities—outages rendered cables mounted on pylons safe to steal.
63. Rosalind Dixon and Theunis Robert Roux, 'Making Constitutional Transitions: The Law and Politics of Constitutional Implementation in South Africa', University of South Australia Law Series 64, 2018, http://classic.austlii.edu.au/au/journals/UNSWLRS/2018/64.pdf, accessed 14/03/25.
64. Haroon Bhorat and State Capacity Research Project, 'Betrayal of the Promise: How South Africa Is Being Stolen', State Capacity Research Project, May 2017, p. 3, https://pari.org.za/wp-content/uploads/2017/05/Betrayal-of-the-Promise-25052017.pdf, accessed 14/03/25.
65. Dixon and Roux, 'Making Constitutional Transitions'.
66. 'Data on Assassinations Shows Stark Reality of Violence in KwaZulu–Natal', Global Initiative Against International Organised Crime, 2024, https://riskbulletins.globalinitiative.net/esa-obs-025/04-data-on-assassinations-shows-stark-reality-of-violence-in-kwazulu-natal.html, accessed 14/03/25. It reported that nearly half were due to internecine war in the taxi industry, whose ubiquitous clusters are mobile monuments to the lack of an integrated public transport system.
67. James W. Messerschmidt, *Masculinities and Crime: Critique and Reconceptualisations of Theory*, Lanham, MD: Rowman & Littlefield, 1993.

68. Motsei, *Kanga and the Kangaroo Court*, p. 14.
69. See Moral Regeneration Movement website: https://www.mrm.org.za, accessed 14/03/25; see Shola Lawal, 'Jacob Zuma's Nine Lives: How South Africa's Ex-president Keeps Coming Back', Al Jazeera, 18/04/24, https://www.aljazeera.com/news/2024/4/18/jacob-zumas-nine-lives-how-south-africas-ex-president-keeps-coming-back, accessed 14/03/25.
70. An African patterned, printed cotton fabric, around 1.5 metres.
71. Motsei, *Kanga and the Kangaroo Court*, p. 153.
72. Thembisa Waetjen, 'Tradition's Desire: The Politics of Culture in the Rape Trial of Jacob Zuma', Association of Concerned African Scholars, bulletin 84, 19/11/09, https://associationofconcernedafricascholars.org/traditions-desire/, accessed 14/03/25.
73. Gill Gifford, 'The Zuma Rape Case: 25 Court Days Later', Independent Online, 30/04/06, https://www.iol.co.za/news/south-africa/the-zuma-rape-case-25-court-days-later-275903, accessed 14/03/25.
74. For the judgment, see https://www.saflii.org/za/cases/ZAGPHC/2006/45.pdf, accessed 14/03/25.
75. Shireen Hassim, 'Why, a Decade on, a New Book about Zuma's Rape Trial Has Finally Hit Home', The Conversation, 5/10/17, https://theconversation.com/why-a-decade-on-a-new-book-on-zumas-rape-trial-has-finally-hit-home-85262, accessed 14/03/25.
76. Wendy Brown, *States of Injury: Power and Freedom in Late Modernity*, Princeton: Princeton University Press, 1995, pp. 21, 68–70.
77. See Beatrix Campbell, *Secrets and Silence*, Bristol: Policy Press, 2023, p. 103.
78. Brown, *States of Injury*, pp. 66–70.
79. Judith Lewis Herman, *Father Daughter Incest*, Cambridge, MA: Harvard University Press, 1981.
80. Judith Lewis Herman, 'Crime and Memory', *Bulletin of the American Academy of Psychiatry and the Law* 23, no. 1 (1995), pp. 57–76, https://jaapl.org/content/jaapl/23/1/5.full.pdf, accessed 14/03/25.
81. Thornberry, *Colonizing Consent*, p. 2.
82. Lisa Vetten, 'Paradox and Policy: Addressing Rape in Post-apartheid South Africa', in Nicole Westmoreland and Geetanjali Gangoli (eds), *International Approaches to Rape*, Bristol: Policy Press, 2012, pp. 169–92.
83. Ibid.
84. 'Mbeki Questions SA Rape Figures', BBC News, 28/10/99, http://news.bbc.co.uk/1/hi/world/africa/492669.stm, accessed 14/03/25.

85. Vetten, 'Re-writing the Script'.
86. Katharine Wood and Rachel Jewkes, 'Violence, Rape and Sexual Coercion: Everyday Love in a South African Township', *Gender and Development* 5, no. 2 (June 1997), pp. 41–6, https://www.jstor.org/stable/4030438, accessed 14/03/25.
87. Rachel Jewkes et al., 'Understanding Men's Health and Use of Violence: Interface of Rape and HIV in South Africa', 2009, https://www.academia.edu/17031683/Understanding_Mens_Health_and_Use_of_Violence_Interface_of_Rape_and_HIV_In_South_Africa, accessed 14/03/25.
88. 'South Africa: Winnie Mandela Joins Campaign against Crime', AP Archive, YouTube, 21/07/15, https://www.youtube.com/watch?v=S1R-_oVKlzY, accessed 14/03/25.
89. 'Tshabalala v The State; Ntuli v The State [2019] ZACC 48', https://www.saflii.org/za/cases/ZACC/2019/48.html, accessed 14/03/25; the men were convicted—some of them on the basis of the doctrine of 'common purpose' that held them culpable even if some individuals did not actually commit rape. Over the next twenty years, that doctrine was challenged until it was finally settled by the Constitutional Court. The judges acknowledged their debt to 'feminist legal theory' and warned that 'legal barriers in our South African jurisprudence' had shown 'a number of embedded patriarchal gender norms in the procedural rules of evidence in relation to rape'. The court ruled that rape was 'characterised with power on one side and disempowerment and degradation on the other'. The origins of rape were 'anchored in the structured imbalance of power between men and women as social groups, that is, in their political relationship'.
90. 'Tshabalala v S; Ntuli v S (CCT323/18;CCT69/19) [2019] ZACC 48; 2020 (3) BCLR 307 (CC); 2020 (2) SACR 38 (CC); 2020 (5) SA 1 (CC) (11 December 2019)', https://www.saflii.org/za/cases/ZACC/2019/48.html, accessed 14/03/25.
91. Vetten, 'Re-writing the Script'.
92. Ibid.
93. Motsei, *Kanga and the Kangaroo Court*, pp. 88–90.
94. David Smith, 'South African Court Finds ANC's Julius Malema Guilty of Hate Speech', *The Guardian*, 15/03/10, https://www.theguardian.com/world/2010/mar/15/anc-julius-malema-guilty-hate-speech, accessed 14/03/25.
95. Ironically, Kasrils was by then a critic of the ANC government's historic compromise with market capitalism to ensure peaceful transition from apartheid.
96. Zelda Venter, 'Zuma's Accuser to Benefit after Kasrils Wins Case', 24/08/16,

IOL, https://www.iol.co.za/dailynews/news/zumas-rape-accuser-to-benefit-after-kasrils-wins-case-2060274, accessed 14/03/25.

97. Carl Collison, 'Women Freedom Fighters Tell of Sexual Abuse in Camps', *Mail and Guardian*, 27/10/17, https://mg.co.za/article/2017-10-27-00-our-women-freedom-fighters-tell-of-sexual-abuse-in-camps/, accessed 14/03/25.
98. Shireen Hassim, 'Violent Modernity: Gender, Race and Bodies in Contemporary South African Politics', *Politikon: South African Journal of Political Studies* 41, no. 2 (2014), https://doi.org/10.1080/02589346.2013.865824, accessed 14/03/25.
99. One in nine referred to the proportion of raped women who report the event to the police.
100. Verashni Pillay, 'Minding the ANC Gender Gap', *Mail and Guardian*, 23/09/10, https://mg.co.za/article/2010–09–23-minding-the-anc-gender-gap/, accessed 14/03/25.
101. Ibid.
102. Stefaans Brmmer et al., 'Spy Boss's Dodgy Business', *Mail and Guardian*, 21/11/08, https://mg.co.za/article/2008–11–21-spy-bosss-dodgy-business/, accessed 14/03/25.
103. Hassim, *ANC Women's League*.
104. 'ANCWL Leaders Quiet on Gender Issues, for Fear of Losing Positions', The Citizen, 7/03/21, https://www.citizen.co.za/news/south-africa/ancwl-leaders-quiet-on-gender-issues-for-fear-of-losing-positions/, accessed 14/03/25.
105. Redi Thlabi, *Khwezi: The Remarkable Story of Fezekile Ntsukela Kuzwao*, La Vergne: Jonathan Ball, 2017, p. 3.
106. Pumla Gqola Motsei, *Rape: A South African Nightmare*, Auckland Park: MFBooks, 2015, p. 37.
107. See 'Women of the Slave Lodge', Ancestors Research South Africa, which draws on research by Prof. Robert Shell, https://slavery.iziko.org.za/excavation/, accessed 14/03/25.
108. Motsei, *Rape*.
109. Thornberry, *Colonizing Consent*.
110. Ibid., p. 4.
111. Winnie Madikizela Mandela, *491 Days: Prisoner Number 1323/69*, Johannesburg: Picador Africa, 2013; Pippa Green, 'Albertina Sisulu's Story of Persecution and Suffering, Love and Triumph', All Africa, 2011, https://allafrica.com/stories/201106090005.html, accessed 14/03/25.

112. Shoshona Felman and Dori Laub, *Testimony: Crises of Witnessing in Literature, Psychoanalysis and History*, London: Routledge, 1992.
113. Beth Goldblatt and Sheila Meintjes, 'Dealing with the Aftermath: Sexual Violence and the Truth and Reconciliation Commission', *Agenda: Empowering Women for Gender Equality* 36 (1997), pp. 7–18, http://www.jstor.org/stable/4066215, accessed 14/03/25.
114. Beth Goldblatt and Sheila Meintjes, 'Women: One Chapter in the History of South Africa? A Critique of the Truth and Reconciliation Report', Wits History Workshop, June 1999, http://hdl.handle.net/10539/7838, accessed 14/03/25.
115. Women's experience is the focus of white Afrikaaner writer and broadcaster Antjie Krog's book, *Country of My Skull*, Johannesburg: Random House, 1999. Truth and Reconciliation Commission of South Africa Report, vol. four, 1999, https://www.sahistory.org.za/sites/default/files/trc_report_volume_4.pdf, accessed 14/03/25.
117. Goldblatt and Meintjes, 'Dealing with the Aftermath'.
118. Mtintso in ibid.
119. 'MK Commander Alleges Sexual Abuse in ANC Exile Camps', South African Press Association, 18/06/96, https://www.justice.gov.za/trc/media/1996/9606/s960618b.htm, accessed 14/03/25.
120. Motsei, *Kanga and the Kangaroo Court*.
121. Carl Collison, 'Women Freedom Fighters Tell of Sexual Abuse in Camps', *Mail and Guardian*, 27/10/17, https://mg.co.za/article/2017-10-27-00-our-women-freedom-fighters-tell-of-sexual-abuse-in-camps/, accessed 14/03/25.
122. Hannah Osborne, 'South Africa Rape Victim Was Disembowelled by Hand', *International Business Times*, 17/10/13, https://www.ibtimes.co.uk/anene-booysen-rape-murder-trial-johannes-kana-514685, accessed 14/03/25.
123. Mia Malan, 'Diepsloot: Where Men Think It Is Their Right to Rape', *Mail and Guardian*, 01/10/15, https://mg.co.za/article/2015-10-01-diepsloot-where-men-think-its-their-right-to-rape/, accessed 14/03/25.
124. Ibid.; Mia Malan, 'Child Rape in Diepsloot: The Shocking Story That Provoked Outrage', *Mail and Guardian*, 24/11/16, https://mg.co.za/article/2016-11-24-child-rape-in-diepsloot-the-shocking-story-that-sparked-outrage/, accessed 14/03/25.
125. Mia Malan, 'A Pandemic Is Not Just a Disease: It's a Political, Social and Economic Crisis Fuelled by Inequality', *The Guardian*, 07/08/23, https://

www.theguardian.com/global-development/commentisfree/2023/aug/07/a-pandemic-is-not-just-a-disease-its-a-political-social-and-economic-crisis-fuelled-by-inequality, accessed 14/03/25.
126. Malan, 'Diepsloot'.
127. In the northern state of Limpopo, lethal 'sanitation' ended the life of five-year-old Michael Komape in 2014: he died in the toilet of a school he'd only attended for three days, having drowned in excrement. His parents took legal action, and in 2018 Limpopo's High Court ordered the state to install safe and hygienic toilets in all of its rural schools, 'Understanding the Michael Komape Judgment', GroundUp, 10/05/18, https://groundup.org.za/article/understanding-michael-komape-judgment/, accessed 14/03/25.
128. Brown Lekekela, interview with the author.
129. See the Green Door Diepsloot Victim Lifeline website: https://greendoor-shelter.org, accessed 14/03/25.
130. Abigail M. Hatcher et al., 'Process Evaluation of a Community Mobilization Intervention for Preventing Men's Partner Violence Use in Peri-urban South Africa', *Evaluation and Program Planning* 78 (2020), https://doi.org/10.1016/j.evalprogplan.2019.101727, accessed 14/03/25. The programme was organised by Witwatersrand University researchers; Diepsloot's only women's shelter, Green Door; and Mia Malan's journalism resource centre, Bhekisisa, which not only distributes evidence-based stories to the national media but mentors journalists and promotes agenda-setting: see 'What Is Bhekisisa?', https://bhekisisa.org/what-is-bhekisisa/, accessed 14/03/25; the programme involved 144 workshops in small local clusters, conducted by trained local activists.
131. Hatcher et al., 'Process Evaluation of a Community Mobilization Intervention'.
132. Ibid.
133. Brenda Madumise-Pajibo, 'Recent Statistics of Crime against Women: Witnesses May Be Complicit', News 24, 24/06/22, https://www.news24.com/news24/Opinions/Columnists/GuestColumn/opinion-brenda-madumise-pajibo-recent-statistics-of-crime-against-women-witnesses-may-be-complicit-20220623, accessed 14/03/25.
134. Ibid.
135. Andries Bezuidenhout and Sakhela Buhlungu, 'Enclave Rustenburg: Platinum Mining and the Post-apartheid Social Order', *Review of African Political Economy* 42, no. 146 (2015); see also 'Nothing Has Changed for the Better: Things Are Worse', Bench Marks, 30/08/22, https://www.bench-marks.org.za/nothing-has-changed-for-the-better-things-are-worse/, accessed 14/03/25.

136. This argument is informed by the work of the pioneering feminist geographer Doreen Massey, particularly her essays 'A Global Sense of Place' and 'A Place Called Home'.
137. David Bruce, 'Submission to the Marikana Commission of Inquiry', 27/10/14, https://www.seri-sa.org/images/Bruce_Submissions.pdf, accessed 14/03/25.
138. Asanda Benya, 'Invisible Hands: Women of Marikana', *African Review of Political Economy* 42, no. 142 (2017).
139. Ibid.; Bridget Ndibongo, 'Women of Marikana: Survival and Struggles', MA thesis, University of Johannesburg, 2015, https://core.ac.uk/download/pdf/43583268.pdf, accessed 14/03/25.
140. Bezuidenhout and Buhlungu, 'Enclave Rustenburg'.
141. Ibid.
142. Nick Davies, 'The Savage Truth behind the Marikana Massacre', *Mail and Guardian*, 21/05/15, https://mg.co.za/article/2015-05-21-the-savage-truth-behind-the-marikana-massacre/, accessed 14/03/25.
143. First and Scott, *Olive Schreiner*, p. 202.
144. Ben Fine and Zavareh Rustomjee, *The Political Economy of South Africa: From the Minerals-Energy Complex to Industrialisation*, London: C. Hurst & Co., 1996; Sam Ashman, 'Racial Capitalism', *New Agenda* 84 (2022).
145. Ashman, 'Racial Capitalism'.
146. Ibid.
147. Ashman and Fine, 'Neo-liberalism, Varieties of Capitalism, and the Shifting Contours of South Africa's Financial System'.
148. Bezuidenhout and Buhlungu, 'Enclave Rustenburg'.
149. Ibid.
150. Beatrix Campbell and Val Charlton, 'Work to Rule', *Red Rag*, 1978; Campbell, 'United We Fall', *Red Rag*, 1980; Campbell, 'Old Fogeys and Angry Young Men', *Soundings* 1 (1995).
151. Lonmin insisted that they did not feature in the bargaining framework agreed with the NUM.
152. Interview with the author.
153. Interview with the author.
154. The company was founded in London in 1909. After the Second World War, it attracted Conservative politicians and members of the royal family but was condemned in 1973 by Prime Minister Edward Heath as the 'unacceptable face of capitalism'.

155. Cyril Ramaphosa was the beneficiary of a 'black empowerment' deal between South Africa's oligarchs and the ANC. He was a non-executive board member of Lonmin and of Oppenheimer's Anglo American.
156. Interview with the author.
157. Interview with the author.
158. Peter Alexander et al., *Marikana: A View from the Mountain and a Case to Answer*, Auckland Park: Jacana Media, 2012; Jared Sachs, 'Marikana Prequel: NUM and the Murders That Started It All', Daily Maverick, 12/10/2012, https://www.dailymaverick.co.za/opinionista/2012-10-12-marikana-prequel-num-and-the-murders-that-started-it-all/, accessed 14/03/25.
159. Alexander et al., *Marikana*.
160. For an exhaustive analysis of the Farlam commission report and its conclusion, and an analysis of the Marikana events, see David Bruce, 'Summary and Analysis of the Farlam Report', Council for the Advancement of the South African Constitution, 18/08/15, https://cisp.cachefly.net/assets/articles/attachments/56154_casac_summary-and-analysis-of-the-report-of-the-marikana-commission-of-inquiry.pdf, accessed 14/03/25.
161. Fazila Farouk and Samantha Hargreaves, 'The Impact of Mining on Women', South African Civil Society Information Service, 2013, https://sacsis.org.za/site/article/1818, accessed 14/03/25.
162. Ndibongo, 'Women of Marikana'. HIV infection rates in mining communities littered around the north-west of the country are higher than average because, women complain, men refuse to wear condoms.
163. A Hippo is now housed in Johannesburg's Apartheid Museum, a signifier of the terror machine.
164. Mandy De Waal, 'Marikana's Theatre of the Absurd Claims Another Life', Daily Maverick, 20/09/12, https://www.dailymaverick.co.za/article/2012-09-20-marikanas-theatre-of-the-absurd-claims-another-life/, accessed 14/03/25.
165. President Jacob Zuma set up a Commission of Inquiry into the massacre, chaired by Supreme Court Judge Ian Farlam, and two years later, when Ramaphosa was giving evidence, Sikhala Sonke organised a memorial event. 'We still have no justice, just tears,' said one of the women.
166. Ndibongo, 'Women of Marikana'.
167. Jodi Polders and Gill Nelson, 'Living Conditions of Mine Workers from Eight Mines in South Africa', *Development Southern Africa* 36, no. 3 (2019), pp. 265–82, https://doi.org/10.1080/0376835X.2018.1456909, accessed 14/03/25.

168. Phia van der Watt and Lochner Marais, 'Implementing Social and Labour Plans in South Africa: Reflections on Collaborative Planning in the Mining Industry', *Resources Policy* 71 (2021), https://doi.org/10.1016/j.resourpol.2021.101984, accessed 14/03/25; 'Everything You Need to Know about Social and Labour Plans', Umsiszi, https://umsizi.co.za/slp-a-z-everything-you-need-to-know-about-social-and-labour-plans/?cn-reloaded=1, accessed 14/03/25.
169. Interview with the author.
170. Asanda Benya, 'Underground Women Miners', Fellows Seminar, Stellenbosch University, 13/12/22, https://stias.ac.za/2022/12/underground-women-miners/, accessed 14/03/25. See also Asanda Benya, 'Personal Experience of Working Underground', 2010, https://www.academia.edu/33737045/2010_Personal_Experience_of_Working_Underground_Asanda_Benya_pdf, accessed 14/03/2015; Benya, 'Women in Mining: A Challenge to Occupational Culture in Mines', MA thesis, University of Witwatersrand, 2009, https://wiredspace.wits.ac.za/server/api/core/bitstreams/1f0a5d69-2d87-4a22-81aa-6865d7272b9e/content, accessed 14/03/25.
171. Van der Watt and Marais, 'Implementing Social and Labour Plans in South Africa'. By 2016, Lonmin acknowledged that 13,500 of its employees—about three-quarters—remained in need of formal housing.
172. 'State and Mining Houses Both Failed Marikana Community', Witwatersrand University Centre for Applied Legal Studies and Amnesty International, 16/08/22, https://www.wits.ac.za/news/sources/cals-news/2022/state-and-mining-houses-both-failed-marikana-community.html; the government's empty rhetoric was palpable in its response to the Farlam Commission: 'Farlam Commission Findings: Steps Taken by the Department of Mineral Resources', 07/09/17, https://pmg.org.za/committee-meeting/23217/, accessed 14/03/25.
173. See International Finance Corporation website: https://www.ifc.org/en/home, accessed 14/03/25.
174. 'South Africa: Lonmin; 02/Marikana', Compliance Advisor Ombudsman, 16/06/15, https://www.cao-ombudsman.org/cases/south-africa-lonmin-02marikana, accessed 14/03/25.
175. Ibid., p. 9.
176. 'Lonmin's Profits Rise as Marikana Community Continues to Suffer', London Mining Network, 26/05/19, https://londonminingnetwork.org/2019/03/press-release-lonmins-profits-rise-as-marikana-community-continues-to-suf-

fer/, accessed 14/03/25. This information was given to the Farlam Commission of Inquiry into the massacre.

177. 'CAO's Investigation of IFC's Environmental and Social Performance in Relation to Investments in Lonmin Plc Platinum Mining Company, South Africa', Compliance Advisor Ombudsman, June 2023, https://www.cao-ombudsman.org/sites/default/files/downloads/CAO%20Compliance%20Investigation%20Report%20SA%20Lonmin%20-%2002%20-%20June%2020%202023%20English.pdf, accessed 14/03/25. It was also 'non-compliant with air emission and groundwater pollution standards'.

178. Sibanye-Stillwater subsequently denied responsibility for the historical commitments.

179. 'Lonmin's Profits Rise as Marikana Community Continues to Suffer'.

180. Bezuidenhout and Buhlungu, 'Enclave Rustenburg', p. 4.

181. Ferial Haffajee, Heather Dodd and Andy Chinnah, 'Re-imagining Johannesburg after the Marshalltown Fire: What's Happened and What's Next?', Daily Maverick webinar, YouTube, 13/10/23, https://www.youtube.com/watch?v=LxbD-IbBJE4, accessed 14/03/25.

182. Nico Kotze and Leani de Vries, 'Resuscitating the African Giant: Urban Regeneration and Inner City Redevelopment Initiatives along the "Corridor of Freedom' in Downtown Johannesburg', *Geographica Polonica* 92, no. 1 (2019), pp. 55–70, https://doi.org/10.7163/GPol.0136, accessed 14/03/25.

183. Haffajee, Dodd and Chinnah, 'Re-imagining Johannesburg'.

184. Interview with the author.

185. Interview with the author.

186. 'Just and Equitable?', SERI, June 2022, https://www.seri-sa.org/images/SERI_Mag_Court_Evictions_report_FINAL_HIGH_RES_FOR_WEB_UPLOAD.pdf, accessed 14/03/25.

187. Most of these buildings had been saddled with massive unpaid municipal debt, which left residents with an ongoing challenge of accessing municipal services, such as water, electricity and waste collection.

188. Interview with the author.

189. Interview with the author.

190. Interview with the author.

191. Interview with the author.

192. Kimberley Mutandiro, 'Marshalltown Fire Survivors to Launch Class Action against City of Johannesburg', GroundUp, 24/08/24, https://groundup.org.

za/article/marshalltown-fire-survivors-to-launch-class-action-against-the-city-of-joburg/, accessed 14/03/25.
193. Jon Boutcher, 'Operation Kenova Northern Ireland "Stakeknife" Legacy Investigation', 2024, https://www.psni.police.uk/sites/default/files/2024–03/Operation%20Kenova%20Interim%20Report%202024.pdf, accessed 14/03/25.
194. The Arabic word for uprising, most commonly associated with Palestinian resistance to Israeli occupation.

6. ICELAND: PARADISE?

1. Iceland gained sovereignty in 1918 and independence in 1944.
2. See Nancy Fraser's provocative charge that elements of second-wave feminism converged with capitalism: 'Feminism, Capitalism and the Cunning of History', *New Left Review* 56 (Mar./Apr. 2009), https://newleftreview.org/issues/ii56/articles/nancy-fraser-feminism-capitalism-and-the-cunning-of-history, accessed 14/03/25.
3. The Vikings came from Scandinavia and settled to farm in Iceland in the 870s.
4. Elisabeth Prugl, '"If Lehman Brothers had been Lehman Sisters …": Gender and Myth in the Aftermath of the Financial Crisis', *International Political Sociology* 6, no. 1 (Mar. 2012), https://academic.oup.com/ips/article-abstract/6/1/21/1787105?redirectedFrom=fulltext, accessed 14/03/25.
5. Home rule was introduced in 1904, but Iceland was not released from union with Denmark until 1944.
6. The ASÍ elected its first female president, Drífa Snædal, in 2018. In 1975, women were not allowed to be members of the national farmers' union.
7. Interviews with the author.
8. Prugl, '"If Lehman Brothers Had Been Sisters"', pp. 21–35.
9. Hannes Hólmsteinn Gissurarson interview with the author.
10. Their mentors were the Austrian Friedrich Hayek, beloved of the UK's Conservative Party leader Margaret Thatcher; his teacher Ludwig von Mises; and the American Milton Friedman. Hayek and Friedman were the men of the moment—both were awarded the Nobel Prize for economics in the mid-1970s—who provided the theory for unfettered capitalism that fired up the global political economy at the end of the Cold War.
11. Will Davies, *The Limits of Neoliberalism*, London: Sage, 2015.
12. David Harvey, *A Brief History of Neo-liberalism*, Oxford: Oxford University Press, 2007.

13. Andrew Gamble, 'The Two Faces of Neo-liberalism', in Richard Robison (eds.), *The Neo-liberal Revolution*, London: Palgrave Macmillan, 2006, pp. 20–1, https://link.springer.com/chapter/10.1057/9780230625235_2, accessed 14/03/25.
14. Andrew Gamble, 'Why Is Neoliberalism so Resilient?', *Critical Sociology* 45, nos. 7–8 (2019), https://journals.sagepub.com/doi/abs/10.1177/0896920519832648, accessed 14/03/25.
15. Silla Sigurgeirsdóttir and Robert Wade, 'Lessons from Iceland', *New Left Review* 65 (2010), https://newleftreview.org/issues/ii65/articles/robert-wade-silla-sigurgeirsdottir-lessons-from-iceland, accessed 14/03/25.
16. Ibid.
17. Ibid.
18. Ibid.
19. Interview with the author.
20. Sigurgeirsdóttir and Wade, 'Lessons from Iceland'.
21. Janine R. Wedel, *Shadow Elite: How the World's New Power Brokers Undermine Democracy, Government and the Free Market*, New York: Basic Books, 2009, p. 35.
22. Ibid., p. 71.
23. Janet Elise Johnson, Þorgerður Einarsdóttir and Gyða Margrét Pétursdóttir, 'A Feminist Theory of Corruption: Lessons from Iceland', *Politics and Gender* 9, no. 2 (2013), https://www.researchgate.net/publication/259433714_A_Feminist_Theory_of_Corruption_Lessons_from_Iceland, accessed 14/03/25.
24. Wedel, *Shadow Elite*, p. xi.
25. Johnson, Einarsdóttir and Pétursdóttir, 'Feminist Theory of Corruption'.
26. Colin Crouch, *The Strange Non-death of Neoliberalism*, Cambridge: Polity Press, 2011.
27. Þröstur Olaf Sigurjónsson, 'Privatisation and Deregulation', University of Iceland, 2011.
28. Bibler: 'The Central Bank had given away the country's meagre foreign currency reserves' to Kaupthing bank 'just hours before it collapsed'.
29. Report of the Special Investigation Commission, 12/04/08, https://www.rna.is/eldri-nefndir/addragandi-og-orsakir-falls-islensku-bankanna-2008/skyrsla-nefndarinnar/english/, accessed 14/03/25.
30. Thorvaldur Gylfason, 'Iceland's Special Investigation: The Plot Thickens', Centre for Economic Policy Research, 12/04/10. Ten out of Iceland's sixty-three MPs, including leaders of the Independence Party, owed an average of 9 million euros.

31. Steven Erlanger, 'Iceland's Prime Minister Steps Down amid Panama Papers Scandal', *New York Times*, 05/04/16, https://www.nytimes.com/2016/04/06/world/europe/panama-papers-iceland.html, accessed 14/03/25.
32. Amanda Erikson, 'How Iceland's Government Was Brought Down by a Letter from PM's Father Demanding Paedophile's Pardon', *The Independent*, 18/09/17, https://www.independent.co.uk/news/world/europe/iceland-paedophile-brought-down-government-bright-future-coalition-hjalti-sigurjon-hauksson-benedikt-sveinsson-bjarni-benediktsson-a7952721.html, accessed 14/03/25; the cover-up provoked the Bright Future party to withdraw from the coalition because of 'corruption and dishonesty'.
33. Marie Louise Stig Sørensen, 'Gender, Material, Culture and Identity', *Viking and Medieval Scandinavia* 5 (2009).
34. Margaret Willson, *Seawomen of Iceland*, Seattle: University of Washington Press, 2016.
35. Ibid.
36. Ibid.
37. Doreen Massey, *Space, Place and Gender*, Cambridge: Polity Press, 1994.
38. Madeleine Gustavsson, 'Women's Changing Productive Practices, Gender Relations and Identification in Fishing through a Critical Feminisation Perspective', *Journal of Rural Studies* 78 (Aug. 2020), pp. 36–46.
39. Enrico Alonso-Población and Anke Niehof, 'On the Power of a Spatial Metaphor: Is Female to Land as Male Is to Sea?', *Maritime Studies* 9, no. 3 (2019), pp. 249–57, https://research.wur.nl/en/publications/on-the-power-of-a-spatial-metaphor-is-female-to-land-as-male-is-t, accessed 14/03/25.
40. Ibid.
41. Elena Finkbeiner interview: Kiley Price, 'In Fishing Industry, Women Face Hidden Hardships', Conservation International, 29/04/21, https://www.conservation.org/blog/in-fishing-industry-women-face-hidden-hardships-study, accessed 14/03/25.
42. Valdur Ingimundarson, 'Fighting the Cod Wars in the Cold War: Iceland's Challenge to the Western Alliance in the 1970s', *The RUSI Journal* 148, no. 3 (2003), pp. 88–94.
43. Willson, *Seawomen of Iceland*; Birgir Runolfsson and Ragnar Arnason, 'Individual Transferrable Quotas in Iceland', Fraser Institute, https://www.fraserinstitute.org/sites/default/files/FishorCutBaitIndividualTransferableQuotas.pdf, accessed 14/03/25.

44. Hannes Holmsteinn Gissurarson, 'Liberalism in Iceland in the Nineteenth and Twentieth Centuries', *Econ Journal Watch* 14, no. 2 (2017).
45. Fiona McCormack, 'Quota Systems: Repositioning Value in New Zealand, Iceland and Irish Fisheries', in Luis Fernando Angosto-Ferrandez and Geir Henning Presterudstuen (eds), *Anthropologies of Value: Cultures of Accumulation across the Global North and South*, London: Pluto Books, 2016, https://www.researchgate.net/publication/306280890_, accessed 14/03/25.
46. The allocation of ITQs to individual firms and vessels did not, however, give irrevocable property rights. Advocates of privatisation argue that this created uncertainty around the permanence and exclusivity of the ITQs and undermined their economic effectiveness.
47. Courtney Carothers and Catherine Chambers, 'Fishers Privatisation and the Remaking of Fisheries Systems', *Environment and Society* 3, no. 1 (2012).
48. Eva Munk-Madsen, 'The Norwegian Fishing Quota System: Another Patriarchal Construction?', *Society and Natural Resources* 11, no. 3 (2008), pp. 229–40.
49. Organisation of Economic Co-operation and Development, 'Sustaining Iceland's Fisheries through Tradeable Quotas', Policy Paper no. 9, 2017, https://www.oecd.org/environment/resources/Policy-Paper-Sustaining-Iceland-fisheries-through-tradeable-quotas.pdf, accessed 14/03/25.
50. Becky Mansfield, 'Privatisation: Property and the Remaking of Nature–Society Relations', *Antipode* 39, no. 3 (2007).
51. Anna Karlsdóttir, 'Not Sure about the Shore! Transformation Effects of Individual Transferrable Quotas on Iceland's Fishing Economy and Quotas', in Marie E. Lowe and Courtney Carothers (eds), *Enclosing the Fishers: People, Places and Power*, Bethesda, MD: American Fisheries Society, 2008.
52. Ragnar Arnason, 'The Icelandic Individual Transferable Quota System: A Descriptive Account', *Marine Resource Economics* 8, no. 3 (1993).
53. Evelyn Pinkerton, 'Groundtruthing Individual Transferrable Quotas', in E. Paul Durrenberger and Gísli Pálsson (eds), *Gambling Debt: Iceland's Rise and fall in the Global Economy*, Boulder: University Press of Colorado, 2014.
54. McCormack, 'Quota Systems'.
55. Matt Eliason, 'A Fish Stock Market: Iceland's Controversial Quota System', *Iceland Magazine*, 15/09/14.
56. Anna Karlsdóttir, 'Are Living Fish Better than Dead Fillets? The Power and Invisibility of Women in Aquaculture and the Icelandic Fishing Economy', in Joanna Kafarowski (ed.), *Gender, Culture and the Northern Fisheries*, Edmonton:

Canadian Circumpolar Institute Press, 2009. One exception is the wealthy businesswoman Guðbjörg Matthiasdottir, who inherited quotas from her late husband.
57. Ibid.
58. Karlsdóttir, 'Not Sure about the Shore!'; Timothy Heleniak and Hjördis Sigurjonsdottir, 'Once Homogenous, Tiny Iceland Opens Its Doors to Immigrants', Migration Policy Institute, 18/04/18, https://www.migrationpolicy.org/article/once-homogenous-tiny-iceland-opens-its-doors-immigrants, accessed 14/03/25.
59. Willson, *Seawomen of Iceland*, p. 91.
60. Karlsdóttir, 'Not Sure about the Shore!'
61. Pinkerton, 'Groundtruthing Individual Transferrable Quotas'. See also Catherine Chambers and Courtney Carothers, 'Thirty Years after Privatisation: A Survey of Icelandic Small-Boat Fishermen', *Marine Policy* 80 (June 2017), pp. 69–80.
62. Karlsdóttir, 'Are Living Fish Better than Dead Fillets?', pp. 67–84.
63. McCormack, 'Quota Systems', p. 80.
64. Jelena Ćirić, 'Fishing Industry Profits Spark Wealth Distribution Debate', *Iceland Review*, 31/05/22, https://www.icelandreview.com/politics/fishing-industry-profits-spark-wealth-distribution-debate/, accessed 14/03/25.
65. Becky Mansfield, '"Modern" Industrial Fisheries and the Crisis of Over-Fishing', in Richard Peet, Paul Robbins and Michael Watts (eds), *Global Political Ecology*, London: Routledge, 2010, pp. 84–99.
66. Ingi Freyr Vilhjálmsson, 'An Icelandic Fishing Company Bribed Officials in Namibia and Used Norway's Largest Bank to Transfer 70 Million Dollars to a Tax Haven', *Stundin*, 12/11/19, https://stundin.is/grein/9920/an-icelandic-fishing-company-transferred-70-million-dollars-through-a-tax-haven-in-norways-largest-bank/, accessed 14/03/25. According to the whistle-blower, Jóhannes Stefánsson, the bribes had been authorised by Samherji chief executive Thorsteinn Már Baldvinsson. The whistle-blower's story was aired jointly by the Icelandic paper *Stundin*, TV investigative programme *Kveikur* and Al Jazeera in November 2019.
67. Alexander Elliott, 'Samherji Tried to Track RÚV Journalist through Ministry', RÚV, 27/05/21, https://www.ruv.is/frett/2021/05/27/samherji-tried-to-track-ruv-journalist-through-ministry, accessed 14/03/25; Samherji complained to the police. The story ran and ran in the Icelandic media, until, finally, the police closed the case in 2024.

68. Jelena Ćirić, 'Fishing Industry Profits Spark Wealth Distribution Debate', *Iceland Review*, 31/05/22, https://www.icelandreview.com/politics/fishing-industry-profits-spark-wealth-distribution-debate/, accessed 14/03/25.
69. Andie Sophia Fontaine, 'Fishrot Files: The Response in Iceland So Far', Grapevine, 14/11/19, https://grapevine.is/news/2019/11/14/fishrot-files-the-response-in-iceland-so-far/, accessed 14/03/25.
70. Iceland had recovered its reputation after the 2008 banking crash and by 2018 ranked thirteenth in the Transparency International Corruption Perceptions Index; though globally rated as relatively clean, it was now the most corrupt Nordic country. In 2022, Transparency International warned that Samherji's pursuit of journalists sent a 'dangerous message' to the entire country: 'Iceland Investigations against Journalists Reporting on Samherji Undermine Press Freedoms and Anti-corruption Efforts', Transparency International, 16/02/22, https://www.transparency.org/en/press/iceland-investigations-against-journalists-fishrot-samherji-undermine-press-freedoms-anti-corruption, accessed 14/03/25.
71. US aircraft and navy monitoring of Russian submarines was only abandoned in 2006. With no army of its own, Iceland became one of the few nations without a military presence.
72. Although the president's role is largely ceremonial, it involves the power to assemble a government. Finnbogadóttir used the role to promote the reforestation of this bleak, largely treeless terrain.
73. In 1999, it dissolved. Some members joined two other parties, the Social Democratic Alliance and the Left-Green Movement.
74. John Nichols, 'Iceland's Left-Wing, Environmentalist, Feminist Prime Minister', *The Nation*, 08/03/18.
75. Ásdís Aðalbjörg Arnalds et al., 'Paid Parental Leave in Iceland', in Caroline de la Porte (ed.), *Successful Public Policy in Nordic Countries*, Oxford: Oxford University Press, 2022.
76. Interview with the author.
77. Þorgerður Einarsdóttir, 'Culture, Custom and Caring: Men's and Women's Possibilities to Parental Leave', Akureyri, Centre for Gender Equality in Iceland, 2004.
78. Interview with the author.
79. Arnalds, Eydal and Gíslason, 'Paid Parental Leave in Iceland'.
80. 'Response to the UN's "Call for inputs—custody cases, violence against women

and children"', Life without Violence, December 2022, https://www.lifanofbeldis.is/blog-1/statement-responding-to-the-uns-call-for-inputs-custody-cases-violence-against-women-and-children, accessed 14/03/25.

81. Stephanie J. Dallam, 'The Parental Alienation Syndrome: Is It Scientific?', Leadership Council on Child Abuse & Interpersonal Violence, 1999; see also Dallam, 'Dr Richard Gardner: A Review of His Theories and Opinions on Atypical Sexuality, Paedophilia and Treatment Issues', *Treating Abuse Today* 8, no. 1 (1998), https://web.archive.org/web/20211116075945/http://www.leadershipcouncil.org/1/res/dallam/2.html, accessed 14/03/25; Andrew Gumbel, 'Dr Richard A. Gardner, Child Psychiatrist Who Developed the Theory of Parental Alienation', *The Independent*, 31/05/03, https://www.independent.co.uk/news/obituaries/dr-richard-a-gardner-36582.html, accessed 14/03/25.

82. 'Household Work during the COVID-19 Pandemic', Statistics Iceland, https://statice.is/publications/experimental-statistics/householdwork-tt/, accessed 14/03/25.

83. 'The Gender Pay Gap Decreased between 2019 and 2023', Statistics Iceland, 21/01/25, https://statice.is/publications/news-archive/wages-and-income/gender-pay-gap-2019-2023/, accessed 14/03/25.

84. Ivana Kottasová, 'The World's "Best Place to Be a Woman" Sued for Misogyny', CNN, 25/12/21, https://edition.cnn.com/2021/12/20/europe/iceland-domestic-violence-intl-cmd/index.html, accessed 14/03/25.

85. Judith Lewis Herman, *Trauma and Recovery: The Aftermath of Violence; From Domestic Abuse to Political Terror*, New York: Basic Books, 2015.

86. Iris Marion Young, *Justice and the Politics of Difference*, Princeton: Princeton University Press, 2011.

87. Beatrix Campbell, *The Iron Ladies: Why Do Women Vote Tory?*, London: Virago, 1987.

88. Sigrún Sif Jóelsdóttir and Grant Wyeth, 'The Misogynist Violence of Iceland's Female Paradise', *Foreign Policy*, 15/07/20, https://foreignpolicy.com/2020/07/15/the-misogynist-violence-of-icelands-feminist-paradise/, accessed 14/03/25.

89. Drífa Jónasdóttir et al., 'Women and Intimate Partner Violence: Prevalence of Hospital Visits and Nature of Injuries in the Icelandic Population', 2021, https://www.researchgate.net/publication/340795841_Women_and_intimate_partner_violence_Prevalence_of_hospital_visits_and_nature_of_injuries_in_the_Icelandic_population, accessed 14/03/25.

90. 'One in Four Women Raped or Sexually Assaulted', University of Iceland, 2018,

https://english.hi.is/research/one-four-women-has-been-raped-or-sexually-assaulted, accessed 14/03/25.

91. Kottasová, 'World's "Best Place to Be a Woman" Sued for Misogyny'.
92. Katrin Hohl and Elizabeth E. Stanko, 'Five Pillars: A Framework for Transforming the Police Response to Rape and Sexual Assault', *International Criminology* 2, no. 4 (2022), pp. 222–9, https://www.researchgate.net/publication/360638609_Five_Pillars_A_Framework_for_Transforming_the_Police_Response_to_Rape_and_Sexual_Assault, accessed 14/03/25.
93. Jennifer Temkin, *Rape and the Legal Process*, Oxford: Oxford University Press, 2022, pp. 22–3.
94. Beatrix Campbell, *Secrets and Silence*, Bristol: Policy Press, 2023.
95. Originally formed by Tarana Burke in Selma, Alabama, against sexual abuse and adopted in 2017 in response to allegations against movie mogul Harvey Weinstein. The conference was held under the auspices of the Nordic Council of Ministers, of which Jakobsdóttir was president.
96. Kate Connolly, 'Iceland Hosts First Major International #MeToo Conference', *The Guardian*, 17/09/19, https://www.theguardian.com/world/2019/sep/17/metoo-conference-hopes-to-relegate-harassment-to-history, accessed 14/03/25.
97. Interview with the author.
98. Interview with the author.
99. 'Application no. 59809/19, R.E. against Iceland and 3 Other Applications', European Court of Human Rights, 2021, https://hudoc.echr.coe.int/eng#{%22itemid%22:[%22001-209021%22]}, accessed 14/03/25.
100. Interview with the author.
101. Türkiye was the first to ratify the treaty in 2012, and the first—and only state—to withdraw in 2021. The treaty came into force in 2014. According to the Council of Europe, by 2025 there were thirty-nine signatories and accessions. Council of Europe, 'Chart of Signatories and Ratifications of Treaty 2010', 16/03/25, https://www.coe.int/en/web/conventions/full-list?module=signatures-by-treaty&treatynum=210, accessed 14/03/25.
102. I am borrowing this idea from leading clinician Richard Krugman's description of paediatricians' dilemmas in responding to suspicions of child sexual abuse in under-resourced child protection systems, see Campbell, *Secrets and Silence*, p. 77.
103. Susan Bordo, 'Feminism, Postmodernism, and Gender Scepticism', in Linda J. Nicholson (ed.), *Feminism/Postmodernism*, London: Routledge, 1990.

104. Interview with the author.
105. Andie So'phia Fontaine, 'Most Icelanders Unhappy with Islandsbanki Sale, Believe Law Was Broken', Grapevine, 29/04/22, https://grapevine.is/news/2022/04/29/most-icelanders-unhappy-with-islandsbanki-sale-believe-law-was-broken/, accessed 14/03/25.
106. Ibid.
107. Catherine Fulton, 'Minister of Finance Bjarni Benediktsson Resigns', Grapevine, 10/10/23, https://grapevine.is/news/2023/10/10/minister-of-finance-bjarni-benediktsson-resigns/, accessed 14/03/25.
108. Ibid.
109. Iryna Zubenko, 'Iceland's New Government Formed, Priorities Revealed', Grapevine, 23/12/24, https://grapevine.is/news/2024/12/23/icelands-new-government-formed-priorities-unveiled/, accessed 14/03/25.
110. Janet Elise Johnson, *The Gender of Informal Politics: Russia, Iceland and Twenty-First Century Male Dominance*, Basingstoke: Palgrave Macmillan, 2018.

7. ROJAVA: 'THE STREET WAS OPEN TO THE WOMEN'

1. Memed Aksoy, session on revolutionary change and the Kurdish movement at 'Reimagining Democracy' conference, organised by Assemblies for Democracy, 28/03/15, https://assembliesfordemocracy.org/london-programme/london-march-28/, accessed 14/03/25.
2. Author interview on Skype with Dilar Dirik, 09/11/16.
3. David R. Croteau, William D. Hoynes and Charlotte Ryan, Rhyming Hope and History: Activists, Academics, and Social Movement Scholarship, Minneapolis: University of Minnesota Press, 2005, p. 223.
4. Stuart Hall, 'Encoding/Decoding', in Stuart Hall et al. (eds), *Culture, Media, Language*, London: Hutchinson, 1980, pp. 128–38 (p. 138).
5. David A. Snow and Robert D. Benford, 'Ideology, Frame Resonance, and Participant Mobilization', *International Social Movement Research* 1 (1998), pp. 197–217.
6. Jim Muir, 'Sykes–Picot: The Map that Spawned a Century of Resentment', BBC, 16/05/16, http://www.bbc.co.uk/news/world-middle-east-36300224, accessed 19/01/18.
7. Luke Mogelson, 'Dark Victory in Raqqa', *The New Yorker*, 06/11/17, https://www.newyorker.com/magazine/2017/11/06/dark-victory-in-raqqa, accessed 16/05/2024.

8. Veysi Dag, 'What Are Syrian Mercenaries Doing in Azerbaijan?', openDemocracy, 02/10/20, https://www.opendemocracy.net/en/north-africa-west-asia/what-are-syrian-mercenaries-doing-azerbaijan/, accessed 10/09/24.
9. Shahrzad Mojab, 'The Politics of "Cyberfeminism" in the Middle East: The Case of Kurdish Women', *Race, Gender & Class* 8, no. 4 (2001), pp. 42–61 (p. 49).
10. Michael Knapp, Anya Flach and Ercan Ayboga, *Revolution in Rojava: Democratic Autonomy and Women's Liberation in Syrian Kurdistan*, London: Pluto Press, 2016, p. 37.
11. Harriet Allsopp, *The Kurds of Syria: Political Parties and Identity in the Middle East*, London: I. B. Tauris, 2014, p. 40.
12. Author interview on Skype with Dilar Dirik, 09/11/16.
13. Knapp, Flach and Ayboga, *Revolution in Rojava*, pp. 48–9.
14. Ibid., p. 50
15. Ibid., pp. 51–5.
16. Quoted in Meredith Tax, *A Road Unforeseen: Women Fight the Islamic State*, New York: Bellevue Literary Press, 2016, p. 168.
17. Author interview on Skype with Dilar Dirik, 09/11/16.
18. Kongra Star was previously known as Yekitya Star, when its membership was open to Kurdish women only. The new name was adopted at their sixth congress in February 2016 to signal their openness to all women regardless of ethnicity.
19. Sakine Cansız, *Sara: My Whole Life was a Struggle*, trans. Janet Biehl, London: Pluto Press, 2018.
20. Ibid., p. 292.
21. Ibid., p. 226.
22. Author interview on Skype with Dilar Dirik, 09/11/16.
23. Ibid.
24. Constanze Letsch, 'Sakine Cannszi: "A Legend among PKK Members"', *The Guardian*, 10/01/23, https://www.theguardian.com/world/2013/jan/10/sakine-cansiz-pkk-kurdish-activist, accessed 13/02/18.
25. Knapp, Flach and Ayboga, *Revolution in Rojava*, p. 37.
26. Author interview with Frederike Geerdink via Skype on 23/07/18.
27. Interview with David Graeber: 'Real Media: Syria, Anarchism and Visiting Rojava', TRNN, 01/07/17, https://therealnews.com/rm0629dgraeber, accessed 24/07/18.

28. In 2014, 40,000 Yazidis were trapped in the mountains of Sinjar, Northern Iraq, when ISIS laid siege—5,000 men were killed and 7,000 women and girls taken as sex slaves, raped and tortured. John Beck, 'Iraq's Yazidis Living in Fear on Sinjar Mountains', Al Jazeera, 26/07/16, http://www.aljazeera.com/news/2016/07/iraq-yazidis-living-fear-mount-sinjar-160726063155982.html, accessed 24/07/18.
29. Email from Kongra Star spokesperson, dated 01/10/16.
30. Dilar Dirik, 'Feminist Pacifism or Passive-ism' openDemocracy, 07/03/17, https://www.opendemocracy.net/en/5050/feminist-pacifism-or-passive-ism/, accessed 04/04/18.
31. 'DAANES' Social Contract, 2023 Edition', 14/12/23, https://rojavainformationcenter.org/2023/12/aanes-social-contract-2023-edition/, accessed 10/09/24.
32. Author interview with Walîda Botî, 05/03/16.
33. Rahila Gupta, 'It's Raining Women', openDemocracy, 26/04/16, https://opendemocracy.net/5050/rahila-gupta/rojava-revolution-it-s-raining-women, accessed 05/12/16.
34. Rahila Gupta, 'Rojava's Commitment to Jineolojî: The Science of Women', openDemocracy, 11/04/16, https://www.opendemocracy.net/rahila-gupta/rojava-s-commitment-to-jineoloj-science-of-women, accessed 09/10/17.
35. Wes Enzinna, 'A Dream of Secular Utopia in ISIS' Backyard', *New York Times*, 24/11/15, http://www.nytimes.com/2015/11/29/magazine/a-dream-of-utopia-in-hell.html?_r=0, accessed 30/11/15.
36. Rahila Gupta, 'Rojava Revolution: How Deep Is the Change?', openDemocracy, 20/06/16, https://www.opendemocracy.net/5050/rahila-gupta/rojava-revolution-how-deep-is-change, accessed 14/12/16.
37. Cole Bunzel, 'From Jihadi to Islamist: Ahmed al-Sharaa and His Critics', Jihadica, 03/01/25, https://www.jihadica.com/from-jihadi-to-islamist/, accessed 10/01/25.
38. 'Full Speech of Dr. Bashar al-Assad President of the Syrian Arab Republic, Damascus 06/01/2013', YouTube, 06/01/13, https://www.youtube.com/watch?v=JGeGHVAjG5c, accessed 20/04/16.
39. 'Charter of the Social Contract', Peace in Kurdistan, https://peaceinkurdistancampaign.com/charter-of-the-social-contract/, accessed 20/02/18.
40. Alexandra Zavis, 'Feminism, Syria-Style: Conservative Tribesmen Freed from Islamic State Emerge into a World Where Women Have Rights', *Los Angeles Times*, 08/01/18, http://www.latimes.com/world/middleeast/la-fg-syria-culture-clash-20170108-story.html, accessed 19/12/18.

41. Rod Nordland, 'Women Are Free, and Armed, in Kurdish-Controlled Northern Syria', *New York Times*, 24/02/18, https://www.nytimes.com/2018/02/24/world/middleeast/syria-kurds-womens-rights-gender-equality.html, accessed 23/03/18.
42. 'DAANES' Social Contract'.
43. Author interview on Zoom with Berivan Şaredariye, 25/09/24.
44. 'Women's Village: Jinwar', Internationalist Commune, 26/09/17, https://internationalistcommune.com/jinwar/, accessed 06/07/18.
45. Julie Bindel, 'The Village Where Men are Banned', *The Guardian*, 16/08/15, https://www.theguardian.com/global-development/2015/aug/16/village-where-men-are-banned-womens-rights-kenya, accessed 06/07/18.
46. Nadje Al-Ali and Isabel Kaiser, 'Jineolojî and the Kurdish Women's Freedom Movement', *Politics and Gender* 18, no. 1 (Mar. 2022), pp. 212–43, https://doi.org/10.1017/S1743923X20000501, accessed 19/01/21.
47. Catharine A. Mackinnon, *Towards a Feminist Theory of the State*, Cambridge, MA: Harvard University Press, 1991, p. 136.
48. Author interview with Given Erzîngen, 03/10/16.
49. Nasrin Ramazanali, 'Fighting an Islamic Regime', in Houzan Mahmoud (ed.), *Kurdish Women's Stories*, London: Pluto, 2021.
50. Rahila Gupta, 'Women on the Front at Raqqa', openDemocracy, 14/02/17, https://www.opendemocracy.net/5050/rahila-gupta-women-on-front-at-raqqa, accessed 31/07/18.
51. Tax, *Road Unforeseen*, pp. 143–4.
52. Author interview with Anya Flach, 17/04/17.
53. Author interview with Frederike Geerdink via Skype on 23/07/18.
54. 'The Women's Movement in Rojava', Co-Operation in Mesopotamia, https://mesopotamia.coop/the-womens-movement-in-rojava/, accessed 13/01/25.
55. Rahila Gupta, 'Women's Cooperatives in Qamişlo, Rojava', Co-operative Economy, 20/04/16, https://cooperativeeconomy.info/womens-co-operatives-in-rojava/, accessed 09/10/17.
56. Interview with Delal Afrin, 06/03/16.
57. Interview with Hediye Yusuf.
58. Salvador Zana, 'Rojava's Economics and the Future of the Revolution', Co-operation in Mesopotamia, 01/07/17, https://mesopotamia.coop/rojavas-economics-and-the-future-of-the-revolution/, accessed 10/01/25.
59. Author interview with Dr Alan Semo, 21/11/17.
60. Janet Biehl, 'Revolutionary Education: Two Academies in Rojava', Co-operation

in Mesopotamia, 03/01/21, available at Revolutionary Education – Co-operation in Mesopotamia accessed 02/04/25.
61. Knapp, Flach and Ayboga, *Revolution in Rojava*, p. 181.
62. Ibid., p. 182.
63. Gupta, 'Rojava's Commitment to Jineolojî'.
64. Knapp, Flach and Ayboga, *Revolution in Rojava*, p. 44.
65. Gupta, 'Rojava's Commitment to Jineolojî'.
66. 'Revolutionary Education', Andrea Wolf Institute of Jineolojî, Rojava, 2019, p. 38.
67. Ibid.
68. Ibid.
69. Rahila Gupta, 'Before Iran, the Kurdish Feminist Revolution', *New Internationalist*, 23/02/23, https://newint.org/immersive/2023/02/23/iran-kurdish-feminist-revolution, accessed 20/09/24.
70. Luke Mogelson 'Dark Victory in Raqqa', *The New Yorker*, 30/10/17, https://www.newyorker.com/magazine/2017/11/06/dark-victory-in-raqqa, accessed 01/11/17.
71. Murray Bookchin, 'Libertarian Municipalism: The New Municipal Agenda', http://dwardmac.pitzer.edu/Anarchist_Archives/bookchin/libmuni.html, accessed 05/08/24.
72. Ahmet Hamdi Akkaya and Joost Jongerden, 'Reassembling the Political: The PKK and the Project of Radical Democracy', in Renée In der Maur and Jonas Staal (eds), *Stateless Democracy*, Utrecht: BAK, 2015, p. 187.
73. Abdullah Öcalan, *Liberating Life: Woman's Revolution*, n.p.: International Initiative Edition, 2013, pp. 8, 10–11, http://www.freeocalan.org/wp-content/uploads/2014/06/liberating-Lifefinal.pdf, accessed 18/03/16.
74. Dr Lina Khatib, head of Middle East and North Africa Programme, Chatham House, said this in a Q&A at a public meeting organised by RUSI, 27/10/17.
75. *Liberating Life*, pp. 10–11.
76. 'The Combahee River Collective Statement', Apr. 1977, http://circuitous.org/scraps/combahee.html, accessed 24/06/20.
77. 'DAANES' Social Contract'.
78. Rahila Gupta, 'Rojava Revolution: Reshaping Masculinity', openDemocracy, 09/05/16, https://www.opendemocracy.net/en/5050/rojava-revolution-reshaping-masculinity/, accessed 05/07/18.
79. *Liberating Life*, p. 54.

80. Author interview on Skype with Dilar Dirik, 09/11/16.
81. Rahila Gupta, 'Treaties Alone Can't Protect Women from Violence', CNN, 26/09/20, https://edition.cnn.com/2020/09/26/opinions/violence-against-women-turkey-intl/index.html, accessed 22/09/24.
82. Quoted by Tax, *Road Unforeseen*, p. 284.
83. Ibid., p. 284.
84. Knapp, Flach and Ayboga, *Revolution in Rojava*, p. xviii.
85. Ibid., pp. xvi–xvii.
86. *Liberating Life*, p. 13.
87. Ibid., p. 30.
88. Ibid., p. 49.
89. Gupta, 'It's Raining Women'.
90. Tax, *Road Unforeseen*, p. 124.
91. *Liberating Life*, p. 22.
92. Ibid., p. 50.
93. Author interview with Hediye Yusuf.
94. 'Beyond the Frontlines', Rojava Information Center, https://rojavainformation-center.org/storage/2021/06/Beyond-the-frontlines-The-building-of-the-democratic-system-in-North-and-East-Syria-Report-Rojava-Information-Center-December–2019-Web-version.pdf, accessed 22/09/24.
95. 'Turkey Target Civilian Infrastructure in Rojava and Kurdish Territories', Impact International, 27/10/23, https://impactpolicies.org/news/347/turkey-target-civilian-infrastructure-in-kurdish-territories, accessed 22/09/24.
96. Jenni Keasden and Natalia Szarek, *Worth Fighting For: Bringing the Rojava Revolution Home*, Bristol: Active Distribution Publishing, 2023, p. 29.
97. 'Beyond the Frontlines'.
98. 'Iran Update', Institute of War, 16/12/24, https://www.understandingwar.org/backgrounder/iran-update-december-16-2024, accessed 11/01/25.
99. 'New Syrian Justice Minister Involved in Executions of Women in 2015', Medya News, 05/01/2025, https://medyanews.net/video-new-syrian-justice-minister-involved-in-executions-of-women-in-2015/, accessed 12/01/25.

CONCLUSION

1. Bobby Bannerjee, 'Necrocapitalism', *Organization Studies* 29, no. 12 (Dec. 2008), pp. 1541–63, https://www.researchgate.net/publication/247734777_Necrocapitalism, accessed 06/02/25.

2. Naomi Klein, *The Shock Doctrine: The Rise of Disaster Capitalism*, London: Penguin, 2008.
3. Shoshanna Zuboff, *The Age of Surveillance Capitalism: The Fight for a Human Future at the New Frontier of Power*, London: Profile Books, 2019.
4. Interview with Yanis Varoufakis: 'Technofeudalism: What Killed Capitalism?', The Chris Hedges Report, 29/01/25, https://chrishedges.substack.com/p/technofeudalism-what-killed-capitalism, accessed 02/02/25.
5. Koh Ewe, 'The Ultimate Election Year: All the Elections around the World in 2024', *Time*, 28/12/23, https://time.com/6550920/world-elections-2024/, accessed 28/04/24.
6. Timothy Mitchell, 'McJihad: Empire and Islam between the US and Saudi Arabia?', Verso Books, 2017, https://www.versobooks.com/en-gb/blogs/news/3256-mcjihad-empire-and-islam-between-the-us-and-saudi-arabia?, accessed 08/03/24.
7. Rana Dasgupta, 'The Demise of the Nation State', *The Guardian*, 05/04/19, https://www.theguardian.com/news/2018/apr/05/demise-of-the-nation-state-rana-dasgupta, accessed 05/04/18.
8. Rahila Gupta interview with Abdullah Alaoudh via Zoom, 09/04/24.
9. Tim Jonze, 'The Nepo Baby Who Made Good: Rob Reiner on Trump, Family—and His Brilliant, Beloved Movies', *The Guardian*, 29/02/24, https://www.theguardian.com/film/2024/feb/29/the-nepo-baby-who-made-good-rob-reiner-on-trump-family-and-his-brilliant-beloved-movies, accessed 29/02/24.
10. India Today Newsdesk, 'God Chose Me for This: What PM Modi Said about the Women's Reservation Bill', *India Today*, 23/09/19, https://www.indiatoday.in/india/story/parliament-special-session-pm-modi-said-on-womens-reservation-bill-2437655-2023-09-19, accessed 28/02/24.
11. Madawi al-Rasheed, *A Most Masculine State: Gender, Politics, and Religion in Saudi Arabia*, New York: Cambridge University Press, 2013, p. 292.
12. Kate Nash, 'The Cultural Politics of Human Rights and Neoliberalism', *Journal of Human Rights* 18, no. 5 (2019), pp. 490–505.
13. Colin Hay and Michael Lister, 'Introduction: Theories of the State', in Colin Hay, Michael Lister and David Marsh (eds), *The State: Theories and Issues*, 2nd edn, London: Bloomsbury, 2022, p. 10.
14. Sylvia Walby, *Theorising Patriarchy*, Oxford: Blackwell, 1990, p. 159.
15. Catharine A Mackinnon, *Towards a Feminist Theory of the State*, London: Harvard University Press, 1989, pp. 160–1.

16. Johanna Kantola, *Feminists Theorize the State*, London: Palgrave Macmillan, 2006, pp. 4–5.
17. Anna M. Zajicek and Toni M. Calasanti, 'Patriarchal Struggles and State Practices: A Feminist, Political-Economic View', *Gender and Society* 12, no. 5 (Oct. 1998), pp. 505–27 (p. 507).
18. Kantola, *Feminists Theorize the State*, p. 10.
19. Quoted by Hans Asenbaum in an interview with Anne Phillips, 'The Politics of Presence Revisited', *Democratic Theory* 10, no. 2 (Winter 2023), pp. 80–9 (p. 80).
20. 'Global Gender Gap Report 2023', World Economic Forum, 20/06/23, https://www.weforum.org/publications/global-gender-gap-report-2023/digest/, accessed 02/08/24.
21. Rahila Gupta interview with Clanci Rosa, 22/08/23.
22. Al-Rasheed, *Most Masculine State*, p. 29.
23. Ibid., p. 293.
24. Rahila Gupta interview with Deysi Cheyne, 18/08/23.
25. Walby, *Theorising Patriarchy*, pp. 159–60.
26. Ibid., p. 159.
27. Ibid., p. 51.
28. Cynthia Enloe, 'The Persistence of Patriarchy', *New Internationalist*, 01/10/17, https://newint.org/columns/essays/2017/10/01/patriarchy-persistence, accessed 15/11/23.
29. 'Global Gender Gap Report 2020', World Economic Forum, n.d., p. 6, https://www3.weforum.org/docs/WEF_GGGR_2020.pdf, accessed 06/02/25.
30. Ibid.
31. Felix Richter, 'Gender Pay Gap Widens with Education Levels', Statista, 18/09/23, https://www.statista.com/chart/31893/female-to-male-earnings-ratio-in-the-united-states/, accessed 02/02/25.
32. Clara Martínez-Toledano, 'World Inequality Report 2022', Imperial College London and World Inequality Lab, 2022, https://www.bankofengland.co.uk/-/media/boe/files/events/2022/june/workshop-hf-and-martinez-toledano-slides.pdf, accessed 04/02/25.
33. Orlando Figes, *A People's Tragedy: The Russian Revolution 1891–1924*, London: Pimlico, 1996, p. 332.
34. Benjamin Ziemann, 'Peace Movements in Western Europe, Japan and USA since 1945: Introduction', *Mitteilungsblatt des Instituts für soziale Bewegungen* 32 (2004), pp. 5–19.

35. Quoted by Nira Yuval Davis, *Gender and Nation*, London: Sage, 1997, p. 124.
36. Thomas Piketty, *A Brief History of Inequality*, London: Belknap Press of Harvard University Press, 2022.
37. 'Feminist Foreign Policy: Where do France, Spain and Italy stand? Summary of the Latest Gender in Geopolitics Institute Report', Focus 2030, 05/02/24, https://focus2030.org/Feminist-foreign-policy-where-do-France-Spain-and-Italy-stand-Summary-of-the, accessed 06/02/25.
38. 'Inside Raqqa: Syrian Women Secretly Film to Show Life under ISIS', YouTube, 18/03/16, https://www.youtube.com/watch?v=cKmAYIZ2Hj8, accessed 31/03/20.

INDEX

abaya, 114, 117, 119
Abd al-Wahhab, 113
Abdsalam, Mona, 312
Abdullah, King of Saudi Arabia, 115
abortion
   in El Salvador, 5, 15, 35, 43, 51, 53, 56–7, 67, 73, 74, 77, 79–83, 352
   in Russia, 136–7, 142, 150, 169, 172, 177, 346
abortion, 5, 15, 35, 36, 43, 51, 53, 56–7, 67, 73, 342
Abu Bilel, 99, 104
Adrianiva, Anna, 21–2, 143, 178
advertising, 297–8
Afghanistan, 8, 10, 86, 92, 111, 114, 137, 138, 352
African National Congress (ANC), 220, 224, 225–30, 259
   corruption, 230–33, 237
   Marikana massacre (2012), 248–50
   neoliberalism, 225–30

   representation in, 237–8
   uMkhonto we Sizwe, 240
   Zuma rape trial (2005–6), 233–7, 238, 239, 240
Afrin, Delal, 318
Afrin, Rojava, 300, 329
AIDS, 222–3, 230, 234, 243–4
Aksoy, Mehmet, 296
Alaoudh, Abdullah, 128
alcohol
   in El Salvador, 68
   in Islamic State, 94
   in Russia, 146, 147, 168
   in Saudi Arabia, 87, 114, 122
Aldossari, Maryam, 124, 128
Alerta Raquel, 76
Algeria, 7, 33
Alianza Republicana Nacional (ARENA), 59, 75, 80
Alibaba, 204
All-China Women's Federation (ACWF), 180, 183, 184, 191, 192, 195, 199, 209, 211, 217

INDEX

World Women's Conference (1995), 204–8, 209
All-Russian Women's Forum, 166
ALQST, 118, 119
Alyokhina, Maria, 9, 154
Aminah, 119
Amini, Mahsa Jina, 1
Amnesty International, 33, 118
Andors, Phyllis, 185
Anglo American Corporation, 225
Anti-Corruption Foundation, 164
Anti-Cybercrime Law (Saudi Arabia, 2007), 117
Antonsdóttir, Hildur Fjóla, 289, 290
Apartheid South Africa (1948–93), 8, 36, 219–30, 235, 239–40, 248–9, 258–9
    Black Consciousness Movement, 224, 229, 259
    capitalism and, 225–30
    pass laws, 221, 223–4
    Sharpeville massacre (1960), 220–21, 249
    Soweto uprising (1976), 249
    Truth and Reconciliation Commission, 240
apostasy, 95, 100, 103
Apple, 202
Arab nationalism, 91, 113
Arab Spring (2011), 9, 89, 112, 114–15, 124, 298, 302–3
Aramco, 91–2, 111
Argentina, 35
Armand, Inessa, 140

Armenia, 176
Armenian people, 298
Ásgeirsdóttir, Berglind, 281–2
Ashman, Sam, 225, 253
Asian tigers, 184
Asmal, Kader, 221
Asociación de Mujeres de El Salvador (AMES), 47–8, 51–9
al-Assad, Bashar, 89, 298–303, 311, 319, 320, 321, 335, 336, 337
assault, *see* physical violence
Assiri, Yahya, 119
al-Atawneh, Muhammad, 110
authoritarianism, 2, 3, 6, 35, 37, 341, 342–3

Ba'athism, 7
Baai, Gandhi, 220, 224, 229, 245
baby towers, 182
baby-loss leave, 15
al-Baghdadi, Abu Bakr, 87, 93
Baghouz, Syria, 90
Bakur, 301, 304
Barber, Matthew, 100
Barrett, Michèle, 15
Barrio-18 gang, 44, 59–60, 61
Barsukov, Vladimir, 165
Barzani clan, 336
Bashkortostan, Russia, 133
Batalina, Olga, 167
de Beauvoir, Simone, 29
Bedouin, 112
Begin–Sadat Center, 108
Begum, Shamima, 95

INDEX

Beijing University's Law School, 208
Beijing Yirenpeng Centre (BYC), 210
Beijing, China
    Tiananmen Square massacre (1989), 183, 184
    UN 4th World Conference on Women (1995), 81, 181, 184, 204–8
    Victory over Violence protest (2012), 208
'Believe Together' law (2018), 78
Benediktsson, Bjarni, 272, 293
Bennoune, Karima, 96
Benya, Asanda, 246, 252
bereavement, 15
Berlin Wall, fall of (1989), 7, 24
Beslan school massacre (2004), 167
Bezuidenhout, Andries, 253
Bibler, Jared, 272
Biehl, Janet, 321
Biko, Steve, 229
Bin Laden family, 86, 114, 121
Bin Laden, Osama, 10, 87, 92
Bin Ladin, Carmen, 86, 112, 114, 122
Bitcoin, 72
Biyela, Thobeka, 257
Black Consciousness Movement, 224, 229, 259
Black Economic Empowerment (BEE), 231
Black Lives Matter, 38
Black Venus, 10
Blank, Gary, 13
Bollywood, 324
Bolsheviks, 29, 135–41, 144
Bookchin, Murray, 325–6
Booysen, Anene, 241
Botî, Walîda, 310
breastfeeding, 78
Buhlungu, Sakhela, 253
Bukele, Nayib, 6, 21, 39, 45, 50, 71–2, 75, 83–4, 341, 347
    abortion laws, 43, 77
    Bitcoin and, 71–2
    homicide rates and, 41–2, 341
    LGBT+ and, 77
    mano dura policies, 6, 21, 41, 51, 60–61, 64–5, 84, 347
    masculinity and, 21, 75
    prostitution and, 39, 64
    sex education laws, 78
    Territorial Control Plan (2019–), 65, 66
Bushveld, 245
Butler, Judith, 325
Byline, xii

Çağlayan, Handan, 316
Callimachi, Rukmini, 90
Cameroon, 84
Camp Bucca, Iraq, 88
Campo Rebelde, 58
Canada, 287
Cansiz, Sakine, 305–6, 325, 333
Cao Ju, 210
capitalism, 2, 3, 6, 7–8, 12–17, 20, 28, 37, 40, 54–5, 80, 297–8

INDEX

China and, 7, 181, 184, 189, 195, 197–204
communism and, 18, 139–40, 145, 150, 186
democracy and, 339–40
Iceland and, 6, 262–73, 275–6, 280, 292–3
Islam and, 91
necro-capitalism, 66, 84
pornography and, 28, 147
prostitution and, 29, 145
Rojava and, 297–8, 327
South Africa and, 225–30, 245–54, 352
see also neoliberalism
care work, 13, 14, 18–21
'Careful, Religion!' (2003 exhibition), 154
Carter, Jimmy, 70
Cathedral of Christ the Saviour, Moscow, 132–3
Catholicism, 35, 43, 74, 81–2, 155, 342
liberation theology, 48–51
celibacy, 315, 334
Central Intelligence Agency (CIA), 7, 91–2
Centre for Applied Legal Studies, 251, 253
Chatham House, 326
Chechen people, 298
Chechnya, 156, 161, 167
Chengdu, Sichuan, 203
Cheyne, Deysi, 54, 83
child marriage, 311

child support, 70, 80
childcare, 14, 17, 347
in China, 184–5, 187, 202
in El Salvador, 53, 54, 58, 71
in Iceland, 264, 280–82
in Russia, 138, 143, 149, 168
Chile, 16, 268
China, xiii, 3, 5, 7, 36, 38, 179–217, 341
capitalism in, 7, 181, 184, 189, 195, 197–204
childcare in, 184–5, 187, 202
common prosperity policies, 204
Confucianism, 181, 182, 183, 193, 197
Cultural Revolution (1966–76), 185, 186, 189, 191, 198
democracy and, 183, 204
domestic labour in, 184–5
domestic violence in, 205–9
education in, 186, 188, 189, 196, 199
employment in, 188, 195, 197–204, 348
family in, 180, 191, 193, 199–200, 209, 217
Feminist Five, 211–14
Four Modernisations (1979–80), 7–8, 183–6, 187, 198
Great Leap Forward (1958–62), 189, 191, 198
hukou system, 198–9
human rights in, 34, 206
Iron Girls, 180–81, 193–4

INDEX

Law on Protection of the Rights of Women (1992), 206
lying flat phenomenon (c. 2020–), 204
marriage in, 182, 196–7, 207, 209–10
Marriage Law (1950), 182, 207
migrant labour in, 198–204
Mosuo people, 11
National Programme for Women's Development (2021–30), 196
NGOs in, 181, 207, 208–10, 213, 215, 341
996 regime in, 204
Occupy Men's Toilets protest (2012), 213–14
one-child policy (1979–2015), 187–92, 194–5
pronatalist policies, 15, 199–200
representation in, 216
Safe China mission (2015–), 215
sex ratio in, 5, 187, 190, 194
sexual violence in, 207, 211–13, 214–16
Targeted Poverty Alleviation (2013–), 199
Tiananmen Square massacre (1989), 183, 184
toilet revolution (2019), 214
tradition in, 181–2
UN 4th World Conference on Women (1995), 81, 181, 184, 204–8
Victory over Violence protest (2012), 208
welfare in, 184, 186, 194–5, 216
China Women's Newspaper, 205
Chinnah, Andy, 255
Chomsky, Noam, 52
Christian Committee for the Displaced, 50
Christianity
　Catholicism, 35, 43, 74, 81–2, 155, 342
　Evangelism, 43, 67, 69–70, 74, 155, 342
　liberation theology, 48–51
　Russian Orthodox, 5, 35, 37, 131–5, 138, 144, 153–7, 165, 167, 177, 342
Chuganov, Dmitry, 161
Circassian people, 298
Cizire, Rojava, 311, 319
climate change, 352
Clinton, Hillary, 206
CO-MADRES, 50
Cockburn, Patrick, 91
Cod Wars (1958–76), 274–5
Colectiva Feminista, La, 72
Columbia University, 91
Combahee River Collective, 327
commons, 271
communism, 8, 10, 18, 69, 92
　China, 179–83, 186, 189, 198
　El Salvador, 48
　Soviet Russia, 29, 135–44, 145, 186
Compliance Advisor Ombudsman (CAO), 253

INDEX

Comunidades Eclesiales de Base (CEBs), 49, 51
condoms, 158–9, 160, 234, 244
Confucianism, 181, 182, 183, 197
Connell, Raewyn, 4, 5, 22
Consolidated Gold Fields, 227
Constitution Hill, Johannesburg, 239
contraception, 56, 158–9, 160, 191, 234, 244
Corbyn, Jeremy, 340
corporate social responsibility, 16
corruption
   in Iceland, 263, 269, 270, 293
   in South Africa, 230–33
Cossacks, 133, 135
Costa Rica, 56, 79–80
COVID-19 pandemic, xiii, 1, 20, 123, 132, 142, 169, 196, 214
Crazy English, 207
Crimea, 134, 157, 165
crisis centres, *see* refuges/crisis centres
Crocus City Hall attack (2024), 87
Cuba, 298, 332
Cultural Revolution (1966–76), 185, 186, 189, 191, 198
culture wars, 37

DAANES, *see* Rojava, 319
Dabiq, 93, 97, 98
dar al-reaya, 118–19
Davies, Will, 268
Davin, Delia, 200

Day of Family, Love, and Loyalty, 168
Day of the Unborn Child, 43
De Waal, Mandy 251
Decade of Women (1975–85), 191, 263
Deera Square, Riyadh, 85–6
Deloitte, 15
democracy, xi–xii, 2, 3, 6, 17, 37, 339–53
   China and, 183, 204
   Iceland and, 262, 263, 270, 279–80
   Islamic State and, 106
   Rojava and, 298, 299, 309–14, 318, 325–6, 329–30, 335, 337
   Russia and, 9, 150, 156, 157, 177, 341
   Saudi Arabia and, 126–9, 342–3
   South Africa and, 233, 248, 260, 341
Democratic Republic of the Congo, 31
Democratic Union Party, 299, 302, 320
Deng Xiaoping, 7–8, 183, 186
Department of Non-European Affairs, 254
Desai, Rehad, 249
Development Bank of South Africa, 227
dictatorships, 3, 6
Didion, Joan, 41
Diepsloot, Johannesburg, 241–4
Dignas, Las, 72

INDEX

Dines, Gail, 28
Ding Xuexiang, 217
direct democracy, 298–9, 348
Dirik, Dilar, 298, 304–6, 308, 328, 330
divorce
  in China, 196, 207
  in Iceland, 282
  in Ireland, 342
  in Islamic State, 103
  in Rojava, 328
  in Russia, 18, 137, 142–3, 168, 172
  in Saudi Arabia, 118
  in Syria, 311–12
domestic labour, 13, 14, 18–21
  in China, 184–5
  in El Salvador, 55–6, 62, 71
  in Iceland, 265, 280, 292
  in Rojava, 332
  in Russia, 168
  in Saudi Arabia, 122–4
domestic violence, 16, 25–8
  in China, 205–9
  in El Salvador, 63–4, 73, 74, 78
  in Iceland, 283
  in Rojava, 310, 312–13
  in Russia, 27, 134–6, 144, 146–7, 154, 165, 167, 171–5, 346
  in Saudi Arabia, 118, 120
  in South Africa, 238, 351–2
Donbas, Ukraine, 156
Dong Bian, 185
Dong Yige, 185, 202
dowries, 196, 311, 351

Economic Freedom Fighters, 236
economic violence, 74, 171, 351
Eddy, William, 91–2
Egypt, 7, 91, 113
Einarsdóttir, Þorgerður, 270
Ejército Revolucionario del Pueblo (ERP), 55
Ekaterinburg, Ural, 163
El Faro, 65, 77
El Salvador, 3, 5, 8, 16, 17, 34, 36, 37, 38, 39–84, 332, 341
  abortion laws, 5, 15, 35, 43, 51, 53, 56–7, 67, 73, 77, 79–83, 352
  'Believe Together' law (2018), 78
  civil war (1979–92), 6–7, 8–9, 32, 36, 39, 46–60, 69–70
  disappearances in, 3, 42, 44, 50, 76, 341
  domestic violence in, 63–4, 73, 74, 78
  economic violence in, 74, 351
  emigration, 59–60, 61, 66–7, 68, 70, 80
  family in, 15, 18, 40, 53, 61, 77–8, 80
  femicide in, 27, 42–3, 44, 45, 52, 74, 76, 82, 341
  Fourteen Families, 46
  gangs in, 6, 21, 23, 39–42, 44, 45, 59–69, 75–6, 83, 347
  homicide rates, 41–2, 341
  human rights in, 34, 66
  land distribution in, 46

INDEX

law on gender violence (2011), 73–4
LGBT+ in, 43, 68, 77, 84, 342
Love Turned into Food' law (2022), 78
mano dura policies, 21, 41, 42, 45, 51, 60, 64–6, 75–6, 347
marriage in, 44, 46
masculinity in, 21, 24, 41, 62, 64, 74, 75, 81
motherhood in, 43, 61, 63, 66–7, 68, 71, 77–8, 80
'Nacer con cariño' law (2021), 77, 78
neoliberalism in, 9, 40, 59, 71
Peace Accords (1992), 8–9, 40, 59, 70, 72, 149
religion in, 35, 41, 43, 44, 48–51, 67, 68–70, 74, 77, 80–81, 83
sex education in, 77, 78, 79
sexual violence in, 30, 43, 52, 57, 63, 67, 68, 73, 76–80
single motherhood in, 43, 61, 68, 70, 71, 80
tattoos in, 21, 45, 64
teenage pregnancies in, 76, 77, 78–80
Territorial Control Plan (2019–), 65, 66
US, relations with, 6–7, 47, 49–50, 52, 59–60, 69–72
women's organisations in, 72–7, 149
Elizondo, Edith, 3, 45, 76
employment, 14, 15–16, 151, 264, 267, 280, 283, 348
in China, 188, 195, 197–204, 348
in Russia, 138–44, 151–2, 170
in Saudi Arabia, 124–6
End of Equality, The (Campbell), xi
Ending Violence against Women (2006 report), 26
Engelbrecht, Wynand, 256
Engels, Friedrich, 18, 139, 343
Enloe, Cynthia, 347
Enteo, Dmitry, 154
Erdoğan, Recep Tayyip, 295, 311, 328–9
Erelle, Anna, 98–100, 104
European Court of Human Rights (ECHR), 290
European Network of Migrant Women, 132
European Union (EU), 73
Eurovision Song Contest, 174
Evangelism, 43, 67, 69–70, 155, 342
Eve and the New Jerusalem (Taylor), 13
Everyday Terrorism (Pain), 26
Ezidi people, 100–104, 308

Faisal, King of Saudi Arabia, 106
family, 18–21
in China, 180, 191, 193, 199–200, 209, 217
in El Salvador, 15, 18, 40, 53, 61, 77–8, 80

INDEX

in Russian Federation, 15, 18, 134–5, 149–50, 155–6
in Soviet Union, 19, 138–44, 147
Family Party, 154
family wage, 13–14
Farabundo Martí National Liberation Front (FMLN), 32, 39–40, 43, 47–8, 51–9, 72, 80, 347
   Asociación de Mujeres, 51–9
   Ejército Revolucionario del Pueblo, 55
   Fuerzas Populares de Liberación, 48, 49, 55, 58
   government (2009–19), 60, 71, 75, 82
   liberation theology and, 49
   women in, 47–8, 51–9, 62–3
Farlam Commission (2012), 250
fatawa, 91, 103, 111–12
Feinstein, Andrew, 230
Fem Fest, 166
female genital mutilation (FGM), 101, 120–21, 345
femicide, 5
   in China, 182
   in El Salvador, 27, 42–3, 44, 45, 52, 74, 76, 82–3, 341
   in Iceland, 284
   in Kurdistan, 300, 311, 312
   in Russia, 146–7, 171
   in South Africa, 242–3, 352
feminism, xiii, 2, 3
   capitalism and, xiii, 12–17, 37, 54–5, 150

   resistance, 31–6
   second wave (1960s–70s), 16, 19, 25–6
   Seneca Falls Convention (1848), 12
   socialism and, xiii, 13–14, 16
   unpaid work and, 18–21
   violence and, 25–31
Feminist Anti-War Resistance (FAR), 175–6
Feminist Five, 211–14
fertility treatment, 15
Figes, Orlando, 348
Financial Times, 204
Fine, Ben, 225, 226, 247, 253
Finkbeiner, Elena, 274
Finnbogadóttir, Vigdís, 279
First World War (1914–18), 135, 141, 284, 339
fishing industry, 274–9
Flach, Anja, 307
Floyd, George, 1
foot binding, 182
football, 154, 160, 302
Forbes, 15
forced marriage, 311, 314, 345
Ford Foundation, 245
Forty Forties, 154
Foundation for Social and Cultural Initiatives, 169
Four Modernisations (1979–80), 7–8, 183–6, 187, 198
Foxconn, 202
France, 337, 352
Francis, Pope, 157

INDEX

Fraser, Nancy, xiii, 16
Frazer, Elizabeth, 25, 205, 206–7
Free Syrian Army, 304
Freedom Charter (1955), 224
Friedman, Eli, 211
Friedman, Milton, 225
FSB, 158, 163
Fuerzas Populares de Liberación (FPL), 48, 49, 55, 58
Fundación Sí a la Vida, 81

Gagarin, Yuri, 153
Gamble, Andrew, 268
Gardner, Richard, 283
Gaza, 1
Geerdink, Fréderike, 308, 316–17
gender dysphoria, 15
gender pay gap, 14, 15–16, 151, 264, 267, 280, 283, 348
Girls against the Draft, 161
Gísladóttir, Sigrún Ingibjörg, 290
Gíslason, Ingólfur, 281, 282
Gissurarson, Hannes Hólmsteinn, 267
Global Centre for Countering Extremist Ideology (ETIDAL), 109
Global Gender Gap Report, 345
Global Initiative against Transnational Crime, 233
Global Leaders' Meeting on Women's Empowerment (2015), 211
globalisation, 135, 138
God & Country (2024 documentary), 342

God's Will, 154
Goldberg, Steven, xii
Goldwater, Barry, 268
GONGOs, 166
Gorbachev, Mikhail, 8, 143, 147
Gqola, Pumla, 238, 241
Graeber, David, 308, 330
Great Leap Forward (1958–62), 189, 191, 198
Greece, 195
Green Door, Johannesburg, 239, 242–4
Greenhalgh, Susan, 187, 189
Grímsson, Ólafur Ragnar, 271
Grinda Gonzalez, José, 164
Growth, Employment and Redistribution (GEAR), 225–6, 229
Guangzhou, Guangdong, 203, 210, 213–14
Guatemala, 70
Guðjónsdóttir, Sigríður Björk, 288
Guevara, Ernesto 'Che', 51
Gulf War
  First (1990–91), 111–12
  Second (2003–11), 88, 92
Gunnarsdóttir, Halla, 269, 271, 287, 291, 292
Gunnlaugsson, Sigmundur, 273
Guo Jianmei, 206, 208
Gupta family, 232, 237
Gylfason, Thorvaldur, 279

Haarde, Geir, 271, 272
Hadebe, Ntokozo, 242

INDEX

al-Hadi, Humaydi Daham, 311
Haj, 126
Hall, Stuart, 299
Happy Birthday, Mr Putin! calendar, 159
al-Harithi, Khulud, 98
Hartmann, Heidi, 12–13, 14
Harvey, David, 268
Hassim, Shireen, 226, 228, 238
al-Hathloul, Lina, 117, 118, 122, 129
al-Hathloul, Loujain, 109, 116–17, 119, 127
Hauksdóttir, Arna, 285
Hay'at Tahrir al-Sham (HTS), 300, 304, 312, 335, 337
Hayek, Friedrich, 268
He Guangye, 195
He Zhongyang, 208
hegemonic masculinity, 21–5
Helie-Lucas, Marieme, 33
Her Story (2022 film), 193
Herland (Gilman), 333
Herman, Judith Lewis, 235, 284
Herrera, Morena, 56, 57, 72, 79, 81
Hershatter, Gail, 193, 201
heval, 316
Hêzên Parastina Civakî (HPC), 309
Hêzên Xweparastinê (HXP), 308–9
hijab, *see* veiling
Himmelweit, Susan, 19–20
Hindu nationalism, 37, 341, 342
hippy movement, 19
Hiroshima atomic bombing (1945), 349
hisba, 97, 108
Hitachi, 203
HIV/AIDS, 222–3, 230, 234, 243–4
Hobsbawm, Eric, 182
Holtzman, Zelda, 229, 259–60
#HomeDetainees, 119
homosexuality, *see* LGBT+
Hong Kong, 184
honour killings, 300, 311
horizontal power, 343
House of the People, 310
House, Karen Elliott, 114
Houthis, 126
Huang Xueqin, 216
Huang Yuqin, 200
hukou system, 198–9
Human Rights Commission, Saudi Arabia, 120
human rights, 2, 26, 28, 31, 33–4, 343–4
  in China, 34, 206
  in El Salvador, 34, 66
  in Russia, 34, 156, 157
  in Saudi Arabia, 34, 120
Hungary, 341
Hussein, Saddam, 7, 88, 299
Hutchings, Kimberly, 25, 205, 206–7
hyperinflation, 151

#IAmNotAfraidToSpeak, 178

INDEX

Ibn Saud, 91, 112–13
Ice Age, 10
Iceland, 3, 6, 9, 261–93, 342, 345, 351
  corruption in, 263, 269, 270, 293
  democracy in, 262, 263, 270, 279–80
  domestic labour in, 265, 280, 292
  domestic violence in, 283
  employment in, 264, 267, 280
  Equal Rights Law (1976), 9
  financial crisis (2008–11), 269, 271–3, 282, 293
  fishing industry, 274–9
  gender pay gap in, 264, 267, 280, 283
  immigration in, 277, 292, 293
  neoliberalism in, 6, 262–73, 275–6, 280, 292–3
  parental leave in, 280–83
  policing in, 288–90
  poverty in, 274
  prostitution in, 286–7
  representation in, 264–5, 279–80, 345
  sexual violence in, 27, 264, 283–90
  Slutwalk, 287
  state capture in, 266–71, 342, 351
  Women's Day Off (1975), 9, 263–6, 291
  women's movement, 263–6

Icelandic Libertarian Alliance, 268
Ikhwan, 112
illiteracy, 47, 189
immigration, *see* migration
incels, 22
Independence Party, 266, 268, 272, 273, 280, 293
Independent, The, 103
India, xii, 6, 11, 37, 341, 342
Indignados, 343
Individual Transferable Quota (ITQ), 275–6
Indonesia, 93
Inevitability of Patriarchy, The (Goldberg), xii
Instituto Salvadoreño de Formación Profesional (INSAFORP), 66
International Finance Corporation (IFC), 252, 253
International Labour Organisation (ILO) 210
International Monetary Fund (IMF), 71–2
International Women's Day, 136, 173, 212, 295
International Women's Month, 43
internet, 119–20
invented tradition, 182
iPhone, 202
Iran, 1, 10, 111, 113–14, 126, 137, 295, 299, 336
Iraq
  Ezidi genocide (2014–17), 100, 308

INDEX

Gulf War I (1990–91), 111–12
Gulf War II (2003–11), 88, 92
ISIS caliphate (2014–19), 86, 88, 91, 92, 94, 100–104, 296
Kurdistan, 295, 297, 299, 316, 320, 336
Saddam government (1979–2003), 7, 88, 91–2
Ireland, 342
Iron Girls, 180–81, 193–4
Islam, 6, 10, 35, 86, 87, 349, 352
apostasy, 95, 100, 103, 104–5
dress codes, 1, 93, 94, 95, 104, 114, 117, 155
fatawa, 91, 103, 111–12
Haj, 126
Russia and, 137, 155–6, 350
Salafism, 86, 88, 108, 109
Sharia law, 86, 91, 97, 104, 106, 110–12, 113, 311–12
Shi'ism, 86, 88, 104
Soviet Union and, 137
Sunnism, 86, 88, 104
Ummah, 93, 97
Wahhabism, 88, 93, 106, 108
Islamic State (ISIS), 3, 6, 32, 61, 86–109, 328, 335, 349, 352–3
apostasy in, 95, 100, 103, 104–5
Battle of Raqqa (2017), 296
Crocus City Hall attack (2024), 87
defeat of caliphate (2017–19), 7, 107–9, 296, 313
economic underpinnings, 90–91

education system, 105–7
Ezidi enslavement, 100–104, 308
Kobanî siege (2014), 304
recruitment, 93–100
Saudi Arabia and, 6, 86–8, 89, 92–3, 126
Islamism, 8
Saudi Arabia and, 87, 91–2, 107, 111, 113
Syria and, 300, 303, 337
Íslandsbanki, 293
Israel, 1, 7, 19, 45, 158
Istanbul Convention (2014), 290
Ixchel, 45, 76
Izmaylovo family, 163

Jakobsdóttir, Katrín, 273, 280, 287, 291, 292
Japan, 184, 349
al-Jazeera, 278
jihadi brides, 95
Jineolojî, 323–4
JINHA, 317
Jinwar, Rojava, 11, 314, 333
Johannesburg, Gauteng
Constitution Hill, 239
Diepsloot, 241–4
Usindiso fire (2023), 254–9
Johnson, Janet Elise, 270
Johnson, Kay Ann, 182, 183
Jónsdóttir, Guðrún, 265, 279, 285, 286
Juárez, Silvia, 42, 64, 70, 73, 78, 80
judiciaries, 2, 341

455

INDEX

Júlíusson, Kristján Þór, 278
justice gap, 285–6

kafala system, 122
Kandiyoti, Deniz, 24
Kang Keqing, 185
kanga, 234
Karklins, Rasma, 270
Kasrils, Ronnie, 227, 234, 237
Katsav, Moshe, 158
Kenya, 11, 314
Kerala, India, 11
KGB, 147, 153, 158
Khachaturyan sisters, 134, 175
Khampepe, Sisi, 259
al-Khansaa Brigade, 104
Khashoggi, Jamal, 126
Khatib, Lina, 326
Khomeini, Ruhollah, 10, 113
Khryushi Protiv, 161
Khumalo, Sibongile, 241
Kirill, Patriarch of Moscow, 138, 153, 155, 156, 157, 166, 177
Kobanî, Rojava, 303–4
Kollontai, Alexandra, 29, 136, 142, 144–5, 146
Koma Civakên Kurdistanê (KCK), 302
Kongra Star, 300–301, 305, 308, 309, 310, 322, 323, 329, 332
Kormukhin, Andrei, 154
Kruglov, Artyom, 163
Kurdistan Workers' Party, 18, 24, 58, 299–302, 304–7, 325, 331, 333

Kurds
  ISIS War (2014–19), *see* Islamic State
  liberation movement, 18, 24, 58, 299, 300, 301–2, 304–7, 311, 350
  Rojava, *see* Rojava
Kursk disaster (2000), 159
Kuwait, 111–12
Kuzwayo, Fezekile Ntsukela, 233–7, 238

Last Utopia, The (Moyn), 33
Laub, Dori, 239–40
Law on Protection of the Rights of Women (1992), 206
Lazo, Nubia, 68, 79–80
Le Pen, Marine, 340
Lean In (Sandberg), 17, 37
Leballo, Potlako, 241
Lee, Kim, 207
Left-Green Movement, 271, 273, 278, 280, 292, 293
Lekekela, Brown, 243
Lenin, Vladimir, 136–7, 139, 140–41, 142, 144, 147, 153
Lerner, Gerda, 11–12
LGBT+, 19, 23, 43, 68, 77, 84, 342
  in El Salvador, 43, 68, 77, 84, 342
  in Iceland, 271
  in Islamic State, 94
  in Rojava, 317
  in Russia, 137, 142, 155, 156, 170, 174, 175, 350

456

INDEX

in Saudi Arabia, 109, 122
in South Africa, 234
Li Hua, 192
Li Maizi, 213–14
Li Yang, 207
liberal feminism, 8, 150, 344
Liberal Party, 271
Liberating Life (Öcalan), 327
liberation theology, 48–51
Like a Rolling Stone (2024 film), 193
Lin Delia, 215
literacy, 32, 47, 186
Litvinenko, Alexander, 164
Liu Li, 214
Liu Meng, 214
Lobos, Norma Leticia, 77
loli image, 194
Long March (1934–5), 185
Lonmin, 35, 248–54
Lorde, Audre, 32
Los Angeles Times, 313
'Love Turned into Food' law (2022), 78
Lowe Morna, Colleen, 237
Lu Jun, 210

Ma, Jack, 204
Mackinnon, Catharine, 315, 344
Macro-Economic Research Group, 226
Madikizela Mandela, Winnie, 219–20, 228, 230, 236, 259
Madonsela, Thuli, 231–2
Madumise-Pajibo, Brenda, 244
Magyar, Bálint, 165
mahram, 97, 98, 112
Mail and Guardian, 238, 242
Mala Gel, 310
Malan, Mia, 241–4
Malaysia, 195
Malema, Julius, 236
Mali family, 242–3
Malofeyev, Konstantin, 165
Manbij, Rojava, 313
Mandela, Nelson, 219–21, 226, 227–8, 229, 236, 259
Mandela United Football Club, 259–60
Manizha, 174
Mansfield, Becky, 276
Manuel, Trevor, 226
Manzini, Manala, 238
Mao Zedong, 183, 186, 189, 198
Maoism, 48
Maphatsoe, Kebby, 237
Marikana massacre (2012), 35, 246, 248–50
marriage, 29, 311, 345
in China, 182, 196–7, 207, 209–10
in El Salvador, 44, 46
in Islamic State, 95–100, 103–4
in Rojava, 311, 328
in Russia, 18, 137, 139, 142–4, 168, 172
in Saudi Arabia, 118–19, 121
Marshall Islands, 278
Martinez, Raúl, 54
Marxism, 29–30, 55, 153, 157, 186, 216, 299, 325, 346

INDEX

Marzouki, Moncef, 9
masculinity, 4, 21–5, 340
  in El Salvador, 21, 24, 41, 62, 64, 74, 75, 81
  in Russia, 21–2, 23–4, 133, 134, 157–63, 167, 177
Massey, Doreen, 274
Masuhlo, Paulina, 246, 249, 251
matrilineal societies, 4, 11
matrilocal societies, 4
Matveychev, Oleg, 176–7
Mazzucato, Mariana, 20
Mbeki, Thabo, 222, 226, 227, 229, 230–31, 235–6
Mbembe, Achille, 84
Mecca, Saudi Arabia, 114
  Grand Mosque occupation (1979), 111, 114
  Haj, 126
media, 2
Medina Haj, 126
Medina, Saudi Arabia, 114
Medvedev, Dmitry, 169
Mejía, Domitila Ayala, 32
Mélenchon, Jean-Luc, 340
Mélidas, Las, 82
menopause, 15
#MeToo movement, 16, 22, 214–16, 241, 287
Metropolitan Cathedral, San Salvador, 50–51
metrosexual image, 21
Mexico, 70, 199, 213
Michel, Sonya, 20
Microsoft, 15

Mies, Maria, 168, 325
migration, 15, 20
  China and, 198–204
  El Salvador and, 59–60, 61, 66–7, 68, 70, 80
  Iceland and, 277, 292, 293
  Saudi Arabia and, 93, 95, 115, 122–3, 126–9
  South Africa and, 247, 250–51, 254
Minerals Energy Complex (MEC), 247, 253
misogyny
  in El Salvador, 74
  in Russia, 133, 136
  in South Africa, 236
misogyny, 22, 28
Mitchell, Timothy, 7, 91
Mizulina, Elena, 156, 167
Modi, Narendra, 37, 340, 342
Mohammed bin Salman, Saudi Crown Prince, 85, 93, 116, 123, 125, 126, 128–9, 346
Molodaia Gvardiia Edinoi Rossii, 161
Monaco, 261
Mongolia, 213
Montoya, Ainhoa, 46
Moravian Venus, 10
Morocco, 213
Moscow, Russia
  Cathedral of Christ the Saviour, 132–3
  Crocus City Hall attack (2024), 87

INDEX

Dubrovka Theatre siege (2002), 167
Moscow, Russia, 170
Mosul, Iraq, 89, 105, 107, 296
Mosuo people, 11
motherhood, 14, 17
    in China, 197
    in El Salvador, 43, 61, 63, 66–7, 68, 71, 77–8, 80
    in Iceland, 265, 280–83
    in Russia, 15, 142, 148, 168–9
    see also single motherhood
Mothers of the Plaza De Mayo, 35
Mothers, Comrades, Goddesses (Çağlayan), 316
Motsei, Mmatshilo, 238
Motshekga, Angie, 238
Movement for a Democratic Society, 309
Moyn, Samuel, 33
Mozambique, 213
MS-13 (Mara Salvatrucha), 44, 59–60, 61, 67
Mtintso, Thenjiwe, 240
Mulan (1998 film), 179
Munk-Madsen, Eva, 276
Murphy, Rachel, 199
Musk, Elon, 22, 339
Muslim Brotherhood, 94, 113, 126
mutawa, 114
muzhik, 133, 157–63
Myakayaka-Manzini, Mavivi, 238
Myanmar, 341

al-Naba, 96

Nacer con cariño law (2021), 77, 78
Nagasaki atomic bombing (1945), 349
Naidoo, Jay, 227
Najmabadi, Afsaneh, 349
Namibia, 278
Narodnik movement, 136
Nash, Kate, 33
Nashi, 160–61
Nasser, Gamal Abdel, 7, 113
National AIDS Council, 234
National Union of Mineworkers (NUM), 248–9
nationalism, 15, 23, 31, 37, 326, 340
    in El Salvador, 340–41
    in Iceland, 275
    in India, 37
    in Kurdistan, 336
    in Russia, 169, 340–41
    in Saudi Arabia, 6, 112, 126, 340–41
    in United States, 70
Navalny, Alexei, 164
Navas, María Candelaria, 53
necro-capitalism, 66, 84
neo-Nazis, 154, 160
neoliberalism, 2, 6, 7, 8, 16–17, 20, 28, 297, 340
    in China, 194
    in El Salvador, 9, 40, 59, 71
    in Iceland, 6, 262–73, 275–6, 280, 292–3
    in Russia, 151, 171

INDEX

in South Africa, 225–30, 248, 352
Neolithic period, 318, 323, 330
Nepal, 332
New Economic Policy (1921–31), 186
New Ideas, 75
new wars, 31
New York Times, 90, 116, 311
Newman, Susan, 225
Ngcobo, Sphiwe, 257
Nicaragua, 56, 332
nihilist movement, 136
Niida, Noboru, 182
Nkandla, KwaZulu–Natal, 231–2
No to Violence, 175
non-governmental organisations (NGOs), 2, 341
   in China, 181, 207, 208–10, 213, 215, 341
   in El Salvador, 73
   in Russia, 155, 171–3, 341
non-state actors, 33
non-violence, 31
Northern Ireland, 260
nostalgia, 37, 157
novels, 120
Nuevo Cuscatlán, El Salvador, 43, 75
al-Nusra, 337

O'Sullivan See, Katherine, 171
Obama, Barack, 71, 108
Observatorios de Violencia, 76
Öcalan, Abdullah, 18, 24, 58, 299–302, 305, 311, 314, 322–32, 343
Occupy Men's Toilets protest (2012), 213–14
Occupy movement (2011–16), 343
Oddsson, Davíð, 268, 272
OECD, 14, 195, 280, 282
Öfgar, 288, 290
oil industry, 91–2, 111, 125, 336
Olympic Games
   Beijing (2008), 207
   Sochi (2014), 133
Omar, Amina, 311, 317, 332
One in Nine Campaign, 237
one-child policy (1979–2015), 187–92, 194–5
Operation Big Sister (2011), 286
Oppenheimer, Caroline, 227–8
Oppenheimer, Ernest, 223, 225
Orange Revolution (2004–5), 160
Order of Maternal Glory, 142
organised crime
   in El Salvador, 6, 21, 23, 39–42, 44, 45, 59–69, 75–6, 83
   in Russia, 23, 154, 160–66, 177
   in South Africa, 233
Orientación, 81
Origin of the Family, The (Engels), 18, 139
ORMUSA, 42, 72, 73, 76
al-Otaibi, Manahel, 117
Owen, Margaret, 312–13

pacifism, 31
Padayachee, Vishnu, 225
Palestine, 1, 7, 301
Pan African Congress (PAC), 241

INDEX

Panama Papers leak (2016), 273
Panyu, Guangzhou, 203, 210
parental leave, 15, 143, 280–83
Partiya Karkerên Kurdistanê (PKK), 18, 24, 58, 299–302, 304–7, 325, 331, 333
Partiya Yekîtiya Demokrat (PYD), 299, 302, 320
pass laws, 221, 223–4
Patriarchs, The (Saini), 3, 11, 343
patriarchy, xi–xiii, 2–6
   biology and, xii, 4
   capitalism and, 12–18, 37, 54–5, 80
   contingency, 4
   family and, 18–21
   hegemonic masculinity, 21–5
   origins, 10–12
   public vs private spheres, 3, 5
   violence and, 25–31
patrimonial violence, 74, 351
Pegasus, 45
Pelicot, Gisèle, 2, 30
Peña, Lorena, 82
Peng, Ito, 20
pensions, 15
People's Protection Units, 101, 303
Personal Status Law (Saudi Arabia, 2022), 117–18
Peterson, Dahlia, 215
Pétursdóttir, Gyða Margrét, 270
Philippines, 93, 341
Phillips, Anne, 216, 345
physical violence, 22, 26, 27, 28
   in China, 208
   in El Salvador, 63
   in Islamic State, 102
   in Russia, 134, 167
   in South Africa, 238
pigeons, 104
Pigs Don't Agree, 161
Pinkerton, Evelyn, 276
Pinochet, Augusto, 268
polygyny, 103–4, 234, 235, 300, 311, 313, 337, 343
Popova, Alena, 167
population, 14–15, 80–81
   in China, 5, 15, 187–92, 194–5, 199–200, 204
   in Russia, 15, 141–2, 160, 168–9
populism, 2, 15, 21, 37, 45, 75, 168, 340, 351
pornography, 16, 28, 103, 147, 149
post-conflict societies, 30
poverty
   in China, 186, 198, 199
   in El Salvador, 40, 47, 49, 51, 59, 62, 63, 70, 71, 81, 146
   in Iceland, 274
   in Russia, 144, 145, 146
   in Saudi Arabia, 121, 122, 124, 125–6
   in South Africa, 221, 222, 229, 230, 231, 242–4
Pravda, 142
Price Waterhouse Coopers (PwC), 14
Prigozhin, Yevgeny, 23, 134, 162, 164–5

INDEX

prisons, 162
privatisation, 16, 20
  in China, 185, 187
  in El Salvador, 46, 59
  in Iceland, 268, 270, 275–6, 293
  in Saudi Arabia, 125
  in South Africa, 229
Progressive Party, 271
Progressive Women's League, 237
pronatalism, 15
  in China, 15, 199–200
  in Russia, 15, 142, 160, 168–9
Property Owners and Managers Association, 256
prostitution, 16, 28, 29, 84
  in Iceland, 286–7
  in Russia, 29, 136, 144–6, 148, 169–70
Pu Wei, 205
Pushkina, Oksana, 154, 170
Pussy Riot, 9, 132–3, 152, 154, 158–9, 173, 175, 346
Putin, Vladimir, 21, 23–4, 132, 133, 135, 151, 152–78, 340, 346
  anti-LGBT laws, 170, 175
  masculinity and, 23–4, 133, 157–62, 167, 340
  organised crime and, 163–6
  Orthodox Church and, 37, 132, 134, 152–7

al-Qaeda, 94, 109, 311, 337
  in Iraq (AQI), 88
  September 11 attacks (2001), 114

al-Qahtani, Saud, 109
Qamişlo, Rojava, 296–7, 303, 317, 328
Qandil Mountains, 307–8, 316
Qianqian Law Firm, 208
Quest for Democracy, 127–8
Qur'an, 35, 87, 106, 115, 352

Racioppi, Linda, 170–71
racism, 15, 255, 337, 344
radicalism, 349
Ramadan, 87
Ramaphosa, Cyril, 245, 249
Ramirez, Lesly, 79
Ranger, Terence, 182
rape, 14, 28, 29, 30–31
  in El Salvador, 43, 52, 57, 63, 67, 68, 73, 77–80
  in Iceland, 264, 283–90
  in Islamic State, 100–104
  in Rojava, 315–17
  in Russia, 144, 158, 166, 172
  in Saudi Arabia, 120–21, 123
  in South Africa, 233–7, 238–45
Raqqa, Syria, 89, 101, 107, 296, 297, 313, 353
al-Rasheed, Madawi, 110, 115, 120, 128, 343, 346
Rathbone, Eleanor, 13
Reagan, Ronald, 7, 69–70, 268
refuges/crisis centres, 25–6
  in Russia, 171–2
  in Saudi Arabia, 118–19
  in South Africa, 242–4, 245, 254
regressive modernisation, 3

INDEX

Reiner, Rob, 342
religion, 5, 8, 31, 33, 35
   see also Christianity; Islam
remittances, 70–71, 200
representation
   in China, 216
   in Iceland, 264–5, 279–80
   in South Africa, 237–8
reproductive rights, 14–15, 36, 40
   in El Salvador, 5, 15, 35, 43, 51, 53, 56–7, 67, 73, 77, 79–83, 352
   in Russia, 136–7, 142, 150, 169, 172, 177
   in South Africa, 244
Resistencia Nacional (RN), 72
Revista la Brújula, 42, 44
Revolution in Rojava (Flach), 307
Reykjavik Theatre Company, 279
Rhodes, Cecil, 223, 247
Rimelan, Rojava, 322
Rivers, Angela, 256
Riyadh, Saudi Arabia, 85–6
Road Unforeseen, A (Tax), 316, 331
Roe v. Wade (1973), 36
Rofel, Lisa, 192
Rojava, xii, 3, 6, 7, 9, 11, 32, 36, 101, 295–338, 343, 352–3
   democracy in, 298, 299, 309–14, 318, 325–6, 329–30, 335, 337, 343
   domestic labour in, 332
   domestic violence in, 310, 312–13
   economy, 318–21, 334–5

   femicide in, 300, 311, 312
   football riots (2004), 302, 303
   ideological training in, 321–4
   ISIS ideology in, 107–8
   ISIS War (2014–19), *see* Islamic State
   sexual violence in, 315–17
Rojava Information Centre (RIC), 334–5
Romero, Óscar, 48, 49–51
Rosa, Clanci, 42, 44, 346
Rossman, Ella, 34, 350
Rowbotham, Sheila, 136, 141
Russian Civil War (1917–23), 135, 141
Russian Federation (1991–), xiii, 3, 5, 8, 16, 34, 36–8, 131–5, 148–78, 340, 341, 346–7, 351
   abortion laws, 150, 169, 172, 177, 346
   anti-NGO law (2006), 172
   Beslan school massacre (2004), 167
   blasphemy law (2013), 152
   Chechen Wars (1994–2009), 156, 161, 167
   conscription in, 161, 169
   constitutional crisis (1993), 149
   Crimea annexation (2014), 134, 157, 165
   Crocus City Hall attack (2024), 87
   democracy and, 9, 150, 156, 157, 177, 341
   domestic violence in, 27,

134–6, 144, 146–7, 154, 165, 167, 171–5, 346, 350
Donbas War (2014–), 156
Dubrovka Theatre siege (2002), 167
employment in, 151–2, 170
family in, 15, 18, 134–5, 149–50, 155–6
faux feminism in, 166
football hooligans in, 154, 160
gangs in, 23, 154, 160–63
human rights in, 34, 156, 157, 341
hyperinflation (1992), 151
IWD protests (2006), 173
Kursk disaster (2000), 159
LGBT+ in, 137, 142, 155, 156, 170, 174, 175, 350
liberal feminism, 8, 150
mafia in, 163–6, 177
masculinity in, 21–2, 23–4, 133, 134, 157–63, 167, 177
neo-Nazis in, 154, 160
neoliberalism in, 151, 171
NGOs in, 155, 171–3, 341
pronatalism in, 15, 142, 160, 168–9
prostitution in, 146, 148, 169–70
Pussy Riot, 9, 132–3, 152, 154, 158–9, 173, 175, 346
religion in, 5, 35, 37, 131–5, 138, 152–7, 165, 167, 177
Rojava, relations with, 337
sex ratio in, 168
sexual violence in, 134, 144, 158, 166, 172, 174, 178
single motherhood in, 137, 138, 168
Snow Revolution (2011–13), 9, 156
Sochi Winter Olympics (2014), 133
Ukraine War (2014–), 23–4, 134, 142, 156, 161, 169, 170, 175–6, 178, 346
Western values and, 135, 138, 150, 168
women's organisations in, 166–7, 170–77
Russian Orthodox Church, 5, 35, 37, 131–5, 138, 144, 153–7, 165, 167, 177, 342, 346
Russian Revolution (1917), 135–6, 141
Russo-Ukrainian War (2014–), 23–4, 134, 161, 169, 178, 346, 350
  anti-war movement, 350, 175–6, 346, 350
  Crimea annexation (2014), 134, 157, 165
  Donbas War (2014–), 156
  masculinity and, 23–4
  Order of Maternal Glory, 142
  Orthodox Church and, 156
  prostitution and, 170
  Wagner Group, 23, 134
Rustenburg, South Africa, 245–54
Rustomjee, Zavareh, 247

INDEX

RÚV, 278
Rwanda, 341

Sachs, Albie, 221
Saini, Angela, 3, 11, 343
Salafism, 86, 88, 108, 109
Salman, King of Saudi Arabia, 85
same-sex marriage, 29, 159
Samherji, 278
San Salvador, El Salvador, 45, 50–51, 58–9, 71, 75
Sánchez-Cerén, Salvador, 73
Sandberg, Sheryl, 17, 37
Sanders, Bernie, 340
SARA, 312
Şaredariye, Berivan, 314, 335
Saudi Arabia, xiii, 3, 6, 9–10, 35–8, 85–8, 110–29, 341, 346, 352
    Anti-Cybercrime Law (2007), 117
    class in, 114, 121–6
    dar al-reaya, 118–19
    diaspora, 125–9
    domestic labour in, 122–4
    domestic violence in, 118, 120
    driving ban (1990–2017), 109, 111, 115, 116–17, 346
    education system, 106–7
    emigration, 95, 126–9
    employment in, 124–6
    executions in, 85–6
    fatawa in, 91, 111–12
    guardianship system, 117–18, 121
    Gulf War (1990–91), 111–12
    Haj, 126
    human rights in, 34, 120
    internet in, 119–20
    Islamic State War (2014–19), 108–9
    Islamism and, 87, 91–2, 107, 111, 113
    kafala system, 122
    Khashoggi murder (2018), 126
    liberalisation policies, 108, 109, 110, 115–18, 123, 128
    mahram system, 97, 98, 112
    marriage in, 118–19, 121
    Mecca Mosque occupation (1979), 111, 114
    migrant labour in, 93, 115, 122–3
    National Family Protection Programme, 120
    novels in, 120
    oil industry, 91–2, 111, 125, 336
    pendulum of freedoms, 110–21
    Personal Status Law (2022), 117–18
    religious nationalism, 6, 112, 126
    Saudisation policies, 93, 115, 123, 124
    September 11 attacks (2001), 114
    sexual violence in, 120–21, 123
    Shura Council, 110–11, 115
    Soviet–Afghan War (1979–89), 92, 114
    temporary marriages in, 103, 112

INDEX

tourism, 125, 129
United States, relations with, 91–2, 111–12, 114, 129
Vision 2030 programme, 123, 125, 126, 129
Wahhabism, 88, 93, 106, 110
Save the Children, 105
Schreiner, Olive, 247
Scottish Women's Aid, 26
Seawomen of Iceland (Willson), 274, 275, 276
'Second Coming, The' (Yeats), 339
Second Vatican Council (1962–5), 48–9
Second World War (1939–45), 132, 142, 168
second-wave feminism (1960s–70s), 16, 19, 25–6
secularism, 35, 152, 207, 300, 307, 312, 327, 331
Sejake, Wellington, 240
Seljan, Helgi, 278
Semo, Alan, 320, 321
Sen, Amartya, 190
Seneca Falls Convention (1848), 12
September 11 attacks (2001), 114
sex education, 77, 78, 79
sex ratios
  in China, 5, 187, 190
  in Russia, 141, 168
sex-positive activism, 28
sexual harassment, 16, 23, 28
  in China, 202, 211–13, 214–16
  in Russia, 136, 152
  in Saudi Arabia, 124
  in South Africa, 252
sexual violence, 14, 25, 26, 28–31
  in China, 207, 211–13, 214–16
  in El Salvador, 43, 52, 57, 63, 67, 68, 73, 76–80
  in Iceland, 264, 283–90
  in Islamic State, 100–104
  in Rojava, 315–17
  in Russia, 134, 144–6, 158, 166, 172, 174, 178
  in Saudi Arabia, 120–21, 123
  in South Africa, 30, 233–7, 238–45
Shaanxi, China, 201
Shaik, Schabir, 231
al-Sharaa, Ahmed, 312
shareholder activism, 15
Sharia law, 86, 91, 97, 104, 106, 110–12, 113, 311–12
Sharpeville massacre (1960), 220–21, 249
Shi'a Islam, 86, 88, 104
al-Shura Council, 110–11, 115
Sibanye-Stillwater, 253
Siglufjörður, Iceland, 275
Sigurðardóttir, Jóhanna, 271, 273
Sigurgeirsdóttir, Silla, 269
Sihle, Kenneth, 258
Sikhala Sonke, 251
Singapore, 197
single motherhood, 347
  in China, 193
  in El Salvador, 43, 61, 68, 70, 71, 80

INDEX

in Russia, 137, 138, 168
Sinjar, Iraq, 100, 308
Sisulu, Albertina, 239
Sithole, Moses, 236
Slave Lodge, Cape Town, 239
Slovo, Joe, 230
Slutwalk, 287
Smith, Joan, 27
Snow Revolution (2011–13), 9
Sochi Winter Olympics (2014), 133
Social Democratic Alliance, 271, 293
social reproduction, 19, 184, 193, 217, 222, 247
socialism, xiii, 3, 13–14, 16, 29–30, 107
see also communism; Marxism
Socio-Economic Rights Institute (SERI), 251, 253, 256
Solovey, Vanya Mark, 173–4
Sonke Gender Justice, 237
Sonti, Primrose, 246, 249–51, 254
South Africa, 3, 5–6, 8, 17, 199, 219–60, 351–2
apartheid (1948–93), *see* Apartheid South Africa
arms industry in, 230–31
Black Consciousness Movement (c. 1960–), 224, 229, 259
Black Economic Empowerment (1994–), 231
Constitutional Court, 232
constitutional law in, 222–3
corruption in, 230–33
democracy in, 233, 248, 260, 341
domestic violence in, 238, 351–2
femicide in, 242–3, 352
gangs in, 233
healthcare in, 228, 229
HIV/AIDS and, 222–3, 230, 234, 243–4
housing in, 222, 228, 230, 245, 247, 254–9
Marikana massacre (2012), 35, 246, 248–50
migrant workers in, 247, 250–51, 254
mining industry, 223, 245–54
Moral Regeneration Movement, 234
poverty in, 221, 222, 229, 230, 231
representation in, 237–8
sexual violence in, 30, 233–7, 238–45, 351–2
state capture in, 222, 231–3
Truth and Reconciliation Commission, 240
Usindiso fire (2023), 254–9
welfare in, 228
Zondo Commission (2018), 232
Zuma rape trial (2005–6), 233–7, 238, 239, 240
South African Commission on Gender Equality, 237
South Korea, 184, 197

INDEX

South Sudan, 30
South Yemen (1967–90), 7
Southall Black Sisters, 28
Soviet Russia/Union (1917–91), 7, 8, 19, 135–52, 170, 333, 345, 347, 348
   abortion laws, 136–7, 142
   Afghan War (1979–89), 8, 10, 92, 114
   collapse (1989–91), 7, 8, 70, 147–52, 159
   direct democracy in, 348
   employment in, 138–44, 170
   family in, 19, 138–44, 147
   glasnost/perestroika (c. 1985–91), 8, 147
   liberal feminism in, 8, 150
   New Economic Policy (1921–31), 186
   nostalgia for, 157
   pronatalism in, 142
   prostitution in, 29, 136, 144–6
   religion in, 153
Soviet Women's Committee (SWC), 148
Soweto uprising (1976), 249
Soyapango, El Salvador, 61
Spain, 343, 352
spatial–social relationship, 274
Sperling, Valerie, 23–4, 149, 150, 152, 156, 158
Sri Lanka, 332
St Petersburg, Russia, 131, 136, 162, 170, 174
Stal, 161

Stalin, Joseph, 132, 135, 141, 146, 148, 157
State Capture (Madonsela), 232
state capture
   in Iceland, 266–71
   in South Africa, 222, 231–3
state, shrinking of, 15, 16
Stephenson, Svetlana, 158
Steyn City, Johannesburg, 243
Steyn, Douw, 227
Stígamót, 285, 287, 290
StopKham, 161
strip clubs, 286
Stundin, 278
Sultana, Saudi Princess, 100, 122
Sun Yat-sen University, 212
Sunni Islam, 86, 88, 104
Surkov, Vladislav, 160
Svavarsdóttir, Svandís, 278
Sweden, xii, 286, 352
Sykes–Picot Agreement (1916), 299
Syria Arabisation policy, 299, 323
Syria, 340
   Civil War (2011–), 300, 304, 319, 336
   ISIS caliphate (2014–19), *see* Islamic State
   Revolution (2011), 9, 89, 298, 302–3
   Rojava, *see* Rojava
Syriac people, 298
Syrian Democratic Forces (SDF), 89, 296

Taliban, 86, 111

INDEX

Tatarstan, Russia, 133
Tate, Andrew, 22
tattoos, 21, 45, 64
Tax, Meredith, 316, 331
Taylor, Barbara, 13
technofeudalism, 340
teenage pregnancies, 76, 77
    in El Salvador, 76, 77, 78–80
    in South Africa, 236
Telegram, 176, 177
temporary marriages, 103, 112
Tereshkova, Valentina, 148
TEV-DEM, 309, 329
Thailand, 341
Thatcher, Margaret, 7, 268, 346
theocracy, 3, 6, 110
Third World, 80, 190
Thornberry, Elizabeth, 239
Tiananmen Square massacre (1989), 183
Times, The, 108
Tlhabi, Redi, 238
toilets, 214
Tomsk, Russia, 174
Torfason, Hörður, 271
trade unions, 13, 29
transgender people, 84
Trevaskes, Susan, 215
Trotsky, Leon, 138–9
Trump, Donald, 2, 21, 37, 72, 232, 339, 340, 342
Truth and Reconciliation Commission, 240
Tsargrad TV, 165
Tuktasheva, Anna, 155
Tunisia, 9
Türkiye, 137, 199, 295, 299–302, 304–6, 307, 323, 328–9
    Rojava invasion (2019), 108, 304, 309, 321, 329, 334–7, 341
Turkmen people, 298
Twitter, 119

Ukraine
    Crimea annexation (2014), 134, 157, 165
    Donbas War (2014–), 156
    Orange Revolution (2004–5), 160
    Russian War (2014–), *see* Russo-Ukrainian War
ulama, 110–11
uMkhonto we Sizwe, 240
Umm Sumayyah, 98, 103
Ummah, 93
Umoja, Kenya, 11, 314
Union of Communities in Kurdistan, 302
Union of Free Women of Kurdistan, 307
Union of Municipalities, 314
Union of Russia's Women (URW), 148–9
United Democratic Front (UDF), 224, 226, 228, 231, 259
United Kingdom
    childcare in, 347
    Cod Wars (1958–76), 274–5
    immigration laws, 344–5

INDEX

neoliberalism in, 7, 268
Northern Ireland conflict (c. 1968–98), 260
Occupy movement (2011–16), 343
Rojava, relations with, 337
second-wave feminism (1960s–70s), 16, 25
violence in, 14, 25–6, 27, 74, 171, 286, 347
United Nations
apartheid, resolution on (1976), 225
Commission on the Status of Women, 110
Committee on the Elimination of Discrimination, 216
Decade of Women (1975–85), 191, 263
Ending Violence against Women (2006 report), 26
Global Leaders' Meeting on Women's Empowerment (2015), 211
Human Rights Commission, 283
Population Conference (1974), 190
Truth Commission for El Salvador (1992–3), 57
World Conference on Population (1994), 80
4th World Conference on Women (1995), 81, 181, 184, 204–8

United States, 2, 6–7, 352
El Salvador, relations with, 6–7, 47, 49–50, 52, 59–60, 69–72
Floyd murder (2020), 1
Gulf War I (1990–91), 111–12
Gulf War II (2003–11), 88, 92
Islamic State War (2014–19), 7, 89, 108
neoliberalism in, 7, 268
Occupy movement (2011–16), 343
peace movement in, 349
Quest for Democracy conference (2024), 127–8
Roe v. Wade (1973), 36
Rojava, relations with, 337
Saudi Arabia, relations with, 91–2, 111–12, 114, 129
Seneca Falls Convention (1848), 12
September 11 attacks (2001), 114
Soviet–Afghan War (1979–89), 10
Trumpism, 2, 21, 36, 37, 72, 232, 339, 340, 341, 342
violence in, 14, 25–6, 286
University of London, 46
unpaid labour, 13, 14, 18–21, 184, 202, 264, 265, 291
Urquilla, Carmen, 42
USAID, 73
Usindiso fire (2023), 254–9
Üstündağ, Nazan, 329
Uzbekistan, 137

INDEX

Valdimarsdóttir, Unnur Anna, 285
Van Niekerk, Robert, 225
Vatican, 48–9, 261
veiling, 1, 93, 94, 95, 104, 114, 117, 155
Venezuela, 340, 341
Venus of Dolni Vestonice, 10
Venus of Hohle Fels, 10
Vetten, Lisa, 236
Vezhevatova, Liliya, 176
Víglundsson, Þorsteinn, 283
Vikings, 262, 263, 267, 271, 273, 275
Villalobos, Joaquín, 48
violence, 17, 24, 25–31, 73–4
　see also domestic violence; femicide; sexual violence
violent democracy, 233
Vision 2030 programme, 123, 125, 126, 129
Voronezh, Russia, 174
vory v zakone, 162

Wade, Robert, 269
Wagner Group, 23, 134, 162–3, 164–5
Wahhabism, 88, 93, 106, 108
Walby, Sylvia, 5, 344, 347
walking marriage, 11
Walters, Natasha, 115
Wang Zingjuan, 205
warfare, 30–31, 341, 349
Watson, Peggy, 24
Wedel, Janine, 270
welfare systems, 2, 15, 347, 351
　in China, 184, 186, 194–5, 216
　in Iceland, 280
　in Russia, 149, 157
　in South Africa, 228
WikiLeaks, 164
Williams, Fiona, 20–21
Willson, Margaret, 274, 275, 276, 292
Witwatersrand University, 240, 253
Wollstonecraft, Mary, 29
Women, the Family and Peasant Revolution (Johnson), 182, 183
Women Living Under Muslim Laws, 33
Women of China, 185
Women of Russia, 148–9
Women's Hotline, 205
Women's Hour, 333
Women's Legal Research and Service Centre, 208
Women's Liberation Movement, 19, 25–6, 191, 263, 284
Women's List/Women's Alliance, 279
Women's Research Institute, 205
World Bank, 9, 59, 70, 252
World Conference on Population (1994), 80
World Cup (2018), 288
World Economic Forum, 225, 280
World Health Organization (WHO), 26
World Women's Conference (1995), 81, 181, 184, 204–8
Worldwide Russian People's Council, 166

INDEX

Wu Xiaogang, 195

X, 119
Xi Jinping, 180, 197, 199–200, 204, 211, 214, 215, 217
Xiaoguwei Island, Guangzhou, 203

Yang Yuan, 204
Yeats, William Butler, 339
Yekîneyên Parastina Gel (YPG), 101, 303, 315, 332
Yekîneyên Parastina Jin (YPJ), 101, 308, 309, 314, 315
Yekitiya Azadiye Jinen Kurdistan (YAJK), 307
Yeltsin, Boris, 148, 149, 151, 152, 161
YOLO (2024 film), 193, 194
Young Communist League, 197
Young Guard of United Russia, 161
Young, Iris Marion, 284
Younge, Gary, 38, 48
Your Fatwa Does Not Apply Here (Bennoune), 96

Yr Þorbergsdóttir, Sonja, 291
Yuan Feng, 205
Yusuf, Hediye, 311, 319, 322, 334
Yusupova, Marina, 162

al-Zarqawi, Abu Musab, 88
Zetkin, Clara, 140, 142
Zhang Ying, 206
Zhangzhou, Fujian, 187
Zheng Churan, 212
Zheng Tiantian, 209
Zheng Wang, 180, 188, 191, 206, 211
Zhengzhou, Henan, 202
Zhenotdel, 136, 137
Zhou Xiaoxuan, 214
Zhu De, 185
Zhu Jun, 214
Zhu Xiaomei, 203
Zobnina, Anna, 131
Zondo Commission (2018), 232
Zuckerberg, Mark, 22
Zuma, Jacob, 227, 231–7, 238, 239, 240, 259, 341
Zuptas, 232, 237